Sexual Violence Against Global Politics

Sexual violence against men is an under-theorised and under-noticed topic, though it is becoming increasingly apparent that this form of violence is wide-spread. Yet despite emerging evidence documenting its incidence, especially in conflict and post-conflict zones, efforts to understand its causes and develop strategies to reduce it are hampered by a dearth of theoretical engagement. One of the reasons that might explain its empirical invisibility and theoretical vacuity is its complicated relationship with sexual violence against women. The latter is evident empirically, theoretically, and politically, but the relationship between these violences conjures a range of complex and controversial questions about the ways they might be different, and why and how these differences matter.

It is the case that sexual violence (when noticed at all) has historically been understood to happen largely, if not only, to women, allegedly because of their gender and their ensuing place in gender orders. This begs important questions regarding the impact of increasing knowledge about sexual violence against men, including the impact on resources, on understandings about, and experiences of masculinity, and whether the idea and practice of gender hierarchy is outdated. This book engages this diverse set of questions and offers fresh analysis on the incidences of sexual violence against men using both new and existing data. Additionally, the authors pay close attention to some of the controversial debates in the context of sexual violence against men, revisiting and asking new questions about the vexed issue of masculinities and related theories of gender hierarchy.

The book will be of great interest to students and scholars of sex, gender, masculinities, corporeality, violence, and global politics, as well as to practitioners and activists.

Marysia Zalewski is Professor at Cardiff University, Wales, United Kingdom.

Paula Drumond is Assistant Professor, Institute of International Relations at the Pontifical Catholic University of Rio de Janeiro (IRI/PUC-Rio), Brazil.

Elisabeth Prügl is Professor at the Graduate Institute of International and Development Studies, Geneva, Switzerland.

Maria Stern is Professor at the University of Gothenburg, Sweden.

Interventions
Edited by:
Jenny Edkins
Aberystwyth University
and
Nick Vaughan-Williams
University of Warwick

The Series provides a forum for innovative and interdisciplinary work that engages with alternative critical, post-structural, feminist, post-colonial, psychoanalytic and cultural approaches to international relations and global politics. In our first five years, we have published sixty volumes.

We aim to advance understanding of the key areas in which scholars working within broad critical post-structural traditions have chosen to make their interventions, and to present innovative analyses of important topics. Titles in the series engage with critical thinkers in philosophy, sociology, politics, and other disciplines and provide situated historical, empirical, and textual studies in international politics.

We are very happy to discuss your ideas at any stage of the project: just contact us for advice or proposal guidelines. Proposals should be submitted directly to the Series Editors:

- Jenny Edkins (jennyedkins@hotmail.com) and
- Nick Vaughan-Williams (N.Vaughan-Williams@Warwick.ac.uk).

'As Michel Foucault has famously stated, "knowledge is not made for understanding; it is made for cutting". In this spirit The Edkins–Vaughan-Williams Interventions series solicits cutting edge, critical works that challenge mainstream understandings in international relations. It is the best place to contribute post-disciplinary works that think rather than merely recognize and affirm the world recycled in IR's traditional geopolitical imaginary.'

Michael J. Shapiro, University of Hawai'i at Manoa, USA

For a full list of available titles, please visit www.routledge.com/series/INT

Writing the Self and Transforming Knowledge in International Relations
Towards a Politics of Liminality
Erzsébet Strausz

Sexual Violence Against Men in Global Politics
Edited by Marysia Zalewski, Paula Drumond, Elisabeth Prügl, and Maria Stern

Sexual Violence Against Men in Global Politics

Edited by Marysia Zalewski,
Paula Drumond, Elisabeth Prügl, and
Maria Stern

Routledge
Taylor & Francis Group

LONDON AND NEW YORK

First published 2018
by Routledge

2 Park Square, Milton Park, Abingdon, Oxfordshire OX14 4RN
52 Vanderbilt Avenue, New York, NY 10017

Routledge is an imprint of the Taylor & Francis Group, an informa business

First issued in paperback 2020

British Library Cataloguing-in-Publication Data
A catalogue record for this book is available from the British Library

Library of Congress Cataloging-in-Publication Data
Names: Zalewski, Marysia, editor.
Title: Sexual violence against men in global politics / edited by Marysia
Zalewski [and three others].
Description: Abingdon, Oxon ; New York, NY : Routledge, 2018. |
Series: Interventions | Includes bibliographical references and index.
Identifiers: LCCN 2017060473| ISBN 9781138209909 (hardback) |
ISBN 9781315456492 (ebook)
Subjects: LCSH: Male rape–Political aspects. | Sex crimes–Political
aspects. | Rape as a weapon of war. | War crimes.
Classification: LCC HV6558 .S4975 2018 | DDC 364.15/320811–dc23
LC record available at https://lccn.loc.gov/2017060473

ISBN: 978-1-138-20990-9 (hbk)
ISBN: 978-0-367-59096-3 (pbk)

Typeset in Times New Roman
by Wearset Ltd, Boldon, Tyne and Wear

Contents

List of illustrations   viii
Notes on contributors   ix
Acknowledgements   xv

Introduction: sexual violence against men in global politics   1
MARYSIA ZALEWSKI, PAULA DRUMOND, ELISABETH PRÜGL,
AND MARIA STERN

'Tribulations'   20
NZIZA HAROUNA D. NZISABIRA

PART I
Provocations   23

1 **Provocations in debates about sexual violence against men**   25
MARYSIA ZALEWSKI

2 **Battle-induced urotrauma, sexual violence, and American**
  servicemen   43
CHRIS HENDERSHOT

3 **Masculinity, men, and sexual violence in the US military**   57
ELIZABETH MESOK

4 **Languages of castration – male genital mutilation in conflict**
  and its embedded messages   71
HENRI MYRTTINEN

5 Medical approaches to sexual violence in war, in guidelines, and in practice   89
   CAROLINE COTTET

6 The political economy of sexual violence against men and boys in armed conflict   102
   SARA MEGER

Reflections   117

   Reflections on sexual violence against men and boys in global politics   119
   PAUL HIGATE AND NIVI MANCHANDA

   Homo interruptus   122
   PAUL KIRBY

   Can our intellectual curiosity on gender cause harm?   126
   MADELEINE REES

   Gender, sex, and sexual violence against men   129
   LAURA J. SHEPHERD

   Not for the faint of heart: reflections on rape, gender, and conflict   132
   LARA STEMPLE

PART II
Framing   135

7 Uncovering men's narratives of conflict-related sexual violence   137
   MICHELE LEIBY

8 Sex, violence, and heteronormativity: revisiting performances of sexual violence against men in former Yugoslavia   152
   PAULA DRUMOND

9 'Only a fool ...' why men don't disclose conflict-related
sexual violence in an age of global media   167
CHRIS DOLAN

10 Masculine subjectivities in United Nations discourse on
gender violence (1970–2015): absent actors, deviant
perpetrators, allies, and victims   184
GIZEH BECERRA

11 Sexual violence or torture?: The framing of sexual violence
against men in armed conflict in Amnesty International and
Human Rights Watch reports   198
THOMAS CHARMAN

12 Conflict-related male sexual violence and the international
criminal jurisprudence   211
PATRICIA VISEUR SELLERS AND LEO C. NWOYE

Reflections   237

Familiar stories, the policing of knowledge, and other
challenges ahead   239
MARIA ERIKSSON BAAZ

Reflections on the slippery politics of framing   243
HARRIET GRAY

Male victims: a blind spot in law   246
CHARU LATA HOGG

Sexual violence against men and boys in the Congo   249
ILOT MUTHAKA

SGBV against men and boys as a site of theoretical and
political contestation   251
JILL STEANS

'People You May Know'   254
KEVIN KANTOR

Index   256

Illustrations

Figures

| 1.1 | Marché d'esclaves | 36 |
| 7.1 | Author photograph, CVR n.d. | 140 |

Tables

7.1	Comparing figures on CRSV	139
7.2	Probability that PTRC interviewers mark 'sexual violence' in testimony, by victim sex, sexual violation type, and interviewer sex	143
7.3	Probability that PTRC interviewers mark 'sexual violence' in testimony, by victim sex and sexual violation type	146
7.4	Most frequent types of CRSV against men and women	147

Contributors

Gizeh Becerra is currently pursuing a PhD degree at the Gender Studies Institute of the University of Geneva. Her doctoral research examines the conceptualisation of violence against women (VAW) in the United Nations system from the 1970s to the present day. Her thesis analyses the issue's emergence as an international public problem and the effects of institutionalisation on problem framing. Her research focuses on the interactions of women's social movements, experts, and UN officials, and how these exchanges shaped VAW norms over time, influencing our current understanding of the problem. Ms Becerra has also worked with international organisations and NGOs developing research and awareness-raising campaigns to combat VAW.

Thomas Charman is a PhD student in the School of Social and Political Science at the University of Edinburgh. His research focuses on analysing how sexual violence against men in armed conflict is framed by nongovernmental organisations and international legal tribunals, and the conceptual and practical implications that stem from the use of particular frames.

Caroline Cottet is the co-founder and coordinator of the Refugee Women's Centre, a non-profit organisation that supports women, families, and unaccompanied minors in the refugee camps of Northern France. Alongside her activism, she partakes in academic research by writing and editing. Namely, she is an editor for the Encounters section of *Critical Military Studies* and an Editor-at-Large, specialising in gender and sexuality theory, for E-International Relations.

Chris Dolan is the Director of Refugee Law Project, Makerere University Kampala, and a Visiting Professor at the Transitional Justice Institute and INCORE, Ulster University. He works extensively with refugee and IDP survivors of sexual violence in conflict settings, as well as conducting research and global advocacy on the need for inclusive approaches to gender-based violence, particularly for male and LGBTI survivors of such violence. Recent articles include 'Inclusive Gender: Why Tackling Gender Hierarchies Cannot be at the Expense of Human Rights and the Humanitarian Imperative', *International Review of the Red Cross* and 'Victims Who Are Men' in *The Oxford Handbook of Gender and Armed Conflict* (Oxford University Press, 2017).

Paula Drumond is Assistant Professor at the International Relations Institute at the Pontifical Catholic University of Rio de Janeiro (IRI/PUC-Rio). Paula holds a PhD in International Relations/Political Science from the Graduate Institute of International and Development Studies (IHEID, Geneva). Her research focuses broadly on gendered dynamics of violence, peace, and security.

Maria Eriksson Baaz is Professor in Peace and Development Research at the School of Global Studies, University of Gothenburg and a senior lecturer at the Department of Government, Uppsala University, Sweden. Her research interests are in civil–military relations, gender and security, and post-colonial theory. In addition to numerous articles and book chapters, she is the co-author (with Maria Stern) of *Sexual Violence as a Weapon of War? Perceptions, Prescriptions, Problems* (2013) and the author of *The Paternalism of Partnership: A Postcolonial Reading of Identity in Development Aid* (2005).

Harriet Gray is a Lecturer in International Relations at the University of York, UK. Her research focuses primarily on sexual and gender-based violence in military and conflict spaces, and in particular on the gendered political processes through which various harmful acts come to be understood (or, do not come to be understood) as 'violence', as 'sexual violence', and as 'conflict-related sexual violence'. Her work has been published in journals including *Gender, Place and Culture*, *Feminist Review*, *Feminist Studies*, and *Critical Military Studies*.

Chris Hendershot works as a Research Associate at York University where he completed his PhD on private military and security corporations. He has previously published on issues of militarisation, embodiment, gender, and sex.

Paul Higate is Professor in Conflict and Security at the University of Bath. He has written on the gendered culture of the military with a focus on masculinities and gendered relations. He is currently looking at the militarisation of British society. He is the UK editor of the journal *Men & Masculinities* and associate editor of the journal *Critical Military Studies*.

Charu Lata Hogg is Visiting Michael D. Palm Fellow at the Williams Institute and Founding Director of the All Survivors Project. She was Policy and Advocacy Director and previously Asia Program Manager at Child Soldiers International, formerly the Coalition to Stop the Use of Child Soldiers. She has been Associate Fellow in the Asia Programme at Chatham House since 2004, where she covers political and human rights developments in South and South-East Asia. She is the Chair of the Board of Trustees of the Sri Lanka Campaign for Peace and Justice. She worked as the South Asia researcher for Human Rights Watch until 2009 and documented violations of international human rights and humanitarian law in Nepal and Sri Lanka.

Kevin Kantor is a performance and teaching artist based in Denver, CO, and the founder and former artistic director of SOAPbox Production.

Paul Kirby is a Research Fellow at the Centre for Women, Peace and Security at the London School of Economics and Political Science and Lecturer in International Security at the University of Sussex. His research focuses predominantly on theories of wartime sexual violence and he has published on these issues in the *European Journal of International Relations* and *Men and Masculinities*, and on policy responses to conflict-related sexual violence in *International Affairs* and the *International Feminist Journal of Politics*.

Michele Leiby is an Associate Professor in Political Science at the College of Wooster, Ohio. Her research addresses pressing questions concerning gender, political violence, and human rights advocacy. Her work is methodologically diverse, including large-N statistical analysis, interview and archival research, experimental and survey design, and extensive fieldwork in Latin America and the USA, and has been published in *American Political Science Review*, *International Studies Quarterly*, *Politics and Society*, *Revista Memoria*, as well as various edited volumes.

Nivi Manchanda is a Lecturer in International Politics at Queen Mary, University of London. Her abiding interests are the politics of race and coloniality. She is the co-convenor of the Colonial, Postcolonial, Decolonial (CPD) BISA working group and the co-editor of *Race and Racism in International Relations: Confronting the Global Colour Line* (London: Routledge, 2015).

Sara Meger is a Lecturer in International Relations at the University of Melbourne. Her research focuses on the intersection of gender, political economy, and international security. She is the author of *Rape Loot Pillage: The Political Economy of Sexual Violence in Armed Conflict* (New York: Oxford University Press, 2016).

Elizabeth Mesok is an independent scholar whose research focuses on gender, race, and militarism. Her current book project examines the emergence of all-female counter-insurgency teams in Iraq and Afghanistan and the US military's instrumentalisation of gender difference for global military campaigns. Her work has been published in *Radical History Review* (2015) and *Feminist Studies* (2016).

Ilot Muthaka is originally from the Democratic Republic of Congo and has over fifteen years of experience working directly with communities focusing on human rights, gender equality, sexual and gender-based violence, masculinities, and conflicts. He holds a degree in sociology from Cepromad University and, in 2019, expects to complete a graduate certificate in Humanitarian Actions Leadership from Eastern Mennonite University, Virginia, USA, which he pursues via distance learning. As the Founder and Director of the Congo Men's Network, he frequently travels to the rural and urban communities of North and South Kivus, Kinshasa, and Ituri to conduct gender trainings for human and women's rights organisations and activists. He is actively engaged in creating awareness on different national and international instruments like the DRC law 06/07-06/July/2006 on sexual violence, the

Convention on the Elimination of All Forms of Discrimination against Women (CEDAW), and Security Council Resolution 1325.

Henri Myrttinen is the Head of Gender and Peacebuilding with International Alert, a London-based peacebuilding organisation. He has around fifteen years of experience of working on gender, peace and security, with a focus on critically engaging with masculinities as well as on researching and addressing sexual and gender-based violence. He holds a PhD from the University of KwaZulu-Natal, South Africa in Conflict Resolution and Peace Studies.

Leo C. Nwoye is a former Assistant Appeals Counsel in the Office of the Prosecutor at both the Mechanism for International Criminal Tribunals (Arusha Branch) and the International Criminal Tribunal for Rwanda. He holds an LLM (with Distinction) from Northumbria University. He is an accredited mediator and also a PhD candidate within the School of International Relations at the University of St Andrews.

Nziza Harouna D. Nzisabira is vice-secretary of 'Men of Peace', an association of male survivors of conflict-related sexual violence based in the Nakivale refugee settlement, Southwest Uganda.

Elisabeth Prügl is Professor of International Relations at the Graduate Institute of International and Development Studies in Geneva where she directs the Institute's Gender Centre. Her research focuses on gender in international governance, including in the areas of economic development, agriculture, and peacebuilding.

Madeleine Rees is a British lawyer and current Secretary General of the Women's International League for Peace and Freedom. In the UK, she worked on behalf of both the Commission for Racial Equality and the Equal Opportunities Commission, mainly developing strategies to establish rights under domestic law. In 1998, Madeleine was appointed as Head of the Office of the High Commissioner for Human Rights and their gender expert in Bosnia and Herzegovina. From September 2006 to April 2010, Madeleine served as the Head of the Women's Rights and Gender Unit for the Office of the High Commissioner for Human Rights. Madeleine was appointed Officer of the Order of the British Empire (OBE) in 2014 for services to women's rights and international peace and security. She was awarded an honorary doctorate from the University of Edinburgh in 2015 and is now a Professor of Practice at the London School of Economics.

Patricia Viseur Sellers, Esq., is the Special Advisor for Prosecution Strategies for the Prosecutor of the International Criminal Court. She also is a Visiting Fellow at Kellogg College, University of Oxford, where she teaches international criminal law and human rights law. Previously, she was the Legal Advisor for Gender, Acting Head of the Legal Advisory Section and a prosecutor at the Yugoslav (ICTY) Tribunal from 1994 until February 2007. She has authored numerous articles, including: 'Wartime Female Slavery:

Enslavement?' *Cornell University Journal of International Law* 44, 1: (2011); 'Rape and Sexual Violence', in the critically received, *A New Commentary to the Geneva Conventions* (Oxford University Press, 2015); and '(Re)Considering the Gender Jurisprudence' in *The Oxford Handbook of Gender and Armed Conflict* (Oxford University Press, 2017).

Laura J. Shepherd is Professor of International Relations at the University of Sydney. Her primary research focuses on the United Nations Security Council's 'Women, Peace and Security' agenda and she has written extensively about the formation, implementation, and politics of this policy architecture. Laura is particularly interested in post-structural accounts of gender, politics, and security. Much of her work investigates concepts and performances of authority, legitimacy, and power through this theoretical framework, and she also has strong interests in pedagogy and popular culture. Laura is the author/editor of several books, including *Gender, Peacebuilding and the Politics of Space* (Oxford University Press, 2017) and *Gender Matters in Global Politics: A Feminist Introduction to International Relations* (Routledge, 2nd edn, 2015).

Jill Steans is currently Senior Lecturer in International Relations Theory at the University of Birmingham. An experienced researcher in the field of gender in International Relations, she currently holds a grant from the Economic and Social Research Council (UK), which allows her to pursue research on gender-based violence against LGBTI people in the Great Lakes Region. She has previously served as an expert witness on the UK House of Lords Select Committees on Sexual Violence in Conflict (2015–2016). Jill is currently writing a book on *War Stories* that engages with narrative approaches to conflict and war.

Lara Stemple is the Assistant Dean for Graduate Studies and International Student Programs at UCLA School of Law, where she oversees the law school's LLM and SJD degree programmes and directs the Health and Human Rights Law Project. She teaches and writes in the areas of human rights, global health, gender, sexuality, and incarceration.

Maria Stern is Professor in Peace and Development Studies at the School of Global Studies, University of Gothenburg. Her research interests include feminist security studies, security-development, and the international political sociology of violence. Recently her work has focused on the questions of sexual violence. She is the co-author (with Maria Eriksson Baaz) of *Sexual Violence as a Weapon of War?: Perceptions, Prescriptions, Problems in the Congo and Beyond* (Zed Books, 2013). Additionally, she has written and co-edited several books and her articles have appeared in leading international academic journals. She is currently Associate Editor of *Security Dialogue*.

Marysia Zalewski is Professor of International Relations at Cardiff University. Her research focuses on feminist enquiry and she is currently working on critical projects on sexual violence against men, the future of sexual violence, sexed violence and terrorism, performance and knowledge production in international politics and creative writing in International Relations. Key publications include: her 2013 book *Feminist International Relations: Exquisite Corpse* (Routledge); the '*Man Question*' books with Jane Parpart; and a range of essays including most recently those co-authored with Maria Stern, 'Feminist Fatigue(s): Reflections on Feminism and Familiar Fables of Militarization', *The Review of International Studies*, 2009); and with Anne Sisson Runyan, 'Taking Feminist Violence Seriously in Feminist International Relations', *International Feminist Journal of Politics* (2013) and 'Unthinking Sexual Violence in a Neoliberal Age of Spectacular Terror', *Critical Studies on Terrorism* (2015).

Acknowledgements

Co-edited books are quite a challenge to bring to final completion, and in these acknowledgements we offer our grateful thanks to a range of people and organisations who have all played a part in helping us to move beyond the challenge, to the point when we can finally press 'send' and breathe a sigh of relief (even if only momentarily).

First, we thank every one of our contributors for their hard work, insightful contributions, and patience. We are also grateful to our reflections authors for their willingness to participate in this experiment, for their thoughtful meditations, and for putting up with delays and short deadlines. We thank Nziza Harouna D. Nzisabira and Kevin Kantor for authorising the publication of their poems/voices/stories in what must be for them an unusual outlet. And we all offer our very grateful thanks for some wonderful editorial assistance from Laís Meneguello Bressan at the Graduate Institute's Gender Centre. Finally, thanks to Lucy Frederick at Routledge for her patience and good humour and to the Intervention Series editors, Jenny Edkins and Nick Vaughan-Williams, for their very welcome support for our project.

The whole editing process has been (eventually) deeply rewarding and also surprising. Our book has emerged as much more than the sum of its parts and we, as editors, have learned a great deal from working together. We all agree that this book symbolises more than the outcome of years of research and academic compromise. It is very much a product of a concerted and unswerving feminist spirit of friendship and mentorship, all under Marysia's wise leadership. The beauty and magic of our collaborative work became so much more visible when we recognised our own and each other's voices emerging, and merging in a chorus of oftentimes very different voices that have joined together here.

Paula's research was made possible by a doctoral scholarship from CAPES, the Brazilian Coordination for the Improvement of Post-Graduate Training. Our work also benefited enormously from an International Exploratory Workshop grant provided to Paula and Elisabeth by the Swiss National Science Foundation (grant number IZ32Z0 160275). And Maria thanks the Swedish Research Council and the Swedish Foundation for Humanities and Social Science for their generous support.

We dedicate this book to all the survivors and victims of sexual violence, and to all the people who try to help.

Introduction

Sexual violence against men in global politics

Marysia Zalewski, Paula Drumond, Elisabeth Prügl, and Maria Stern

Largely ignored for centuries and typically understood as part of the 'spoils of war', sexual violence is now evidentially ubiquitous, most notably in conflict and war zones. Indeed, in the last few decades interest in, and concern about sexual violence has increased exponentially, especially in the realm of high politics. In part, this intensified interest has resulted from the widespread incidence of wartime rape in Bosnia-Herzegovina in the early 1990s and in Rwanda in 1994. Extensive empirical evidence and reporting has helped bring to a halt the long-standing political inattention to this form of violence. The new attention has been welcomed by many. That we can now speak of sexual violence as a global and severe harm has been neither easy nor straightforward; it has required years of intense feminist scholarship and activism. Yet despite this and the high political attention, the egregious harm of sexual violence persists worldwide with people often suffering in relative silence and far removed from the purview of the global media, the policy world, and the scholarly work aimed to address it. Moreover, the exponential globalised attention appears to have accomplished little in regard to the recognition of the different kinds of victims, and the complex range of needs for redress in both the short and long term. And there remains scanty understanding of the contextual and complex relations of power and the material circumstances that produce sexual violence. As such, as editors, we sensed that there were still many gaps in the ways we think about, understand, or try to 'do something about' sexual violence – whether in theory, politics, or legislation; indeed, this is a political and intellectual scene of some impoverishment.

Into this fraught terrain has entered the increasing visibility of sexual violence against men[1] – the central concern of this book.[2] Though sexual violence against men has received some fleeting comments in international documents, as in the 2013 Security Council Resolution 2106, for the most part the focus on sexual violence has *not* included a significant focus on men as victims and survivors.[3] The Resolution, which has been celebrated as the first-ever explicit recognition of sexual violence against men by the UN Security Council, makes but a sole and peripheral reference to the issue in its preamble:

> Noting with concern that sexual violence in armed conflict and post-conflict situations disproportionately affects women and girls, as well as groups that

are particularly vulnerable or may be specifically targeted, while also affecting men and boys and those secondarily traumatized as forced witnesses of
sexual violence against family members.

(UNSC Res. 2106 2013)

For many scholars and activists, it is becoming increasingly apparent that male
victims of this form of violence have been overwhelmingly rendered invisible,
both in research and policy papers produced by international organisations.
Moreover, international legal instruments have been developed in a way that
often explicitly exclude men as a class of victims of sexual violence (Lewis
2009; Stemple 2009; Dolan, Fletcher, and Oola 2013; Dolan 2014c; Sivakumaran 2010; Sellers and Nwoye, Ch. 12 in this volume). The legal treatment of
sexual abuses against men as 'inhumane acts', 'cruel treatment', 'torture', and
'persecution' – rather than 'sexual violence' – in places like the former Yugoslavia and Kenya, for example, epitomises the persisting difficulties in surfacing
the sexual vulnerability of male bodies (Sivakumaran 2007, 2013; Stemple 2009;
Lewis 2009; Oosterveld 2014; Mouthaan 2013; Sellers and Nwoye, Ch. 12 in
this volume). Prosecution and investigation mechanisms are often ineffective for
reasons that range from reporting barriers to narrow understandings of rape as
vaginal penetration. Moreover, policy discourses and practices in international
organisations continue to operationalise sexual violence as male-on-female
(Grey and Shepherd 2012; Sivakumaram 2010) and portray male rape as aberra-
tional (Cohen 2014). At the same time, the paucity of data on the issue due to
under-reporting and lack of interest on the part of stakeholders has been critical
in maintaining a pervasive silence (Leiby, Ch. 7 in this volume; Charman, Ch. 11
in this volume).

Accompanying this is a noticeable stance of incomprehension, discomfort,
and puzzlement when faced with the increasing claims of widespread incidences
of sexual violence against men, especially in conflict zones. Some have finger-
pointed at feminist groups, holding them responsible for the persisting lethargy
surrounding male victimisation (Jones and Del Zotto 2002: 3) and arguing that a
'female-specific approach to rape' (Stemple 2009: 628) as well as the fear of
diverting already scarce funding from female victims have hindered attention to
male victimhood (Sivakumaran 2013: 82). Others have insisted that arguments
to include men equally into considerations of and programming on gender-based
violence ignore the reality of masculine domination and pervasive gender hierarchy (Goetz 2014; De Brouwer 2005; Ward 2016). While knowledge about
sexual violence in general is vast and growing, this *still* remains almost entirely
in the context of assuming that sexual violence is perpetrated *against* particular
subjects, namely, women and girls, and that it is perpetrated *by* particular subjects, namely, men and boys. This classic gendered framing has perhaps contributed to the sense or belief that sexual violence against men is both overly
difficult to categorise or comprehend in implied contradistinction to what it is
believed is already known about sexual violence against women. Additionally,
and somewhat contradictorily, the analysis of sexual violence against men often

rests on what we know about sexual violence from these familiar gendered framings (Drumond 2017). This, despite that many argue what we know about sexual violence against women is also partial, unstable, and circumscribed by our limited frames of understanding (e.g. Eriksson Baaz and Stern 2013; Heberle and Grace 2009; Zalewski and Runyan 2015).

Consequent to our thinking on this range of issues, in this Introduction, we signal our curiosities about a set of interrelated conundrums that shape the overall text. These include: the tensions that arise through different approaches to the politics and ethics of framing sexual violence against men, as well as to the epistemological and theoretical bases of such framing; the puzzles that our imaginaries of war and peace pose in trying to make sense of sexual violence against men; the uneven politics of knowledge production; and the differing agendas and vantage points that emerge from addressing sexual violence against men from the positionality of both academics and practitioners. Our inevitably brief summation of these conundrums is woven throughout this Introduction, which we have divided into two main sections. In Part I – *placing this book in the field(s)* – we open up and explicate the range of puzzles we have introduced, and reflect on how we place our volume in relation to these. The second part introduces the *shape and content of the book* and our intentions and hopes informing that construction. Overall, in this volume, we aim to highlight and interrogate some of the complexities and discomforts around sexual violence against men, to offer fresh analysis on the incidences of sexual violence against men using both new and existing data, to revisit the question of masculinity and theories of gender hierarchy, and to contribute to the growing body of knowledge of this issue in the arena of global politics, specifically related, but not limited to, armed conflict, military power, and institutions.

A specific instigating moment for this collection was a workshop on 'Sexual Violence against Men and Boys in Conflict' hosted by the Graduate Institute in Geneva in February 2015.[4] Participants at the workshop included both practitioners and academics. The range of papers and the ensuing discussions made it distinctly apparent that there is limited available research on this kind of violence (particularly in conflict, as this was the focus of the workshop), but also, significantly, that many questions and tensions that arise out of the conundrums noted above were not engaged and/or were under-explored. We open with a specific acknowledgement of these tensions given our intention to use them productively in this book, not least as all contributors share a commitment to exploring, understanding better, and acting – if in often very different ways – on the visceral harms that this manner of violence elicits.

In the time that it has taken to produce this volume, both the available research and the tensions have increased as sexual violence against men has become further established as a valid area of concern and intervention. For instance, the second edition of the *International Protocol on the Documentation and Investigation of Sexual Violence in Conflict*, issued in March 2017, now features an entire chapter on sexual violence against men and boys (UK Foreign & Commonwealth Office 2017: 265–281). Another vivid example came in March

2016 with the International Criminal Court (ICC) conviction of Jean-Pierre Bemba for crimes committed by the former Congolese vice-president and his troops in the Central African Republic. In a landmark judgement, the ICC made a leading contribution to international jurisprudence in charging incidents of sexual violence against men under the rubric of rape.[5] A good number of books, reports, articles, and guidelines for investigation have been recently published, which work to uncover and respond to the vulnerability of men and boys in wartime in relation to sexual violence (e.g. IICI 2016; Kapur and Muddell 2016; Edström, Dolan, Shahrokh, and David 2016; Ferrales, Brehm, and McElrath 2016). Yet, many of the tensions noted earlier still manifest, alongside the persistence of a range of problematic and simplistic assumptions about subjects and objects of such violence, and around the forms such violence takes. These will be discussed in a variety of ways in the contributing chapters of this book.

Placing this book in the field(s)

The marked differences in theorising or explaining sexual violence against men were apparent at the workshop in Geneva. Questions – for instance, about how to define this form of violence, how to measure it, how to understand it, and what to do about it – generated different responses and were suggestive of different approaches and analyses. Of course, this is to be expected, and our intention is not to resolve or eviscerate these differences, but rather to render them visible and facilitate spaces for their further exploration. As editors, we sensed that it mattered – it mattered a great deal to do this, not least given the emotion that accompanied the different forms of thinking and theorising about sexual violence against men and the accompanying expectations about 'what to do'.

When we speak of placing the book 'in the field(s)', we mean both situating it, however loosely, in ongoing conversations within academia, as well as in relevant fields of practice globally. However, we do not intend to secure this book or the work in it to a particular academic discipline. That said, we recognise that as editors we share a particular point of departure in our engagement with the subject of this volume. We work primarily within the academic discipline of International Relations (IR), and, although each of us has a different focus, our work has been closely associated with critical feminist theory. Marysia Zalewski (Cardiff University, UK) focuses primarily on critical feminist enquiry especially in the context of knowledge production about international politics. Paula Drumond (IRI/PUC-Rio, Brazil) has written a PhD dissertation devoted to unpacking the phenomenon of conflict-related sexual violence against men, combining insights from feminist theory with systematic empirical evidence from case studies on former Yugoslavia, Peru, and the Democratic Republic of the Congo (DRC). Elisabeth Prügl (Graduate Institute, Geneva, Switzerland) comes to the issue through her work on the development of gender expertise in international institutions. And Maria Stern (University of Gothenburg, Sweden) has worked on sexual violence in warfare particularly in the DRC context, asking how the issue is framed and understood, and to what effect. Our intended audience, however, is not limited to the field of IR (or a narrowly conceived critical feminist IR); instead, we hope to engage scholars and practitioners across a wide range of disciplines, interests, and expertise in (re)theorising, (re)thinking, and engaging in helping prevent and redress sexual violence against men.

While our intent is thus inclusive, the politics and practices of knowledge production clearly curtail the questions we might ask, the voices and perspectives we include, the cases we study, and the conclusions we draw. The consequent exclusions and differential positionalities should not be underestimated. We are investigating the issue from the vantage point of academics in various institutions in Western Europe, although one of us now teaches in Brazil. This location no doubt orients our gaze, directing us to the research of academics in our networks (largely in the Anglophone Global North) and to phenomena discussed in international forums. This inevitably engenders a range of lacunae, one of the most gaping of which is the lack of an explicit treatment of race, although international narratives of sexual violence against men are suffused with racial imaginaries. Other fissures remain, fissures which we hope will impel further conversations that draw examples from other sites and other themes not figuring in these pages.[6]

Sexual violence in war and peace

Reflecting our disciplinary location in International Relations, we approach the topic of sexual violence against men from a global perspective and focus primarily on conflict-related sexual violence, yet this too comes with problems. The distinction between war and peace serves as one of the basic underlying grammars of the modern liberal state system and the political imaginaries that sustain it, including the ways that we imagine the subjects, logics, forms, and effects of sexual violence. The immensely influential work of the UN's Women, Peace, and Security (WPS) agenda solidly fixes our attention on sexual violence in conflict and war. The Global Summit to end Sexual Violence *in conflict* and the UN multi-agency campaign 'Stop Rape Now'[7] are perhaps glaring examples of how international policy efforts to prevent and respond to incidents of sexual violence centralise their discourses in the landscape of war(s), leading to an overall inconspicuousness of peacetime rape as a global phenomenon worthy of international attention and political mobilisation. This is the case even more so when it comes to sexual violence against men. Sexual violence against women is addressed in a range of human rights instruments and UN programming; in contrast, sexual violence against men appears only in the context of a Security Council resolution and gradually in humanitarian action in conflict situations. As such, we are aware that the growing global attention to sexual violence inevitably reflects the drawing of distinct boundaries between wartime logics and peacetime ones, so much so that speaking of 'conflict-related', or 'wartime' sexual violence signifies that these are distinct phenomena, with unique logics and effects. This dominant framing of wartime sexual violence in both policy arenas, as well as in academic research, casts it as a strategic, symbolic, and visceral weapon of war, which is targeted at the enemy population through the abuse of individual bodies. In addition to the physical injuries inflicted upon these bodies, the harms that ensue depend on gender and the ways in which gender intersects with other power relations that make up the particular warscape (Drumond, Ch. 8 in this volume). Often, the 'target' of such violent acts includes the collective to which the individual survivor belongs. 'Cultural' repercussions and stigmatisation of victims/survivors, for instance, often follow as effects of these acts. Sexual violence, so the conventional story has it, in peacetime settings in 'Western' liberal states, is considered a criminal act and evidence of deviant behaviour in official discourse and legislation, despite its widespread occurrence (cf. Gavey 2005; #metoo[8]). The harms that these acts cause are mediated through this framing, and are directed, to a large degree, at the individual person subjected to this violence, instead of at the collective. While feminist work in International Relations and other academic disciplines (for instance, in anthropology and history), has convincingly problematised any tidy lines drawn between war and peace and called attention to the ways in which racialised gendered violences inform each other along a 'war–peace continuum' (for a good overview, see Boesten 2017), the notion that war and peace are distinct spheres strongly persists. There is, of course, a corresponding growing attention to 'peacetime' sexual violence, which is reflected in debates over (national) jurisprudence and the role of consent in distinguishing sex from violence (e.g. Halley 2008; Fischell 2016). There is, also, a growing body of literature that reinvigorates debates about the war–peace continuum and shows the intersections and interconnections between different forms and contexts of sexual and gender-based violence (e.g. Davies and True 2015; Boesten 2014).

This volume joins such efforts. As noted above, the contributing chapters hone in on sexual violence that is committed *against men* that occurs in relation to armed conflict and to military power and institutions. Yet, and importantly, this focus serves as a point of departure for also exploring the ways that such violence transgresses 'peacetime' and 'wartime' settings, and refuses any neat dichotomy between wartime and peacetime (Halley 2008). Thus, our book offers entry points for further probing this dichotomy in specific relation to sexual violence against men.

Scholarly framings

Theorisations of masculinity and militarised ideologies play a key role in scholarly framings and analyses of sexual violence against men. Goldstein (2001), Zarkov (2001), Sivakumaran (2007), and others suggest that practices of sexual violation, ranging from penile penetration to castration, encode the symbolic placing of male opponents in positions of subordination and feebleness commonly attributed to femininity (see also, Scarce 1997; Abdullah-Khan 2008; Lewis 2009). Literature on men and masculinities also focuses on processes of gendering and on the construction of violent masculinities in particular (see

Dawes 2014; Kirby and Henry 2012; Dolan 2002, 2011; Messerschmidt 2012; Zalewski and Parpart 1998; Parpart and Zalewski 2008).

Connell's concept of hegemonic masculinity has been particularly influential in the literature on sexual violence against men (Connell 2005 [1995]). Understanding masculinity as a social construct and a power relation, the concept of hegemonic masculinity brings into sharp relief the coexistence of complex intra-masculine hierarchies, which often rely on the vilification of women and the feminine (Connell 2005 [1995]: 77; Beasley 2008: 88; cf. Belkin 2012). Military or militarised masculinities constitute a variant of hegemonic masculinity that incorporates homophobic, racist, and misogynist identifications and practices (Belkin 2012; Higate 2003; Whitworth 2004; Kronsell 2015; Zalewski 2017; Chisholm and Tidy 2017). It emerges from violent socialisation processes, such as soldier trainings and hazing rituals, that reinforce a sense of masculine entitlement not only over women, but also over other (less privileged) groups of men (Whitworth 2004: 159–163; Peterson 2010). Viewed in this light, sexual violence has been regularly understood as constitutively related to dominant constructions of manhood, which are normalised and promoted by social institutions, such as the state and the military (Goldstein 2001; Skjelsbæk 2001). Yet, these accounts often problematically treat masculinity as a fixed 'set of properties' (Hutchings 2008: 394) or 'a (gender) "thing"' (Stern and Zalewski 2009: 619) that is applied to diverse contexts and manifestations of conflict-related sexual violence. Indeed, the slipperiness of the concept has led some authors to contest its explanatory power, denouncing its use as a buzzword or a fixed list of attributes to explain 'a wide variety of social phenomena' (Hearn 1996: 203; Pankhurst 2010: 157).

Like masculinity more broadly, hegemonic masculinity (including military masculinity) is not universal, deterministic, or constant through time (for a critique of hegemonic masculinity, cf. Whitehead 2002; Beynon 2002; Beasley 2008). Some authors in this vein have engaged with masculinity as a discursive process, always in the making and never fully achieved (Eriksson Baaz and Stern 2009, 2013; Hutchings 2008). Eriksson Baaz and Stern's study on perpetrators' narratives conducted in the DRC, for instance, demonstrated how soldiers commonly justify their behaviour by alluding to more complex stories of human suffering and unaccomplished constructions of masculinity in face of their social and economic disempowerment (Eriksson Baaz and Stern 2009). Drawing on such insights and contributions, this volume invites us to rethink the complex, 'surprising', and sometimes paradoxical entanglements of masculinity, sex, and violence in global politics (Kirby and Henry 2012: 446–447; Parpart and Zalewski 2008).

Practitioners' framings

The relationship of policy and practice to theory raises further perplexing questions that resonate with those noted above and that together motivate the production of this volume. These include questions about the value of theories embedded in feminist and gender scholarship in shedding light on the incidence of sexual violence against men; persistent questions about the vexed and arguably sullied relationship between feminist theory and gender-focused international policy; and, crucially, questions about how to help victims bring perpetrators to justice, and to more effectively work to prevent (at best), or lessen (at worst) these kinds of violent acts.

It is significant that the topic of sexual violence first appeared on the international agenda as one of various forms of 'violence against women' identified by activists and adopted into human rights language (Joachim 1999). It developed from General Recommendation 19 of the Committee on the Elimination of Discrimination against Women in 1992, the Declaration on the Elimination of Violence against Women in 1993, and the Beijing Platform for Action in 1995, through to a raft of UN Security Council Resolutions (1325 [2000]; 1820 [2008]; 1888 [2009]; 1960 [2010]; 2106 [2013])[9] to the Global Summit to End Sexual Violence in 2014, and the 2015 Global Study on the implementation of Resolution 1325.[10] General Recommendation 19 defined 'gender-based violence' as 'violence that is directed against a woman because she is a woman or that affects women disproportionately' and suggested that this includes 'acts that inflict physical, mental or sexual harm (...)' (CEDAW 1992: para. 6). The Declaration on the Elimination of Violence against Women (1993) similarly viewed sexual harm as one type of violence being done to women and subsequent instruments adopted this framing. This entry point matters because it has authorised women as the subjects for whom to claim rights or demand intervention; it has specified the 'root causes' of sexual and gender-based violence to lie in patriarchy and identified solutions accordingly; it has generated associated tools and institutionalised respective procedures for intervention; and it has directed the corresponding allocation of resources. Practitioners work within these realities, which exceed any simplistic notion of feminist conspiracy to occlude sexual violence against men (Jones and Del Zotto 2002: 3).

Feminist theories oftentimes relate uneasily to the arguments between activists and practitioners that seek to make visible violence against men on the one hand, while fearing to lose an analysis of patriarchal power relations on the other (Ward 2016). As evidence of male violation proliferates – mostly consisting of data collected by practitioners in human rights investigations, international court proceedings, and NGO interventions – the urgency to 'do something' is palpable (Dolan 2014b, 2015). And yet, feminist theorising invites us to step back, to critically reflect on the underlying gendered assumptions that go into demands that 'men too' are victims of gender-based violence, that 'men too' should have access to services (Dolan 2014c) in similar ways that we reflect on the politics of casting women as (always already) victims. Familiar dilemmas emerge between the impetus to heed the call for immediate and strategic action on the one hand, and for critical, analytical inquiry on the other. Nevertheless, this does raise questions about continuing to justify the problematisation of the productivity of gender in this context of violation, as well as insisting on questioning the meaning of the sexual in light of unceasing atrocities. Does this kind of focus beckon an inadvertent reinstatement of sociobiological notions of sexual violence as somehow inevitable (Eriksson Baaz and Stern, forthcoming)?

One of aims in this book is to expose and unpack the range of questions and puzzles that we introduce here. Though there is a growing literature on sexual violence against men, our view is that the deeper questions have not been fully explored, and oftentimes have been ignored. This is perhaps not surprising given that many of the puzzles we introduce here are infused with a range of political and intellectual tensions, which emerge as all the more difficult, given the very visceral context of broken bodies, minds, and lives ripped apart. Yet it is for that very reason that we were motivated to collate this volume.

Shape and content of the book

This is a multi-textured text; the two main parts each consist of six chapters followed by a 'reflections' section, which we will discuss in a moment. Opening and closing the volume are poems by Nziza Harouna D. Nzisabira and Kevin Kantor, both survivors of sexual violence. Harouna is a Congolese Refugee in Uganda and is the vice-secretary of 'Men of Peace', an association of male survivors of conflict-related sexual violence based in the Nakivale refugee settlement. Kantor is a performance and teaching artist based in Denver, Colorado, and the founder and former artistic director of SOAPbox Production.

Part 1: Provocations. This title gestures towards the range of tensions and controversies we introduce above. Our aim in this section is to initiate the process of opening up, exploring and discussing some of these. In the opening chapter, Marysia Zalewski begins with a reflection on the troubling and enigmatic duo – 'sex and violence'. The relationship between the two remains a notoriously unsettled one with any explicit connection between them typically presented by more conservative institutions as a deviation from 'correct' versions of sex. Yet 'sex and violence' seem melded together in ways that continue to defy many imaginations and theorisations. From this initial rumination, Zalewski moves to reconsider some of the debates around sexual violence against men. Specifically she discusses what she regards as vexatious and perturbing forms of analyses and theorising in this realm, hinting at an intellectual and political landscape of 'complexities shrouded in simplicity'. She concludes with a consideration of what might be at stake.

In Chapter 2, Chris Hendershot conducts a discursive analysis of how battle-induced urotrauma becomes sexualised. Battle-induced urotrauma involves injuries to the genitals, urinary tract, renal system, and perineum resulting from the explosive, concussive, and blunt forces produced by and through combat and is estimated to account for '0.5–4.2% of all war injuries'. Hendershot specifically focuses on the genital harm suffered by American servicemen during combat operations in Afghanistan and Iraq between 2001 and 2013. He argues that urotrauma becomes sexualised through the reiteration of heteronormal, phallic, and able-bodied discourses. To suggest that urotrauma becomes sexualised is a semantic method of recognising how the meaning of harmed genitalia and male embodiment come to matter iteratively through the repetition, ritualisation, and/ or reimagining of language, images, emotions, and flesh.

Elisabeth Mesok draws our attention to incidents of sexual violence against men outside conflict zones. Focusing on the US military, her chapter highlights how the issue of sexual violence has largely been characterised as a 'women's issue' by the military, advocacy organisations, and the media alike, despite the fact that more men than women are sexually assaulted each year. However, Mesok identifies that over the last few years there has been an increase in attention to male sexual assault survivors, with the Department of Defense developing plans to address male victimisation and outreach. Specifically her chapter analyses discourses around male sexual violence in the US military to consider the gendered constructs that shape dominant conceptualisations of male–male sexual violence. Mesok approaches male–male sexual violence as a mode – both physical and discursive – through which military masculinity is negotiated, as real and symbolic violence enacted in an attempt to enforce the unenforceable boundaries of masculinity. Ultimately, her chapter argues that sexual violence against men is constitutive rather than disruptive of the project of military masculinity, a cultivated process whereby the abject feminine is continually engaged, rather than merely rejected, in an attempt to secure the borders of masculine and feminine.

Henri Myrttinen takes a corporeal approach in his chapter, honing in the 'messages' embedded in violence against male genitalia and the belief systems that motivate these acts as well as render these messages intelligible. Through this focused approach, Myrttinen's chapter interrogates and fleshes out the core of some of the 'work' that sexual violence against men and boys can do, namely, humiliate, dehumanise, and both literally and figuratively emasculate the victim, destroying his reproductive capacity and underscoring the power of the perpetrator. Furthermore, his particular focus on male genital mutilation invites us to carefully consider the range of forms of sexual violence against men and to resist the dominant characterisation of this manner of violation as being equivalent to anal penetration – a narrow focus that hinders adequate understanding of and response to other forms of violence which might have equally severe physical, emotional, psychological, and social implications for the victim/survivor.

In Chapter 5, Caroline Cottet opens with a commentary on a scene from a film *Men Can Be Raped Too*. The film tells a story of increasing incidents of men and boys being victims of sexual violence in conflict, and the lack of effective responses especially from medical organisations. Reflecting on this lack of effective response, Cottet traces some of the historical connections between medical science and understandings of sexual violence against men, focusing especially on the remnants of biological determinism in medical science. She then moves to focus on the medical assistance available during the war in the former Yugoslavia, as described in the medical guidelines put forth by the UNHCR and the practices of doctors on the ground. Her argument is that there is a very strong link between the guidelines and practices regarding sexed bodies, which is important as it has direct implications for the ways in which male victims of sexual violence are treated. She concludes that there remains a strong bias in the medical field deriving from biological determinism, which she argues has distorted understandings of sexual violence against men, and this is exacerbated in war.

Sara Meger's chapter begins with something of a controversial judgement in debates around sexual violence against men, which was articulated by the UN Special Representative of the Secretary General on Conflict-Related Violence, Zainab Bangura. She said that sexual violence was 'no longer a gender issue'. Working with some of the conceptual tools of feminist political economy (FPE), Meger argues that an FPE approach has the capacity to shed important new light on the causes and consequences of sexual violence against men and boys by uncovering the ways in which violence inscribes and exploits differential values on bodies in times of war.

It is the case that, as Les Back puts it, 'writing fixes thought' (2016: 52), but as a book of 'writing' we cannot escape that dilemma here. However, we wanted to include a conversational element or reflective tone to offer a different articulation of the questions and puzzles we are working with in this volume. To assemble these intervening segments, the set of chapters from each section were sent to a range of people, who were asked to say what most provoked, or enlightened them, or indeed irritated them about the varied writings. These interventions were not intended to be 'reviews' of the work, and we did not impose a standard format. Our intention was to stay as close as possible in a book of writing to a more conversational, organic tone. Overall we wanted to offer an additional, perhaps more interrogative route to open up and address the puzzles around sexual violence against men, to add 'texture', and to raise additional important questions and more theoretical nuance.[11] The authors of reflections in this section include: Paul Higate and Nivi Manchanda, Paul Kirby, Madeleine Rees, Laura J. Shepherd, and Lara Stemple.

Part II: Framing. By focusing on the framing of sexual violence against men, we hope to unsettle the notion that it pre-exists its enactment and representation and that it can easily be documented and treated. Chapters in this section thus invite us to consider the way in which sexual violence against men has been performed and conceptualised in specific contexts. The first three chapters embed the phenomenon in the local contexts of Peru, former Yugoslavia, and Sudan. They show how sexual violence against men gains meaning through the way it is staged, and how interventions are constrained by local and transnational interpretations in the social media and in truth and reconciliation efforts. The second three chapters analyse the ways this form of violence is being constructed through international law and policy discourses. The authors address how the phenomenon has been circumscribed in UN discourses on sexual violence against women, in the framings of non-governmental organisations, and in the stumbling interpretive efforts of international jurisprudence. The section provides a sense of sexual violence against men gaining facticity as a social, political, and legal phenomenon that can be known and is subject to intervention.

The denial of sexual violence against men continues inadvertently in statistical practices. In her chapter, Michele Leiby examines data collected from more than 2,000 testimonies of violence during the Peruvian civil war (1980–2000), to document how frequently and in what contexts men were targeted for sexual humiliation, torture, mutilation, and rape. She presents descriptive statistics on the patterns of sexualised violence against men, and discusses why this evidence remains absent from the dominant narratives of conflict-related sexual violence in Peru. Contrary to the conventional wisdom, her study finds that men comprised approximately 30 per cent of all victims of conflict-related sexual violence. The study also demonstrates that these narratives of male sexual trauma are much more likely to be missed or mischaracterised by human rights scholars and advocates, especially if the sexual offence described is not penetrative rape, and if the interviewer/researcher is also male. The chapter concludes by providing a few guidelines for investigators to ensure that male voices of conflict-related sexual violence are heard.

Among a wide range of examples, the genocide in the former Yugoslavia (1991–1995) became one of the most notorious cases in which men were systematically targeted by sexual violence. Drawing on extensive archival research of cases handled by the International Criminal Tribunal for the former Yugoslavia (ICTY) since its creation, Paula Drumond investigates performances of sexual violence against men as they were enacted in the conflicts in Bosnia (1992–1995) and Croatia (1991–1995). The chapter makes visible the 'grammars' of violence that underpin two distinctive forms of sexual violence against men: oral rape and genital violence. From this analysis, Drumond argues that as a social performance driven by heteronormativity, sexual violence against men gains its meaning through the aversion and abjection evoked by a penetrated/ un-phallic/emasculated body. While illuminating how heteronormative tropes of sex and sexuality work as enablers of sexual violence against men, the chapter also demonstrates how it is performed in intimate articulation with local cartographies of enmity, which in former Yugoslavia were shaped by a genocidal ethno-national ideology.

Like Drumond, Chris Dolan explores sexual violence against men as embedded in a social context that facilitates it and that, moreover, is amplified by social media. Working closely with victims and survivors of sexual violence, he is concerned about the difficulty of obtaining evidence on the phenomenon and lists the extensive obstacles for men to disclose the crime. His chapter explores the toxic online reactions to two broadcasts on sexual violence against men in Sudan, which included him together with two survivors. Online reactions from around the world discredited the experiences shared, interpreting male rape as a sign of homosexuality foreign to Sudan and imported from the West. While there were also expressions of acknowledgement and solidarity, the conflation of sexual violence with rape narrowed down the issue, invited disbelief, and denied the survivors' experience.

Calls for recognising sexual violence against men are reactions to the preoccupation of international actors with sexual violence against women; thus its meaning cannot be separated from UN framings. Gizeh Becerra traces the evolving construction of masculine subjectivities in different gender violence discourses, from their invisibilisation in discourses on trafficking and domestic violence, to the representation of perpetrators as pathologically dysfunctional or socially isolated, to the emerging representations of men and boys as allies for the prevention of violence against women and as victims of sexual violence in conflict and post-conflict situations. In particular, Becerra argues that problem representations that do not acknowledge the gendered roots of various forms of violence tend to obscure the systemic nature of gendered power imbalances. Failure to recognise that violence occurs as a result of imbalances in social power structures leads to a focus on the role individuals play, either as perpetrators or victims, and narrows down the conversation to arguments over which groups deserve to be recognised as subjects of policy.

Thomas Charman takes up the issue of how sexual violence against men is framed in the activist language of international non-governmental organisations. His chapter analyses reports by Amnesty International and Human Rights Watch from 2000 to 2016 and finds a pronounced tendency to subsume sexual violence against men under the category torture. This is in stark distinction to sexual violence against women. Yet context matters: sexual violence against men is most often recorded in the context of detention in conjunction with other mistreatments recognised as torture. Another difference pertains to explanation: sexual violence against women is associated with gender subordination, but no such association is offered in the case of male violation, where gender is largely deemed irrelevant. Charman calls for recognising the gender dimension of sexual violence against men while problematising its framing through the lens of sexual violence against women.

In the final chapter, Patricia Sellers and Leo Nwoye provide a comprehensive overview of the jurisprudence hitherto on conflict-related male sexual violence (CRMSV) from the international courts (ad hoc, hybrid, and permanent). The consideration of CRMSV partly stems from the crucial advocacy work and gender analysis by women's rights activists, which may have also inadvertently led to the uneven, piecemeal, and sometimes, exclusionary approach adopted by the international courts. While identifying insufficiencies and missed opportunities, their chapter also discusses treatments of sexual violence against men as psychological torture, rape, persecution, and a foreseeable part of ethnic cleansing. And it reviews issues of command responsibility and political liability. The authors posit that international criminal tribunals should tackle sexual violence more collectively and coherently, because incidents of conflict-related sexual violence (CRSV) against men and women, while individually distinct, are conceptually interconnected. The combined CRSV experiences of both sexes comprehensively contain the rationale for their persistent occurrence.

Following the final chapter is our second collection of reflection pieces by Maria Eriksson Baaz, Harriet Gray, Charu Hogg, Ilot Muthaka, and Jill Steans. Our overall aim in this book has been to expand the range of questions being asked about sexual violence against men, not least in conflict and war zones, and to open up the exploration of different sites in which this manner of violence is perpetrated. And crucially, our intention has been to offer thoughtful analyses and reflections as a way to more deeply probe both the actuality of sexual violence against men, but also its historical, epistemological, and popularised routes and avenues of (re)presentation and (re)production. We close the book with a poem by Kevin Kantor, *People You May Know*.

Notes

1 Since we are not working with a demarcation of age in this volume (unless specifically stated), men should be read to include boys.
2 Most of existing work on sexual violence against men has been concerned with documenting and explaining male exposure to sexual assault in varied settings, such as prisons, war zones, university fraternities, and military institutions (e.g. Scarce 1997; Abdullah-Khan 2008; Sivakumaran 2007; Mezey and King 2000; Christian, Safari, Ramazani, Burnham, and Glass 2011; Dolan 2014a; Cohen 2014).
3 Throughout the book, we use the terms victim and survivor interchangeably, well aware of the baggage that comes with these terms. We are sympathetic to the idea that the term survivor avoids the sense of passivity inherent in the notion of a victim; but we also are aware that accepting victim status gains recognition and entitlements and are wary of suggesting that survivors are in some way empowered by their experience.
4 Paula Drumond, 'Sexual Violence against Men during Conflict: Bridging the Gap between Theory and Practice.' Scientific Report of an Exploratory Workshop. Programme on Gender and Global Change, Graduate Institute, Geneva, 2015. http://grad uateinstitute.ch/files/live/sites/iheid/files/sites/genre/shared/Genre_docs/2342_TRavaux EtRecherches/Report_SVAM_%20Workshop.pdf.
5 *The Prosecutor* v. *Jean Pierre Bemba Gombo*. Case No. ICC-01/05-01/08-3343, Judgement pursuant to Article 74 of the Statute, 21 March 2016.
6 For instance, further exploration of sexual violence against migrant and refugee men and a discussion of the role of religion in fostering and responding to the phenomenon are strongly needed.
7 'Stop Rape Now' is a campaign led by the UN Action Against Sexual Violence in Conflict (UN Action), a multi-agency effort to improve programming and advocacy work to prevent and respond to conflict-related sexual violence. See www.stoprape now.org/about/.
8 A hashtag set up by the actor Alyssa Milano in 2017 in the wake of sexual abuse allegations involving film producer Harvey Weinstein. Milano invited anyone subject to similar abuse to use #metoo to tell their stories. Over a period of days, millions did so. For further information, see www.theguardian.com/world/2017/oct/20/women-worldwide-use-hashtag-metoo-against-sexual-harassment.
9 Building on the call to fight 'rape and other forms of sexual abuse' raised by Resolution 1325, four UN Security Council Resolutions (UNSCR) deal with the issue of sexual violence in armed conflicts. In 2008, UNSCR 1820 unanimously recognised sexual violence as a matter of international peace and security, urging the creation of mechanisms for its prevention and response. More recently, Resolutions 1888 (2009), 1960 (2010), and 2106 (2013) advanced institutional mechanisms to punish and prevent the occurrence of sexual violence in conflict and post-conflict situations. Resolution 1888 (2009) creates the office of the UN Secretary-General's Special Representative on Sexual Violence in Conflict and calls for the appointment of Women's Protection Advisors (WPAs) for peacekeeping missions. Resolution 1960 (2010) recommends the establishment of monitoring, analysis, and reporting mechanisms on

conflict-related sexual violence. Resolution 2106 (2013) focuses on the operationalisation and strengthening of mechanisms to respond to sexual violence, including efforts to end impunity for such crimes.

10 See 'Preventing Conflict, Transforming Justice, Securing the Peace' – A Global Study on the Implementation of United Nations Security Council Resolution 1325, http://wps.unwomen.org/.

11 One or two of the chapters arrived too late to send to our 'reflections writers', and in the final construction of the book we moved some chapters to different parts, hence reference is occasionally made to chapters which now appear in a different part.

References

Abdullah-Khan, Noreen. 2008. *Male Rape: The Emergence of a Social and Legal Issue*. New York: Palgrave Macmillan.

Back, Les. 2016. *Academic Diary: Or Why Higher Education Still Matters*. London: Goldsmiths Press.

Beasley, Christine. 2008. 'Rethinking Hegemonic Masculinity in a Globalizing World'. *Men and Masculinities* 11(1): 86–103.

Belkin, Aaron. 2012. *Bring Me Men: Military Masculinity and the Benign Facade of American Empire, 1898–2001*. London: C. Hurst & Co.

Beynon, John. 2002. *Masculinities and Culture*. Buckingham, PA: Open University Press.

Boesten, Jelke. 2014. *Sexual Violence during War and Peace: Gender, Power, and Post-Conflict Justice in Peru*. London: Palgrave Macmillan.

Boesten, Jelke. 2017. 'Of Exceptions and Continuities: Theory and Methodology in Research on Conflict-Related Sexual Violence'. *International Feminist Journal of Politics* 19(4): 506–519.

CEDAW – UN Committee on the Elimination of Discrimination Against Women. 1992. *CEDAW General Recommendation No. 19: Violence Against Women*. Accessed 5 November 2017. www.refworld.org/docid/52d920c54.html.

Chisholm, Amanda and Joanna Tidy (eds). 2017. 'Masculinities at the Margins'. Special Issue, *Critical Military Studies* 3(2): 99–102.

Christian, Mervyn, Octave Safari, Paul Ramazani, Gilbert Burnham, and Nancy Glass. 2011. 'Sexual and Gender Based Violence against Men in the Democratic Republic of Congo: Effects on Survivors, Their Families and the Community'. *Medicine, Conflict and Survival* 27(4): 227–246.

Cohen, Claire. 2014. *Male Rape is a Feminist Issue: Feminism, Governmentality and Male Rape*. London: Palgrave Macmillan.

Connell, Raewyn W. 2005 [1995]. *Masculinities*, 2nd edn. Berkeley, CA: University of California Press

Davies, Sara E. and Jacqui True. 2015. 'Reframing Conflict-Related Sexual and Gender-Based Violence: Bringing Gender Analysis Back in'. *Security Dialogue* 46(6): 495–512.

Dawes, James. 2014. *Evil Men*. Cambridge, MA: Harvard University Press.

De Brouwer, Anne-Marie. 2005. *Supranational Criminal Prosecution of Sexual Violence: The ICC and the Practice of the ICTY and the ICTR*. Antwerp: Intersentia.

Dolan, Chris. 2002. 'Collapsing Masculinities and Weak States: A Case Study of Northern Uganda'. In Frances Cleaver (ed.), *Masculinities Matter!: Men, Gender and Development*. London: Zed Books.

Dolan, Chris. 2011. *Social Torture: The Case of Northern Uganda, 1986–2006*. New York: Berghahn Books.

Dolan, Chris. 2014a. 'Letting Go of the Gender Binary: Charting New Pathways for Humanitarian Interventions on Gender-Based Violence'. *International Review of the Red Cross* 96(894): 485–501.

Dolan, Chris. 2014b. 'Into the Mainstream: Addressing Sexual Violence against Men and Boys in Conflict'. A briefing paper prepared for the workshop held at the *Overseas Development Institute*, London, 14 May 2014. www.warchild.org.uk/sites/default/files/Into-the-Mainstream.pdf.

Dolan, Chris. 2014c. 'Has Patriarchy Been Stealing the Feminists' Clothes? Conflict-Related Sexual Violence and UN Security Council Resolutions'. *IDS Bulletin* 45(1): 80–84.

Dolan, Chris. 2015. 'Letting Go of the Gender Binary: Charting New Pathways for Humanitarian Interventions on Gender-Based Violence'. *International Review of the Red Cross* No. 894.

Dolan, Chris, Laurel E. Fletcher, and Stephen Oola. 2013. 'Promoting Accountability for Conflict-Related Sexual Violence: A Comparative Legal Analysis of International and Domestic Laws Relating to IDP and Refugee Men in Uganda'. *Refugee Law Project Working Paper No. 24*.

Drumond, Paula. 2015. 'Sexual Violence Against Men during Conflicts: Bridging the Gap between Theory and Practice'. Scientific Report. Geneva: The Graduate Institute. Accessed 19 February 2018. http://graduateinstitute.ch/files/live/sites/iheid/files/sites/genre/shared/Genre_docs/2342_TRavauxEtRecherches/Report_SVAM_%20Work shop.pdf.

Drumond, Paula. 2017. 'Embodied Battlefields: Uncovering Sexual Violence against Men in War Theaters'. PhD diss., The Graduate Institute, Geneva.

Edström, Jerker, Chris Dolan, Thea Shahrokh, and Onen David. 2016. 'Therapeutic Activism: Men of Hope Refugee Association Uganda Breaking the Silence over Male Rape in Conflict-related Sexual Violence'. *IDS Evidence Report 182*. March 2016. Accessed 19 February 2018. https://opendocs.ids.ac.uk/opendocs/bitstream/handle/123456789/9995/ER182_TherapeuticActivismMenofHopeRefugeeAssociationUganda BreakingtheSilenceoverMaleRapeinConflictrelatedSexualViolence.pdf;jsessionid=4E3 352983E856ACAAA5053376D97095E?sequence=1.

Eriksson Baaz, Maria, and Maria Stern. 2009. 'Why Do Soldiers Rape?: Masculinity, Violence, and Sexuality in the Armed Forces in the Congo (DRC)'. *International Studies Quarterly* 53(2): 495–518.

Eriksson Baaz, Maria and Maria Stern. 2013. *Sexual Violence as a Weapon of War?: Perceptions, Prescriptions, Problems in the Congo and Beyond*. London: Zed Books.

Eriksson Baaz, Maria and Maria Stern. Forthcoming. 'Curious Erasures: The Sexual in Wartime Sexual Violence'. Under review at the *International Feminist Journal of Politics*.

Ferrales, Gabrielle, Hollie Nyseth Brehm, and Suzy McElrath. 2016. 'Gender-Based Violence Against Men and Boys in Darfur: The Gender-Genocide Nexus'. *Gender and Society* 30(4): 565–589.

Fischell, Joe. 2016. *Sex and Harm in the Age of Consent*. Minneapolis, MN: University of Minnesota Press.

Gavey, Nicola. 2005. *Just Sex? – The Cultural Scaffolding of Rape*. New York: Routledge.

Goetz, Anne Marie. 2014. Preventing Violence Against Women: A Sluggish Cascade? *Open Democracy*. 25 November. Accessed 25 February 2018. www.opendemocracy.net/5050/anne-marie-goetz/preventing-violence-against-women-sluggish-cascade.

Goldstein, Joshua S. 2001. *War and Gender: How Gender Shapes the War System and Vice Versa*. Cambridge: Cambridge University Press.

Grey, Rosemary, and Laura J. Shepherd. 2012. ' "Stop Rape Now?" Masculinity, Responsibility, and Conflict-Related Sexual Violence'. *Men and Masculinities* 16(1): 115–135.

Halley, Janet. 2008. 'Rape at Rome: Feminist Interventions in the Criminalization of Sex-Related Violence in Positive International Criminal Law'. *Michigan Journal of International Law* 30: 1–123.

Hearn, Jeff. 1996. 'Is Masculinity Dead?: A Critical Account of the Concepts of Masculinity and Masculinities'. In Mairtin Mac An Ghaill (ed.), *Understanding Masculinities: Social Relations and Cultural Arenas*. Buckingham: Open University Press, 202–217.

Heberle, Renée J. and Victoria Grace. 2009. *Theorizing Sexual Violence*. New York: Routledge.

Higate, Paul. 2003. *Military Masculinities: Identity and the State*. Westport, CT: Praeger.

Hutchings, Kimberly. 2008. 'Making Sense of Masculinity and War'. *Men and Masculinities* 10(4): 389–404.

IICI (Institute for International Criminal Investigations). 2016. 'Guidelines for Investigating Conflict-Related Sexual Violence against Men and Boys'. *The Hague: Institute for International Criminal Investigations (IICI)*. www.iici.info/uploads/docs/160229_IICI_InvestigationGuidelines_ConflictRelatedSGBVagainstMenBoys.pdf.

Kirby, Paul and Marsha Henry (eds). 2012. 'Rethinking Masculinity and Practices of Violence in Conflict Settings'. Special Issue, *International Feminist Journal of Politics* 14(4): 445–449.

Kronsell, Annika. 2015. 'Sexed Bodies and Military Masculinities: Gender Path Dependence in EU's Common Security and Defense Policy'. *Men and Masculinities* 19(3): 311–336.

Joachim, Jutta. 1999. 'Shaping the Human Rights Agenda: The Case of Violence Against Women'. In Mary K. Meyer and Elisabeth Prügl (eds), *Gender Politics in Global Governance*. Lanham, MD: Rowman & Littlefield, 142–160.

Jones, Adam, and Augusta Del Zotto. 2002. 'Male-on-Male Sexual Violence in Wartime: Human Rights' Last Taboo?' Paper presented at the *Annual Convention of the International Studies Association*. New Orleans, 23–27 March.

Kapur, Amrita and Kelli Muddell. 2016. 'When No One Calls It Rape: Addressing Sexual Violence Against Men and Boys'. *International Center for Transitional Justice* (ICTJ). www.ictj.org/publication/sexual-violence-men-boys.

Lewis, Dustin A. 2009. 'Unrecognized Victims: Sexual Violence Against Men in Conflict Settings Under International Law'. *Wisconsin International Law Journal* 27(1): 1–49.

Messerschmidt, James W. 2012. *Gender, Heterosexuality, and Youth Violence: The Struggle for Recognition*. Plymouth: Rowman & Littlefield.

Mezey, Gillian C. and Michael B. King (eds.) 2000. *Male Victims of Sexual Assault*. 2nd edn. Oxford: Oxford University Press.

Mouthaan, Solange. 2013. 'Sexual Violence against Men and International Law – Criminalising the Unmentionable'. *International Criminal Law Review* 13(3): 665–695.

Oosterveld, Valerie. 2014. 'Sexual Violence Directed Against Men and Boys in Armed Conflicts and Mass Atrocities: Addressing a Gendered Harm in International Criminal Tribunals'. *Journal of International Law and International Relations* 10: 107–128.

Pankhurst, Donna. 2010. 'Sexual Violence in War'. In Laura J. Shepherd (ed.), *Gender Matters in Global Politics: A Feminist Introduction to International Relations*. London: Routledge, 148–160.

Parpart, Jane L. and Marysia Zalewski (eds). 2008. *Rethinking the Man Question.* London: Zed Books.

Peterson, V. Spike. 2010. 'Gendered Identities, Ideologies, and Practices in the Context of War and Militarism'. In Laura Sjoberg and Sandra Via (eds), *Gender, War, and Militarism: Feminist Perspectives*. Santa Barbara, CA: ABC-CLIO, LLC, 17–29.

Scarce, Michael. 1997. *Male on Male Rape: The Hidden Toll of Stigma and Shame*. New York: Basic Books.

Sivakumaran, Sandesh. 2007. 'Sexual Violence Against Men in Armed Conflict'. *European Journal of International Law* 18(2): 253–276.

Sivakumaran, Sandesh. 2010. 'Lost in Translation: UN Responses to Sexual Violence against Men and Boys in Situations of Armed Conflict'. *International Review of the Red Cross* 92(877): 259–277.

Sivakumaran, Sandesh. 2013. 'Prosecuting Sexual Violence Against Men and Boys'. In Anne-Marie de Brouwer, Charlotte Ku, Renee Romkens, and Larissa van den Herik (eds), *Sexual Violence as an International Crime: Interdisciplinary Approaches*. Cambridge: Intersentia, 79–97.

Skjelsbæk, Inger. 2001. 'Sexual Violence and War: Mapping Out a Complex Relationship'. *European Journal of International Relations* 7(2): 211–237.

Stemple, Lara. 2009. 'Male Rape and Human Rights'. *Hastings Law Journal* 60: 605–645.

Stern, Maria, and Marysia Zalewski. 2009. 'Feminist Fatigue(s): Reflections on Feminism and Familiar Fables of Militarisation'. *Review of International Studies* 35(3): 611–630.

UK Foreign & Commonwealth Office. 2017. *International Protocol on the Documentation and Investigation of Sexual Violence in Conflict*, 2nd edn, March. www.gov.uk/government/uploads/system/uploads/attachment_data/file/598335/International_Protocol_2017_2nd_Edition.pdf.

UN General Assembly. 1993. *Declaration on the Elimination of Violence against Women*. 20 December 1993, A/RES/48/104. Accessed 7 November 2017. www.refworld.org/docid/3b00f25d2c.html.

UN Security Council. 2000. *Security Council Resolution 1325 (2000)* [On Women and Peace and Security]. 31 October 2000, S/RES/1325 (2000). Accessed 7 November 2017. www.refworld.org/docid/3b00f4672e.html.

UN Security Council. 2008. *Security Council Resolution 1820 (2008)* [On Acts of Sexual Violence Against Civilians in Armed Conflicts]. 19 June 2008, S/RES/1820 (2008). Accessed 7 November 2017. www.refworld.org/docid/485bbca72.html.

UN Security Council. 2009. *Security Council Resolution 1888 (2009)* [On Acts of Sexual Violence Against Civilians in Armed Conflicts]. 30 September 2009, S/RES/1888 (2009). Accessed 7 November 2017. www.refworld.org/docid/4ac9aa152.html.

UN Security Council. 2010. *Security Council Resolution 1960 (2010)* [On Women and Peace and Security]. 16 December 2010, S/RES/1960(2010). Accessed 7 November 2017. www.refworld.org/docid/4d2708a02.html.

UN Security Council. 2013. *Security Council Resolution 2106 (2013)* [On Sexual Violence in Armed Conflict]. 24 June 2013, S/RES/2106 (2013). Accessed 7 November 2017. www.refworld.org/docid/51d6b5e64.html.

Ward, Jeanne. 2016. 'It's Not about the Gender Binary, It's about the Gender Hierarchy: A Reply to "Letting Go of the Gender Binary."' *International Committee of the Red Cross* 98(1): 275–298.

Whitehead, Stephen M. 2002. *Masculinities: Key Themes and New Directions*. Cambridge: Polity.

Whitworth, Sandra. 2004. *Men, Militarism, and UN Peacekeeping: A Gendered Analysis*. Boulder, CO: Lynne Rienner Publishers.

Zalewski, Marysia. 2017. 'What's the Problem with the Concept of Military Masculinities?'. *Critical Military Studies* 3(2): 200–205.

Zalewski, Marysia and Jane L. Parpart (eds). 1998. *The 'Man' Question in International Relations*. Boulder, CO: Westview Press.

Zalewski, Marysia and Anne Sisson Runyan. 2015. ' "Unthinking": Sexual Violence in a Neoliberal Era of Spectacular Terror'. *Critical Studies on Terrorism* 8(3): 439–455.

Zarkov, Dubravka. 2001. 'The Body of the Other Man: Sexual Violence and the Construction of Masculinity, Sexuality and Ethnicity in Croatian Media'. In Caroline O. N. Moser and Fiona C. Clark (eds), *Victims, Perpetrators or Actors: Gender, Armed Conflict and Political Violence*. London: Zed Books, 69–82.

'Tribulations'[1]

Nziza Harouna D. Nzisabira

Here is an anxious male survivor of sexual violence
I don't have hope that we shall one day be assisted neither have a decent life
Why can't the service providers make it simultaneously just to avoid too many tribulations?
There I am at the health center, clinic, hospital while sitting on the bench
Then I saw some of the uncomfortable patients who were waiting to be consulted
whom couldn't sit for long
whom couldn't stand for long
whom couldn't look at people for long
And I wonder why they can't be assisted
In fact I can't keep myself from thinking about it while I am dissimulating despite too much tribulations
I am saying this with a heavy heart that I have been detained by the culture of silence for so long
Henceforth, it is time to advocate, act, talk, speak out
So then the services and the treatment of sexual violence could be simultaneously
So then and we therefore can get rid of too much tribulations
Although I have spoken out as a male survivor of sexual violence
I constantly request you to stop rejecting us
Indeed we really to be listened and assisted accordingly
I don't care even if it will take a hundred or million days to start recognizing us
As we also deserve decent life so then we shall escape these too much tribulations
I, as a male survivor of sexual violence, who was denied adequate services
I can assure you that we are very delicate
Therefore you don't have to treat us like vanity

Because we have been suffering henceforward

Before even the first South-South Institute, which took place in Uganda

But up to now nothing significant has been produced as the sign of recognizing us

Despite our hurting events we are hoping that the healing events are likely and due

We hope we are approaching the end of Tribulations

Note

1 Poem prepared as a special dedication to all the participants of the second South-South Institute in Cambodia. https://richardhoffman.org/2015/05/24/south-south-institute-on-sexual-violence-against-men-boys/. The author's recitation of the poem is available at: https://docs.google.com/file/d/0B87P6WxtSTzvVGxuMlZ4TjAzbWs/edit.

Part I

Provocations

1   Provocations in debates about sexual violence against men

Marysia Zalewski

Opening comments

It should be straightforward. It seems obvious that sexual violence is unquestionably abhorrent in any circumstances. It would then also seem obvious that attempts to effectively deal with its effects and prevent its future occurrence should be at the core of political and theoretical interventions. Yet the couplet 'sexual violence' – in practice and in theory – remains troublingly enigmatic. The relationship between 'sex' and 'violence' is a notoriously unsettled one, any connection between the two typically presented by more conservative institutions as a deviation from 'correct' versions of sex which are usually related to procreation, sometimes love. Women in many of these traditional narratives appear as simply containers for procreation, men as providers. The corporeal experiences of sex typically understated and at the same time often assumed. Here, men as active and women as passive (in all their varied physical and psychic permutations) conventionally materialise as paramount (see Chapters 2 and 5 by Hendershot and Cottet). I open this chapter with these observations in part because a plethora of paradoxes and what we might call 'complexities shrouded in simplicity' seem to mark representations of sexual violence, as well as its theorisations and attempts at its obliteration. The question or spectre of an intimate relationship between sex and violence is one that will largely remain unanswered, at least explicitly, in this volume. But it is the intellectual spirit of this opening chapter to 'unfold' paradoxes as a way to raise some questions about the inflection of debates about sexual violence. To do this, I will first briefly explain how I became interested in the issue of sexual violence against men, and then offer my reflections on a series of issues that perturb me about debates about sexual violence against men.

Introduction

I initially became interested in the incidence of sexual violence against men through an interest in the hyper-celebrity fuelled attention to sexual violence against women. This manner of violence has been subject to a great deal of theorising, policy construction, and political discussion, and current international governance attention is intense. The United Nations presents as something of a paragon of virtue in this context from the 'ground-breaking' Security Council Resolution 1325 to more recent developments including the creation of UN Women,[1] the Sustainable Development Goals,[2] the 2014 Global Summit to End Sexual Violence,[3] the latest Security Council resolutions (two of the most recent relevant ones include SCR 2106 and SCR 2122 both in 2013),[4] and the 2015 Global Report reviewing progress since UNSCR 1325.[5] These are preceded, accompanied by, and variably indebted to the multiple archives of feminist scholarship, theorising, and activism most obviously since the 1960s, at least in its documented Western frames. As such, a central reason for the abundant attention to women in this context is attributed to domination of feminist writers who have worked very hard to 'highlight the sexual victimisation of women' (Graham 2006: 188) especially as this was an 'everyday occurrence' (Brownmiller 1975; Stanko 1990; Leatherman 2011).

But we know that gender is not only about women, thus the apparent lack of sustained theoretical and political interest in sexual violence against men is curious. Humans are capable of all manner of violent acts and this kind of violence is not unusual. It is also not that sexual violence against men, especially in zones of conflict, has not visibly featured across the centuries. Goya's *Disasters of War* etchings tell explicit stories about sexually violated men.[6] Though it is true to say that sexual violence against women drenches artistic, literary, and public imaginations. The list here would be a lengthy one: the *Rape of the Sabine Women*, Jack the Ripper, tales of everyday domestic violence and the 'sex slaves' of contemporary 'extremist groups'. The prevalence of sexual violence against women seemingly increases in war and conflict scenarios, its reporting (especially currently) is immediate (more or less), its salacious presence at the top of international political agendas assuring good press and attention from researchers and policymakers alike. It's a very 'sexy' topic; a disturbing paradox perhaps. It is now not news that rape, sexual assault, and sexual mutilation have become among the 'preferred methods' of inflicting pain in wars/conflict; 'war' offers permission to deliver a whole host of inventive and brutal levels of pain. However, given current increasingly noticed incidences of sexual violence against men, the imbalance of gendered attention is causing concern – 'Everybody has heard the women's stories. But nobody has heard the men's' (Storr 2011). Men suffer from sexually violent attacks – why not simply include them in as serious ways as female victims? It should be straightforward, though it seems it is not and the reasons why are complex, some of which I will point to in this chapter (and other authors in the book will take these complexities up in varied ways).

The remainder of this chapter works with what Barbara Tomlinson describes as the 'scene of argument' (2010), or, simply the framing of debates, specifically here around some of the reasons made (even if via assumption) for the theoretical and conceptual inclusion of men and boys made in debates around the gender(ing) of sexual violence. My discussion here will focus on a range of inter-connected issues, though these sections will be brief, more akin to 'snap-shots' and in some ways are intentionally 'unfinished'. The issues are ones that that have vexed me in my readings around a variety of debates and discussions on sexual violence against men.[7] By way of a conclusion, I reflect on what I think might be at stake.

That description is (almost) enough (data speaks first)

What do we think when we read about sexual violence? What can we think? I open a book on sexual violence in conflict and I am usually immediately assailed by a searing list of sexually violent incidents. The detail has become familiar. But what does the list prove – that the facts 'speak for themselves'? 'Facts', certainly as critical scholars understand them, never speak for themselves, but are ventriloquised through 'sedimented layers of previous interpretations' (Jameson 2001: 101), or some facts, as Tomlinson puts it, 'seem already true before the moment of argument' (2010: 1). But it's not that 'the list' of sexual violations doesn't have impact – perhaps more affective than cognitive – though we might ask how certain or clear the separation between 'feeling' and 'thinking' is. When I show an image from Goya's *Disaster of War*[8] in classes and talks, one (of the many) which depicts the act of severing a man's penis, many in the audience wince; unsurprisingly. How does this sensory reaction affect or even constitute how we can think about sexual violence against men?

Of course, providing a long list of sexually violent acts to demand attention and reparation is something that feminist scholars and activists have made much use of to illustrate the gendered and sexed damage done to women and girls. The foundational conceptual work of, for example, Mary Daly and Andrea Dworkin (and a host of others in the realm of what can still be called Anglo-American radical feminism), still, surprisingly I think for many, provide the basis for a good deal of the 'gender thinking', concepts, and semantic tactics underpinning a wide range of internationalised policies on gender, perhaps especially those targeting sexual violence. There are many problems with this, not least the persistent tethering of injury to the category of woman (and the bodies of women), 'forever' placing woman in a (categorised) site of pain and bloodied victimhood – women as 'always rapeable' (Marcus 1992). Sexual violence has a particular place in this rendition, with women so often figuratively positioned as (always) at the mercy of patriarchal power and the vicious ways that violence could get hidden in the frames of love or sex. The verification of such injuries *as* injury became a crucial way in which feminist scholars and activists could both prove the truth of the violence of patriarchal power and gain the right to pursue justice and hopefully reform (Bumilller 2008). The facts of violence against women, not least sexual violence, did, it seems, begin to 'speak for themselves'. Importantly so, as Emily Martin made clear some time ago, women's stories of violence 'are not trivial (...) they are radical, they are threatening, they would mean revolution' (1988: 20). Could it be just the same for men? That the facts of sexual violence against men simply but powerfully need to be afforded visibility and credibility, opening up chances for justice and reparations to follow? Can gender be so conceptually simple especially when it has seemed to belong (only) to women despite decades of more nuanced and attentive theorising? Erring on the side of theoretical and sensory caution is usually sound advice as Gunne and Brigley Thompson reminds us that:

> A powerful subject like rape [or sexual violence] can be a trap ... we can be so seduced into thinking the material itself is so strong ... we don't have to engage with it very deeply – an outpouring of emotion or an emphasis on graphic detail will suffice.
>
> (Gunne and Brigley Thompson 2010: xix)

Sexual violence against men and boys is (almost) as frequent as that against women and girls

This simple proposition invokes a glut of questions, for instance, what is to be counted in the frame of 'sexual violence'? How would this be measured? Is the claim related to sexual violence in war, conflict and post-conflict zones (and when is it decided that a country/nation/state/society is beyond any of these warring states?), or sexual violence in 'peace-time'? Some of these questions will be taken up in other chapters in this book; to recall, my aim here is only to open up some of the complexities summoned by the empirical levelling of the incidence of sexual violence across the traditional gender-binary, most notably in relation to sexual violence associated with conflict/post-conflict. In this context, it is surely the case that men have conventionally been largely ignored in narratives around sexual violence (though this is also credibly claimed to be the case in 'peace-time'), as the *Guardian* headline introduced earlier about the 'darkest secret of wars' infers. Others also make this point, as Graham notes, 'male victims [of sexual violence] are largely neglected' (2006: 187), and for Sivakumaran, 'relatively little material exists on the subject [sexual violence against men in armed conflict] and the issue tends to be relegated to a footnote' (2007: 253). Though despite centuries of depictions of sexual violence against both men and women in times of conflict (especially as depicted in art), it is only in the last few decades that this kind violence has been acknowledged as 'wrong' or indeed (and crucially) as even *noticeable* as different in some way to the 'regular' violence of war – or even *as* violence at all. But it is the case that this 'new' attention has largely focused on sexual violence against women. At least that is how it seems and is generally reported in the academic literatures, related legislation and policies, and in the media. As stated earlier, perhaps a central reason for the focused attention on sexual violence against women is because of the decades of work by feminist writers who have worked very hard to highlight the sexual victimisation of women. Has this work and its ensuing influence on policy hidden the facts about sexual violence against men, designating such violence as a paradigmatically feminised injury, making masculinised ownership conceptually and psychically very difficult, oftentimes impossible?

The complexities invoked here also emerge in the atmosphere of incredulity about the veracity of claims that incidences of sexual violence are (more or less) equally divided (or suffered) by both genders.[9] Many continue to insist that 'women and girls are the primary victims of this [sexual] violence' (Ward 2016: 296).[10] However, work over the last decade or so has clearly unearthed and made visible (empirically, conceptually, legislatively) sexual violence against men in a range of conflict and post-conflict zones as the work in this volume testifies. Men are indeed a gender too and their vulnerability to violence associated with gender (notably that to which the label of 'sexual' get attached) surely must be recognised as such. Though this does beg a specific question about gender, which is: are men the same (kind of) gender as women? The answer must be no, as gender, despite its varied appearance and impact across the binary, implies difference – minimally sexual difference (Zalewski 2010; Irigaray 1993). The markers of femininity and masculinity, notwithstanding their considerable variations over time and cultures, are, it seems, indelibly marked by their difference to each other (Kramer 2000). And their constructed character enhances infinite possibilities. Thus, to make claims about the gender of specific forms of violence named sexual is to invoke, however ephemerally, the workings of gender in their differentially masculinised and feminised shapes. And the ways that masculinity and femininity in all their constructed and shifting pluralities are conjured, have different kinds of implications (to each other). Think of Hélène Cixous's provocative comment, 'when we say to a woman that she is a man or to a man that he is a woman, it's a terrible insult. This is why we cut one another's throats' (quoted in Sellers 2004: 200).

The sense of Cixous' comment is more forcefully clarified when we consider some of the ways in which narratives about sexual violence against men mobilise ideas about masculinity and what it means to be 'a man'. At the trial of Jean-Pierre Bemba,[11] one of the witnesses reported that his rapist had said after the attack, 'you are a woman now'. The forced removal of a man's 'manliness' through an act of sexual violence is powerfully invoked here. This is especially the case given the further detail supplied – his wife left him because he 'wasn't a man' anymore. Or for Dhia al Shweiri, a former prisoner in Abu Ghraib,

> we are men. It's OK if they beat me. Beatings don't hurt us: it's just a blow. But no one would want [his] manhood to be shattered. They wanted us to feel as though we were women, the way women feel, and this is the worst insult, to feel like a woman.
>
> (Puar 2007: 89)

Masculinity here is presented as the conduit through which to (fatally) damage a man, even if the body still lives. In this sense, perhaps we can say that masculinity (really does) 'make a man' (Berger, Wallis, and Watson 1995). Though this is not to say that masculinity is just something that is 'in the head', or a 'simple' matter of personal identity (Connell 1995), much less choice (Parpart and Zalewski 2008). Rather masculinity extends into the world, merging as it travels. Masculinity as a 'thing', as something which 'does (do) work', as something which is contradictorily harmful, welcome and necessary, as a thing which, despite *so* many moves away from so-called 'essentialism', constantly re-emerges as possessive of some 'deep essence', or at least if not that, so deeply lodged in the constitution of lives, feelings, laws, and corporeality, its budging is impossible, perhaps except when a man 'becomes' a woman through an act of sexual violence. This is serious.

Do we dare to ask if a woman who is raped becomes a man? This appears as 'nonsense'. Perhaps more 'sensible' and gender conforming is that a woman who is raped is (once again) confirmed as a woman (Marcus 1992; Gunne and Brigley Thompson 2010). Does this signify a (radical) distance between masculinity and femininity as well as their differentially temporal, spatial, and corporeal places? Do femininity and masculinity materialise in different sites and with different vulnerabilities – corporeally, physically, psychically, and imaginatively? Is there something about masculinity which desires, needs, or invites an 'intactness' which femininity can more easily let go of, or have opened up, like a hymen? Is damage to masculinity, even as an idea or ideal, too difficult to suture, unlike a vagina? Thus masculinity's 'falling apart' emerges as 'too much to bear'? Powerful heteronormative structuring completing the 'impossibility' of deconstruction here – posing questions about the masculine woman, for example, become problematic, perhaps impossible, inviting closer a question that prowls in discussions around the sexual violation of men – is it worse for men?

> Penetration of the female body remains 'less shocking' than that of the male body, because the definition of the male corporeal boundary is contradicted directly by such penetration, in a way that the boundaries of the female body are not.
>
> (Graham 2006: 198)

Feminist work conceals women's violence and the violence of feminism

Women, like men, are capable of perpetrating all kinds of violence; and women do commit all kinds of violence. Though it is probably right to say that the women and men tend, oftentimes, to commit different kinds of violence – attributable in part to the consequences of gendering. There is, however, a persistently lingering sense of feminist (and by association female) innocence, which in turn is stickily connected to women's 'peace-work' and traditionally secured associations with (motherly) nurturing (Zalewski and Runyan 2015; Sjoberg and Gentry 2007). This may indeed affectively and repeatedly (re)position women, and by feminised connection, feminists, as being too far removed from the possibility of violence. And potentially even *further* removed from enacting sexual violence, given this has so firmly been traditionally placed in the realms of heterosexualised masculine desire. Rightly or wrongly is not really the point. And further, it can be argued that the putative innocence of feminist scholarship, traditionally presented as an emancipatory justice project, works to conceptually conceal not only women's proclivities to violence, including sexual violence, but also to conceal the 'truth' of male victimhood (Halley 2006; Zalewski and Runyan 2013). The veracity of all of these claims might easily be challenged (or confirmed), yet there is surely something about the gendered focus on women and all her epistemological, ethical, ontological scaffolding that might go some way in explaining why there has been so little attention to sexual violence against men, at least until very recently. Again, their truth is not quite the point here, rather the lingering suspicion that these claims or intuitions may either be true, or that the dominance of feminist work in this area steers thinking about gender in these directions which place feminism and women in persistent places of imagined peacefulness and always more victims than perpetrators.

It is clear that feminism has a long history of, and association with violent militancy both epistemic and activist, and to forget this effectively places feminism in the realm of (feminised) innocent knowledge-making. Moreover, historically, feminists have worked hard to strategise around their explicit use of violence, regularly making decisions about when violence is an appropriate tactic or strategy to resist and overturn patriarchal violence (Frazer and Hutchings 2014). Perhaps more obvious is the destabilising epistemological work of feminism, even if the word violence is not typically attached to resistant knowledge-making practices. Feminist theorists have undoubtedly had the intention of overturning conventional knowledge bases in regard to gender/sex, including the bases of professionalised knowledge (such as the law, science, medicine, and education), and historical and theoretical knowledge (including philosophy, political theory, and history), as well as that powerful knowledge source – 'common sense'. It is thus surprising at one level that feminism is so clearly much more associated with peace (Sylvester 2013), as a goal and as a mode of non-violent activism. Yet a question still remains: how has feminist work contributed to making invisible the violences of concern in this volume? Conversely, feminism is consistently engineered as an easy target for violence:

> Over time, forces threatened by feminist violations of oppressive conventions and social orders have done everything, from muzzling, imprisoning, torturing, and killing assumed feminists (often 'simply' women) to ignoring, trivializing, expropriating, and excoriating feminist ideas while periodically and hopefully pronouncing feminist dead.
>
> (Zalewski and Runyan 2013: 298)

The sense that gender is a neutral tool as if sexual politics had been settled once and for all

I've pondered a lot over Anne Marie Goetz's challenging suggestion that, 'the recent focus on male victims of war rape can have the unfortunate effect of further postponing the feminist social change project' (2014). On Goetz's account, we might agree with Joanna Bourke in that, 'feminists are right to be wary' (2007: 246) about increasing the focus on men. Or as White puts it, 'to talk about men and masculinities was *dangerous*, risking the hard-won gains of feminism and chronically open to co-option, since patriarchal values and practices remain dominant in both society and development institutions' (Cornwall and White 2000: 34). Might it really be the case that what we might call 'conventional gendered favouritisms' would induce the usual patriarchal dirty work in such a difficult context, such that resources, attention, and agenda setting would begin to funnel over to men? Rosi Braidotti presciently reminds us, 'my entire conditioning, enforced by a whole socio-political system, pushes me to rejoicing at having yet another opportunity to think talk dream about "men"' (1987: 239).

This tenor of thoughts might not feel appropriate in the context of such violence. And yet if the sense is that the (feminist) use of gender can result in serious gender inequities such that feminist work has resulted in egregious bias (Misra 2015), its balancing might be appropriate to consider – perhaps to 'add men and stir' (Drumond 2017). The idea of 'gender inclusivity' is key here. Though as the idea and practice of 'adding women and stirring' has been thoroughly criticised as ultimately (and minimally) failing to deal with or properly understand structural discrimination, questions about similar problems with the idea of 'adding men and stirring' might be raised. If the arguments turn on the (feminist) bias of gender theory (and practice), and men are 'a gender too', there is a compelling if simple logic to 'adding men and stirring'. Indeed, a strong sense of justice to this as argued by those who advocate for 'gender inclusivity' (Jones 2009; Dolan 2014). Chris Dolan articulates it well, 'to reverse the current malfunction of gender as an analytical, practical and political engine, we must replace women and girls as the default at-risk group with more gender-inclusive formulations' (2014: 500). One of Dolan's central arguments is that 'conceptual barriers' have led to the assumption that gender power and inequality is unidirectional with the result that gender power is believed to always have 'the same biological targets and the related view that (sexual) violence against women and children is the paradigmatic expression of these unidirectional inequalities' (Dolan 2014: 500). Yet, as he says, if gender is a social construct, it follows that men can be vulnerable too. This manner of reasoning fuels the argument for a flattening out of gender, or rather an equalising of gender in debates around sexual violence against men.

In her discussion about politics and pain, Sara Ahmed notes that the production of equivalence (of pain) allows injury to become an entitlement, going on to stress the need to 'attend to the different ways "wounds" enter politics' (2004: 32–33). This may be important work to do in the context of sexual violence, not least given the questions that might be raised in regard to claiming the vulnerability of the 'Other' invoked in arguments about gender inclusivity; there is something curious about claiming the vulnerability of 'the Other' as might be seen when 'white people' claim racist injury. Though it is credible to claim women have traditionally been presented as the 'weaker sex' in need of protection, even if this materialises oftentimes as akin to a 'protection racket' (Eisenstein 1983; Young 2003; Sjoberg and Peteet 2011; Zalewski and Runyan, forthcoming), it is also the case that the male subject is classically the privileged site of anxiety. And as the aesthetic and corporeal repository of masculinity, re-inscribing masculinity perhaps too easily becomes a site of priority. We might continue to ask questions about sexual politics here as the latter can reveal the ways in which gender remains structured by hierarchical power, which conventionally reserves/preserves 'special' places for those positioned along gender binaries:

> With sexual politics consigned to the past (…) gender inequalities are renewed and patriarchal norms reinstated.
>
> (O'Neill 2015: 102)

The biological 'truth' of sex organs

Are there sex organs really? Of course, the answer must be yes at one level given the centuries of knowledge-building that has gone into firming up the boundaries and borders of what we call the human body in all its variations, though always with a standard or centre, even as this shifts. I pause here to note that my questions, especially those that are more seemingly abstract and conceptually focused, might seem inappropriate, insensitive when bodies are broken, lives ripped apart. Yet how gender and its intimate relations – sex, violence, rafts of other identity markers, and makers/breakers of lives – have life breathed into them matters. And how these markers, with gender as one example, work to extinguish life or make lives unliveable matters deeply. Another way to think about all this is through the concept (and work) of *social construction*. This concept, or idea about the productive character of life, living, feeling, and thinking with all its attendant material consequences has found a fairly comfortable place in the lexicon of critical theorising, though I wonder if the idea of social construction has largely failed to make its conceptual and material mark (Vance 1996), at least within the discipline of International Relations[12] and specifically in regard to gender and feminist theorising. Of course, sexual violence can break lives; though concepts (simultaneously) can break (or make) them too (see Hendershot, Ch. 2 in this volume).

The sense or construction of the 'truth' of the body – through biology, medicine, science, religion, and 'common sense' – has conjured a morass of ways to 'fix', ignore, or condemn types of bodies that don't 'fit' or don't 'work appropriately (according to tradition and imposed standards). Critical analysis of the allegedly 'disabled' body, for example, reveals myriad ways in which sexual identity or sexual sensation is denied to those bodies without (working) conventional sexual organs or parts (see Hendershot, Ch. 2 in this volume), despite protestations to the contrary from the inhabitants of those bodies (see Shildrick 2009; Shakespeare 2017). Differently marked (and constructed) bodies are persistently awarded differential treatment.

One way in which this has been noted in debates around the lack of attention to sexual violence against men, is in regard to medical specialisms and particularly that those medical specialisms for women by default harm men as there is no equivalent to obstetrics and gynaecology. This is an interesting observation. The history of the development of medical specialisms related to specific diseases or parts of the body is intriguing and important. And it is surely the case that obstetrics and gynaecology are both historically and currently a significant part of medical science and practice. Obstetrics relates to pregnancy, childbirth and midwifery; gynaecology is the branch of medicine, which deals with the functions and diseases specific to women and girls, especially those affecting the reproductive system. Regarding the relationship with sexual violence, the sheer amount of skill, knowledge, and expertise available, has surely made 'easier' the restoration of women's bodies consequent to overt (physical) damage done to sexual/reproductive parts through sexual violence. Where does this figure in the 'gender debate' or 'scene(s) of argument' at issue here? It is the case that there is not a similar medical specialism or major field dedicated to the reproductive parts of men's bodies. One might say that this development would be logical given the life endangering complications that have marked childbirth for millennia, even today in all parts of the world, if very differentially. But there are other gendered stories to tell about the history of the development of the fields of obstetrics and gynaecology though, many indelibly marked by histories of control and management of women's reproductive functions, desires, and possibilities. In part, this might be attributed to women's perceived inferiority (to men), circling back to the 'truth' of sex-reproductive organs and parts. As Nancy Tuana articulates it, 'for centuries, Western science accounted for women's perceived inferiority by referring to her role in reproduction' (1993: 111). And it might also be noted that the term or identity of 'gynaecologist' emerged from 'man-midwife' consequent to the massacre of 'witches/wise women' in the European/American 'witch-hunts' of the sixteenth–nineteenth centuries (Daly 1987: 224). The history of the development of gynaecology, fuelled by increasingly popular 'sciences' including Freudian psychoanalysis, is littered with savage removals of parts of women's bodies as a way to reduce or annihilate their gendered 'threat levels', most notably through the removal of ovaries, clitorises, and wombs.

However, it remains credible to claim there is a preponderance of medical specialisms geared towards women's sexual and reproductive body parts and functions. But in what ways does this knowledge or 'reality' help to better explain incidences of sexual violence against men, or to more effectively help in the recuperation of men's sexually violated bodies? What roles do the powerful underlying and simultaneously often overwhelming gendered and sexed narratives of such truths have to play? Are these gendered trenches of knowledge, which illustrate viscerally clear markers of differentially gendered trajectories ready to be discarded?

> The physiology of orgasm and penile erection no more explain a culture's sexual schema than the auditory range of the human ear explains its music.
>
> (Vance 1996: 47)

Persistent Othering of those outside the conventional gender binary

If men are a footnote, 'other' genders/sexes are even more 'relegated' or rendered invisible. This despite the evidence that LGTBQI+ people are more likely to suffer from violent attacks – typically targeting their perceived 'wrong' sexual or gendered presentation.[13] But where can other (genders/sexes) be placed in the conceptual vortex of the gender binary, a binary which is doing a good deal of work in these debates. Is this 'category' (is it one really?) of people simply to be slotted in, 'added in' as men might be? A different tenor of questions begins to emerge here, less to do with the injustices of inclusion/exclusion in regard to the gender binary, and more to do with the types of sense that can be made of a binaried sexed system, if all distinctions should be flattened out (no trans, bi, queer, gay, gender fluid, female, male – just sexually violated bodies). Though of course, what 'sex' is being violated then, perhaps leading to the question: are we asking the right questions at all?

Perhaps the preoccupation with inclusion/exclusion in regard to gender/sex is something of a red herring. Despite seeming otherwise, the 'additive' endeavour erases some of the most serious work that categories perform; it might even assist these erasures. The hope in moving those from the holding pattern of parentheses (as in a footnote or brackets – literally, metaphorically, grammatically, empirically, theoretically) into the main body (of a sentence, a policy, a conceptual framework) is perhaps misplaced. This dream of inclusion displays an extraordinary faith in, bizarrely, the idea of equality in the realm of sexed categories. And a belief that such categories are 'simply' about corporeal/psychic identity and not entangled in the labyrinthine mire of larger concepts and constructs of the political. An illustration of one 'complexity shrouded in simplicity' here, is the simplistic idea that the inclusion of LGTBQI+ people into the frame of protection from sexual violence in conflict can only be an 'absolute good'. Yet as those scholars working with queer theory argue, when the international political spotlight falls upon those bodies which disturb conventional sexed boundaries, caution is advised (Puar 2007; Weber 2016; Drumond 2017). The seemingly benign inclusion of LGTBQI+ people can instead work to sanction unwarranted interventions. This is perhaps similar to the notorious use of gender in relation to women's vulnerability, typically as a rationale for intervention of all kinds as in the military invasion of Afghanistan in 2001, which was partly justified on the grounds of 'women's rights'.[14] In the context of LGTBQI+ people, the transmission of the Global North's rhetorics around allowable sexed and gendered relationships and roles can easily morph into future rationales for all manner of interventions:

> We also know that any single-axis identity politics is invariably going to coagulate around the most conservative, normative construction of that identity.
>
> (Puar, Pitcher, and Gunkel 2008)

... and that leaves race ... (as it is so often 'left')

Figure 1.1 Marché d'esclaves.

Source: http://autourduperetanguy.blogspirit.com/archive/2011/04/04/le-guide-du-commerce-de-l-amerique-principalement-dans-le-po.html.

One of the most extraordinary and most brutal incidences of historically lingering sexual violence that might be encountered is one that was violently produced through the pitiless prisms of race, gender, and colonialism. This violence was enacted on the woman known as both Sara Baartman and 'the Hottentot Venus'. Born on the South African frontier in the 1770s where she lived for nearly three decades, she then spent five years in Europe before dying in Paris in 1815 (Crais and Scully 2009). Images of her 'as' the Hottentot Venus are easily locatable via the internet, most usually ones showing her being inspected by white colonial men peering curiously and excitedly at her 'excessively large' buttocks – 'a supposedly paradoxical freak of race and sexuality, both alluring and primitive' (Crais and Scully 2009: 1). The last few years of her short life have been relentlessly presented as standing in for 'the whole', but even on death, she did not escape violation. Her corpse was dissected by the then revered scientist Georges Cuvier who remade her into a plaster cast – she was seemingly always available to be made, unmade, and remade – accessible for tens of thousands to see, indeed millions given the throngs who attended the Universal Exhibition in Paris in 1889. 'Even while dead the female still engenders her sexual punishment' (Bumiller 2008: 23). Her brain, skeleton, and sexual organs remained on display in a Paris museum until 1974 and her remains were not repatriated and buried until 2002, when Nelson Mandela arranged for her return and burial.

I chose not to show an image of Sara Baartman here, mindful of Avery Gordon's words about a slave belonging to a white man in nineteenth-century America, who had been ordered to pose nude for the benefit of scientific studies, 'she was just a piece of data waiting for his words to write her up, to pass her down to us as social science' (2001: 185). Or as Trinh T Minh-ha articulates, 'it's as if everywhere we go, we become Someone's private zoo' (1987: 7). The image I do show here is from the Afro-American Slave Trade and depicts a similar, if less well-known site (and sight) of colonial and racial inspection.[15] This image, discussed at length by Frederik Charles Staidum Jr, has the caption which states, 'A Britishman licks the chin of a Negro to verify his age and to discover, by the taste of his sweat, if he is ill' (2007: 59). As Staidum claims,

> Penetration figures heavily within this image, as the European enslaver pries the African male's mouth open and peers in. Like the use of the tongue in the previous engraving, this act of insertion is seemingly asexual, but the White man's ability to trespass on to and into the Black male body speaks to absolute power to transcend any boundary.
>
> (Staidum 2007: 82)

Staidum goes on to describe the scene as an 'uninvited transgression' given the unsought licking of the flesh, elaborating;

> He licks the flesh of the African, in order to determine the African's state of health, which is not an uncommon act for the time period (…) the forced exchange of bodily fluids is tainted with the threat of sexualized violence.
>
> (Staidum 2007: 76)

In contemporary imaginaries, the chin, nose, or ears do not readily appear as a potential corporeal site of sexual assault, yet as Staidum states, 'in nineteenth-century inconographics [sic] and physiognomy, ears were constructed, as were genitalia, as organs that exposed pathological essence, particularly of prostitutes and sexual women' (2007: 187). Thus, within the world of nineteenth-century medical conventions and aesthetics, a sexual value was attached to facial anatomy. Examining the ear or other facial features, then, is likened to examining the genitalia for reproductive potential or sadistic pleasure.

What might we take from this instance of violation? How does it help us with our questions about sexual violence against men? Perhaps it might provoke us to ask more rigorous questions about what counts *as* a sexual organ, and what the consequences are of being so deeply in the thrall of conventional and contemporarily defined sexual parts and acts; recall Gayle Rubin's insight that sexual acts are 'burdened with an excess of significance' (1984: 151). We might want to further pursue analytical failures in regard to the idea of 'social construction'; recall Carol Vance's comment mentioned earlier, 'the physiology of orgasm and penile erection no more explain a culture's sexual schema than the auditory range of the human ear explains its music' (1996: 47). We might also reconsider how we vastly underestimate, despite academic appearances to the contrary, the ways in which bodies and subjectivities are exhaustively and microscopically constituted through the heavily textured range of identity categories that we periodically appear to 'know' (and do) something about. Queered and raced bodies persistently disappearing in this analytic scenario, slipping so often away from the 'secured' realm of the 'unviolatable'. The popular concept of 'intersectionality' has seemed, especially in academic vernacular, to seductively offer a way out of this dilemma. Yet it is the very familiar binary of sex–gender (Stern and Zalewski 2009) that persistently navigates its way to the surface of attention in debates around sexual violence.

Concluding discussion

'Inevitably, a work is always a form of tangible closure. But closures need not close off; they can be doors opening onto other closures and functioning as ongoing passages to an elsewhere (-within-here)' (Minh-ha 1991: 15). I opened this chapter saying I aimed to unfold paradoxes and raise some questions about the inflection of debates about sexual violence. One motivation for this discussion (and book) was the historical lack of empirical, political, or theoretical concern for sexual violence against men especially in conflict and post-conflict zones. There has been a marked change in this over the last decade or so with much more work being done on this violence as many of the authors in this volume discuss. As men suffer from sexually violent attacks, it makes contemporary sense to include them in as serious ways as female victims. The attention to sexual violence especially that relating to conflict, has grown exponentially over the last several decades, most clearly targeting that violence meted out to women and girls. Variations of patriarchy, sexism, and misogyny – whether freshly present or the heavy lingering of decaying vestiges – are singled out as causes for sexual violence against women and count as central reasons for ardent theoretical and political attention. Serious epistemological points hover in the background and nurture the foreground of these simple assertions; though we might ask what use is epistemology when medicine, surgery, or simple care of all kinds is what is needed in the time of pain and injury. What worth is there in debating the conceptual intricacies of gender/sex ordering? When faced with men or boys in pain, damaged, broken, sometimes destroyed in the wake of sexual violence – conceptual and epistemological questions are indeed temporally useless, obscene even. Though this is not to say that they are absent in the making of the moment and the pain, and the 'unmaking' of a man. But in the moment of need, that need is all that matters.

But there is more to say here. More could be said about how gender and sex are made, about how they become, and how they might be unmade. And there is much more to say about the direction of travel in regard to concepts and theory, and gender, sex, and violence. But as I said at the beginning of this chapter, my aim here has only been to (begin to) open up paradoxes and questions, and flag up 'complexities shrouded in simplicity'; the substantive work can only be touched on or gestured towards here, to be taken up more deeply in further work by many of the contributors to this volume here and in other work. So, I finish by briefly pondering on a quotation from Lawrence Kramer – 'the tendency to sexual violence seems lodged in the very core of ordinary subjectivity like a bone in the throat' (2000: 2). Kramer's provocation may at first glance seem to imply inevitability and necessity which regularly emerge as akin to an 'evil duo' pitted against the earnest endeavours of those of us who place so much hope in the value of telling the 'right' stories, or advocating for sociologically and behaviourally inspired remedies and cures. But Kramer's intention is more nuanced and interrogatory than this suggests; he offers a very powerful hint about the untapped force of connections between sex, gender, and violence, despite apparent abundant data and knowledge. Many questions about sexual violence have persistently been asked, but given the range of potential 'complexities shrouded in simplicity' gestured towards in this chapter, we might consider radically overhauling the kinds of questions that we ask about this egregious and relentless form of human harming.

Notes

1 See the UN Women website, www.unwomen.org/en.
2 See the UN's Sustainable Development Goals, www.un.org/sustainabledevelopment/sustainable-development-goals/.
3 See Global Summit to End Sexual Violence in Conflict, London, 2014, www.gov.uk/government/topical-events/sexual-violence-in-conflict.
4 See 'Security Council Adopts Resolution 2122 (2013), Aiming to Strengthen Women's Role in All Stages of Conflict Prevention, Resolution', United Nations, 18 October 2013, www.un.org/press/en/2013/sc11149.doc.htm; and United Nations Peacekeeping, www.un.org/en/peacekeeping/issues/women/wps.shtml.
5 See 'Preventing Conflict, Transforming Justice, Securing the Peace' – A Global Study on the Implementation of United Nations Security Council Resolution 1325, http://wps.unwomen.org/.
6 To view the 82 prints by Francisco Goya in the series *The Disasters of War*, dating from 1810–1820, see www.richardharrisartcollection.com/portfolio-view/francisco-goya-2/.
7 These vexations have emerged from a wide set of my readings on sexual violence against men. A range of associated references will be included throughout.
8 *The Disasters of War* (*Los desastres de la guerra*) is a series of eighty-two prints created between 1810 and 1820 by the Spanish painter and printmaker Francisco Goya.
9 And the conventional binary remains paramount in these discussions.
10 For further reflections, see Cottet (Ch. 5 in this volume).
11 The former Congolese vice-president, Jean-Pierre Bemba, who was brought to trial by the International Criminal Court for Crimes of Sexual Violence in War. See Bowcott (2016).
12 Which is the discipline I am most familiar with.
13 See 'Responding to Transgender Victims of Sexual Assault', Office for Victims of Crime, June 2014, www.ovc.gov/pubs/forge/sexual_numbers.html; and 'Sexual Assault and the LGBTQ Community', Human Rights Campaign, www.hrc.org/resources/sexual-assault-and-the-lgbt-community.
14 See James Gerstenzang and Lisa Getter, 'Laura Bush Addresses State of Afghan Women', *Los Angeles Times*, 18 November 2018, http://articles.latimes.com/2001/nov/18/news/mn-5602.
15 Laurent, fec. Illustration for [Chambon], Le commerce de L'Amérique par Marseille (Avignon, 1764), vol. II, pl. XI, facing p. 400: Marché d'esclaves. Copper engraving. Page: 249 × 190 mm. The image is available in the public domain.

40 *Marysia Zalewski*

References

Ahmed, Sara. 2004. *The Cultural Politics of Emotion*. Edinburgh: Edinburgh University Press.

Berger, Maurice, Brian Wallis and Simon Watson (eds). 1995. *Constructing Masculinity*. London: Routledge.

Bourke, Joanna. 2007. *Rape: A History from 1860 to the Present*. London: Virago.

Bowcott, Owen. 2016. 'Congo Politician Guilty in First ICC trial to Focus on Rape as a War Crime'. *Guardian*, 21 March. Accessed 12 November 2017. www.theguardian.com/world/2016/mar/21/icc-finds-ex-congolese-vice-president-jean-pierre-bemba-guilty-of-war-crimes.

Braidotti, Rosi. 1987. 'Envy: Or with Your Brain and My Looks'. In Alice Jardine and Paul Smith (eds), *Men in Feminism*. New York: Methuen.

Brownmiller, Susan. 1975. *Against Our Will. Men, Women and Rape*. New York: Fawcett Books.

Bumiller, Kristin. 2008. *In an Abusive State: How Neoliberalism Appropriated The Feminist Movement Against Sexual Violence*. Durham, NC: Duke University Press.

Connell, Raewyn W. 1995. *Masculinities*. Berkeley, CA: University of California Press.

Cornwall, Andrea and Sarah C. White. 2000. 'Men, Masculinities and Development Politics, Policies and Practice'. *IDS Bulletin* 31(2): 1–6.

Crais, Clifton and Pamela Scully. 2009. *Sara Baartman and the Hottentot Venus: A Ghost Story and a Biography*. Princeton, NJ: Princeton University Press.

Daly, Mary. 1987. *Gyn-Ecology: The Metaethics of Radical Feminism*. Boston, MA: Beacon Press.

Dolan, Chris. 2014. 'Letting Go of the Gender Binary: Charting New Pathways for Humanitarian Interventions on Gender-Based Violence'. *International Review of the Red Cross* 96(894): 485–501.

Drumond, Paula. 2017. 'Embodied Battlefields: Uncovering Sexual Violence against Men in War Theaters'. PhD diss., The Graduate Institute, Geneva.

Dworkin, Andrea. 1987. *Intercourse*. London: Arrow Books.

Eisenstein, Hester. 1983. *Contemporary Feminist Thought*. London: Harper Collins.

Frazer, Elizabeth and Kimberly Hutchings. 2014. 'Feminism and the Critique of Violence: Negotiating Feminist Political Agency'. *Journal of Political Ideologies* 19(2): 143–163.

Goetz, Anne Marie. 2014. Preventing Violence Against Women: A Sluggish Cascade? *Open Democracy*, 25 November 2014.

Gordon, Avery F. 2001. *Ghostly Matters: Haunting and the Sociological Imagination*, Minneapolis, MN: University of Minnesota Press.

Graham, Ruth. 2006. 'Male Rape and the Careful Construction of the Male Victim'. *Social & Legal Studies* 15(2): 187–208.

Gunne, Sorcha and Zoë Brigley Thompson. 2010. *Feminism, Literature and Rape Narratives*. London: Routledge.

Halley, Janet. 2006. *Split Decisions: How and Why to Take a Break from Feminism*. Princeton, NJ: Princeton University Press.

Irigaray, Luce. 1993. *An Ethics of Sexual Difference*. Translated by Carolyn Burke. London: The Athlone Press.

Jameson, Frederic. 2001. 'The Political Unconscious'. In Steven Seidman and Jeffrey Alexander (eds), *The New Social Theory Reader*. London: Routledge, 101–107.

Jones, Adam. 2009. *Gender Inclusive: Essays on Violence, Men, And Feminist International Relations*. London: Routledge.

Kramer, Lawrence. 2000. *After the Lovedeath: Sexual Violence and the Making of Culture*. Los Angeles, CA: University of California Press.

Leatherman, Janie. 2011. *Sexual Violence and Armed Conflict*. Cambridge: Polity Press.

Marcus, Sharon. 1992. 'Fighting Bodies, Fighting Words: A Theory and Politics of Rape Prevention'. In Judith Buther and Joan Scott (eds), *Feminists Theorize the Political*. London: Routledge, 385–403.

Martin, Emily. 1988. *The Women in the Body: A Cultural Analysis of Reproduction*. Milton Keyes: Open University Press.

Minh-ha, Trinh T. 1987. 'Difference: A Special Third World Women Issue'. *Feminist Review* 25: 5–22.

Minh-ha, Trinh T. 1991. *When the Moon Waxes Red: Representation, Gender and Cultural Politics*. London: Routledge.

Misra, Amalendu. 2015. *The Landscape of Silence: Sexual Violence Against Men in War*. London: Hurst & Co.

O'Neill, Rachel. 2015. 'Whither Critical Masculinity Studies?: Notes on Inclusive Masculinity Theory, Postfeminism, and Sexual Politics'. *Men and Masculinities* 18(1): 100–120.

Parpart, Jane L. and Marysia Zalewski. 2008. *Rethinking the Man Question*. London: Zed Books.

Puar, Jasbir K. 2007. *Terrorist Assemblages: Homonationalism in Queer Times*. Durham, NC: Duke University Press.

Puar Jasbir, Ben Pitcher and Henriette Gunkel. 2008. 'Q&A with Jasbir Puar [Interview]'. *Darkmatter*, 2 May. Accessed 12 November 2017. www.darkmatter101.org/site/2008/05/02/qa-with-jasbir-puar/.

Rubin, Gayle S. 1984. 'Thinking Sex: Notes for a Radical Theory of the Politics of Sexuality'. In Carol Vance (ed.), *Pleasure and Danger: Exploring Female Sexuality*. London: Routledge.

Sellers, Susan. 2004. *The Hélène Cixous Reader*. London: Routledge.

Shakespeare, Tom. 2017. *Disability: The Basics*. London: Routledge.

Shildrick, Margaret. 2009. *Dangerous Discourses of Disability, Subjectivity and Sexuality*. London: Palgrave Macmillan.

Sivakumaran, Sandesh. 2007. 'Sexual Violence Against Men in Armed Conflict'. *European Journal of International Law* 18(2): 253–276.

Sjoberg, Laura and Caron Gentry. 2007. *Mothers, Whores and Monsters: Women's Violence in Global Politics*. London: Zed Books.

Sjoberg, Laura and Julie Peteet. 2011. 'A(nother) Dark Side of the Protection Racket'. *International Feminist Journal of Politics* 13(2): 163–182.

Staidum, Frederick Charles Jr. 2007. 'Too Filthy to be Repeated: Reading Sexualized Violence Against Enslaved Males in U.S. Slave Societies'. Master thesis, Cornell University.

Stanko, Elisabeth A. 1990. *Everyday Violence: How Women and Men Experience Sexual and Physical Danger*. London: Harper Collins.

Stern, Maria and Marysia Zalewski. 2009. 'Feminist Fatigue(S): Reflections on Feminism and Familiar Fables of Militarization'. *Review of International Studies* 35(3): 611–630.

Storr, Will. 2011. 'The Rape of Men: The Darkest Secret of War'. *Observer – Guardian*, 17 July. Accessed 12 November. www.theguardian.com/society/2011/jul/17/the-rape-of-men.

Sylvester, Christine. 2013. *War as Experience*. London: Routledge.

Tomlinson, Barbara. 2010. *Feminism and Affect at the Scene of Argument*. Philadelphia, PA: Temple University Press.

Tuana, Nancy. 1993. *The Less Noble Sex*. Bloomington, IN: Indiana University Press.

Vance, Carole S. 1996. 'Social Construction Theory and Sexuality'. In Maurice Berger *et al.* (eds), *Constructing Masculinity*. London: Routledge, 37–48.

Ward, Jeanne. 2016. 'It's Not about the Gender Binary, It's about the Gender Hierarchy: A Reply to "Letting Go of the Gender Binary"'. *International Committee of the Red Cross* 98(1): 275–298.

Weber, Cynthia. 2016. *Queer International Relations*. Oxford: Oxford University Press.

Young, Iris Marion. 2003. 'The Logic of Masculinist Protection: Reflections on the Current Security State'. *Signs: Journal of Women in Culture and Society* 29(1): 1–25.

Zalewski, Marysia. 2010. '"I Don't Even Know What Gender Is": A discussion of the Relationship Between Gender Mainstreaming and Feminist Theory'. *The Review of International Studies* 36: 3–27.

Zalewski, Marysia and Anne Sisson Runyan. 2013. 'Taking Feminist Violence Seriously in Feminist International Relations'. *International Feminist Journal of Politics* 15(3): 293–313.

Zalewski, Marysia and Anne Sisson Runyan. 2015. 'Unthinking Sexual Violence in a Neoliberal Age of Spectacular Terror'. *Critical Studies on Terrorism* 8(3): 1–17.

Zalewski, Marysia and Anne Sisson Runyan. Forthcoming. 'Feminist Violence and the In/Securing of Women and Feminism'. In Caron Gentry, Laura J. Shepherd, and Laura Sjoberg (eds), *Routledge Handbook on Gender and Security*. London: Routledge.

2 Battle-induced urotrauma, sexual violence, and American servicemen

Chris Hendershot

In this chapter, I conduct a discursive analysis of how battle-induced urotrauma becomes sexualised. Battle-induced urotrauma can be defined as any injury to the genitals, urinary tract, renal system, and perineum resulting from the explosive, concussive, and blunt forces produced by and through combat and is estimated to account for '0.5–4.2% of all war injuries' (Waxman, Beekley, Morey, and Soderdahl. 2009: 145). It is regularly experienced as a polytrauma, in which multiple appendages, organs, and flesh are damaged (VA/DoD 2016). My focus in this chapter is on the genital harm suffered by American servicemen during combat operations in Afghanistan and Iraq between 2001 and 2013. Drawing on the articulations of injured and non-injured American servicemen, their families, medical professionals, journalists, and digital content providers, I contend that urotrauma becomes sexualised through the reiteration of heteronormal, phallic, and able-bodied discourses. In becoming sexualised as such, urotrauma also becomes an injurious experience through which male embodiment is naturalised through and for masculinist and militarised meanings. I use the phrase 'becomes sexualised' to gesture towards performativity in which notions and practices of flesh, physiology, gender, and sex interact to determine what genitalia mean and how genitalia matter (Butler 1993; Barad 2007). Accordingly, this chapter works from the premise that the genitalia of American servicemen, and male embodiment more broadly, have a (re-)iterative and not a natural or ahistorical meaning. To suggest that urotrauma becomes sexualised is a semantic method of recognising how the meaning of harmed genitalia and male embodiment come to matter iteratively through the repetition, ritualisation, and/or reimagining of language, images, emotions, and flesh.

The relevance of my analysis to this collection on sexual violence against men and boys is that the discursive context of battle-induced urotrauma presents a contemplative opportunity to further understand how the iterative sexualising (and masculinising and militarising) of male bodies is an injurious process. Understood as such, sexual violence becomes something else than the intention, method, and/or consequence of a single or widespread action that exploits the sexualised being/becoming of men and boys (Sivakumaran 2007). This chapter contends that the violence of sexualising cannot only be understood as specific injuries, harm, mutilations, or humiliations. The sexualising of men and boys, that is, the iterative distinguishing and entangling of embodiment and desire, also causes harm by naturalising, that is, obscuring iteration, how men and boys should embody male bodies, for example, use penises and testicles. To be sure, the harms affected by the naturalising of male bodies do not equate to the harms and exclusions manifested through the feminising (Davis 2002), queering (Halberstam 2008), dis-abling (McRuer 2010), and racialising (Richter-Montpetit 2014) of other('s) bodies. The natural male body is a political iteration that privileges those people that can claim, enact, or embody it – often to violent denial and policing of others. To question the conceptual and political basis of the natural male body as an iteratively injurious process is to open further possibilities of contesting the violence that makes, breaks, and remakes a multiplicity of embodied beings and becomings.

By focusing on urotrauma, this chapter undertakes an analysis of how the sexualising of men and boys is reiterated and enacted through a battle-induced injury. For instance, the sexualising of urotrauma through phallic discourses, that is, discourses that attach the symbolic power of the phallus to bodies adorned with penises and testicles, reiterates the meaningfulness of male bodies as 'impenetrable, war-[bodies] simultaneously armed and armoured, equipped for victory' (Waldby 1995: 268). In other words, the discursive normalising, phallusising, and abling of battle-induced urotrauma as a specifically problematic injury for male servicemen obfuscates how reiterations of male-being as normal, phallic, and able are exceedingly pernicious embodiments of and for men and boys.

This chapter will demonstrate that the discursive context of urotrauma offers little space to understand battle-induced genital injuries as moments of rupture in which a reimagining of men, genitals, and violence can be iterated. As Butler writes, 'we may seek recourse to matter in order to [demonstrate] a set of injuries [...] only to find that *matter itself is founded through a set of violations,* ones which are unwittingly repeated in the contemporary invocation' (1993: 29). Understanding how battle-induced injuries become sexualised is insightful for discussions of sexual violence against men and boys because it works as an analogous caution against presuming that sexualised injuries can become moments to contest the reiterative possibilities of injuring men and boys. It is crucial to recognise that 'much of what is traditionally associated with masculinity is in fact generative of impairment' (Shakespeare 1999: 63). Hence, to sexualise genital injuries through discourses that naturalise what it means to be a man or a boy ignores how the making of natural (and normal) bodies is also an injurious process.

To demonstrate how urotrauma becomes sexualised and how this becoming reiterates the injurious embodiments of men and boys this chapter is divided into three sections. The first section goes into further detail on how many American servicemen were injured in Afghanistan and Iraq, as well describing how urotrauma becomes a combat injury. The second section delves into an analysis of how American servicemen become sexualised. This section presents the broad sexual and militarised contexts through which the sexualising of urotrauma comes to matter. The third section concentrates on how articulations of lost potential, reproductive capacities, and conjugal intimacy sexualise urotrauma through heteronormal, phallic, and able-bodied discourses. To conclude, I re-emphasise the conceptual and political need to question the naturalising of male bodies when those bodies become injured. Such a questioning is necessary in order to open (more) possibilities to iterate the sexualised (and masculinised) meaning of men and boys through non-injurious practices and processes.

Battle induced urotrauma

To understand how urotrauma becomes sexualised, I will first focus on how (many) American servicemen have suffered urotrauma as a result of combat operations in Afghanistan and Iraq. In terms of casualty numbers, the *New York Times* reports, 'From 2001 to 2013, 1,367 men in [American] military service suffered wounds to the genitals' (Grady 2015). Per another *New York Times* report,

> Most of the wounded men – 94 percent – were 35 or younger and more than a third of the men had at least one injury that was considered severe; 129 lost one of their testes, 17 lost both and 86 had severe injuries to the penis. Fewer than five lost the penis.
>
> (Grady 2017)

A study specifically focusing on the urotrauma caused by improvised explosive devices (IED), notes that between 2001 and 2011 IEDs were primarily responsible for seriously injuring 448 American servicemen (Banti, Walter, Hudak, and Soderdahl 2016).

American servicemen are not the only people to have suffered urotrauma. A study in the *Arab Journal of Urology* notes that between 2004 and 2008, 504 Iraqi patients were admitted to the Al-Yarmouk Hospital in Baghdad with urogenital injuries (Al-Azzawi and Koraitim 2014: 149). Likewise, men, penises, and testicles do not exclusively suffer urotrauma. Although American servicewomen have also suffered urotrauma, they have received far less attention than their male colleagues (Poppe 2014). The Trauma Outcomes and Urogenital Health or TOUGH project is, however, studying the effects of battle-induced urotrauma on women, which will hopefully begin to rectify this empirical discrepancy (Grady 2017). Critically, I anticipate that the TOUGH project will, however, be another source in which the meaning of urotrauma, whether the injured are men or women, is articulated through heteronormal, phallic, and able-bodied discourses.

How these thousand plus young men suffer urotrauma depends on several factors. Bodily harm is initiated through the concussive and searing forces of explosions and the penetrating, blunt, slicing, and infecting impacts of metal, plastic, sand, fabric, bone, flesh, and bacteria. These impacts are in turn, sheered and shaped by the physical specificities of military tactics and battle space [,] by the kinds of armor [*sic*] the military constantly redesigns to keep soldiers from dying [and] by the responsiveness of battlefield medicine, which finds new ways to [... try ...] to keep soldiers alive.

(Wool 2016: 401)

The effect of these harming, protecting, and healing forces and interventions means that despite being generally classified as urotrauma, battle-induced genital injuries are embodied individually by American servicemen. Specific manifestations of this harm as expressed by servicemen and medical professions include: (1) ' "Part of [a] testicle is gone, and [the] urethra was severed. The tissue died. There was no chance of repairing the pathways completely" ' (Urology Care Foundation 2011); (2) ' "[the] urinary system was in shreds. [The] testicles were destroyed. [The] penis was attached to his body by only 'a little thread of skin" ' (Jones 2013: 47); and (3) 'tiny metal shards in one testicle and [...] five pieces of shrapnel "the size of a pea or larger" embedded in his penis. "Two of those pieces are actually in the tip" ' (Roberson 2011).

As mentioned, urotrauma is also regularly embodied and endured as a polytrauma. This means a serviceman can have both his legs broken, a broken arm, portions of his hands damaged, shrapnel embedded in a shoulder, and one testicle that is completely 'ripped away' and a third of the other testicle that is torn off (Kime 2014). Enduring these injuries means living through the (unreconciled) economic and social constraints of debility. For instance, alongside the unsettling realization that US Department of Defense insurance policies dispense $25,000 per injured testicle and $50,000 for penises (Horton 2011), the costs of long-term and/or specialised care required to treat polytrauma often exceed these pay-outs and 'health insurance coverage for some of the [other] consequences of [urotrauma] is also limited' (Wilcox, Schuyler, and Hassan 2015: 4). The violent instance of urotrauma is realized in mere seconds, but the harm is borne out over months and years.

To be shot, burnt, or blown-up is excruciatingly painful. Likewise, the harmfulness of the injuries that American servicemen can and do suffer in combat extends while beyond the battlefield. What this pain and harm means in terms that are not simply referencing the immediate causes and effects of an injury are not as straightforward nor as apolitical as urotrauma has been discussed to this point in the chapter. How the harm of urotrauma comes to matter is an iterative process of entangling the meanings of genitalia, masculinity, and sexuality through the militarised bodies of American servicemen. The (sexualised) meaning of urotrauma also does not begin at the moment of injury. American servicemen, injured or not, are already sexualised in particular ways that legitimate the enacting of militarised violence.

Militarised sexuality

In situations of violence, sexualising processes are ever swirling among the bodies of combatants and among the meanings and motivations of violence. In a militarised American context, sexualising is a process through which the violence of the American military becomes a desirable enactment for the body-politic – that is, the nation, the state, and the people that fund and populate the military. Militarised sexuality iterates possibilities that combat can be fought with 'our' normal, powerful, and capable bodies against the perverse, impotent, and queer bodies (Puar and Rai 2002; Puar 2005) of the enemy. Militarised sexuality manifests desires for violent embodiments as well as the appeal, the sexiness, of enacting violence on others. As combat is also the 'ultimate test of manhood' (Cohn 1999: 460), militarised sexuality is also a key method of making the American military appealing to men and boys desiring to become a man that is more than one's self.

To become an American serviceman is to become an 'object of desire' while simultaneously sublimating a submissiveness to militarised and nationalised desires:

> Upon graduation from the total institution of basic training, troops are taught to take enormous pride in their new bodies, stripped of excess, and their new sense of self. From uniforms to finely toned muscles to posture, the military works to produce a new body with a new identity. The broader culture reinforces these messages, treating soldiers as embodiments of confidence, and their muscles, weapons, and uniforms as sexy. The transformed citizen, submissive to the state, is rewarded with the sex appeal that only massive symbolic power can bestow. From loving 'a man in uniform' to 'weapons porn' […], militarization and sexuality are mutually implicated.
>
> (Crane-Seeber 2016: 49)

This process of sexualising Servicemen becomes meaningful through multiple expressions of personal, general, and national desires for visually attractive, bodily confident, and competent men. Disciplined, protective, and heroic men become the guardians of the nation, whom one can take home to meet the family. Muscular, armed, and violent men become the necessary bad-boys, whom one can bed for a night of carnal bliss. Committed and duty-bound men become appealing symbols of sacrifice, as they are willing to put their bodies in harms way. This broad sexualising of the Hero, Bad-Boy, and/or Sacrificer reiterates the entangled meaningfulness of being and becoming a man through such institutions as work, the family, the military, and the nation.

Combat injuries pose a particularly troubling problem for the iterative sexualising of American servicemen. The appeal of fighting for the American military is that it sexualises one's body in such a way as to make it both individually/personally and generally/nationally desirable. However, combat also makes 'bodies that are unruly and at odds with common sense notions of proper, whole bodies, conceived psychologically, physically, and otherwise' (Achter 2010: 49). Or as Wool writes, 'the grievously injured American soldier thus presents a particular problem: a figure of exceptionally worthy heteronational citizenship and iconic masculinity captured in an emasculated and "invalidated" form' (2016: 400).

Combat injuries are iteratively volatile because the masculinising and sexual-ising process of military service/combat cannibalises the bodies of servicemen. Combat injuries can disrupt militarised sexuality by unmaking male bodies rather than reaffirming their fleshy desirability and masculine potential. An injured serviceman may still have a generalisable appeal by virtue of their bodily sacrifice. However, if combat injuries impair reproductive and erectile functions as well as altering aesthetic attractiveness, personal desires to become a milita-rised man as well personal desires of militarised male bodies may be diminished. Or as one American Serviceman laments, ' "Who's going to want to be with me now?" ' (Wood 2012). Without national or personal desires for Servicemen, institutionalised manhood and the military lose a key discursive method of making themselves, or being made, appealing. To maintain the appeal of the military and the sexiness of institutionalised manhood the rhetorical, medical, and socio-cultural rehabilitation of injured servicemen becomes necessary. Or in a more reiterative phrasing, in order to honour the sacrifice of injured servicemen, the 'goal is to heal, to care for and to restore our wounded warriors to their maximum potential' (Callahan 2012: 5).

Rehabilitation does more than heal the injured servicemen. Rehabilitation also reiterates the 'natural' possibilities for male bodies. Those natural possibil-ities are that injured bodies need to be made whole and functional again in order to be and perform a whole and functional manhood. As Wool contends, 'Norm-ative forms of productive masculinity have [...] been key to' the rehabilitation of American servicemen (2016: 400). Moreover, Linker asserts that in the United States,

> Rehabilitation was thus a way to restore social order after the chaos of war by (re)making men into producers of capital. Since wage earning often defined manhood, rehabilitation was, in essence, a process of making a man manly. Or, as the World War I 'Creed of the Disabled Man' put it, the point of rehabilitation was for each disabled veteran to become 'a MAN among MEN in spite of his physical handicap'.
>
> (Linker 2011: 4)

Simultaneously, debility as a result of war has been distinguished from congeni-tal debility wherein the tragedy of battle-induced injury becomes a marker of 'one's service to the modern state, to industrial capitalism, to warfare: it helps the veteran's body preserve patriotic values and masculinity' (Serlin 2003: 162). This distinction between battle-induced and congenital debility is not simply an empirical recognition of differing times, spaces, and causes of debility. It also furthers the political import of naturalising by distinguishing those bodies that desire to be masculinised and those that cannot.

An example of normalising and nationalising servicemen injured in Afghan-istan and Iraq comes through the aesthetics of the photobook *Always Loyal* (Caso 2016). This book which features eroticised visuals of the injured servicemen 'entangles sexual politics, physical disability, and militarism through the homoerotic sexualization of the disabled veteran. This produces the normali-zation of militarized bodies [...] as a way of celebrating the sacrifice of soldiers who fight for the nation' (Caso 2016: 3). Through the eroticised visuals, this book is also a moment of celebrating the ability of the injured servicemen to overcome and to reassert their sexuality – a sexuality that despite being visual-ised through a body broken in combat does not break away from the appeal of militarised sexiness.

What is key for an analysis of urotrauma is recognising how rehabilitation reiterates militarised sexuality through injury – thereby reinscribing the natural possibilities of and for male bodies. Rehabilitation marks combat injury as an impairment that represents a challenge to reclaim, reattach, and reiterate the appeal of militarised sexuality. The bodies of the injured servicemen may be unruly, but rehabilitative efforts are interventions that ward off feminising, queering, trans-itioning or debilitating possibilities. Servicemen may no longer be able to fight for their country through combat, but they can continue to fight for their manhood by not allowing their injury to be emasculating and enfee-bling. Rehabilitation reiterates military sexuality by manifesting the post-combat and post-injury possibility of embodying the desirability of being/becoming men in the American military.

The entanglement of militarised sexuality and rehabilitation through the injured bodies of American servicemen is a significant demonstration of how bodily harm can become a moment of reiteration. Manifestation of injuries is not necessarily a contestation of the militarised and sexualised contexts that motivate the violent circumstances that make battle injuries possible. The attractiveness of a man in uniform, the appeal of combat, and the desirability of a man who is willing to sacrifice can all be reiterated through the bodies and performances of injured servicemen. Nonetheless, urotrauma poses an acute sexualised problem. That problem is that even though other forms of combat injury can and do impair the sexual capabilities of servicemen, the sexualised, and naturalised, being of men is unquestionably iterated through whole and functional genitalia.

Servicemen's expressions of ' "How's my dick look?" ' (Roberson 2011), ' "Is my junk all together?" ' (Brown 2011), and ' "It's the male instinct, the first thing you care about" ' (Wood 2012), coincide with descriptions of urotrauma as 'one of war's cruelest injuries' (Huffington Post 2012) and 'uniquely devastating' (Grady 2017), reiterating the centrality of whole and functional genitalia to being and becoming a man. In causing harm to genitalia, urotrauma exposes the possibility that: 'far from stabilizing traditional concepts of masculinity, the vol-atility of the penis actually destabilizes these from within' (Stephens 2007: 87). In damaging dicks and balls, urotrauma opens the possibility that genitalia become unreliable appendages through which to iteratively anchor militarised sexuality, being a man, and/or becoming a man through combat.

Indeed even 'having whole and functional genitalia' does not simply mean that a person can effectively be or become a whole or functional man. Soft and hard, short and long, thick and narrow, straight and curved, hooded and cut are only the visible differences among penises that depending upon one's skin colour, religion, age, occupation, and desires have been variously seized to engender phallic anxiety and exclusion or worse (Spongberg 1997; Richter-Montpetit 2014). Susceptibility to touch, temperature, stress, fatigue, and circulation also render penises to be anything but the on-demand rigid protrusion demanded of phallic-masculinity (Bordo 1999).

Recognising that genitalia can fail to stand 'in for and up for the man' (Potts 2000: 85) offers a conceptual challenge to ideas of 'the universalized male body' (Stephens 2007: 86), the 'metonymical relation' between penis and phallus (Potts 2001: 144), and the centrality of penises and testicles to being and becoming a man. As I am arguing that meanings of urotrauma, genitalia, and male embodiment are made (re-)iteratively, then it is also important to acknowledge that exposing the vulnerability of genitalia may not matter politically. By this I mean to say, the vulnerability exposed by and through urotrauma is, as demonstrated through the above discussion of rehabilitation, readily reiterated through discourses that buttress, rather than contest, militarised sexuality, masculinity, and the naturalness of male being.

Sexualising urotrauma

Analysing how urotrauma becomes sexualised through the articulations and expressions of injured and non-injured American servicemen, their families, medical professionals, journalists, and digital content providers can be an uncomfortable task. Urotrauma, like other combat injuries and the harm rendered through sexual violence, is a life-changing experience. The altering of genital form and function means that everyday activities such as urinating, getting and sustaining an erection, and ejaculating become planned, medicated, difficult, and painful acts. Urotrauma, especially that which is also endured as a polytrauma, also seriously affects the emotional, economic, and mobility capacities of injured servicemen. It is not my intention to dismiss the seriousness of the lived reality of urotrauma. In suggesting that the sexualising of urotrauma is iterated through heteronormal, phallic, and able-bodied discourses, I potentially open this chapter to accusations of a callous or insensitive reading of the laments, frustrations, and sympathetic articulations and expressions that I am citing.

The pondering of a doctor that: '"sometimes you wonder what you're sending back to the family"' (Woodward and Eggertson 2010: 1159) or the lamentation of a wife that: '"I sent this handsome young man to war and I don't know who came back with his name"' (Murphy 2013: 7) can be read as sincere expressions of the serious embodied alterations that result from battle-induced urotrauma. These articulations must also be read as able-bodied iterations that only whole and functional bodies have clear, reliable, and desirable meaning. Furthermore, to equate injury with a loss of meaning or a lack of knowing iterates a naturalness to whole and functional bodies – naturalness that obfuscates how bodies are iteratively realized, while circumscribing the political possibilities of engaging bodies in trans-ition. In the case of these two articulations, to withhold criticism on the basis that they are sympathetic, is to risk perpetuating subtle forms of trans-phobia (Wool 2016) that question what people are when their bodies and aesthetics appear to confound normalised and naturalised expectations of sexed and gendered embodiment.

Instances in which sympathy reiterates other problematic meanings appear in articulations that foreground the lost potential. When a medical professional suggests that: '"an 18 to 20 year old kid coming back without any genital urinary function is prone to being hopeless"' (Koebler 2016), genital debility is couched among phallic temporalities that hold youth to be in '"their peak years of sexual development and reproductive potential"' (Grady 2017). Similarly, to maintain that: 'If one has a genital injury all of a sudden one is rocketed forward to a much older age in which one is dealing with lost productivity' (Ursano 2012: 10) is to uphold phallic and ageist desires for the virility of youth. Sexualising urotrauma as an injury that diminishes the potential of the sufferer reiterates possibilities that the 'male body at the height of its productive capacities is [the] ideal form' (Slevin and Linneman 2010: 487). Associating 'lost productivity' be it sexualised or economic, also naturalises the temporal development of male bodies. It makes possible a militarised sexuality that needs boys to (want to) grow and develop into men. To reiterate and rephrase, the test of combat is to prove manhood and for an American military to be 'a young and vigorous force' (Wilcox, Redmond, and Hassan 2014: 2537) combat must be(come) an attractive practice for boys seeking to become men. To sexualise urotrauma as in injury of lost time, energy, and potential reasserts a sexiness of youth, the temporal possibilities of male bodies, and the politicised ideal that whole and functional bodies are bodies of potential. Medical interventions such as erectile dysfunction drugs, genital transplants, and tissue regeneration (Lawler 2016) do offer (masculinised) 'hope' for urotrauma sufferers. These forms of medical rehabilitation also become entangled among desires for conjugal sex.

An injured serviceman rehabilitating at Walter Reed Memorial Hospital conveys to Wool that: 'he was on Levitra because that way he could have sex with his wife, but [...] it wasn't really sex, it wasn't nice, it was just penetration, like some kind of mandatory exercise for his penis and his marriage' (2015: Kindle Locs 1334–1336). Here phallic and heteronormal meaning manifests as a conjugal duty. Having sex with one's wife not only proves the possibility of a manhood recovered (2015: Kindle Locs 1334–1336), but it is also a reclamation of the natural and normal duty of men to participate in penetrative conjugal sex – even if it is no longer pleasurable. Of worth noting, veteran's advocates do provide non-penile-centric sex possibilities for injured soldiers. As a sexual health professional coyly ponders, '"Does he have a tongue, and can he be taught?"' (Roach 2016: 57). This non-penile-centric sex advice does eschew the able-bodied imaginary that debility means asexuality or undesirability (Rodríguez 2011) as well as opening the potential that carnal pleasure is not bound to a penis's capacity to be a rigid protrusion. Heteronormal preferences for conjugal coupling are not eschewed, however,

I was blown away with the imaginative and resourceful ways this couple found to overcome the challenges of [urotrauma] [...] the emotional bond forged in a battle they weren't sure they'd win, (given the high military divorce rate), is particularly sweet.

(Sabih 2012)

Conjugal success, whether it involves penile-penetrative-sex or other forms of intimate touch, also reaffirms militarised sexuality. By becoming sexually active, post-combat and post-injury urotrauma sufferers and their partners become celebrated examples of how conjugal couplehood is tested, yet strengthened in militarised circumstances.

The struggle to remain in a conjugal relationship is intensified when urotrauma impairs the reproductive capacities of injured servicemen. As an American medical profession suggests,

Although each of the functional challenges that result from damage to the genitourinary organs is life altering, perhaps one of the most profound is loss of fertility [...] shattering a dream of many – to begin a family of their own.

(Gatty 2013)

The heteronormal imperative to reproduce 'the next generation of humans' and 'specific ways of being a man' (Wentzell and Inhorn 2011: 307–308) is abundantly clear in the articulations of the injured, their families, journalists, and politicians. Notable articulations include: (1) '"I couldn't think of anything more devastating than not being able to have kids"' (Urology Care Foundation 2011); (2) 'If the issue of infertility is not adequately addressed for the young men and women in uniform, it will be adding insult to injury' (Zumatto 2015: 1); and (3) 'Although veterans appreciate this [$100/month] benefit it does not adequately compensate the veteran for the unique nature of an injury that prevents their ability to have a family' (Tritten 2016). The phrase 'prevents their ability to have a family' is a particularly troublesome reiteration of the male desire to father and parent their own progeny. Articulated as such, the heteronormal imperative to reproduce sexualises urotrauma as an impairment of a natural desire for men to make their own family. That the notion of adoption, being an uncle, or some other form of responsible family figure is virtually absent from discussions of urotrauma further suggests that male being is incomplete when naturalised capacities to reproduce are impaired.

Loss of meaning and potential and impairment of conjugal sex and reproductive capacities are not experiences that anyone should be forced to endure. To express sympathy towards injured servicemen is to acknowledge that battle-induced genital injury is traumatic. To express a critical hesitancy with how battle-induced urotrauma is sexualised is to acknowledge that violence does alter the form and functionality of bodies, but it does not necessarily injure the process of reiterating meaning. It may seem absurdly abstract to contend that the sexualising of urotrauma through heteronormal, phallic, and able-bodied discourses should matter as much as the 'actual injury'. The injury or harm is, however, unknowable and thus not possible without a body that can be harmed. As has been demonstrated simultaneously throughout this chapter, urotrauma harms a male body that is presumed to have a natural form and function. This naturalising of how men and boys can be(come) embodied needs to be understood as an injurious process.

A de-naturalising conclusion

Over the course of this chapter, I have empirically, argumentatively, and semantically pushed the notion that the sexualising of battle-induced urotrauma, which requires a sexed, gendered, and militarised body to be injured, is an iterative process that affects a naturalised meaning for male embodiment. My repeating that the sexualising, gendering, and militarising of urotrauma, American servicemen, and the male body is an iterative process presents a conceptual and political challenge to naturalised notions of what men and boys are and can be. Challenging naturalised notions is key to a thorough understanding of how men and boys are and can be harmed. The harms of urotrauma as well other forms of battle-induced genital injury can certainly be understood and rehabilitated without acknowledging an iterative meaning making process. This, however, risks re-naturalising the bodies that come to be injured – through combat. The difficulty with naturalised bodies is that conceptually they are not possible and politically the naturalisation process limits possibilities.

By limiting the possibilities of how men and boys can embody maleness, naturalising processes limit the performativity of possibilities. Harm and injury can be realized through the natural male body insofar as violence is simultaneously reiterated as the only or as an appealing practice of achieving or demonstrating manhood. If joining the military, participating in combat, and/or committing an act of sexual violence are valued as practices that permit certain men and boys to achieve manliness, at the masculine expense of other men and boys (which is to say nothing of the violent possibilities directed at the 'other' bodies), then the naturalising of male bodies injuriously limits what men and boys can become. It is therefore imperative that the male body becomes de-naturalised. Battle-induced urotrauma, much like genital mutilation and other forms of sexual violence, do produce possibilities to see the iterative embodiment of men and boys. To prevent and heal these injuries, however, it must be understood that the heteronormality, phallocentric, and able-bodiedness of the naturalised male body is an entangled realization of circumstances that permit men and boys to be male and manly through injury.

References

Achter, Paul. 2010. 'Unruly Bodies: The Rhetorical Domestication of Twenty-First-Century Veterans of War'. *Quarterly Journal of Speech* 96: 46–68.

Al-Azzawi, Issam S. and Mamdouh M. Koraitim. 2014. 'Urethral and Penile War Injuries: The Experience from Civil Violence in Iraq'. *Arab Journal of Urology* 12: 149–154.

Banti, Matthew, Jack Walter, Steven Hudak, and Douglas Soderdahl. 2016. 'Improvised Explosive Device–Related Lower Genitourinary Trauma in Current Overseas Combat Operations'. *Journal of Trauma and Acute Care Surgery* 80: 131–134.

Barad, Karen. 2007. *Meeting the Universe Halfway: Quantum Physics and the Entanglement of Matter and Meaning.* Durham, NC: Duke University Press.

Bordo, Susan. 1999. *The Male Body: A New look at Men in Public and Private.* New York: Farrar, Straus and Giroux.

Brown, David. 2011. 'Amputations and Genital Injuries Increase Sharply Among Soldiers in Afghanistan'. *Washington Post*, 4 March. Accessed 26 August 2016. http://wapo.st/2bnSa0h.

Butler, Judith. 1993. *Bodies that Matter: On the Discursive Limits of 'Sex'.* New York: Routledge.

Callahan, Charles. 2012. 'Introduction: Therapuron'. In Mary Lee Dichtel (ed.), *Evaluation and Treatment of Genital Injuries in Combat Warriors (Artiss Symposium)*, 5. Bethesda, MD: Centre for Traumatic Stress.

Caso, Federica, 2016. 'Sexing the Disabled Veteran: The Homoerotic Aesthetics of Militarism'. *Critical Military Studies*, DOI: 10.1080/23337486.2016.1184420.

Cohn, Carol. 1999. 'Missions, Men and Masculinities'. *International Feminist Journal of Politics* 1: 460–475.

Crane-Seeber, Jesse Paul. 2016. 'Sexy Warriors: The Politics and Pleasures of Submission to the State'. *Critical Military Studies* 2: 41–55.

Davis, Kathy. 2002. ' "A Dubious Equality": Men, Women and Cosmetic Surgery'. *Body & Society* 8: 49–65.

Gatty, Bob. 2013. 'UroTrauma Bill may have Platform for Passage'. *Urology Times*, June. Accessed 27 August 2016. http://bit.ly/2bQ9xHM.

Grady, Denise. 2015. 'Penis Transplants Being Planned to Help Wounded Troops'. *New York Times*, 6 December. Accessed 27 August 2016. http://nyti.ms/2bFhGyp.

Grady, Denise. 2017. 'Study Maps "Uniquely Devastating" Genital Injuries Among Troops'. *New York Times*, 13 January. Accessed 24 February 2017. http://nyti.ms/2mtz9fA.

Halberstam, Judith. 2008. 'The Anti-Social Turn in Queer Studies'. *Graduate Journal of Social Science* 5: 140–156.

Horton, Alex. 2011. 'Traumatic Injury Protection Now Covers Genital Injuries'. *US Department of Veteran Affairs*, 5 December. Accessed 27 August 2016. http://bit.ly/2bp57cJ.

Huffington Post. 2012. 'Wounded Warriors Experience Increase in Genital Wounds (How You Can Help)'. *The Huffington Post*, 21 March. Accessed 25 February 2017. http://huff.to/2bX2RF8.

Jones, Anne. 2013. *They Were Soldiers: How the Wounded Return from America's Wars – The Untold Story.* Chicago, IL: Haymarket Books.

Kime, Patricia. 2014. 'Wounded Troops Battle Obstacles to Sex and Intimacy'. *Military Times*, 29 December. Accessed 28 August 2016. http://bit.ly/1IwbhgJ.

Koebler, Jason. 2016. 'The Doctors Who Did the First US Penis Transplant Explain How It All Works'. *Motherboard*, 16 May. Accessed 18 September 2016. http://bit.ly/2d0YL3Y.

Lawler, David. 2016. 'US Military Funds Research into Lab-Grown Testicles for Wounded Soldiers'. *Telegraph*, 8 January. Accessed 18 September 2016. http://bit.ly/1SJlopa.

Linker, Beth. 2011. *War's Waste: Rehabilitation in World War I America.* Chicago, IL: University of Chicago Press.

McRuer, Robert. 2010. 'Disabling Sex Notes for a Crip Theory of Sexuality'. *GLQ: A Journal of Lesbian and Gay Studies* 17: 107–117.

Murphy, Timothy. 2013. 'The Impact of Trauma/Injury on Our Veterans and Congressional Oversight'. In Mary Lee Dichtel (ed.), *Evaluation and Treatment of Genital Injuries in Combat Warriors (Artiss Symposium)*. Bethesda, MD: Centre for Traumatic Stress, 7–8.

Poppe, Tessa. 2014. 'The Injury Afflicting Veterans That No One Wants to Talk About'. *Task & Purpose*, 23 December. Accessed 25 August 2016. http://taskandpurpose.com/injury-afflicting-veterans-no-one-wants-talk/.

Potts, Annie. 2000. ' "The Essence of the Hard On" Hegemonic Masculinity and the Cultural Construction of "Erectile Dysfunction" '. *Men and Masculinities* 3: 85–103.

Potts, Annie. 2001. 'The Man with Two Brains: Hegemonic Masculine Subjectivity and the Discursive Construction of the Unreasonable Penis-Self'. *Journal of Gender Studies* 10: 145–156.

Puar, Jasbir K. 2005. 'Queer Times, Queer Assemblages'. *Social Text* 23: 121–139.

Puar, Jasbir K. and Amit Rai. 2002. 'Monster, Terrorist, Fag: The War on Terrorism and the Production of Docile Patriots'. *Social Text* 20: 117–148.

Richter-Montpetit, Melanie. 2014. 'Beyond the Erotics Orientalism: Lawfare, Torture and the Racial-Sexual Grammars of Legitimate Suffering'. *Security Dialogue* 45(1): 43–62.

Roach, Mary. 2016. *Grunt: The Curious Science of Humans at War*. New York: W.W. Norton & Co.

Roberson, Laura. 2011. 'War is Hell (on Fertility)'. *Men's Health*, 18 October. Accessed 14 September 2016. http://bit.ly/2cMm7qA.

Rodríguez, Juana María. 2011. 'Queer Sociality and Other Sexual Fantasies'. *GLQ: A Journal of Lesbian and Gay Studies* 17: 331–348. DOI 10.1215/10642684-1163427.

Sabih, Jennifer. 2012. 'Beyond the Battlefield ... Into the Bedroom'. *The Huffington Post*, 21 March. Accessed 18 September 2016. http://huff.to/2cV1usj.

Serlin, David. 2003. 'Crippling Masculinity: Queerness and Disability in US Military Culture, 1800–1945'. *GLQ: A Journal of Lesbian and Gay Studies* 9: 149–179.

Shakespeare, Tom. 1999. 'The Sexual Politics of Disabled Masculinity'. *Sexuality and Disability* 17: 53–64.

Sivakumaran, Sandesh. 2007. 'Sexual Violence Against Men in Armed Conflict'. *European Journal of International Law* 18: 253–276.

Slevin, Kathleen F. and Thomas J. Linneman. 2010. 'Old Gay Men's Bodies and Masculinities'. *Men and Masculinities* 12: 483–507.

Spongberg, Mary. 1997. 'Are Small Penises Necessary for Civilisation?: The Male Body and the Body Politic'. *Australian Feminist Studies* 12: 19–28.

Stephens, Elizabeth. 2007. 'The Spectacularized Penis Contemporary Representations of the Phallic Male Body'. *Men and Masculinities* 10: 85–98.

Tritten, Travis J. 2016. 'Bill Would Provide $20,000 to Troops with Injured Genitals'. *Stars and Stripes*, 13 April. Accessed 28 August 2016. http://bit.ly/2bt8Lge.

Urology Care Foundation. 2011. 'Urotrauma: A Devastating but Little-Known Injury of War'. *Patient Magazine*, Spring. Accessed 15 September 2016. http://bit.ly/2d3aVrz.

Ursano, Robert J. 2012. 'Trauma and its Impact on One's Psyche and Soma'. In Mary Lee Dichtel (ed.), *Evaluation and Treatment of Genital Injuries in Combat Warriors (Artiss Symposium)*. Bethesda, MD: Centre for Traumatic Stress, 9–13.

VA/DoD (Department of Veteran Affairs and Department of Defence). 2016. *Department of Veteran Affairs Department of Defence Report to Congress Care Transition of Members of the Armed Forces with Urotrauma*. Washington, DC: Department of Defense.

Waldby, Catherine. 1995. 'Destruction: Boundary Erotics and Refigurations of the Heterosexual Male Body'. In Elizabeth Grosz and Elspeth Probyn (eds), *Sexy Bodies: The Strange Carnalities of Feminism*. New York: Routledge, 266–277.

Waxman, S., A. Beekley, A. Morey, and D. Soderdahl. 2009. 'Penetrating Trauma to the External Genitalia in Operation Iraqi Freedom'. *International Journal of Impotence Research* 21: 145–148.

Wentzell, Emily and Marcia C. Inhorn. 2011. 'Masculinities The Male Reproductive Body'. In Frances E. Mascia-Lees (ed.), *A Companion to the Anthropology of Body and Embodiment*, 1st edn. Malden, MD: Blackwell Publishing, 307–319.

Wilcox, Sherrie L., Sarah Redmond, and Anthony M. Hassan. 2014. 'Sexual Functioning in Military Personnel: Preliminary Estimates and Predictors'. *The Journal of Sexual Medicine* 11: 2537–2545.

Wilcox, Sherrie L., Ashley Schuyler, and Anthony M. Hassan. 2015. *Genitourinary Trauma in the Military: Impact, Prevention, and Recommendations*. Los Angles, CA: Center for Innovation and Research on Veterans & Military Families.

Wood, David. 2012. 'Beyond the Battlefield: Afghanistan's Wounded Struggle With Genital Injuries'. *The Huffington Post*, 22 March. Accessed 26 August 2016. http://huff.to/2bnjluX.

Woodward, Cal and Laura Eggertson. 2010. 'Homemade Bombs and Heavy Urogenital Injuries Create New Medical Challenges'. *Canadian Medical Association Journal* 182: 1159–1160.

Wool, Zoe. 2015. *After War: The Weight of Life at Walter Reed*. Kindle edn. Amazon.ca. ASIN: B0179G19I4.

Wool, Zoe. 2016. 'Attachments of Life: Intimacy, Genital Injury, and the Flesh of US Soldier Bodies'. In Veena Das and Clara Han (eds), *The Anthropology of Living and Dying in the Contemporary World*. Oakland, CA: University of California Press, 399–417.

Zumatto, Diane M. 2015. *Statement for the Record of Diane M. Zumatto AMVETS National Legislative Director for the Senate Committee on Veterans' Affairs*. Lanham, MD: AMVETS.

3 Masculinity, men, and sexual violence in the US military

Elizabeth Mesok

The first time Heath Phillips was sexually assaulted was in a hotel room in New York City. Just out of boot camp, Heath had been invited by his fellow shipmates to join a weekend excursion to the city while on leave from the ammunition ship USS *Butte*, stationed just off the coast of New Jersey. Heath, seventeen years old and from a small town in upstate New York, was raised to believe that the military was family, and he was eager to get to know his new comrades. After absorbing the sights and sounds of the bustling city, the group of men returned to the hotel room where Heath, despite having had prior experience with alcohol, passed out after just two small cups of beer. Upon regaining consciousness, he felt his pants being pulled down by one man and another grabbing at his penis, and saw a third man standing over him, masturbating. Heath fought off his assailants and escaped to the bathroom; later, the men explained that they were just initiating him, that this was something all new guys have to deal with, and that they would kill him if he told anyone what happened. Despite this threat, Heath immediately reported the attack to the master-at-arms upon returning to the ship the next morning, who responded: 'I think you're lying. I think you just want to go back home.' Labelled a 'baby' and a 'momma's boy', Heath's claim that he had been raped was met with ridicule and disbelief. Trapped on a ship with his assailants, Heath was repeatedly raped and tortured for the next six months.[1]

Heath described the decades following his brief yet violent time in the Navy as a 'twenty-year nightmare', marred by untreated post-traumatic stress disorder, drug and alcohol abuse, broken relationships, incarceration, and suicidal ideation. In order to get off the ship and away from his rapists, Heath was forced to accept an other-than-honourable discharge, which technically prevented him from receiving disability pay and mental health treatment from the US Department of Veterans Affairs (VA). In 2009, however, Heath got sober and, through the support of organisations advocating for the survivors of military sexual assault, stayed sober.[2] By the time I spoke to Heath nearly ten years later, he had dedicated his life to the myriad issues surrounding sexual violence in the military, working closely with veteran's organisations to raise awareness and with members of Congress to introduce legislative reform.[3] He has served as a panellist on a Congressional caucus on male military sexual trauma, spoken at military bases across the USA, testified at Senate hearings, and been featured in major news publications such as *Time* and *GQ* magazines. One of his greatest hopes, he told me, is that people will begin to understand that sexual violence is not a 'gender-specific issue' that only affects women. At the close of our conversation, Heath implored me: 'Just make sure you explain it should never be a gendered thing.'

Heath's insistence that rape 'should never be a gendered thing' recalls a larger critique of feminist scholarship and activism that has centred women as the universal victims of rape, foreclosing analyses of sexual violence wrought against men.[4] Indeed, his adamance that 'non-gendered legislation' and 'non-gendered verbiage' are necessary is born of frustration with the ways in which advocacy organisations and military policy have largely approached military sexual violence as a 'women's issue', an allegedly recent phenomenon attributable to women's increased presence, yet unequal treatment, in the armed forces in the twenty-first century.[5] In recent years, however, there has been a sharp increase in political discourse addressing the fact that military sexual violence is not exclusively a 'women's issue'. The emergence of this discourse, including Congressional hearings, government reports, and action plans released by the Department of Defense (DOD), marks a historically unprecedented moment, where sexual violence against men has received more attention in just a few years than in the entire history of the US military.[6]

In this chapter, I analyse the discourse regarding male–male sexual violence that emerged between 2014 and 2016 alongside Heath's individual narrative in order to critically explore the gendered constructs that shape dominant conceptualisations of male–male sexual violence. Even as the issue of male–male rape refutes the notion that rape is only ever about men dominating women, sexual violence against men remains predominately theorised through essentialist gender binary logic, where the masculine is understood as seeking to secure dominance over the feminine.[7] As Miranda Alison argues,

> Much of the feminist work on rape, including wartime rape, presents the issue purely in the context of male–female gendered power relations. Rape is seen as motivated by a universal male tendency towards indiscriminate violence against women and a generalised masculine desire to maintain a system of social control over all women.

> (Alison 2007: 78)

Here, however, I analyse rape as being productive of the very gendered categories that are said to pre-exist the act of violence, as one of many violent processes through which 'men', 'masculinity', and 'masculine' are constructed.

The emergence of this political discourse regarding male–male sexual violence is evidence of a new historical moment in the ever-shifting project of American military masculinity. Broadly speaking, I understand military masculinity – the particularly militarised iteration of masculinity – as a political technology, a historically contingent and discursively produced mechanism through which the bodies and institutions central to war-making are made to have meaning. Given the ways male military personnel have long figured as the embodiment of manliness in the American imaginary, it might be tempting to read male military rape victims as the most extreme symbolic representation of injured masculinity possible, and thus the discourse around male sexual violence as posing a threat to the coherence of military masculinity. However, rather than understanding the increased discourse around male–male sexual violence in the military as directly counter to the normative ideals of masculinity, I approach this moment as an adaptive response to the unresolvable tensions inherent within military masculinity. In other words, instead of seeing male–male sexual violence as threatening military masculinity, I consider the ways in which it operates as a mode – both physical and discursive – through which military masculinity is negotiated, as real and symbolic violence enacted in an attempt to enforce the unenforceable boundaries of masculinity. Ultimately, I argue that male–male sexual violence is constitutive rather than disruptive of the project of military masculinity, a cultivated process whereby the abject feminine is continually engaged, rather than merely rejected, in an attempt to secure the borders of masculine and feminine.[8]

'Warriors show strength by seeking help': the revision of American military masculinity

In the midst of waging protracted wars across the globe, the US military was forced to publicly confront what has been labelled an 'epidemic' of sexual violence (Schwellenbach 2013). Due to the tireless activism of military civil rights organisations and veteran advocacy groups, by 2011, mainstream media outlets were regularly covering stories of US servicemembers – predominately women – who had been raped by their comrades. The movement reached a fever pitch when, in the spring of 2013, the DOD released a report that an estimated 26,000 servicemembers – 14,000 men and 12,000 women – had experienced 'unwanted sexual contact' during the year prior (US Department of Defense 2013). The response was swift: the media widely covered victims' stories; legislation was introduced to reform the military judicial system; congressional hearings were held; and President Barack Obama issued a sobering warning to Pentagon leaders and military officials that sexual assault in the armed forces undermines military effectiveness and, in turn, jeopardises national security (The White House 2013).

While victim advocates and members of Congress seized this moment to mobilise against what Defense Secretary Chuck Hagel called a 'scourge' of military sexual violence, others were sceptical about the validity of the estimated number of victims as well as the methodology of the study; in particular, they questioned whether measuring the seemingly broad category of 'unwanted sexual contact' inflated the estimated number of sexual assault victims (Hagel 2013). In response to this scrutiny, the DOD commissioned the RAND Corporation in early 2014 to independently assess sexual assault, sexual harassment, and gender discrimination within the military. The RAND Military Workplace Study (RMWS) confirmed that the rate of sexual assault had not been overstated as some critics has suggested, but rather, that the previously conducted surveys had actually *underestimated* the proportion of servicemembers who experienced sexual assault as well as the severity of those assaults (Morral, Gore, and Schell 2016: 87). In addition to reinforcing that the military did, indeed, have a problem with sexual assault (estimating that 10,600 servicemen and 9,600 servicewomen were sexually assaulted in 2013), the RMWS identified 'a substantially greater number of serious assaults among men' and further, found that men 'experienced' sexual assault differently than women (Morral *et al.* 2016: xxvi).

In the two years following the December 2014 release of the RMWS's preliminary results, there was a sharp increase in the production of military and political discourse around male sexual violence. For instance, in March 2015, the Government Accountability Office (GAO), an independent government agency that reports to Congress, issued a report to the House Committee on Armed Services which claimed that US military culture, albeit 'unofficially', was 'defined by exaggerated characteristics of stereotypical masculinity' and 'linked to values and customs that perpetuate rape' (US Government Accountability Office 2015: 1). In December 2016, the DOD unveiled a seventeen-page plan to address the sexual assault of men in the military; the plan attributed the low incidence of men reporting sexual assault (an estimated 10 per cent of men compared to 38 per cent of women in the military) to military 'cultural norms' that shape the way that men understand acts of violence as well as 'stereotypes of masculinity' which prevent men from identifying as victims (US Department of Defense 2016: 3). Given the US's history of normalising sexual assault against men in the military, the publication of government commissioned studies and Pentagon plans that posited a direct correlation between military culture, masculinity, and rape was not just unprecedented – it was shocking.

Rather than accept the political denouncement of sexual violence against men in the military as a progressive or even feminist moment, I read this discourse as productive of a newly revised version of the ever-shifting project that is American military masculinity.[9] At a symbolic level, the recent political discourse regarding male–male sexual violence works to condemn the hyper-assaultive masculinity that jeopardises the readiness and cohesion of the armed services and threatens American military power, privileging a masculinity that is judicious and rational in its enactment of violence.[10] Indeed, from the widely publicised torture of Iraqi prisoners at Abu Ghraib in 2004 to the Marine Corps photo scandal in 2017 – in which servicemembers posted hundreds, if not thousands, of photographs of naked military women, often with sexually violent comments – the US military has faced public criticism of its misogynistic and violent culture fuelled by an aggressive masculinity. This is by no means an exhaustive list of the evidence that demonstrates the military's culture of hyper-aggressive masculinity, nor do I mean to suggest that such culture is historically particular to the post-9/11 era. However, it is important to note that these highly publicised 'scandals', along with the widely reported rates of sexual violence, have occurred simultaneous to the military's attempt to rebrand itself as an equal-opportunity employer in order to widen the pool of potential recruits and thus meet the labour needs of an all-volunteer force taxed by endless warfare. Indeed, over the last decade, the military has worked to establish itself as an institution committed to equality and inclusivity, repealing the combat exclusion policy for women, and lifting the bans on gay and transgender service members.[11] While some might argue that such policy changes indicate a feminisation and thus a weakening of the military (e.g. van Creveld 2000), I see them instead as adaptations to the ever-shifting parameters of military masculinity, a revisionary process that is always partial and incomplete.

These revisions of American military masculinity speak to a cultural moment of heightened anxiety around men, masculinity, and even maleness. For instance, consider the following statement by Army Maj. Gen. Camille Nichols, director of the DOD Sexual Assault Prevention and Response Office: 'Unfortunately, most men would rather be silent than report a sexual assault. We are working to encourage men by emphasizing that warriors show strength by seeking help' (Lyle 2016: 1). This statement, along with the larger discourse around male–male rape in the military, works to make the act of 'seeking help' for sexual violence a characteristic of a strong, male 'warrior'. Indeed, the discourse critiques the 'stereotypical masculinity' which both leads to rape and prevents men from reporting: 'Male survivors of sexual assault may have difficulty reconciling their masculine identity – normatively associated with strength and control – with the experience of being a victim' (US Department of Defense 2016: 15). Such discourse rejects a normative, 'stereotypical masculinity' and posits that one can be both a 'victim' and a 'warrior'. This revision of what it means to be strong, to be a warrior, indeed to be a man, is emblematic of a larger historical moment in which the military is attempting to, in Belkin's (2012) terms, smooth over the contradictions inherent within military masculinity.

' "Real" men don't get raped': sexual violence and the production of 'men'

Immediately after Heath reported his first attack and was ridiculed for it, he received his room assignment: a bunk in the same berthing area where his attackers slept. In the close confines of the ship, Heath could not avoid the abuse. The attacks often happened at night: Heath would be pulled from his bunk and the men would stick their fingers in his eyes and nose to force his mouth open, which they would then penetrate with their penises. Heath was always bothered by the fact that no one responded to the commotion: 'I'm screaming, yelling, fighting, and nobody is even moving their curtains to look' (Penn 2014). Heath made a report each time he was assaulted, and each time was met with responses such as, 'this didn't happen', 'you're a liar', and 'where's your proof?' A month later, after having been raped several times and forced to swallow his attackers' semen, Heath tried hanging himself in a storage room. 'I had been humiliated, beaten, robbed; I wasn't sleeping,' he explained. A petty officer found him and cut him down, only to immediately hit him: 'This guy smacked me and told me I needed to become a man and stand up to these guys. So right then and there I knew: people know that this is happening. So why is nobody helping me?' Desperate, Heath went AWOL, living on the streets and stealing food in order to avoid arrest. After being caught and confined to a naval brig, Heath was ordered to return to the USS *Butte* where he was immediately greeted by the ship's commanding officer. Chastised for leaving, the officer insisted that Heath must not have reported the previous attacks. Heath was then sent back to sleep in the same berthing area, where his attackers were waiting.

In this narrative, it is clear that Heath's shipmates and superiors knew about the assaults; the close quarters of the ship would have made it impossible for such violence to occur completely undetected. The acts of denying and of feigning ignorance align with the pervasive myth that 'men cannot be raped', a belief addressed by both the GAO report and the DOD Plan. For instance, the GAO report states that 'traditional gender stereotypes' prevent men from reporting sexual assault because they must 'contend with myths of male strength and sexuality which lead many to believe that "real" men do not get raped' (US Government Accountability Office 2015: 35). The DOD Plan confirms that within the military, 'sexual assault is widely considered to be a trauma only experienced by women' (US Department of Defense 2016: 12). The categorical denial of male rape is, in part, a result of feminist theorisations of rape as universally about men exerting social and political control over women. For instance, Susan Brownmiller argued that rape is 'nothing more or less than a conscious process of intimidation by which *all men* keep *all women* in a state of fear' (1976: 15). Catherine MacKinnon similarly defines rape as 'an act of dominance over women that works systematically to maintain a gender-stratified society in which women occupy a disadvantaged status as the appropriate victims and targets of sexual aggression' (1991: 1302). A theoretical framework that defines rape as the mechanism through which men physically and politically subordinate women renders Heath's subject position as a male rape victim completely illegible. Male rape victims will always remain ontological impossibilities within analytical approaches that maintain that rape is always already motivated by men's desire to oppress women, not as individuals but as a class.

Understanding rape as, definitively, the means by which men oppress women forecloses an analysis of the ways that sexual violence is actually productive of 'men' as gendered subjects. For instance, the petty officer who slapped Heath after his suicide attempt inadvertently admitted that he knew the assaults had occurred. However, the officer's admonishment 'to buck up and become a man and fight back,' implied that Heath was raped because he was not 'a man' (Ackerman 2016). The problem was not the rape itself, but that Heath had refused or been unable to prove his own manliness within the context of it – either toughening up to prevent the rape, or perhaps, quietly enduring it. As Brownmiller writes, rape is 'the ultimate test of [man's] superior strength, the triumph of his manhood' (1976: 15). The subject position 'man' is both an effect of rape and its precondition; a recognition that a man can indeed be raped threatens to reveal the fictiveness of a gendered order, which promises masculinity as the natural and exclusive property of men.

Ultimately, theorising rape as violence perpetrated by men as a means to dominate women reproduces what Sharon Marcus calls a 'rape script', a naturalised narrative of masculine power and feminine powerlessness that is both the precondition for rape and its result (1992: 391). This 'rape script' assumes that sexual violence is inherently and universally about men securing masculine dominance through a suppression of the feminine. This cultural script must be interrupted for, as Marcus argues, 'To take male violence or female vulnerability as the first and last instances in any explanation of rape is to make the identities of rapist and raped pre-exist the rape itself' (1992: 391). Analysing rape through a predetermined cultural script prevents an understanding of how gendered – as well as racialised, ethnic, and national – subjects are produced through sexual violence.[12] Instead, how might we imagine sexual violence against men as invested in producing both 'men' and 'masculinity', as attempting to enforce the unenforceable boundaries of masculinity and femininity? Masculinity, particularly in a militarised setting, must be theorised as a structure of identification invested in maintaining the naturalness of the signifier 'men', an investment that is heightened within the military institution, which depends upon such gendered signification for war. However, the relationship between masculinity, men, and violence is neither natural nor straightforward but a dialectical process whereby each gains and produces meaning in relationship to the other, a relationship that male–male sexual violence simultaneously threatens and underwrites.

'It wasn't for gratification, it was for torturing me': hazing and hetero-masculinity

After Heath was forced to return to the ship, the abuse intensified. 'From that point on it was just like "game on" with these guys,' Heath recalled. 'The assaults before were bad, but these were worse, the violence was more escalated. And it wasn't for gratification, it was for torturing me.' Heath endured ten months of being threatened, beaten, and raped. The final and most vicious attack occurred in a bathroom when Heath's attackers pulled him out of the shower and started beating him, repeatedly kicking him in the head and anally raping him with a shampoo bottle when one of the attackers was unable to maintain an erection. Heath passed out from pain that 'felt like an iron' inside of him. Upon regaining consciousness, he realised what was causing the pain:

> I had a toilet brush handle shoved inside of me as far as they could shove it. I went straight to medical 'cause I was in so much pain. Naked. I walked through the ship naked, covered in crap. Naked.

After examining him, the doctor diagnosed him with a ruptured haemorrhoid, despite Heath stating that he had been attacked. 'I don't know what you're talking about,' he recalls the doctor saying as he stood there naked, beaten, and covered in faeces. 'That's when I snapped,' Heath remembered. 'I went back to my area, I got dressed and I walked off my ship. And I didn't look back.'

This graphic description of extreme violence stands in stark contrast to Heath's assailants' characterisation of the attack in New York City as merely something that 'all new guys deal with'. The spectrum of violence that Heath endured, from the first act of 'initiation' to the retributive attacks that followed, including the final rape on the bathroom floor, require an examination of how and why male–male sexual violence in the military is often characterised as 'hazing'. Indeed, the GAO report, the RMWS, and the DOD Plan all argued that sexual assault against men requires special attention because it often occurs under the guise of hazing, resulting in men not recognising and thus not reporting the event as 'sexual assault'. For instance, the DOD Plan, drawing on the RMWS data, reports:

> that many of these acts [of sexual violence] are confused with hazing and meant to humiliate or degrade the victim. Men in these circumstances may not want help from a sexual assault program because they may perceive their experience as a cultural norm and unrelated to sexual misconduct.
>
> (US Department of Defense 2016: 5)

Indeed, 34 per cent of men described their sexual assault as hazing, compared to just 6 per cent of women, with men more likely to 'describe the event as serving to humiliate or abuse them as opposed to having a sexual intent' (Morral *et al.* 2016: xix). Overall, the study found that: 'sexual assaults against men often involve repeated, physically violent assaults that occur in a context of bullying, abuse, or hazing' (Morral *et al.* 2016: 90). These findings suggest that essentialist constructions of sexual violence as something that only happens to women have resulted in both the military and individual victims misunderstanding 'rape' as 'hazing', which in turn allowed a wide spectrum of sexual violence to be normalised and embedded in the military institution as a 'cultural norm'.

For instance, Heath believed he had initially been targeted because he was viewed as 'weak': 'And in the military you're supposed to be tough, because if we're going to war, you got to be tough,' he explained. 'So someone like me who went in at 17, weighing 130 pounds, I was not *tough*. Even though I fought back, I was not *tough*.' Heath's emphasis on the word 'tough' indicates the importance of this signifier in his own understanding of what happened; he recognised that lacking this ostensible characteristic of masculinity made him a target for other men to express their dominance. Here, Heath's understanding of his assaults is in line with the RMWS's definition of hazing as 'things done to humiliate or toughen up people prior to accepting them into a group' (Morral *et al.* 2016: 114). In this context, 'hazing' functions as a normalising category where the enactment of sexual violence is sanctioned as disciplinary, as a means of producing tough, yet compliant, subjects upon their entry into the military institution – a means of producing 'men'. Whether they are able to resist or protect themselves from violence is perhaps less important than whether they accept the violence as a constitutive part of their military experience. Indeed, Belkin argues that the ability to endure penetration in the military, in instances characterised as both hazing and rape, functions as a test of manliness: 'men have proven their warrior status when they were penetrated in the anus, hence demonstrating their toughness and ability to take it like a man' (Belkin 2012: 87). Steven Zeeland similarly writes, 'Marines view being penetrated not at all as female, but as a *manly* test of endurance that, successfully withstood, leaves the bottom with *more* power' (quoted in Belkin 2012: 87). Jane Ward finds that in the context of the military, 'being penetrated takes on new meaning as it is imbued with the power to toughen up the male body and put the male character to an extreme test' (2015: 164). In these analyses and Heath's narrative, male–male sexual violence as 'hazing' works to produce 'men' and to secure, rather than threaten, the boundaries of masculinity.

However, in the recent discourse on sexual violence against men in the US military, the coherence of 'hazing' as a concept depends on a clear disarticulation of sexual assault that is intended to 'abuse, humiliate, harass, or degrade any person', and sexual assault intended to 'arouse or gratify the sexual desire of any person' (USC 10 2012, para. 920 – Art. 120). The survey questions asked in the RMWS required respondents to indicate whether 'the event was intended for either a sexual purpose, to abuse, or to humiliate' (Morral *et al.* 2016: 9). Given the pervasive myth that: 'males raped by another man must be homosexual' (US Government Accountability Office 2015: 35) and the military's policy of discharging men who identified as homosexual up until 2011 (Turchik and Wilson 2010), it is unsurprising that 70 per cent of men indicated that they believed their sexual assault was intended to abuse or humiliate as opposed to having a sexual intent (Morral *et al.* 2016: 15). Problematically, the very design of the survey questions falsely suggests that rape intended to humiliate or abuse cannot also be sexual. However, by analytically separating the motivations for rape into those that are sexual and those that are non-sexual, the hetero-masculinity of the perpetrators, the victims, and the military institution itself are left unquestioned.

For instance, the DOD plan identified 'widely endorsed myths and misconceptions about male sexual assault' that prevent men from reporting, including the belief that 'male on male sexual assault is about homosexuality rather than power' (US Department of Defense 2016: 7). In insisting that rape is about power – the power to humiliate, to abuse, to control – rather than sexual desire, the DOD is utilising a radical feminist argument that emerged in the 1970s to politicise rape and resist the notion that rape was explainable by men's natural and uncontrollable desire for women. However, I would argue that the DOD's employment of this argument functions to protect the sexuality of the perpetrator and the victim; by identifying male–male sexual violence as hazing, queer desire is sanctioned as heterosexual. As Ward writes, hazing, which includes 'dominance, humiliation, anality, and repulsion (…) is not simply a practice; it is also a hetero-erotic trope, one that facilitates access to homosexual activity while inscribing this activity with heterosexual meaning' (2015: 156). In this sense, we can understand hazing as working to secure the military's hetero-masculinity on both a material and a symbolic level. Hazing as the physical, material enactment of sexual violence involves the interplay of power, pleasure, and revulsion through an active engagement with feminine abjection, negotiating the ever-shifting boundaries of masculinity. On the symbolic level, the reports and studies that analyse male–male sexual violence in the military can be understood as part of a new iteration of American military masculinity, one that seeks to revise the hyper-aggressive, assaultive violence that characterises the armed forces while simultaneously protecting the hetero-masculinity of the institution.

Inspired by the trauma that he endured, Heath has dedicated his life to ending the stigma against male sexual assault. His plea that rape 'should never be a gendered thing' is understandable given the way in which sexual violence is predominately characterised in both the civilian and military world as something that happens only to women. However, sexual violence is, indeed, a 'gendered thing', which must be analysed as productive of the very gendered subjects upon which it acts. Disarticulating normative weddings of sex and gender is necessary to understand how sexual violence functions as a process of sexual differentiation without assuming the outcome of such differentiation. Further, it is crucial to acknowledge that sexual violence is necessary for and beneficial to militarism, with sexual violence against men functioning as an integral part of the construction of military masculinity. Attending critically to the gendered dynamics at play in male sexual violence allows us to develop further theoretical insights into how such violence is deeply invested in the production of both men and masculinity, as well as how masculinity rearticulates and reproduces itself in the service of US militarism.

Notes

1 Heath Phillips, phone interview by the author, Basel, Switzerland, 17 February 2017. All quotations attributed to Phillips are from this interview unless otherwise cited.
2 In this chapter, I use the term 'survivor' when reflecting the linguistic choices of Heath's narrative. However, in the rest of the chapter, I use the term 'victim', not as an identity category but as a descriptor, in part to resist the idea that individuals who are raped are always transformed and empowered by their experience.
3 For instance, Heath was influential in the passage of the Fairness for Veterans Act in 2016, which requires military discharge review boards to take into account diagnoses of traumatic brain injury or post-traumatic stress disorder in connection with combat or sexual trauma. This allows veterans with other-than-honourable discharges, like Heath, to petition for their discharge status to be upgraded and thus to gain access to the healthcare benefits offered by the VA.
4 For instance, the legal scholar Bennett Capers argues that 'rape has been gendered for too long' (2011: 1259) and critiques feminist scholars who, in their attempts to reform traditional rape laws, have 'inadvertently legitimized and contributed to the very gender distinctions of which they have been so critical. In response to one form of subordination, they have entrenched another. (...) As a consequence, male victims have suffered' (2011: 1265). Holly Henderson similarly calls for feminism to 'rethink naturalized versions of sexual violence': 'If these essentialized conceptions of rape gain and retain meaning through a continued deployment *by* feminism, might feminism be unwittingly reinforcing rather than breaking down sexist and gender-stereotypic assumptions?' (2013: 227, emphasis in original). For scholarly critiques of

essentialist constructions of rape in war, which naturalise men as perpetrators of sexual violence and women as universal victims, see Alison 2007; Sivakumaran 2010; Stemple 2009; Grey and Shepherd 2012; and Vojdik 2014.

5 For instance, in 2013, the former Chairman of the Joint Chiefs of Staff, General Martin E. Dempsey, suggested that fully integrating women into all military occupational specialties, including ground combat, would reduce the incidence of sexual violence (Panetta and Dempsey 2013). This claim, which was echoed by military women's advocacy organisations and feminist activists, suggests that denying women full military equality institutionalises sexism, which in turn sanctions and normalises sexual violence against women. Such a conceptualisation, however, problematically suggests that military sexual violence is only ever the result of women's subordination and thus resolvable through liberal equality. For further analysis of the limitations of tying the campaign to eradicate military sexual violence to a campaign for military women's equality, see Mesok 2016.

6 Although the Department of Defense began researching the rates of sexual assault and sexual harassment against servicemen in the early 1990s, it was not until 2012 that the Office of Sexual Assault Prevention and Response identified the need to 'promote initiatives that address sexual assault against male victims' (US Department of Defense 2013: 17). For a review of reported prevalence and incidence rates of military sexual assault against men, see Hoyt, Rielage, and Williams 2011.

7 For instance, rape during war remains largely theorised as a process whereby the perpetrator seeks to secure his masculine dominance by raping, and thus feminising the enemy. For example, see Vojdik 2014; Bond 2013; Eriksson Baaz and Stern 2013; Jones 2006; Goldstein 2001; and Skjelsbæk 2001. This a priori assumption that sexual violence is always already a means to feminise the victim and cohere the masculinity of the perpetrator forecloses an analysis of sexual violence as the practice through which 'masculine' and 'feminine' are produced as gendered constructs *and* through which the sexual differentiation of 'men' and 'women' takes place. Here I am following Henderson, who understands rape as 'a sexualized and gendered attack which imposes sexual difference along the lines of violence' (2013: 232).

8 Here I am following Aaron Belkin's argument that military masculinity depends on negotiating with and even embracing the feminine. Belkin argues that 'the production of masculine warriors has required those who embody masculinity to enter into intimate relationships with femininity, queerness and other unmasculine foils, not just to disavow them' (2012: 4). Here Belkin is intervening in scholarship that characterises military masculinity as cohered through the absolute disavowal of the feminine. See, for instance, Goldstein 2001; Bayard de Volo 2012; Jeffords 1989; and Theidon 2009. For an important exception, see Dietrich Ortega's excellent analysis of the construction of military masculinities through an active engagement with – not the rejection or devaluation of – femininities in insurgent militias in Latin America (2012).

9 In the 1980s, for instance, a hyper-aggressive iteration of masculinity was projected onto the American public through popular culture, in response to the perceived feminisation of the nation vis-à-vis the failure of the Vietnam War (Jeffords 1989, 1993). In the following decade, the Persian Gulf War saw a turn 'toward a more sentimentalized masculinity' focused on domesticity, family, and emotionality (Wiegman 1994). One iteration, however, never fully replaces another. Instead, military masculinity acts dialectically as both a regulatory practice and its resultant ideal, constantly responding to new political and cultural moments, yet always characterised by irreconcilable tensions.

10 This narrative of American military masculinity projects a vision of strength, courage, and rational violence enacted benevolently, for the good of the global community and always in contradiction to the presumed irrationality and incoherence of insurgent and terrorist violence. In this iteration, as in all iterations, American military masculinity is an inherently racialised construction.

11 For instance in 2011, the Military Leadership Diversity Commission released the final report of the first commission to study equal rights and opportunities in the US military since 1962. The Commission recommended that the Armed Forces diversify its leadership to better reflect the racial, ethnic, and cultural make-up of the United States, in part by promoting greater recruitment and retention of women and people of colour. Later that same year, the policy barring gay, lesbian, and bisexual service-members from serving openly was officially lifted. In 2013, the former Secretary of Defense, Leon Panetta, rescinded the policy banning women from ground combat positions. In June 2016, the former Secretary of Defense, Ashton Carter, announced that transgender individuals would be able to openly serve. However, during the following summer, President Donald Trump announced via Twitter that the United States government would no longer allow transgender individuals to serve in the armed forces. Immediately following Trump's announcement, which reportedly caught military leaders by surprise, the chairman of the Joint Chiefs of Staff General Joseph Dunford stated that no modifications would be made to the current policy until the Secretary of Defense issued an official plan for implementation. Given the military's significant strides towards representing itself as an inclusive and just organisation, it seems unlikely that a ban will be instated without significant resistance.
12 Indeed rape also serves as a mode of racialisation (e.g. Davis 1983; Collins 2000), and a means to police ethnic boundaries and construct national identities (e.g. Zarkov 2001; Russell-Brown 2003; Alison 2007; Mookherjee 2008; Rejali 1998).

References

Ackerman, Spencer. 2016. '"It Savaged My Life": Military Sexual Assault Survivors Fighting to Become Visible'. *Guardian*, 11 October. www.theguardian.com/society/2016/oct/11/military-sexual-assault-survivors-epidemic.

Alison, Miranda. 2007. 'Wartime Sexual Violence: Women's Human Rights and Questions of Masculinity'. *Review of International Studies* 33: 75–90.

Bayard de Volo, Lorraine. 2012. 'A Revolution in the Binary?: Gender and the Oxymoron of Revolutionary War in Cuba and Nicaragua'. *Signs* 37: 413–439.

Belkin, Aaron. 2012. *Bring Me Men: Military Masculinity and the Benign Façade of American Empire, 1898–2001*. New York: Columbia University Press.

Bond, Johanna. 2013. 'A Decade after Abu Ghraib: Lessons in Softening Up the Enemy and Sex-Based Humiliation'. *Law and Inequality: A Journal of Theory and Practice* 31: 1–36.

Brownmiller, Susan. 1976. *Against Our Will: Men, Women, and Rape*, 2nd edn. New York: Penguin Books.

Capers, Bennett. 2011. 'Real Rape Too'. *California Law Review* 99: 1259–1308.

Collins, Patricia Hill. 2000. *Black Feminist thought: Knowledge, Consciousness, and the Politics of Empowerment*. New York: Routledge.

Davis, Angela. 1983. 'Rape, Racism, and the Myth of the Black Rapist'. In *Women, Race, and Class*. New York: Vintage, 172–201.

Eriksson Baaz, Maria and Maria Stern. 2013. *Sexual Violence as a Weapon of War?: Perceptions, Prescriptions, Problems in the Congo and Beyond*. New York: Zed Books.

Goldstein, Joshua. 2001. *War and Gender: How Gender Shapes the War System and Vice Versa*. Cambridge: Cambridge University Press.

Grey, Rosemary and Laura J. Shepherd. 2012. '"Stop Rape Now?": Masculinity, Responsibility, and Conflict-Related Sexual Violence'. *Men and Masculinities* 16: 115–135.

Hagel, Chuck. 2013. 'United States Military Academy Commencement'. Speech, West Point, New York, 25 May. US Department of Defense, http://archive.defense.gov/Speeches/Speech.aspx?SpeechID=1782.

Henderson, Holly. 2013. 'Feminism, Foucault, and Rape: A Theory and Politics of Rape Prevention'. *Berkeley Journal of Gender, Law and Justice* 22: 225–253.

Hoyt, Tim, Jennifer Klosterman Rielage, and Lauren F. Williams. 2011. 'Military Sexual Trauma in Men: A Review of Reported Rates'. *Journal of Trauma and Dissociation* 12: 244–260.

Jeffords, Susan. 1989. *The Remasculinization of America: Gender and the Vietnam War*. Bloomington, IN: Indiana University Press.

Jeffords, Susan. 1993. *Hard Bodies: Hollywood Masculinity in the Reagan Era*. New Brunswick, NJ: Rutgers University Press.

Jones, Adam. 2006. 'Straight as a Rule: Heteronormativity, Gendercide, and the Noncombatant Male'. *Men and Masculinities* 8: 451–469.

Lyle, Amaani. 2016. 'DoD Unveils Plan to Broaden Sexual Assault Support to Men'. *DoD News, Defense Media Activity*. 15 December. www.defense.gov/News/Article/Article/1030795/dod-unveils-plan-to-broaden-sexual-assault-support-to-men/.

MacKinnon, Catherine A. 1991. 'Reflections on Sex Equality Under Law'. *The Yale Law Journal* 100: 1281–1328.

Marcus, Sharon. 1992. 'Fighting Bodies, Fighting Words: A Theory and Politics of Rape Prevention'. In Judith Butler and Joan Scott (eds), *Feminists Theorize the Political*. New York: Routledge, 385–403.

Mesok, Elizabeth. 2016. 'Sexual Violence and the US Military: Feminism, US Empire, and the Failure of Liberal Equality'. *Feminist Studies* 42: 41–69.

Mookherjee, Nayanika. 2008. 'Gendered Embodiments: Mapping the Body-Politics of the Raped Woman and the Nation in Bangladesh'. *Feminist Review* 88: 36–53.

Morral, Andrew R., Kristie L. Gore, and Terry L. Schell (eds). 2016. 'Sexual Assault and Sexual Harassment in the U.S. Military. Volume 2. Estimates for Department of Defense Service Members from the 2014 RAND Military Workplace Study'. Santa Monica, CA: RAND Corporation.

Ortega, Luisa Maria Dietrich. 2012. 'Looking Beyond Violent Militarized Masculinities: Guerrilla Gender Regimes in Latin America'. *International Feminist Journal of Politics* 14: 489–507.

Panetta, Leon and Martin E. Dempsey. 2013. 'Statement on Women in Service'. Pentagon Press Briefing Room, Washington, DC. 24 January. www.jcs.mil/Media/Speeches/Article/571884/sec-panetta-and-gen-dempseys-media-briefing/.

Penn, Nathaniel. 2014. '"Son, Men Don't Get Raped": In the U.S. Military, More Than Half of Rape Victims are Men'. *GQ*, 12 September. www.gq.com/long-form/male-military-rape.

Rejali, Darius M. 1998. 'After Feminist Analyses of Bosnian Violence'. In Lois Ann Lorentzen and Jennifer Turpin (eds), *The Women and War Reader*. New York: New York University Press, 26–32.

Russell-Brown, Sherrie L. 2003. 'Rape as an Act of Genocide'. *Berkeley Journal of International Law* 21: 350–374.

Schwellenbach, Nick. 2013. 'Fear of Reprisal: The Quiet Accomplice in the Military's Sexual-Assault Epidemic'. *Time*, 9 May. http://nation.time.com/2013/05/09/fear-of-reprisal-the-quiet-accomplice-in-the-militarys-sexual-assault-epidemic/.

Sivakumaran, Sandesh. 2010. 'Lost in Translation: UN Responses to Sexual Violence Against Men and Boys in Situations of Armed Conflict'. *International Review of the Red Cross* 92: 259–277.

70   *Elizabeth Mesok*

Skjelsbæk, Inger. 2001. 'Sexual Violence and War: Mapping out a Complex Relationship'. *European Journal of International Relations* 7: 211–237.

Stemple, Lara. 2009. 'Male Rape and Human Rights'. *Hastings Law Journal* 60: 605–646.

Theidon, Kimberly. 2009. 'Reconstructing Masculinities: The Disarmament, Demobilization, and Reintegration of Former Combatants in Colombia'. *Human Rights Quarterly* 31: 1–34.

Thompson, Mark. 2016. 'Military Sexual Assault Victims Discharged After Filing Complaints'. *Time*, 18 May. http://time.com/4340321/sexual-assault-military-discharge-women/.

Turchik, Jessica A. and Susan M. Wilson. 2010. 'Sexual Assault in the U.S. Military: A Review of the Literature and Recommendations for the Future'. *Aggression and Violent Behavior* 15: 267–277.

USC 10. Uniform Code of Military Justice. 2012. §920 Art. 120.

US Department of Defense. 2016. 'Plan to Prevent and Respond to Sexual Assault of Military Men'.

US Department of Defense, Sexual Assault Prevention and Response Office. 2013. *Department of Defense Annual Report on Sexual Assault in the Military Fiscal Year 2012.* Washington, DC: GPO.

US Government Accountability Office. 2015. *Report to the Committee on Armed Services, House of Representatives.* GAO-15-284. Washington, DC. www.gao.gov/assets/670/669096.pdf.

van Creveld, Martin. 2000. 'Less Than We Can Be: Men, Women, and the Modern Military'. *Journal of Strategic Studies* 23: 1–20.

Vojdik, Valorie K. 2014. 'Sexual Violence Against Men and Women in War: A Masculinities Approach'. *Nevada Law Journal* 14: 923–952.

Ward, Jane. 2015. *Not Gay: Sex Between Straight White Men.* New York: New York University Press.

The White House, Office of the Press Secretary. 2013. 'Remarks by the President After Meeting on Sexual Assault in the Military'. 16 May. https://obamawhitehouse.archives.gov/realitycheck/the-press-office/2013/05/16/remarks-president-after-meeting-sexual-assault-military.

Wiegman, Robyn. 1994. 'Missiles and Melodrama (Masculinity and the Televisual War)'. In Susan Jeffords and Lauren Rabinovitz (eds), *Seeing Through the Media: The Persian Gulf War.* New Brunswick, NJ: Rutgers University Press, 171–187.

Zarkov, Dubravka. 2001. 'The Body of the Other Man: Sexual Violence and the Construction of Masculinity, Sexuality and Ethnicity in the Croatian Media'. In Caroline O.N. Moser and Fiona C. Clark (eds), *Victims, Perpetrators or Actors? Gender, Armed Conflict and Political Violence.* New York: Zed Books, 69–82.

4 Languages of castration – male genital mutilation in conflict and its embedded messages

Henri Myrttinen

Introduction

Slowly but steadily, the issue of sexual violence against men and boys (SVAMB) has been taken up over the past decade as an issue of concern in academic research, policy response, and programming in the emergent field of conflict-related sexual violence (CRSV). The body of literature on SVAMB is increasingly rich but tends to deal mostly with the penetrative anal rape of men and boys, though also acknowledging other forms of violence (e.g. Carpenter 2006; Dolan 2010; Misra 2015; Lewis 2014; Russell 2007; Sivakumaran 2005, 2007; Solangon and Patel 2012). In the policy realm, the focus tends to be much more strongly on rape only, although even gaining space for discussions of SVAMB in the first place has at times been a challenge (Dolan 2015; Kirby 2015). I chose here to focus on violence against male genitalia, as in some ways, it gets to the core of some of the 'work' that SVAMB does: to humiliate, dehumanise, and both literally and figuratively 'emasculate' the victim; destroy his reproductive capacity and underscore the power of the perpetrator (Sivakumaran 2007: 267–275).[1] Second, as the SVAMB debate has focused heavily on penetrational anal rape of men and boys, in particular by other men, I hope to contribute to a broadening of this debate by highlighting other forms of violence. The tendency to not discuss acts of violence against male genital mutilation and its real-life repercussions even where there is evidence of these acts has the potential to render whole categories of victims/survivors invisible (Carlson 2006). Furthermore, the focus on penetrational anal rape with a penis, apart from leaving out other forms of rape and SVAMB, also carries with it the implicit assumption of men as perpetrators, disregarding acts carried out by women and those with non-binary gender identities (Sjoberg 2016).

My hope is that, given the absence of strong research on perpetrator motivations, a better understanding of the messages that perpetrators seek to convey through this particular act, and the belief systems it is embedded in, helps us to better understand what drives sexual violence, be it against men, women, or other gender identities. Echoing Carlson (2006), a lack of a broader understanding of SVAMB and an excessive focus on rape on men and boys only can lead to responders, service providers, researchers, or the judicial system to overlook other forms of violence which might have equally severe physical, emotional, psycho-logical, and social implications for the victim/survivor.

Simultaneously, male genitalia are in many societies and cultures, intimately linked with manhood, and with violence and power – and violence against them can be seen as a direct attack against the 'manliness' of the opponent, both liter-ally and symbolically. Violence against male genitalia is employed as a way of physically and symbolically harming the opponent in male-dominated, masculine-coded theatres of conflict. Castration and penile amputation of van-quished enemy combatants and civilians spans global history from the ancient kingdoms and Empires of Egypt, Dahomey, the Inca, or Persia (Goldstein 2001: 357–359; Misra 2015: 4) to reports coming out of the current conflict in South Sudan (UNICEF 2016). However, although the particular act of violence itself may be the same in different settings, the meaning attached to it by perpetrators, victims/survivors, and broader society is often different, depending on the con-flict context, socio-cultural background, the identity of the perpetrator and that of the victim/survivor.

In this chapter, I explore the various forms of violence directed against male sexual/reproductive organs in different settings of violent conflict and some of the meanings attached to these acts in these contexts by the various people par-taking in the act directly either as victims/survivors, perpetrator, and witnesses or indirectly as audiences. The various forms of violence covered here include full and partial penectomy (the cutting off of the penis), full and partial castra-tion (i.e. cutting off or damaging of the testicles), forced circumcision, and other forms of physical violence against male genitalia such as blunt genital trauma. Some of the acts of violence, such as the deliberate, targeted severing of the testes or the penis, are meant specifically to lead to the loss of or damage to the male sexual organs. In other cases, such as sexualised torture (e.g. electric shocks and beatings administered to the genitalia) or with injuries caused by anti-personnel mines and improvised explosive devices (IEDs), the damage to the penis and testicles may not be the ultimate goal of the violence but rather a collateral 'side-effect'. Furthermore, violence against as well as the mutilation of male sexual organs is committed against both the living and the dead. Some of the examples of the penile amputation and castration that I draw upon below occurred after the death of the people whose bodies were subjected to such violence.

However, regardless of whether, for example, a man's societal standing is seen as actually or merely figuratively linked to his genitalia, it can become a driving factor for penectomy, castration, and other forms of genital mutilation. Furthermore, the acts of violence against male genitalia attributed a great breadth of different meanings, making them a rich area with which to engage theoretically.

For the purposes of this chapter, I use the World Health Organization (2002) definition of sexual violence and include all forms of violence against male geni-talia as sexual violence, which is not an entirely uncontroversial point. Some forms of conflict-related violence against male genitalia ('collateral' damage from improvised explosive devices [IEDs] or small arms fire, blunt trauma) tend to be not regarded as SVAMB, while other forms of sexual violence (e.g. electric shocks to the genitals) have been classified as torture (Al-Azzawi and Koraitim 2014; Carlson 2006; Leiby 2012). A particularly intriguing, and potentially very problematic case of not seeing violence done to male genitalia as sexual violence comes from the International Criminal Court's (ICC) case against Uhuru Muigai Kenyatta, which also covered the forced circumcisions of Luo men. The Pre-Trial Chamber of the ICC ruled that: 'not every act of violence which targets parts of the body commonly associated with sexuality should be considered an act of sexual violence', thus ruling that neither forced circumcisions nor penile amputations were to be classified as sexual violence, but rather as inhumane acts (Grey 2014: 280–282). Classifying an act as sexual violence does not preclude motivations other than sexual ones. As I outline in more detail in the case studies below, the act of violence is often linked to other messages. Sexual violence, as also discussed below in the case studies, can be part of torture and the two are not mutually exclusive.

This chapter proceeds as follows. I first introduce my methodology along with a discussion on the possibilities and difficulties of understanding meanings attached to and conveyed by violence. I then outline in more detail how I use the terms 'message' and 'audience' for the purposes of the chapter, followed by a discussion of several case examples. The purpose of these case examples is to showcase the diversity of meanings attached to the same or similar acts of SVAMB by different actors in different settings. This highlighting of the multiplicity of possible meanings and thereby drivers for a particular act of violence serves to underscore the need for a more contextualised and nuanced examination of why particular acts of violence are perpetrated in a particular setting. I end with a discussion of the 'work' done by SVAMB and the messages it conveys in conflicts.

Methodology and the difficulties of interpretation

This chapter is based mainly on a review of secondary materials, in addition to which some background interviews were conducted with academic researchers and NGO practitioners working on SVAMB as well as informal discussions with investigators working for international agencies. My own understanding of SVAMB is in part informed by my work in the NGO sector on gender issues in conflict-affected societies, including SGBV prevention. I will, for the most part, focus on SVAMB in conflict, but on occasion also refer to some non-conflict related cases where these seemed relevant to me.

Assessing the 'meanings' that these forms of violence take is not straightforward and raises pertinent questions about whether as an outsider to the act I am able to '*really* know' what meanings are being conveyed, in particular when working with second- and third-hand sources.[2]

I have chosen here to approach violence as a 'language' that is seeking to communicate something to a number of audiences, the concept of which I will discuss below. I do not mean this in any esoteric way, nor do I in any way want to belittle or abstract – and thereby sanitise – the very real and often gruesome violence of the acts. Following Jan-Philipp Reemtsma and Chris Cramer, I am examining violence as a form of communication, albeit an extreme one where other forms of communication have broken down (Cramer 2006: 284; Reemtsma 2008: 107).

As with any human act, the acts of violence described here can take on a multiplicity of meanings simultaneously, and there is inevitably a process of interpretation that occurs. An act may be read differently depending on one's vantage point. To use a hypothetical example: an act of cutting off the penis of a dead enemy soldier, for example, may from the point of view of the perpetrator send a message of underscoring her or his victory. Her or his comrades may concur – or may see it as a worrisome sign of excess and loss of control. Civilian bystanders may see it as an act that does not highlight victory, but rather barbarity, while a prosecutor may see the elements of a war crime. For each of these actors, there will likely be other conscious and unconscious emotions and drivers at work, but also meanings: the hypothetical perpetrator, for example, may be seeking to 'shock and awe' the enemy or local population into submission, and/or may seek to send a message of what s/he intends to be of 'ethnic supremacy'. Thus, the meanings of the messages that sexual violence is intended to send and how they are 'read' are multiple, as well as context- and actor-specific.

For the purposes of this chapter, I rely as much as possible on the meanings that are directly stated in the sources I have used, bearing in mind, of course the methodological challenges of attributing meaning that the authors of these sources, in turn, surely faced, as well as the elusiveness of any singular or fixed meaning being attributed to any particular act – even by the perpetrator him/ herself. If, as for example in the Kenyan cases discussed below, the perpetrators directly stated to the intended victim that the act of sexual violence they were about to commit was linked to the victim's ethnicity and their alleged inferior position, and then proceeded to follow through on the act, I then chose to classify this as being an act that aimed to send a message of alleged ethnic inferiority.[3] In cases where the perpetrators did not directly state their message, I have relied on assessments by third parties which I deemed plausible, such as castrations and penectomies committed by militias in Eastern Democratic Republic of Congo (DRC) considered by investigators of the ICC as fitting into broader patterns of terrorising the civilian population. In some cases, such as violence to the male genitals caused by shrapnel from IEDs, I have made the judgement call that unless the IED was directly meant to damage the genitals, there was no message linked specifically to the violence done to the genitals, as the person detonating the IED could not fully control the trajectories of the shrapnel or blast wave. There will, however, be other messages the perpetrator would have been sending, such as resistance against foreign forces or sectarian hatred.

As discussed above, there are likely to be other factors and messages at work as well, but I am not in a position, as an outsider who has not spoken to the various parties, to discern these. Whether or not the second- and third-hand accounts are a 'real' reflection of the intentions of the perpetrators, in as far as the 'real' intentions can be known, is surely a valid question; yet it remains an unanswerable one. However, among the many possible interpretations, I have chosen to relay those that figure in the sources I cite, as they are marked by a sense of credibility.

A further challenge in interpreting possible messages is that I do not necessarily 'speak' the same language as the perpetrator and the intended audiences, that is, I do not have the same frame of reference with which to make sense of the violent acts. If I do not, for example, see the penis and testicles as the literal seat of male power or of witchcraft powers, can I ever fully understand the significance this kind of violence has for those who do? The risk of misinterpretation of the perpetrator's intended messages applies to all audiences, and these problems are not singular to the study of conflict-related violence against male genitalia; they are, perhaps, heightened given its falsely perceived 'exotic' or 'bizarre' nature. These risks are further exacerbated by the lack of comprehensive research, including the dearth of work about women as perpetrators and sexual and gender minorities as victims and/or perpetrators.

The process of collecting the data for this chapter proved to be more difficult than I had anticipated. Although I had over the years come across numerous anecdotes and snippets of news about instances of conflict-related penile amputations and castrations, and mutilations as well as of the ritualistic eating of genitals, verifying their veracity (or at least the shared belief that – and sometimes why – they occurred) through reliable sources was challenging. Unlike the growing literature on SVAMB in general and rape of men in particular, these particular forms of violence seem to have received little serious attention in spite of their ubiquity across time and geographical settings. The sources from which I have gathered my data are diverse and fragmentary.

Another key problem with interpreting the 'languages of castration' is a lack of research on perpetrator motivations as well as on victims' and community members' understandings of the violence and its meanings. Thus, of the audiences I listed above, information on most is not available, unless there is a clear and explicit statement of why the violence is being committed (e.g. Bosnian and Croat men being told by Serb perpetrators that the purpose is to destroy their reproductive capacity or Luo men being mocked for being uncircumcised before the forced circumcision). Much of the available information comes from a more distanced audience: media, academic researchers, judicial staff, and other second- and third-hand authors. While much of the reporting of these forms of violence is of a high quality, the fact that castration and penile amputation, let alone the consumption of body parts, are considered by many to be exotic, taboo, or voyeuristically titillating does colour some of the writing. Consider the following introduction to the book by Henderson (1988), which includes the case of the Vietnamese woman combatant cutting off a US Marine's penis and testicles:

> In the book 'Marine Sniper' by Charles Henderson, He devotes a whole chapter to the Apache Woman, The real life sadistic female VC. The following is an actual torture/castration she performed on a young captured soldier.

The autor [*sic!*] added some dialog for interest as if it needed any more. I think any castration is interesting enough. Just imagine being tied up naked and having an attractive Asian woman approach you with a huge knife, knowing she is going to cut your balls and dick off!!!! Read and enjoy....

(Odd News and Stories 2006)

While this particular paragraph is an extreme example, it does underscore, and in fact openly celebrates, some of the pitfalls of dealing with an issue that is still to a degree seen as being beyond the pale.

As this example clearly shows us, there is a high risk of exoticising and eroticising such violence and projecting it as something that allegedly only 'barbaric Others' do – or Western soldiers do when sent to such 'dark' locales, when discussing such violence that occurs in non-Western societies. Apart from being inaccurate, such narratives also serve to stabilise Western racial and gender identities and their supposed superiority, while doing nothing for the victims and survivors themselves. It is not only 'barbaric' non-Western men, or 'monstrous' women who have carried out these kinds of acts (Sjoberg and Gentry 2007). Rather, these are acts that occur in all societies and that people of all gender identities are capable of.

Messages and audiences of SVAMB

In using the conceptual lens of violence as a communicative tool, we can explore how the violence under scrutiny is intended to send a message to various audiences. As noted above, the messages communicated might be multiple and are not necessarily straightforward or clear, As Laura Sjoberg (2016) points out, these messages are also highly gendered, with different meanings and dynamics at work depending on the gender identities of the victim and the perpetrator – and these gendered dynamics themselves vary between different socio-cultural settings and historical periods.

Acts of violence have several audiences. The first and primary audience is arguably the victim. In some cases, the message or messages are made explicit by the perpetrator, in others, they remain implicit. The victim does not necessarily need to be alive for him to be conceived of as the recipient of a particular message, for example, in cases where the castration or mutilation is posthumous. I would posit as a working hypothesis that, in some of the cases that I address, there was a deliberate infliction of pain, which I would see as being part of the message of powerlessness and subjugation (cf. Dolan 2009, 2010; Sivakumaran 2007). For example, in the Kenyan and Bosnian examples outlined in more detail below, instead of using scalpels/knives and local anaesthesia which would have been readily available in a prison camp (Bosnia-Herzegovina) or urban environment (Kenya), much cruder methods were used, such as broken bottles, teeth, or tying the testicles to a motorcycle.

A second audience is the broader public – be it the community which the victim(s) belong(s) to, that of the perpetrator(s) or those inhabiting the area where the act of violence occurs, or even the wider (global) community who sees or reads about the act via the media. This can be overt, in which case the castration/genital mutilation and/or its effects are made public, be it by displaying mutilated corpses or severed genitalia, or by openly publicising the act and its message (e.g. through radio broadcasts, social media, or by leaving placards around the necks of mutilated victims). At other times, the message is conveyed more surreptitiously through the spread of rumour and innuendo, rather than open messaging. Depending on the audiences, the 'theatre' – to borrow Paula Drumond's term (2017) – and the intentions of the perpetrator, the acts of violence against male genitalia can be public and a form of violent spectacle, hidden from sight completely or somewhere in between.

A third audience group are the peers of the perpetrator(s), and the fourth one is the perpetrator him- or herself. The messages, at least the explicit ones, which are being conveyed to the victims and third parties are to an extent relatively clear, as they are directly articulated by the perpetrator. What exactly the messages are to peers and the self remains less clear, in particular due to a lack of perpetrator and bystander research. For the peers, it may be group cohesion but also establishment of power hierarchies within a unit. For the perpetrators, some of the explicit messages, such as the assertion of one's own dominant position vis-à-vis the victim, or, for example, 'revenge' as punishment of sexual offenders can be relatively clear. What remains under-researched, given a lack of perpetrator research, are more emotional and psychological motivations. As this chapter is based on secondary rather than direct research, and as I am not a trained psychologist, I will not engage with these beyond flagging them as an area for further research.

Languages of genital violence

The messages which the perpetrators seek to convey vary and may be mixed, and sometimes these are explicit and at other times implicit. In the examples here, I aim, as discussed above, to avoid speculation as far as possible, given the dearth of accounts of perpetrator motivations. Instead, I rely on expressed statements linked to the particular acts of violence or on assessments of third parties that I deem as plausible. The different messages presented here are not mutually exclusive – and there are likely others as well that I will have missed, that are beyond my knowledge, or that I am reluctant to put forward given the lack of research on perpetrator's motivation. These latter include, for example, personal, psychological, or sexual motivations for these acts of violence, unless there is direct and stated evidence for these.

Based on the different cases of violence against male genitalia that I was able to find data on in the available literature and background interviews, I have classified the meanings attached to them as follows:

- Destroying the reproductive capacity of the victim;
- The symbolic questioning of masculinity;
- SVAMB as a tool of intimidation and population control;

- SVAMB as a form of revenge;
- Appropriating the masculine-coded power of the victim;
- Indirect messages of SVAMB;
- When violence is not read as SVAMB.

These are based either on perpetrators' reportedly direct statements, or on broader patterns discerned by third parties. These meanings are not mutually exclusive (i.e. there may be – and often are – several of them at work simultaneously), nor is the list exclusive. As discussed above, there may be a range of other conscious and unconscious drivers at work as well.

Destroying the reproductive capacity of the victim

One of the effects of violence against male genitalia often is the destruction of the reproductive capacity of the victim, and this may be one of the intended consequences of this violence. In some contexts, this may occur with a directly genocidal purpose, that is, the intended aim of destroying the reproductive capacity of the ethnic, religious, national, social, or political 'Other'. This has been outlined in the definition of genocide in the 1948 Genocide Convention, reiterated in the International Criminal Tribunal for the Former Yugoslavia (ICTY) and International Criminal Tribunal for Rwanda (ICTR) statutes as well as the ICC Rome Statutes.[4] A widely covered example of this in terms of CRSV is the Bosnian War (1992–1995) where there were repeated instances of violence against Bosnian Muslim and Croat men's genitalia, along with other acts of violence, which can be classified as being genocidal in intent (Bassiouni 1994; Carlson 2006; *Prosecutor* v. *Tadić 1997*; *Prosecutor* v. *Todorović 2001*[5]; Sivakumaran 2005). These were either committed directly by Serb militias or male Bosnian Muslims were forced to commit these acts against other Muslim men. In the *Prosecutor* v. *Tadić* case at the ICTY, a male prisoner was forced to first suck another man's penis and then bite off one of his testicles, with a similar incident reported from another prison camp as well; in the Todorović case, a witness described how he had been forced to bite another man's penis; and in concentration camps, undressed Bosnian Muslim and Croat male prisoners were lined in front of naked Serb women and if any of them had an erection, their penis was cut off (Bassiouni 1994; *Prosecutor* v. *Tadić 1997*; *Prosecutor* v. *Todorović 2001*[6]; Sivakumaran 2005). The genocidal intent of destroying the Croat and Muslim men's reproductive capacity was reportedly at times stated explicitly to the victims by the perpetrators (Carlson 2006). A series of penile amputations and castrations reported over the course of fighting in South Sudan in 2016 may also have had a similar motivation (UNICEF 2016).

The symbolic questioning of the masculinity of the victim/survivor and/or his group

A further key gendered message of sexual violence, Sjoberg (2016) argues, is the feminisation of the victim/survivor and masculinisation of the perpetrator, regardless of the biological sex of the perpetrator and victim/survivor (cf. Alison 2007; Dolan 2010; Puar 2007; Sivakumaran 2005, 2007; Solangon and Patel 2012). Given the social and cultural linking in many societies of male genitalia with symbolic notions of masculinity and virility, and thereby power, castration and penile amputation can become symbolic acts of 'feminisation' and 'emasculation' par excellence. Michael Johnson (2001) relates cases from the Lebanese Civil War 1975–1990, based on his research with local conflict actors. He explains that victorious soldiers of sectarian militias would cut off the genitalia of their dead opponents, leaving the bodies lying around for the public as well as other fighters to see. According to Johnson, the intent of these displays was to send a message of denying the dead victim's – masculine virility, and thereby, by extension, the masculine virility of ethnic/religious community to which the victims belonged.

The underscoring of the 'emasculation' of the losing party through penile amputations and castrations of vanquished enemies has been reported from other geographical regions and historical periods. For example, Goldstein (2001) and Misra (2015) outline cases from Egypt, Dahomey, the Inca Empire, and the Persian Empire. More recently, cases of castration of Kenyan men by British security forces in prison camps during the Kenyan Mau-Mau uprising against colonial rule have been acknowledged by the UK government (Taylor 2012). In the Kenyan case, the public castration of black men by white colonial forces also took on a particular, racialised meaning. As Elkins (2005) outlines, the Mau-Mau uprising led to an active discursive construction in the UK and colonial press of Kenyan men as potentially murderous and sexually predatory threats to white British women. Thus, the sexual violence against these Kenyan men was also linked to an attempt to 'control' the indigenous men's 'dangerous' masculinity and sexuality.

Other forms of violence against male genitalia, such as forced circumcision, can also be used for the purposes of the symbolic and physical humiliation and domination of the Other. This was, for example, the case in the context of the 2007–2008 electoral violence in Kenya, in which ethnic Luo men, who traditionally do not practise circumcision as a rite of passage to manhood, were forcibly subjected to this by supporters of the incumbent Mwai Kibaki (Ahlberg and Njoroge 2013; Corey-Boulet 2011; Oosterveld 2011; *Prosecutor* v. *Kenyatta* 2011[7]). These acts of violence were also covered by the Jomo Kenyatta case of the ICC, in which the pre-trial chamber controversially ruled that the forced circumcisions and penile amputations were not to be considered sexual violence but rather 'that the acts were motivated by ethnic prejudice and intended to demonstrate cultural superiority of one tribe over the other' (Grey 2014: 280).[8] The perpetrators mainly used machetes but also broken soda bottles for the circumcisions; on occasion, however, the whole penis was cut off, in addition to other acts of violence against the victim, including death (Corey-Boulet 2011; *Prosecutor* v. *Kenyatta 2011*[9]). The meanings conveyed by the act were closely linked to symbolic notions of adult masculinity: circumcision among ethnic groups such as the Gikuyu is seen as a central rite of passage to male adulthood and thereby the right to participate in public decision-making, while the term *kihii* (uncircumcised adult man) is considered an extremely grave insult among them (Ahlberg and Njoroge 2013; Corey-Boulet 2011). Thus, a part of the violence was driven by an undercurrent of countering the prospect of uncircumcised men taking political power or even participating in the political process in the first place (Ahlberg and Njoroge 2013; Corey-Boulet 2011).

Humiliation and subjugation of the ethnic Other, as well as the documented spectacle of this humiliation that was shared among peers, were also part of the messages conveyed in another context – that of the sexual violence against Iraqi civilian men – and women – by the US armed forces in Abu Ghraib prison, Iraq in 2003. Although the official US Department of Defense investigation does not specifically mention actual violence against male genitalia, such violence was simulated and threatened in some cases; electrodes were attached to the penis and testicles of prisoners, which is a common torture method (Taguba 2004). These acts of violence and the public reaction to them have been discussed at length by various scholars (e.g. Kassem 2013; Puar 2007; Richter-Montpetit 2007; Sjoberg and Gentry 2007). Interpretations of the 'language' of this violence include those that see it as conveying the following: messages of the subjugation and humiliation of the Arab Muslim Other; the erasure of SGBV against women at US prison sites; as well as the gendered dynamics of the representations of the perpetrators. For the purposes of this chapter, however, I will not revisit the well-documented 'afterlife' of the violence after the scandal broke, although it is a rich case study of how such violence and imagery can be understood differently. I will focus here more on the violence and the images before their unintended publication. In addition to intimidating and terrorising the prisoners, the violence deployed against Arab male prisoners had been specifically designed to humiliate and undermine their sense of masculinity, based on Orientalist readings of 'Arab masculinity' (Kassem 2013; Puar 2007). The images had not been meant for broader publication, although they were possibly meant for blackmailing the victims, and were circulated privately among US troops (Puar 2007; Sjoberg and Gentry 2007). Thus, in addition to the direct victims and the broader Iraqi population (and in the case of abuses at Bagram Air Base, the Afghan population), the perpetrators' peers were a further audience. In the absence of direct statements from the perpetrators or their peers, the messages conveyed by the sharing of these photos remain speculative. However, the poses of the perpetrators (smiling, smoking, giving a 'thumbs up' sign) point in the direction of an additional element of 'entertainment' being involved, but possibly also of building group cohesion and camaraderie (Bourke 2004).

SVAMB as a tool of intimidation and population

Castration and penile amputation, along with other forms of sexual and other violence, can also be used as a tool of intimidation of the local civilian population, as was highlighted in the ICC case concerning the FDLR (*Forces démocratiques de libération du Rwanda*) in eastern Democratic Republic of Congo (*Prosecutor* v. *Callixte Mbarushimana 2011*[10]). The ICC found that various forms of sexual violence against women and girls – but also men and boys – were widespread, including penile amputation. Several witnesses to the ICC reported of a FDLR commander cutting off the penises of civilian victims/survivors and showing these off in public, which fit into a pattern of using acts of violence, including sexual violence, to terrorise the civilian population and thereby control it.

SVAMB as a form of revenge

Castration and penile amputation can also be forms of retaliation against combatants for acts of violence these have committed, with the intent of sending a message to the perpetrator and his peers that such acts are not condoned. In a potentially apocryphal case from the US war in Vietnam, a US Marine's penis and testicles were cut off by a female Viet Cong fighter as part of a broader range of torture, in revenge for sexual violence by US forces against Vietnamese women (Henderson 1988). In an occurrence witnessed and recounted to me by a humanitarian aid worker from the Second Sierra Leone War, a group of villagers had attacked a suspected member of the Rebel United Front (RUF), killed the man, and then paraded the cut-up body through the streets – including an impaled penis, which the villagers apparently gleefully referred to as 'the prick on a stick' (Personal communication 2002). Members of the RUF had themselves been carrying out acts of sexual violence against men and boys, including male genital mutilation (Oosterveld 2011). The 'message' here, I would suggest, was on the one hand a 'post-mortem' one to the dead man and his alleged RUF comrades of community outrage against their violent activities during the war. For the celebrating crowd, the act may possibly have underscored a venting of anger, an act of revenge and of taking control back of lives that had been controlled by armed groups for years.

Jani de Silva (2005) documents how Sri Lankan security forces used various forms of sexual and other violence, including against genitals, against young Sinhala men who had joined the Janatha Vimukthi Peramuna (JVP) insurrection. De Silva sees this violence as an effort to physically destroy the bodies of the young men as punishment for daring to challenge the dominant, gerontocratic, and patriarchal order in which the torturers were often personally invested. The main messages, de Silva argues, were directed against the victims/survivors directly as well as to potential other JVP members. The violence was meant to underscore the high costs that challenging the existing social age- and gender-order would have for any would-be insurrectionists.

A more culturally specific case of revenge through castration/penile muti-lation comes from Northern Maluku, where Nils Bubandt encountered beliefs of vengeful female ghosts, who are the returned spirits of women killed (and in some cases raped) in the Christian–Muslim communal conflict, who then returned to prey on men of the respective other side and 'steal' their genitals (Bubandt 2012). According to Bubandt, two versions of the story circulated: one among Christians that it was a Christian woman's ghost seeking revenge for sexual violence done to her by Muslim militias during the conflict, and one among Muslims that it was a Muslim woman's spirit. In both stories, the message is one of revenge for evils done in the past and a warning not to commit such acts in the future. As such, it fits into a tradition of vengeful female ghosts (*pontianak/kuntilanak*) in the Indonesian archipelago that attack men, and in par-ticular their genitals, in revenge in particular for deaths that involved sexual viol-ence or death during childbirth. The circulation of the post-conflict ghost stories in the local media and between community members, which Bubandt describes also points to an element of titillation for the audience in engaging with the possibility of such supernatural acts.[11]

Appropriating the masculine-coded power of the victim

Particular cultural meanings attached to male genitalia can also be linked to beliefs around the powers thought to be inherent in the organs, not merely in the symbolic, but in very real sense. While the evidence is patchy, there are reports from at least Liberia and DR Congo of genitalia being cut and then partially devoured by fighters in order to appropriate the 'power' of the dead victim (Misra 2015; personal communication with ICC investigators, Geneva, 2015). Here, the message of the act is perhaps mostly to the perpetrators themselves, who can feel empowered through this act of appropriation, and other audiences with whom they may choose to share knowledge of this act.[12]

Indirect messages of SVAMB

In addition to the direct messages of physical 'emasculation', violence against male genitalia, as also other forms of SVAMB, can have the indirect impact – a longer-term message, in a sense – of 'social emasculation', as men and boys are no longer able to fulfil societal expectations placed on men. These include being a breadwinner, participating in community activities, or being sexually active, all of which may be severely restricted due to the long-term physical, emotional, and psychological damage caused by the violence as well as the stigma attached to the damage to or loss of one's genitalia (Dolan 2010; Myrttinen, Khattab, and Naujoks 2016; Refugee Law Project 2011; Schulz 2017). Even though the per-petrators may have moved on and the conflict may have ended, the victims/ survivors as well as their families and communities will be left to deal with the long-term impacts and attendant messages of powerlessness and humiliation (Refugee Law Project 2011).

When violence is not related to SVAMB

Not all violence against male genitalia, however, is as explicitly 'coded' or 'read' as the above examples. Michele Leiby (2012; and Ch. 7 in this volume) has noted a general pattern of systematic under-reporting of SVAMB in her archival research into the Peruvian and Salvadoran truth and reconciliation commissions. Her research uncovers at least one case of castration and penile amputation of a civilian man by the *Sendero Luminoso* guerrilla (2012: 344–345), and the classification of sexual violence as torture only, in particular in the case of male victims/survivors. In addition to the under-reporting that is common to sexual violence, Leiby sees this as, among other things, due to different norms and parameters that were used in the various studies, such as categorising only rape as sexual violence. In part, these were legal parameters (in the case of the Peruvian commission, sexual violence was explicitly limited to rape only), but they were also due to internalised understandings of what is and what is not sexual violence, be it among the victims/survivors, service providers, or those collecting, collating, and reporting the data. Eric Carlson (2006) points out that specifically blunt trauma against male genitals is often disregarded as SVAMB, even seen by some as more of a 'college fraternity prank' than CRSV, in spite of its ubiquity in settings of conflict, detention, and torture. Carlson cites studies from El Salvador where 56 per cent of inmates in one prison had been subjected to blunt trauma to the genitals as had been 44 per cent of a group of male victims/survivors of CRSV in Croatia and Bosnia-Herzegovina. In El Salvador, as Leiby notes, these cases were not reported as sexual violence (2012: 342). Furthermore, Leiby notes that in a case of the torture and murder of four Dutch journalists, trauma to the genitals was not separately recorded as sexual violence (2012: 325).

Conflict-related violence to male genitalia can also be 'collateral', that is, the genitals may not be the primary target of the violence but be harmed nonetheless. How common this can be in modern conflict zones dominated by small arms and IEDs is shown by the following data from one civilian hospital (Yarmouk Hospital) alone in Baghdad during a four-and-a-half-year period from January 2004–June 2008, averaging roughly one case per week:

> Among the 217 patients there were 262 lower GU [genitourinary] injuries involving the bladder in 128 (48.8%) patients, bulbo-prostatic urethra in 21 (8%), penis in 24 (9.2%), and scrotum in 89 (34%). Injuries to the anterior urethra and genitals were inflicted by Improvised Explosive Devices (IEDs) in 53–67% of cases and by individual firearms in 33–47%, while injuries to the posterior urethra and bladder were inflicted by IEDs in 17–22% of cases and by firearms in 78–83%.
>
> (Al-Azzawi and Koraitim 2014: 885)

In the case of small arms fire, some of this may have been deliberately aimed at male genitalia, in which case there was intent behind it. However, as most patients were likely civilians given the nature of the hospital, there is a high likelihood that most small arms-related injuries came from being caught in cross-fires or ricocheting bullets, in which intent was far less likely, as the trajectory of ricocheting bullets cannot be easily controlled. Given the nature of IEDs, the degree to which the blast wave and flight paths of the shrapnel can be directed once the explosive device has been installed is relatively limited. The IED may be positioned in such a way as to attempt to cause maximum damage to the lower body, including the genitals, but direct targeting is far more difficult. Nonetheless, even if the primary intent of the small arms fire or the IED was not to cause damage to the genitalia, the physical, emotional, and social impacts can be similar for the victims/survivors as with violence committed with the explicit focus on the genitals.

Conclusion

As I have sought to outline, although the acts of violence committed against male genitalia are similar, the messages being communicated by the violence and how these are understood by different actors can be quite varied. Sandesh Sivakumaran outlines different forms of 'work' that SVAMB does: establishing the power and dominance of the perpetrator over the victim/survivor, and with power and dominance 'interwoven throughout ideas of emasculation, feminization, homosexualization and the prevention of procreation' (2007: 275) of both the individual victim/survivor and the broader group (e.g. family/clan, military unit ethnic, religious, political, or socio-economic group) that the victim/survivor is seen as representing. Arguably, given the symbolic centrality in many cultures of the penis and testicles to masculinity and masculine-coded values, as well as its biological centrality to men's participation in procreation, violence against male genitalia can convey these messages in the starkest of terms. Based on the examples I have outlined above, other messages may be conveyed as well, with the negotiation or renegotiation of power and dominance interwoven into these as well: symbolic humiliation of the individual and group; revenge; control of sexuality; destroying, removing, or appropriating powers thought to be inherent to the genitals; and the infliction of pain. As mentioned, however, certain forms of conflict-related violence against male genitalia are at times seen by different actors – victims/survivors, service providers, researchers, lawyers, and jurists – as not carrying a particular message at all.

The reason why SVAMB, and perhaps violence against male genitalia in particular, is able to do the work it does lies in the gendered frameworks we use to understand it. As long as male power, masculine identity, and masculine-coded values are considered as symbolically and/or physically/spiritually linked to actual male genital organs, violence against these will be effective in 'emasculating' the victim/survivor. Understanding and deconstructing these links, which vary depending on the context, can help to better comprehend and prevent these forms of violence.

As highlighted above, understandings of SVAMB, in particular beyond penetrational rape, is an area that lacks thorough research at all levels. This includes the understandings of victims/survivors and perpetrators but also of other audiences of the violence; a deeper understanding of the meanings of these forms of violence in non-Western contexts; understanding how the violence relates to sexuality, especially that of the perpetrator; lack of research on female perpetrators; as well as the multiple absences of sexual and gender minority experiences as victims/survivors, perpetrators, and audiences. In part, this is due especially to conflict-related SGBV against men and boys not having been investigated in the past. Furthermore, as Michele Leiby, Eric Carlson, and others have pointed out, SVAMB has and is often not recognised as such but coded differently, for example, as torture or 'mere' blunt trauma. While this is lack of research and more nuanced contextual understandings pertains to SVAMB in general, it seems to be especially the case for violence directed against male genitalia. While it was possible to find individual clues on this form of SVAMB, as well as how and possibly why it was being used from different sources, systematic, contextualised, and in-depth research is missing. It is, however, precisely this kind of nuanced, in-depth, and contextualised research that is required for us to be able to understand the gendered dynamics behind the perpetration of these types of violence.

Notes

1 As, for example, Schulz (2017) rightly points out, the term 'emasculation' is not unproblematic, as it both links socio-culturally constructed masculinities with biological male sex, in this case in particular with male genitalia, and also tends to reinforce gendered notions which value masculinity over femininity. Given its prevalence in the literature, though, I will also use the term here, albeit in quotation marks.

2 That is not to say that primary sources are wholly unproblematic. In my own prior experience of interviewing perpetrators of political violence, the answers often aimed to justify or deny violence as well as to deny culpability (for perpetrator discourses on domestic violence, cf. Hearn 1998: 108–110), and from my own experiences of exposure to violence, I know that my own mind can and will remember details inaccurately.

3 Based on the accounts available, even in these cases where the perpetrator has expressed a direct message which they want to convey, other intended or unintended messages may be at work as well. Furthermore, as with any data, the accuracy of the information can always be put into question, but for the purposes of this chapter, I have chosen to go forward with the working assumption that it does reflect reality to some degree.

4 According to Article 2 of the 1948 Convention on the Prevention and Punishment of the Crime of Genocide, a genocidal act includes:

> Any of the following acts committed with intent to destroy, in whole or in part, a national, ethnical, racial or religious group, as such: killing members of the group; causing serious bodily or mental harm to members of the group; deliberately inflicting on the group conditions of life, calculated to bring about its physical destruction in whole or in part; imposing measures intended to prevent births within the group; [and] forcibly transferring children of the group to another group.

I have explicitly added political groups and socio-economic classes not included in the original convention. Intent here is a key legal term, and one that has often been

difficult to prove in court in the absence of clear and explicit orders (for a more in-depth discussion, see Myrttinen 2017).
5 *Prosecutor* v. *Duško Tadić*, Case No. IT-94-1-T, Sentencing Judgement, 14 July 1997, International Criminal Tribunal for the Former Yugoslavia; *Prosecutor* v. *Todorović*, Case No. IT-95/1, Judgement, 31 July 2001, International Criminal Tribunal for the Former Yugoslavia.
6 Ibid.
7 *The Prosecutor* v. *Uhuru Muigai Kenyatta*, Case No. ICC-01/09-02/11-T-5-Red-ENG 2011, ICC Pre-Trial Chamber III, Transcript, 22 September 2011.
8 As discussed earlier, there is not one single meaning that can be attached to an act of violence and thus the different interpretations of the violence, both the one by the pre-trial chamber and of the acts being sexual violence, can exist simultaneously.
9 Ibid.
10 *The Prosecutor* v. *Callixte Mbarushimana*, Case No. ICC-01/04-10, Pre-Trial Chamber I, Decision, International Criminal Court, 16 December 2011.
11 For a more in-depth discussion on rumours of violence, see, for example, Bubandt (2008) and White (2000).
12 On the use of magic in warfare in Liberia and Sierra Leone, see, for example, Hoffman (2011).

References

Ahlberg, Beth Maina and Kezia Muthoni Njoroge. 2013. '"Not Men Enough to Rule!": Politicization of Ethnicities and Forcible Circumcision of Luo Men During the Postelection Violence in Kenya'. *Ethnicity & Health* 18(5): 454–468.

Al-Azzawi, Issam S. and Mamdouh M. Koraitim, 2014. 'Lower Genitourinary Trauma in Modern Warfare: The Experience from Civil Violence in Iraq'. *Injury, International Journal of the Care of the Injured* 45(5): 885–889.

Alison, Miranda 2007. 'Wartime Sexual Violence: Women's Human Rights and Questions of Masculinity'. *Review of International Studies* 33(1): 75–90.

Bassiouni, Cherif. 1994. Final Report of the United Nations Commission of Experts Established Pursuant to Security Council Resolution 780, S/1994/674. New York: United Nations.

Bourke, Joanna. 2004. 'Torture as Pornography'. *Guardian*, 7 May. www.theguardian.com/world/2004/may/07/gender.uk.

Bubandt, Nils. 2008. 'Rumors, Pamphlets, and the Politics of Paranoia in Indonesia'. *The Journal of Asian Studies* 67(3): 789–817.

Bubandt, Nils. 2012. 'A Psychology of Ghosts: The Regime of the Self and the Reinvention of Spirits in Indonesia and Beyond'. *Anthropological Forum: A Journal of Social Anthropology and Comparative Sociology* 22(1): 1–23.

Carlson, Eric. 2006. 'The Hidden Prevalence of Male Sexual Assault During War Observations on Blunt Trauma to the Male Genitals'. *British Journal of Criminology* 46(1): 16–25.

Carpenter, R. Charli. 2006. 'Recognizing Gender-Based Violence Against Civilian Men and Boys in Conflict Situations'. *Security Dialogue* 37(1): 83–103.

Corey-Boulet, Robbie. 2011. 'In Kenya, Forced Male Circumcision and a Struggle for Justice'. *The Atlantic*, 1 August. Accessed 12 February 2016. www.theatlantic.com/international/archive/2011/08/in-kenya-forced-male-circumcision-and-a-struggle-for-justice/242757/.

Cramer, Chris. 2006. *Civil War Is Not A Stupid Thing – Accounting for Violence in Developing Countries*. London: Hurst & Co.

De Silva, Jani. 2005. *Globalization, Terror & The Shaming of the Nation: Constructing Local Masculinities in a Sri Lankan Village*. Crewe: Trafford Publishers.

Dolan, Chris. 2009. *Social Torture – The Case of Northern Uganda 1986–2006*. Oxford: Berghahn Books.

Dolan, Chris. 2010. *War is Not Yet Over: Community Perceptions of Sexual Violence and its Underpinnings in Eastern DRC*. London: International Alert.

Dolan, Chris. 2015. 'Letting Go of the Gender Binary: Charting New Pathways for Humanitarian Interventions On Gender-Based Violence'. *International Review of the Red Cross* 96(894): 485–501.

Drumond, Paula. 2017. 'Embodied Battlefields: Uncovering Sexual Violence against Men in War Theaters'. PhD diss., The Graduate Institute, Geneva.

Elkins, Caroline. 2005. *Imperial Reckoning: The Untold Story of Britain's Gulag in Kenya*. New York: Henry Holt & Co.

Goldstein, Joshua. 2001. *War and Gender – How Shapes the War System and Vice-Versa*. Cambridge: Cambridge University Press.

Grey, Rosemary. 2014. 'Conflicting Interpretations of "Sexual Violence" in the International Criminal Court'. *Australian Feminist Studies* 29(81): 273–288.

Hearn, Jeff. 1998. *The Violences of Men*. London: Sage Publications.

Henderson, Charles. 1988. *Marine Sniper – 93 Confirmed Kills*. New York: Berkley Publishing.

Hoffman, Danny. 2011. *The War Machines: Young Men and Violence in Sierra Leone and Liberia*. Durham, NC: Duke University Press.

Johnson, Michael. 2001. *All Honourable Men: The Social Origins of War in Lebanon*. London: I.B. Tauris.

Kassem, Ramzi. 2013. 'Gendered Erasure in the Global "War on Terror": An Unmasked Interrogation'. In L. Satterthwaite and J. Huckerby (eds), *Gender, National Security and Counter-Terrorism – Human Rights Perspectives*. London: Routledge, 15–35.

Kirby, Paul. 2015. 'Ending Sexual Violence in Conflict: The Preventing Sexual Violence Initiative and its Critics'. *International Affairs* 91(3): 457–472.

Leiby, Michele. 2012. 'The Promise and Peril of Primary Documents: Documenting Wartime Sexual Violence in El Salvador and Peru'. In Morten Bergsmo, Alf Butenschøn Skre, and Elisabeth J. Wood (eds), *Understanding and Proving International Sex Crimes*. Beijing: Torkel Opsahl Academic E-Publisher.

Lewis, Chloé. 2014. 'Systemic Silencing: Addressing Sexual Violence against Men and Boys in Armed Conflict and its Aftermath'. In G. Heathcote and D. Otto (eds), *Rethinking Peacekeeping, Gender Equality and Collective Security*. London: Palgrave Macmillan, 203–223.

Misra, Amalendu. 2015. *The Landscape of Silence – Sexual Violence Against Men in War*. London: C. Hurst & Co.

Myrttinen, Henri. 2017. 'Men, Masculinities and Genocide'. In Mary Michele Connellan and Christiane Fröhlich (eds), *A Gendered Lens For Genocide Prevention*. London: Palgrave Macmillan.

Myrttinen, Henri, Lana Khattab, and Jana Naujoks. 2016. 'Re-Thinking Hegemonic Masculinities in Conflict-Affected Contexts'. *Critical Military Studies*: 1–17.

Odd News and Stories. 2006. 'Marine's Castration and Torture by Vietong [*sic!*]'. Odd News and Stories, 21 October. Accessed 1 June 2017. http://darkandbizaarestories.blogspot.co.uk/2006/10/marines-castration-and-torture-by.html.

Oosterveld, Valerie. 2011. 'Atrocity Crimes Litigation Year-in-Review: A Gender Perspective'. *Northwestern University of International Human Rights* 9(3): 239–266.

Puar, Jasbir K. 2007. *Terrorist Assemblages: Homonationalism in Queer Times*. Durham, NC: Duke University Press.

Reemtsma, Jan Philipp. 2008. *Vertrauen und Gewalt – Versuch über eine besondere Konstellation der Moderne*. Hamburg: Hamburger Edition.

Refugee Law Project. 2011. 'They Slept With Me'. Video documentary, YouTube, 10 December 2011. Accessed 1 May 2017. www.youtube.com/watch?v=6dxaFqezrXg.

Richter-Montpetit, Melanie. 2007. 'Empire, Desire and Violence: A Queer Transnational Feminist Reading of the Prisoner "Abuse" in Abu Ghraib and the Question of "Gender Equality"'. *International Feminist Journal of Politics* 9(1): 38–59.

Russell, Wynne. 2007. 'Sexual Violence Against Men and Boys'. *Forced Migration Review* 27: 22–23.

Schulz, Philipp. 2017. '"I Felt Useless and Not Man Enough": Deconstructing the Impact of Conflict-Related Sexual Violence on Male Survivors' Masculinities'. Paper presented at the *58th Annual Convention of the International Studies Association (ISA)*, 22–26 February 2017, Baltimore, MD.

Sivakumaran, Sandesh. 2005. 'Male/Male Rape and the "Taint" of Homosexuality'. *Human Rights Quarterly* 27(4): 1274–1306.

Sivakumaran, Sandesh. 2007. 'Sexual Violence Against Men in Armed Conflict'. *European Journal of International Law* 18(2): 253–276.

Sjoberg, Laura. 2016. *Women As Wartime Rapists – Beyond Sensation and Stereotyping*. New York: New York University Press.

Sjoberg, Laura and Caron E. Gentry. 2007. *Mothers, Monsters, Whores: Women's Violence in Global Politics*. London: Zed Books.

Solangon, Sarah and Preeti Patel. 2012. 'Sexual Violence Against Men in Countries Affected by Armed Conflict'. *Conflict, Security & Development* 12(4): 417–442.

Taguba, Antonio, 2004. *Article 15–6 Investigation Of The 800th Military Police Brigade*, Washington, DC: US Department of Defense.

Taylor, Jerome. 2012. 'Government Admits Kenyans were Tortured and Sexually Abused by Colonial Forces During Mau Mau Uprising'. *The Independent*, 17 July. Accessed 1 May 2017. www.independent.co.uk/news/world/africa/government-admits-kenyans-were-tortured-and-sexually-abused-by-colonial-forces-during-mau-mau-7953300.html.

UNICEF 2016. 'Unspeakable Violence Against Children in South Sudan – UNICEF chief'. Press statement, 17 June 2016, Accessed 28 November 2016 at www.unicef.org/media/media_82319.html.

White, Luise. 2000. *Speaking with Vampires: Rumor and History in Colonial Africa*. Berkeley, CA: University of California Press.

World Health Organization (WHO) 2002. 'Sexual Violence'. *World Report on Violence and Health*. Geneva: World Health Organization, 149–172.

5   Medical approaches to sexual violence in war, in guidelines, and in practice

Caroline Cottet

Introduction

Having been raped during war, a man visits a hospital hoping to see a doctor. A nurse seems confused by his presence and asks why he is there. On hearing his explanation, she laughs and says, 'so you mean in Congo, ehm, women are raping men?' A heavy silence follows. The man stares at her seemingly at a loss for words.

This is a scene from the film *Men Can Be Raped Too* (Kithima and King 2015). The film tells a story of increasing incidents of men and boys being victims of sexual violence in conflict, and the lack of effective responses especially from medical organisations. Previous research has identified the same inadequate levels of response across a variety of locations. 'We don't see men, probably because so few get raped,' (Donnelly and Kenyon 1996: 444) was a nurse's comment in an American medical facility where no one had ever seen a male survivor. In a comprehensive study, Augusta Del Zotto and Adam Jones reviewed the activities of 4,076 NGOs that address war rape and sexual violence, and found that 3 per cent mention men in their literature, but hardly any provide services for them (2002: 3). What are we to make of these inadequacies?

In this chapter, I will trace some of the historical connections between medical science and understandings of sexual violence against men, focusing especially on the remnants of biological determinism in medical science. Starting with a brief overview of the trends in publications on sex, gender, and medicine, the introduction seeks to contextualise the relationship between medical and social understandings of sex through the specific example of hormones, if inevitably briefly here. I then focus on medical assistance available during the war in the former Yugoslavia, as described in the medical guidelines put forth by the UNHCR and the practices of doctors on the ground. I claim that there is a very strong link between the guidelines and practices regarding sexed bodies. This is important as it has direct implications for the ways in which male victims of sexual violence are treated. In the conclusion, I suggest that the published guidelines for medical assistance to male victims of sexual violence, shows a slow shift in attitude over the last thirty years. Nonetheless, there remains a strong bias in the medical field deriving from biological determinism, which I argue has distorted understandings of sexual violence against men, and this is exacerbated in war.

Medicine and biological sex

Historically, medical responses to sexual violence have been indebted to particular understandings of gender roles; it is important to remember this in order to understand the context. Publications that connect sex, gender, and medicine point towards a fairly young history of medicine and biological sex in which *social preconceptions* of gender play an important role. A brief look at the literature indicates a clear trend in terms of quantity; when simply counting the number of published books in the field of human sexuality, there were seven before the nineteenth century, five during the entire nineteenth century, and over 1,000 during the twentieth century (Frayser and Whitby 1995: x). There was a significant rise from an average of less than one per year until 1950, to 522 published books between 1980 and 1989 alone (Frayser and Whitby 1995: xi). As the literature on medicine and sex surged in the late twentieth century, so did a considerable interest in the 'nature' of maleness and femaleness.

In terms of some of the content of these publications, *The Evolution of Sex* by Patrick Geddes and J. Arthur Thomson (1889) laid one of the first bricks in the literature on sex and sexualities. Considered 'a definitive account' of the biology of sexual development and reproduction until then, it was also a seminal treatise for the evolution of sex in terms that many still use today (Bederman 1995: 153; Fausto-Sterling 2000: 152; Eckert 2016: 211). What is particularly interesting in that book is, what seems to be, the incorporation of *social* understandings of gender in the biological construction of sexed bodies. The authors explained, for example, that due to their cells, males were catabolic, which means putting out energy, while females were anabolic, meaning they store up and conserve energy. In addition to giving the cells attributes, the terms 'catabolic' and 'anabolic' also described men and women's psychological and social behaviour (Geddes and Thomson 1889: 286–291; Geddes and Thomson 1914: 77–80). The active and passive binary which is directly linked to masculine and feminine 'natures' respectively, is central to the history of medicine and biological sex, as indicated by its central presence in *The Evolution of Sex* and as picked up on and critiqued in later publications (Bederman 1995: 153; Fausto-Sterling 2000: 152; Eckert 2016: 211).

The active/passive binary has rippled through many of the twentieth-century milestone studies on sexed bodies in Europe and North America. One of the most ground-breaking contributors to the field remains the biologist Anne Fausto-Sterling, who has demonstrated through her books that biological differences between sexed bodies have been produced over time through scientific knowledge, suggesting that biology is much more political than often considered (1985, 2000, 2012). In other words, for Fausto-Sterling, scientific conceptions of male and female bodies overwhelmingly rely on cultural understandings of what it means to be male and female. Not only are males considered active both socially and in medical conceptions of the body, in contrast to the female passivity (Bullough 1976: 14; Fausto-Sterling 1997: 220) but pushing the logic further, such medical conceptions have also justified aggressiveness and violence as 'natural' male traits.

Biological justification of gender roles in war: the example of hormones

Aggressiveness, violence, and even war, can be explained from a biological perspective, we are told, as stemming from 'egoistic and dominating behaviour' in the nature of manliness (Thayer 2000: 125). The same mode of thinking has been applied to understandings of parts of the bodies. 'We are assuming,' wrote Steven Goldberg in 1973, 'that there are no differences between men and women except in the hormonal system that renders the man more aggressive' (quoted in Fausto-Sterling 1985: 123). Conversely, the 'myth' of female hormones actively contributes to keeping women in a position of subordination, by making hormones a defining element of femaleness, in a passive and overly emotional interpretation of femininity (DeLuca 2017). Though the concept of hormones was introduced in 1905, sex hormones only attracted wide public attention in the 1970s (Dabbs and Dabbs 2000), when debates about women's inclusion in formerly men-exclusive settings, *especially* the army, came to the forefront of European and American public debates. Arguments based on the idea of a masculine 'natural' aggressiveness and propensity for violence were used to counter the proposition of women joining the ranks, using hormones as part of the reasoning. In the United States, for example, George Gilder from the Reagan Administration argued that: 'the hard evidence is overwhelming that men are more aggressive, competitive, risk-taking ... [and] more combative than women' (Gilder 1979: 44). Indeed the type of hyper-masculinity, justified on biological and thus intrinsic grounds, is central to the very idea of the military and essential to war fighting (Seifert 1996; Goldstein 2001; Belkin 2012).

Yet findings in the discipline of biology that attribute certain behaviours to sexed bodies have been heavily contested. Studies on sex hormones justifying male aggressiveness and violence and those justifying female passivity and subordinate position[1] have all been strongly criticised along two lines: (i) that of attributing behaviours to specific genders; and, (ii) of relying on a non-existent binary. Those two points are very much intertwined: focusing on testosterone and oestrogen, and calling them 'male' and 'female' hormones is actually misleading. Up until the 1920s, the terms 'male hormone' and 'female hormone' were widely used, following the belief that they respectively made boys into men, and girls into women. In 1928, however, scientists realised that 'female hormones' were present in male bodies, and vice versa, with heavily fluctuating levels (Birke 2000: 595). Moreover, the supposed correlation between testosterone levels and aggression is very tenuous (Goldstein 2001: 153), and 'stress-hormones', more generally called adrenaline, are more relevant to stressful situations (like combat) and thus to war, and are not gendered in a biological sense (Goldstein 2001: 157–158). Yet the terminology in sex hormones remains simplistically gendered to this day, as a conscious design in harmony with pre-existing ideas of a sexual duality. It remains within a simple framework trans-latable to research laboratories, pharmaceutical companies, and doctors (Fausto-Sterling 2000, 191; Oudshoorn 1994: 23). This example serves to illus-trate the mechanism of the linkage between biological conceptions of the body and gendered attributes. This in turn has been deployed to justify the behaviours and roles of male and female bodies, not least in the context of sexual violence.

Medical and social understandings of sex

The existing feminist literature on science and gender makes it clear: the dicho-tomy between the medical and the social (like that of sex and gender) is fictive and often misleading. The social project of the gender binary merged with medical understandings of bodies is undeniable and this has consequences for the way sexual violence in war is understood. Most illustrative is the widespread 'natural urge' argument, according to which male soldiers are understood to most likely to rape female civilians due to heterosexual masculine sexual impulses, assumed to be inherent. While numerous studies have debunked this myth, as a belief, it remains prevalent in the armed forces and the public (Seifert 1996: 36; Eriksson Baaz and Stern 2013: 19). The problem is the reinforcement of a public assumption that male heterosexuality is seen as an unstoppable 'natural' or biological force and that its 'satisfaction' can require violence in certain conditions. Consequently, there is a generalised acceptance of men as 'natural' perpetrators of sexual violence and women as 'natural' victims. I will move now to discuss the Guidelines.

PART I Guidelines

During the war in the former Yugoslavia (for which a broader context is pro-vided by Drumond, Ch. 8 in this volume), several international and local organi-sations provided services to victims of sexual violence. As the lead agency, the UNHCR started in late 1991 to provide equipment, training, and guidelines for more than 250 international and local organisations, encompassing over 3,000 personnel on the ground. To reach such a large scale, in 1995, the UNHCR pub-lished guidelines titled 'Sexual Violence Against Refugees: Guidelines on Pre-vention and Response', partially based on the organisation's experience in Yugoslavia up until then, as well as in Rwanda, Somalia, and Vietnam (United Nations 1995: 38; United Nations High Commissioner for Refugees 1995). Hardly any personnel on the ground attended to the male victims of sexual viol-ence, despite the large number of now-known cases.

The invisibility of male victims of sexual violence runs parallel to the gender roles implicitly defined in the UNHCR guidelines. The opening Foreword to the document, written by the then-Special Rapporteur on violence against women for the Commission on Human Rights, Radhika Coomaraswamy, provocatively asks: 'How can the international community prevent sexual violence? How should we respond if a woman becomes pregnant as a result of being raped? What should we do if a child has been sexually attacked?' (United Nations High Commissioner for Refugees 1995: 2). These interrogations begin to indicate the assumptions at work such as the early framing of 'women and children' as a vulnerable category of people, which bears the risk of stigmatising those concerned as innocent, helpless, and voiceless victims. As pointed out by Cynthia Enloe, ' "Womenandchildren" rolls so easily off network [*sic.*] tongues, because in network minds women are family members rather than independent actors, presumed to be almost childlike in their innocence' (1990: 29).

In addition to stigmatising the role of women, these questions also stigmatise the supposed role of men. As made clear in the biological assumptions linked with hormones earlier on, ideas about what it means to be female works hand in hand with ideas about what it means to be male. Considering women as weak and vulnerable, implicitly infers that men are correspondingly strong and dominant. This, once more, falls neatly within the framework of male as perpetrators and women as victims of sexual violence.

The guidelines include a couple of caveats, regarding potential male victims of sexual violence. The first one, in the Preface from Sadako Ogata, United Nations High Commissioner for Refugees in 1995, reads '[w]omen and young girls – and, less frequently, men and boys – are vulnerable to attack' (United Nations High Commissioner for Refugees 1995: 3). 'Attack' here refers to sexual violence generally speaking, as this is the theme of the guidelines. Despite this nod to men, the general narrative in the guidelines does not continue in this inclusive direction. In the Introduction, for example, there is a paragraph titled 'Focus on females', in which the choice of pronouns is explained. 'The pronouns in these guidelines in relation to victims of sexual violence are phrased in the feminine voice and the pronouns in relation to perpetrators of sexual violence are phrased in the masculine voice.' (United Nations High Commissioner for Refugees 1995: 4). This is then no longer addressed in the rest of the guidelines, and the assumption (marked by the choice of pronouns) remains that women are the sole focus. By defining so explicitly the roles in sexual violence, the guidelines suggest to the practitioners where to look for signs and whom to privilege when identifying victims. Although the first passage suggests a possible inclusion of men and boys, the second passage bluntly closes the door on that possibility. Such discrepancies within the guidelines are quite common, and arguably help to perpetuate the exclusion of male victims of sexual violence.

Such a trend is also present in the section in the guidelines on under-reporting of sexual violence. A paragraph explains the probable reluctance of male victims to report as due in part to the scarcity of dedicated legal and social networks. It states that consequently the reported number of cases of sexual violence against men is likely to be quite far from the actual number of cases (United Nations High Commissioner for Refugees 1995: 9). It is therefore difficult to assess whether sexual violence against women is indeed more prevalent than that against men, and if it is, by how much. Yet shortly after, in laying out the causes for sexual violence in war, the assumption is again that men would generally be the perpetrators and women would generally be the victims:

> Male attitudes of disrespect towards women may be instrumental in causing incidents of sexual violence. (…) (…) camp guards and male refugees may look upon unaccompanied women and girls in refugee camps as common sexual property.
>
> Psychological strain on refugee men (…) may cause aggressive behaviour towards women. Many other aspects of refugee life can aggravate this, including idleness, anger at loss of control and power, uncertainty about the future, and frustration with living conditions.
>
> (United Nations High Commissioner for Refugees 1995: 8–9)

Moreover, from these passages, it seems that sexual drive and aggression are understood distinctly, and even *inherently*, as male traits. This echoes the assumed biological attributes of men and women, and consequent behaviours, as debunked in the feminist literature, which I discussed in the Introduction.

As gender roles and assumptions about sexed bodies are strongly interlinked, the boundary between the two is generally quite blurry. One can note such blurriness in the passage quoted above. In the quoted passage, the roles of men and women in sexual violence seem to rely on a particular understanding of male and, by gendered default, female bodies. As explained in the Introduction, the assumption at work here is the 'inherent' aggressiveness, and sometimes even violence, of men, based on a simplified understanding of sexed bodies, seen with the above example of hormones. Such a dominant view is confirmed by the example of the UNHCR guidelines, which blurs the divide between the medical and social understanding of sexed bodies. Making the link between the medical and social understanding of sexed bodies is not new within feminist studies, though its application to sexual violence specifically is less common, as it is otherwise more usually perceived from an exclusively social (e.g. Misra 2015) or biological (e.g. Thornhill and Palmer 2000) viewpoint.

The rest of the UNHCR guidelines exclusively provide information for attending to female victims. In the 'Medical Response' section, the document only discusses the vulnerability of pregnant women, emergency contraception, pregnancy and HIV and STDs, which are only a risk in the case of rape, which is considered unlikely for male victims (United Nations High Commissioner for Refugees 1995: 32). Therefore, the caveats in the guidelines that suggest considering male victims as well (in the introductory section) do not reach the section on medical response. Those notes are only present in the first few pages, but are absent from the medical intervention section, which is the most important in defining the role and actions of practitioners. In fact, the mention of male victims of sexual violence plays such a minor role throughout the document that they might as well go unnoticed by readers.

PART II Practices

Not only are male victims of sexual violence in war invisible in the guidelines, but also in medical practices, by humanitarian organisations on the ground. As described in more depth in Drumond's chapter (Ch. 8 in this volume), Croat and Bosnian male victims of sexual violence in Serbian detention camps were estimated at 4,000 by the Medical Center for Human Rights in Zagreb (Leatherman 1988: 46), and the Association of Concentration Camp Inmates of Sarajevo Canton found that in the Sarajevo Canton alone, 5,000 out of the 6,000 detainees were men, and 80 per cent of them had suffered sexual violence (United Nations Population Fund 2002: 72). Yet, only three organisations attended to male victims, two of which provided medical care: the Medical Center for Human Rights and the International Rehabilitation Council for Torture Victims. Within those organisations combined, no more than four doctors provided services to male victims (Oosterhoff, Zwanikken, and Ketting 2004: 73).

Mladen Lončar was one of those few doctors. Although very few news articles mentioned male victims of sexual violence, those that did included quotes from him (e.g. Borger 1996; and Jaquemet 1995). Dr Lončar notably worked with the Medical Center for Human Rights, an NGO based in Zagreb, Croatia, founded in 1992 by a group of fifteen physicians, social workers, and psychologists. Upon establishment, the centre's primary interest was human rights violations during the wars in the former Yugoslavia. After the end of the wars, the centre shifted its attention to the aftermath of the war, both in psychological and medical terms. Following his experience at the Medical Center for Human Rights, Dr Lončar tried to publish the studies he had carried out on male victims of sexual violence, in order to raise awareness on the underestimated preponderance and to share his knowledge. However, most of Mladen Lončar's studies were never published, and all encountered resistance in various forms (Lončar, Henigsberg, and Hrabać 2010: 201). He explains that the study published in 2010 had been completed fifteen years prior. This long delay was due to lack of funding and reticence from the government, so most of the work was done on a voluntary basis. The Croatian Ministry of Health has not authorised any new study since (Lončar *et al.* 2010: 201). While reasons for such resistance have not been given, the unpopularity of its subject matter and findings may be a likely possibility. Nevertheless, the written traces that he has left, and those of other doctors too, bear witness to the limits of categorising men as perpetrators of sexual violence exclusively, and not as victims. The study highlights the problems in such a framework, despite its convenience and popularity.

Like other victims, men who experienced sexual violence suffered from posttraumatic stress and physical sequelae. Although possible consequences include genital infections, swollen testicles, physical impotence, abscesses, blood in their stools, and ruptures of the rectum, the impact is not always physically observable (Peel, Mahtani, Hinshelwood, and Forrest 2000; Carlson 2006: 22). Doctors like Carlson and van Tienhoven instead recommend looking for other distinctive signs, whether psychosomatic (loss of appetite and weight, headache, sleeplessness), psychological (feelings of guilt, shame, anger, anxiety), or psychosocial (social withdrawal, alcohol and drug abuse, outbursts of anger) (Oosterhoff *et al.* 2004: 71; Carlson 2006). While symptoms are not always easy to unravel, in part because all cases are unique while medical procedures in war are highly standardised (Špirić *et al.* 2010: 411), training health workers to look for those signs when examining male victims would be helpful in moving away from stigma. In contrast, the search of abuse against women sometimes goes too far, as organisations in conflict zones often rely on quantitative data to attract funding, which leads to persistent and sometimes invasive questioning (for more on this, see Quillard 2015; and Sivakumaran 2007: 256 and n. 13).

Harold van Tienhoven makes the important point that, 'some respondents became familiar with sexual violence against women, and because this usually implies rape, they assumed that sexual violence against men would take the same form, namely anal rape' (van Tienhoven 1992: 3). This immediately limits the scope of discussion, since sexual violence against men does not usually take this form (van Tienhoven 1992: 4; Myrttinen, Ch. 4 in this volume). A good illustration of this is Natalia Linos' commentary in the journal *Social Science and Medicine* (2009). My position is similar to hers: by drawing on the literature on sex and gender in the medical sector, she advocates for a greater awareness of gender biases by those providing health services. However, by using 'sexual violence' and 'rape' interchangeably, there is very little evidence to back her point, thus her attempt at explaining the need to look at male victims of sexual violence isn't as strong as it could be.

In a separate study, Petra Brecić and Mladen Lončar found that 20 per cent of male victims of sexual violence in the former Yugoslavia had been raped. Most had suffered trauma to the genitals inflicted by blunt objects, or had been castrated or semi-castrated (in Olujic 1998: 41). Conversely, when interviewing sixty male victims of sexual abuse in Croatia and Bosnia-Herzegovina, Mladen Lončar, Neven Henigsberg, and Pero Hrabać found that only three of them (5 per cent) had been raped (see also Drumond, Ch. 8 in this volume). Yet almost fifty participants had experienced physical torture of genitals, mainly severe beating of testes or penis (Lončar *et al.* 2010: 196). Had the scope been reduced to rape specifically, the pool of interviewed men would have been much narrower. Such was the case in a study on the clients of the Belgrade Centre for Rehabilitation of Torture Victims. In that study, a team of researchers led by Željko Špirić conflated rape and sexual violence, *and* defined rape as an act perpetrated by the opposite sex only. In other words, they defined sexual violence against men as rape perpetrated by women against men, and sexual violence against women as rape perpetrated by men against women. Thus, they found that 13.2 per cent of participating women and 0.2 per cent of the men had suffered from such torture, and concluded that male victims of sexual violence were negligible (Špirić *et al.* 2010).

Such assumptions and definitions of sexual violence against men obviously have implications for the way the victims are treated medically. Mladen Lončar, for example, noted that talking about the incident was generally helpful, because the victim could regain self-confidence with the feeling of contributing to something useful, such as finding the perpetrator – as seen, for instance, in the activities of the organisation Men of Hope, portrayed in *Men Can Be Raped Too* (Kithima and King 2015). Yet in general, the probability of male victims having occasion to seek medical help and to talk about it are extremely low (Monk-Turner and Light 2010). This was also the case in Yugoslavia, considering the small proportion of medical assistance received by male victims of sexual violence. During a workshop in Zagreb, which focused on medical issues concerning male sexual assault, a doctor exclaimed: 'Until I heard the presentation, I thought that the only form of male sexual assault possible was male rape. I must have a lot more patients who were sexual assault victims than I thought' (Carlson 2006: 18). At the same time, some male victims do not report the crime when what happened to them does not fit their conception of sexual violence (Carlson 2006: 23). In addition to being a hindrance to receiving medical attention, such a strong stigma also biases the representation of male victims of sexual violence in quantitative terms. Justifying the lack of attention to male survivors on the basis of numbers, completely ignores the deeply rooted causes for the misrepresentation of the issue.

Conclusion

What has happened since the UNCHR guidelines of 1995 and the war in former Yugoslavia? That point marked the beginning of relatively wide international attention from NGOs in particular to male victims of sexual violence; it also carried a lot of hope in terms of future development and focus on the issue. Yet, in 2002, no international organisation or NGO had yet established a research programme or policy initiative specifically focused on male victims of sexual violence in wartime (Del Zotto and Jones 2002: 6). However, 2008 was marked by a rare research meeting organised by UNOCHA to address the issue of sexual violence against men and boys in conflict (United Nations Office for the Coordination of Humanitarian Affairs 2008; Becerra, Ch. 10 in this volume). It was particularly notable for reviewing the key academic literature on the subject and commissioning additional articles. But very little followed this event, and in 2010, Sandesh Sivakumaran lamented that UN reports on sexual violence in armed conflict are now attuned to the problem and sometimes carry a sentence along the lines that 'men and boys are also subject to sexual violence'. However, such a sentence, if indeed present, is usually the sole reference to men and boys in any report (Sivakumaran 2010: 260).

We had to wait until 2012 for the UNHCR to publish a dedicated document titled 'Working with Men and Boy Survivors of Sexual and Gender-Based Violence in Forced Displacement' (United Nations High Commissioner for Refugees 2012). While it is disappointingly only sixteen pages long with very little information (in contrast to the sixty-page guidelines of 1995), it nevertheless symbolises the acknowledgement of an urgent necessity. More recently, the Institute for International Criminal Investigations (IICI) published a twenty-four-page document called 'Guidelines for Investigating Conflict-Related Sexual and Gender-Based Violence Against Men and Boys' (2016). Although those guidelines are designated for criminal justice and human rights investigators, and so medical attention is considered as forensic investigation primarily, the existence of such guidelines point towards a very slow shift in mentalities around sexual violence against men.

In terms of practice by medical organisations, progress is harder to assess. The attention to male victims of sexual violence has been brought up during the war in former Yugoslavia, and in its aftermath, but without as much development since as would have been hoped. The remarkable efforts of the World Health Organization (WHO) in shedding light on the issue have sadly gone shrouded in the sea of institutional documentation on the former Yugoslavia. For this reason, it is unclear how much the efforts of the WHO have done and what the impact was. A UN document describes a WHO project started in late 1994 called 'The Rehabilitation of War Victims', directly providing support for sexually violated men. However, it appears that lack of funding prevented it from gaining ground, so it remained a localised telephone hotline in Croatia with some data collection (United Nations 1995: 46). None of the studies on the subject of medical assistance to male victims of sexual violence mention this project, or the involvement of the WHO (e.g. Oosterhoff *et al.* 2004; Lončar *et al.* 2010). Yet the WHO guideline publications show a much greater awareness to male victims of sexual violence than other organisations. In 2000, the WHO went as far as controversially stating that:

> Male victims of sexual assault are more likely to suffer significant physical trauma than female victims. Acute treatment of male patients should proceed in a manner that closely parallels female victims, including providing appropriate medical and preventive services based on the medical history and physical examination. Maintenance of an open, non-judgmental attitude is important as this will help to gain the confidence of the individual that has been attacked.
>
> (WHO 2000: 112)

However, the quote was removed in an updated 2003 edition, *Guidelines for Medico-legal Care for Victims of Sexual Violence*. While it admits focusing on women and children, by virtue of likelihood, the 2003 edition also highlights that these 'guidelines address a range of health care issues that apply to individuals of both sexes' and include 'several concerns that are specific to male victims' (WHO 2003: 3); it thus includes the possibility of male and female victims throughout. For example, there are some sample examination record templates in the annex section, where both sketches of male and female bodies can be found for the usage of the practitioner (WHO 2003: 114). While change is taking place, it is doing so at a slow pace, with hopefully a more generalised integration of victims of sexual violence in war, in order to avoid future instances where a male victim of sexual might enter a hospital only to be laughed at by a nurse.

Note

1 For examples of works that critically engage with the justification of male aggressiveness and violence as well as with female passivity, please respectively refer to Fausto-Sterling (1985: 128) and Bleier 1984.

References

Bederman, Gail. 1995. *Manliness and Civilization: A Cultural History of Gender and Race in the United States, 1880–1917*. Chicago, IL: The University of Chicago Press.

Belkin, Aaron. 2012. *Bring Me Men: Military Masculinity and the Benign Facade of American Empire, 1898–2001*. London: Hurst.

Birke, Lynda. 2000. 'Sitting on the Fence: Biology, Feminism and Gender-Bending Environments'. *Women's Studies International Forum* 23(5): 587–599.

Bleier, Ruth. 1984. *Science and Gender: A Critique of Biology and Its Theories on Women*. New York: Teachers College Press.

Borger, Julian. 1996. 'Croats "Raped British Soldiers"'. *Guardian*, 27 July.

Bullough, Vern L. 1976. *Sexual Variance in Society and History*. New York: John Wiley and Sons.

Carlson, Eric Stener. 2006. 'The Hidden Prevalence of Male Sexual Assault During War: Observations on Blunt Trauma to the Male Genitals'. *British Journal of Criminology* 46(1): 16–25.

Dabbs, James McBride and Mary Godwin Dabbs. 2000. *Heroes, Rogues, and Lovers: Testosterone and Behavior*. Blacklick, OH: McGraw-Hill.

DeLuca, Robyn Stein. 2017. *The Hormone Myth: How Junk Science, Gender Politics, and Lies about PMS Keep Women Down*. Oakland, CA: New Harbinger Publications.

Del Zotto, Augusta and Adam Jones. 2002. 'Male-on-Male Sexual Violence in Wartime: Human Rights' Last Taboo?'. Paper presented at the annual convention of the International Studies Association, New Orleans, Louisiana, 23–27 March.

Donnelly, Denise and Stacy Kenyon. 1996. ' "Honey, We Don't Do Men": Gender Stereotypes and the Provision of Services to Sexually Assaulted Males'. *Journal of Interpersonal Violence* 11(13): 441–448.

Eckert, Lena. 2016. *Intersexualization: The Clinic and the Colony*. London: Routledge.

Enloe, Cynthia. 1990. 'Womenandchildren: Making Feminist Sense of the Persian Gulf Crisis'. *The Village Voice* 35(39): 29–32.

Eriksson Baaz, Maria and Maria Stern. 2013. *Sexual Violence as a Weapon of War? Perceptions, Prescriptions, Problems in the Congo and Beyond*. London: Zed Books.

Fausto-Sterling, Anne. 1985. *Myths of Gender: Biological Theories About Women and Men*. New York: Basic Books.

Fausto-Sterling, Anne. 1997. 'How to Build a Man', In Vernon A. Rosario (ed.), *Science and Homosexualities.* New York: Routledge, 219–225.

Fausto-Sterling, Anne. 2000. *Sexing the Body: Gender Politics and the Construction of Sexuality.* New York: Basic Books.

Fausto-Sterling, Anne. 2012. *Sex/Gender: Biology in a Social World*. London: Routledge.

Frayser, Suzanne G. and Thomas J. Whitby. 1995. *Studies in Human Sexuality: A Selected Guide*, 2nd edn. Englewood, CO: Libraries Unlimited.

Geddes, Patrick and John Arthur Thomson. 1889. *The Evolution of Sex*. London: The Walker Scott Publishing.

Geddes, Patrick and John Arthur Thomson. 1914. *Sex*. London: Williams and Norgate.

Gilder, George. 1979. 'The Case Against Women in Combat'. *New York Times Magazine*, 28 January.

Goldstein, Joshua. 2001. *War and Gender: How Gender Shapes the War System and Vice Versa.* Cambridge: Cambridge University Press.

IICI (Institute for International Criminal Investigations). 2016. Guidelines for Investigating Conflict-Related Sexual and Gender-Based Violence Against Men and Boys. The Hague: Institute for International Criminal Investigations.

Inter-Agency Standing Committee. 2004. *Inter-Agency Global Evaluation of Reproductive Health for Refugees and Internally Displaced Persons.* Geneva: Inter-Agency Standing Committee.

Inter-Agency Standing Committee. 2005. *Guidelines for Gender-Based Violence Interventions in Humanitarian Settings: Focusing on Prevention of and Response to Sexual Violence in Emergencies.* Geneva: Inter-Agency Standing Committee.

Jaquemet, Iolanda. 1995. 'Des milliers d'hommes ont été violés en Bosnie: Tabou de guerre'. *Le Nouveau Quotidien*, 10–12 March.

Kithima, Paul Bebhin and Kabafunzaki Darius King. 2015. *Men Can Be Raped Too.* YouTube Film. Directed by Paul Bebhin Kithima. Kampala, Uganda: Refugee Law Project.

Laqueur, Thomas. 1992. *Making Sex: Body and Gender from the Greeks to Freud.* Boston, MA: Harvard University Press.

Leatherman, Janie. 1988. *Sexual Violence and Armed Conflict.* Cambridge: Polity Press.

Linos, Natalia. 2009. 'Rethinking Gender-Based Violence During War: Is Violence Against Civilian Men a Problem Worth Addressing?'. *Social Science and Medicine* 68(8): 1548–1551.

Lončar, Mladen, Neven Henigsberg, and Pero Hrabać. 2010. 'Mental Health Consequences in Men Exposed to Sexual Abuse During the War in Croatia and Bosnia'. *Journal of Interpersonal Violence* 25(2): 191–203.

Misra, Amalendu. 2015. *The Landscape of Silence: Sexual Violence Against Men in War.* London: Hurst.

Monk-Turner, Elizabeth and David Light. 2010. 'Male Sexual Assault and Rape: Who Seeks Counselling?'. *Sexual Abuse: A Journal of Research and Treatment* 22(3): 255–265.

Olujic, Maria. 1998. 'Embodiment of Terror: Gendered Violence in Peacetime and Wartime in Croatia and Bosnia-Herzegovina'. *Medical Anthropology Quarterly* 12(1): 31–50.

Oosterhoff, Pauline, Prisca Zwanikken, and Evert Ketting. 2004. 'Sexual Torture of Men in Croatia and Other Conflict Situations: An Open Secret'. *Reproductive Health Matters* 12(23): 68–77.

Oudshoorn, Nelly. 1994. *Beyond the Natural Body: An Archeology of Sex Hormones.* New York: Routledge.

Peel, Michael, A. Mahtani, Gill Hinshelwood, and Duncan Forrest. 2000. 'The Sexual Abuse of Men in Detention in Sri Lanka'. *The Lancet* 355(9220): 2069–2070.

Quillard, Marion. 2015. 'Que celles qui ont eté violées lèvent la main'. *Numéro XXI* 31: 94–107.

Seifert, Ruth. 1996. 'The Second Front: The Logic of Sexual Violence in Wars'. *Women's Studies International Forum* 19(1/2): 35–43.

Sivakumaran, Sandesh. 2007. 'Sexual Violence Against Men in Armed Conflict'. *The European Journal of International Law* 18(2): 253–276.

Sivakumaran, Sandesh. 2010. 'Lost in Translation: UN Responses to Sexual Violence Against Men and Boys in Situations of Armed Conflict'. *International Review of the Red Cross* 92(877): 259–277.

Špirić, Željko, Goran Opačić, Vladimir Jović, Radomir Samardžić, Goran Knežević, Gordana Mandić-Gajić, and Milorad Todorović. 2010. 'Polne razlike kod žrtava ratne torture s obzirom na vrste mučenja i psihološke posledice' ['Gender Differences in Victims of War Torture: Types of Torture and Psychological Consequences']. *Vojnosanitetski Pregled* 67(5): 411–418.

Thayer, Bradley A. 2000. 'Bringing in Darwin: Evolutionary Theory, Realism, and International Politics'. *International Security* 25(2): 124–151.

Thornhill, Randy and Craig T. Palmer. 2000. *A Natural History of Rape*. Cambridge, MA: MIT Press.

United Nations. 1995. 'Report of the Secretary-General: Rape and Abuse of Women in the Areas of Armed Conflict in the Former Yugoslavia'. *Human Rights Questions: Human Rights Situations and Reports of Special Rapporteurs and Representatives.* United Nations General Assembly A/50/329.

United Nations High Commissioner for Refugees. 1995. *Sexual Violence Against Refugees: Guidelines on Prevention and Response.* Geneva: UNHCR.

United Nations High Commissioner for Refugees. 2003. *Sexual and Gender-Based Violence Against Refugees, Returnees and Internally Displaced Persons: Guidelines for Prevention and Response.* Geneva: UNHCR.

United Nations High Commissioner for Refugees. 2012. *Working with Men and Boys Survivors of Sexual and Gender-Based Violence in Forced Displacement.* Geneva: UNHCR.

United Nations Office for the Coordination of Humanitarian Affairs. 2008. 'The Nature, Scope and Motivation for Sexual Violence Against Men and Boys in Conflict'. Discussion Paper 2 prepared for OCHA experts' meeting: *Use of Sexual Violence in Armed Conflict: Identifying gaps in Research to Inform More Effective Interventions*, UN OCHA Research Meeting. New York, 26 June.

United Nations Population Fund. 2001. *A Practical Approach to Gender-Based Violence: A Programme Guide for Health Care Providers and Managers.* New York: UNFPA.

United Nations Population Fund. 2002. *The Impact of Conflict on Women and Girls: A UNFPA Strategy for Gender Mainstreaming in Areas of Conflict and Reconstitution.* Bratislava: UNFPA.

van Tienhoven, Harold. 1992. 'Sexual Violence, a Method of Torture Also Used Against Male Victims'. *Nordisk Sexologi* 10: 1–8.

WHO (World Health Organization). 2003. *Guidelines for Medico-Legal Care for Victims of Sexual Violence*, Geneva: World Health Organization.

WHO (World Health Organization). 2000. *Reproductive Health During Conflict and Displacement: A Guide for Programme Managers*, Geneva: World Health Organization.

6 The political economy of sexual violence against men and boys in armed conflict

Sara Meger

In 2012, the UN Special Representative of the Secretary General on Conflict-Related Sexual Violence, Zainab Bangura, noted explicitly for the first time that men and boys are also often victims of conflict-related sexual violence (CRSV). Acknowledging the common occurrence of CRSV perpetrated against men and boys led her to declare that wartime sexual violence is 'no longer a gender issue' (UN News 2012). Her sentiments were echoed in the 2012 Human Security Report, which argued that the mainstream narrative and framework for addressing 'rape as a weapon of war' misrepresented the issue, in part because it has neglected to address the perpetration of CRSV against men and boys.

This criticism is not wrong – the international aid, scholarship, and policy on CRSV has long focused on this form of gender-based violence as one of the primary ways that women and girls are affected by war. A 2002 study surveyed more than 4,000 NGO and IGO reports on CRSV and found that a mere 3 per cent acknowledged men and boys as victims, usually only in passing (Del Zotto and Jones 2002). Yet, in nearly every conflict in which sexual violence features, this violence is also perpetrated against men and boys (Russell 2008; Sivakumaran 2007). Thus, the tendency within mainstream advocacy, policy, and scholarship to conflate the 'gender' part of gender-based violence with 'women' has obscured the fact that men and boys may also be victims of sexual violence during war and conflict, and that women and girls may also be perpetrators (Human Security Report Project 2012; Sjoberg 2016).

However, to declare that sexual violence is 'no longer a gender issue' is highly problematic. Since 2012, in an effort to address the silence on CRSV against men and boys, the policy, aid, and scholarship communities have rushed to add men to the analysis of sexual violence in war, resulting in narratives of this violence that in essence *de-gender* CRSV. That is, explanatory frames have shifted from feminist analyses of how gender operates as an axis of power in social, political, and economic life to accounts that minimise (if not trivialise) the influence of hierarchical gender relations as a cause of wartime rape (Cohen, Green, and Wood 2013; Eriksson Baaz and Stern 2013; Carter 2010). The argument goes that men's victimisation or women's perpetration of sexual violence in war is sufficient evidence of an equality between the sexes, or, at least, evidence of the *insufficiency* of hierarchical gender relations as a cause of this violence. Rather than adding more nuance to our understanding of wartime sexual violence, these arguments have further frustrated efforts to understand the determinants of this violence, as well as variations in patterns to its perpetration.

This chapter argues for a feminist political economy (FPE) approach, which provides useful conceptual tools for understanding the motivations and effects of sexual violence in armed conflict. Specifically, by looking at the use of CRSV against men and boys, this approach uncovers the ways in which violence inscribes differential values on bodies in times of war. Not only is the political economy of CRSV apparent 'in the ways that conflicts are often characterised by attempts to gain control over productive and reproductive resources' (Meger 2015: 416), but also in the way that the perpetration of sexual violence represents an exchange in and exploitation of value, both in terms of the bodies involved, and in the violence itself.

This chapter begins by outlining an FPE approach to understanding CRSV and its capacity to shed new light on the causes and consequences of sexual violence against men and boys. I explore the conditions whereby the sexual violation of men and boys elicits symbolic and material value, making it an attractive means by which armed groups achieve particular wartime objectives.[1] I then apply this analysis to two 'types' of CRSV commonly experienced by men and boys: sexual violence as an instrument of torture perpetrated by repressive state forces; and sexual violence as a weapon of war.

The feminist political economy of conflict-related sexual violence

An FPE approach to sexual violence asks the question 'who benefits?' and seeks to uncover the conditions that precipitate and give meaning and value to this violence. Many analyses seek to understand sexual violence solely from the perspective of interpersonal relations (i.e. the micro-level correlates of violence, such as alcohol use, patriarchal family arrangements, or prior exposure to abuse) or cultural dynamics (i.e. the culturally-specific forms of patriarchal control that enable or excuse gendered violence, such as socio-economic class, patriarchal cultural traditions and norms, and honour-based societal arrangements – see Heise 1998). However, an FPE approach redirects our attention to (global) structures as permissive of violence and conflict, and interrogates the links between the socio-cultural *effects* of this violence and the material *objectives* of perpetrators as they are shaped within said structures.

An FPE analysis of CRSV thus helps to uncover the *political* nature and, crucially, *politico-economic value* of gendered violence. It interrogates the possibility that the deployment of this violence is itself a mode of production and reproduction, creating, nurturing, and sustaining political, social, and economic practices. Sexual violence within war zones often operates to ensure compliance, enforce subordination, and/or to challenge prevailing hierarchies. These are not merely *effects* of the violence, but are, in this view, central to the intention that drives its use. That is, regardless of whether the gendered effects of sexual violence are the express intent of the perpetrator, the relatively stable signification of the act as a gendered practice and of gender-based subordination as an effect of the act means that CRSV is always implicated in the (re)production of gender hierarchy. Thus, the focus here is on the material benefits that can be derived from the use of CRSV, and how CRSV, in the aggregate, serves to reconstruct the hierarchical relations on which differential distributions of resources, status, and wealth are based.

The economic politics of sexual violence

Violence has currency in global security. Commonly viewed as merely destructive, violence is also *productive* and – importantly – *reproductive*. Hardt and Negri argue that: 'War has become ... a form of rule aimed not only at controlling the population but producing and reproducing all aspects of social life' (2004: 13). War is not merely a disruption of social, political, and cultural life, but is itself integrally connected to the generation of symbols, meanings, and values associated with life. Feminists have long observed this in the relation between militarisation and gender, both socially, in terms of the influence of militarisation on constructions of masculine and feminine norms, and structurally, in reproducing hierarchical valuation of gendered dualisms, such as the greater value placed on war than peace, on reason than emotion, on toughness than on caring (Enloe 2000).

Applied to the study of CRSV, an FPE lens employs a similar critical reading of militarisation and gender to trace patterns of CRSV to patterns of war, and looks for the value that this specific form of violence may generate for the perpetrating groups. Instead of requiring the explicit *gendered* intent of the perpetrator to be known, this view accepts that:

> acts and practices that show gender hierarchy, that take advantage of gender hierarchy, that reify and reinforce gender hierarchy – acts and practices *of* gender subordination – are then constituted as gender subordination by their genderings, rather than by the intent of the perpetrator or even the (direct or proximate) impact on the (direct or proximate) victim/target/receptor.
>
> (Sjoberg 2016: 177–178)

As such, CRSV is read as a form of political violence. A central device of political violence is humiliation, which may be experienced both at the individual level and collectively by communities/groups. Humiliation 'transmit[s] a highly symbolic and intelligent "message" (...) that reinstate[s] physically, mentally, and emotionally the hierarchy between perpetrator and victim' (Lindner 2006: 5). In the context of armed conflict, humiliating acts of violence are tactics that can be employed by dominant groups to humiliate the subordinate group to maintain hierarchical relations (Giacaman, Abu-Rmeileh, Husseini, Saab, and Boyce 2007), or by subordinate groups to weaken the dominant group and subvert the existing hierarchical relations.

As an emotion, humiliation may not appear at first glance to be the appropriate purview of a political economy analysis. However, as Fattah and Fierke argue, 'emotion is a rational measure of value' (2009: 69). Further, positive emotions such as happiness or joy relate to the presence of the valued subject or object and the ability to realize one's objectives and goals, while negative emotions related to humiliation or betrayal arise from a loss of dignity, value, safety or agency and a subsequent inability to flourish.

(Fattah and Fierke 2009: 70)

Humiliation is of particular interest to an FPE analysis as it takes place within a relationship wherein one party experiences a loss or lowering in status/value (Saurette 2005).

However, the *value* of humiliation can only really be understood through an analysis of its gendered determinants and effects. As humiliation invokes devaluation, its logics are arguably best understood through the FPE frame of *feminisation*. Peterson explains feminisation as a process of devalorisation, arguing:

Not only subjects (women and marginalized men), but also concepts, desires, tastes, styles, 'ways of knowing', cultural expressions (art, music), roles, practices, work, nature, and so on can be feminized – with the effect of reducing their legitimacy, status and value. Importantly, this devalorisation is simultaneously ideological (discursive, cultural) and material (structural, economic).... This de-valorisation normalizes – with the effect of legitimating – the marginalization, subordination, and exploitation of feminized practices and persons.

(Peterson 2010: 19–20)

Peterson's framework is clearly exemplified in stories about men who have experienced sexual violence. Men in detention often narrate their experiences of degradation and sexual abuse as being made to 'feel like a woman' (Franks 2014). One of the detainees held at Abu Ghraib explained, ' "We are men. Beatings don't hurt us; it's just a blow. But no one would want their manhood shattered. [Our captors] wanted us to feel as though we were women, the way women feel ..." ' (Franks 2014: 569). For the detainee, Dhia al-Shweiri, being treated as a woman was to be stripped naked and *looked at*, an experience he describes as 'the worst insult'. The depth of that humiliation, for al-Shweiri, was worse than the beatings and torture experienced at the hands of Saddam Hussein's regime, and a fate worse than death (Franks 2014: 569).

The experience of humiliation as 'a fate worse than death' may be so because, rather than recognising the subjective autonomy and superior value of a militarised, masculine body, that body is stripped of its sovereignty, rendered as both an object for consumption and as an 'Other' to the phenomenological standpoint of the masculine subject (de Beauvoir 1949). Being treated *like a woman* is to be objectified by the masculine subjective gaze and treated as a commodity not with inherent use-value, but meaningful only in social relation. Feminisation, thus 'condemn[s] the victim to dishonour and the loss of the status of a complete man and a citizen (...)' (Bourdieu 2001, in Franks 2014: 577). It renders a man as an object, whose value is realisable only in its exchange.

The exchange value generated by CRSV depends on the social and cultural significance of *bodies* themselves, and subsequently of transgressing the boundaries of particular bodies (Misra 2015). In one of the first in-depth analyses of CRSV against men, Misra argues that a central reason that men are victims of this violence is because 'the key underlying objective of the violator is to defile the body that is at its prime' (Misra 2015: 24). Particularly when the targeted body is also militarised, the ability to reduce this body to a lower status on the gender hierarchy through sexual violation and feminisation may be an effective means by which to demobilise the enemy. Telling here is the gendered *loss of value* that is experienced by the 'body that is at its prime', which connotes the way that value is socially constructed in ways that rely on dichotomous gendered symbols. Only those objects which are associated with or approximate traits of hegemonic masculinity are of *value*, socially, politically, and economically, while those which are feminine or feminised are devalued.

The sexual politics of sexual violence

After the infamous Abu Ghraib photos were leaked to the public in 2004, the world became aware of the routine use of humiliation as a tactic against men detained in the US-led 'War on Terror'. Saurette summarises the treatment:

> Prisoners were forced to strip and then stand naked, or march around naked. They were forced into sexual poses and ridiculed in front of fellow prisoners and American guards. They were forced to simulate sex with one another, in front of female American guards, and were then photographed in these contexts.
>
> (Saurette 2007: 13)

These tactics were not torturous for their physical effects on the prisoners (pain or exposure), but because each practice 'works on specific cultural sensitivities about what it means to be an honourable, self-respecting subject in that culture' (Saurette 2007: 14). Fattah and Fierke (2009) argue that the public humiliation of Abu Ghraib prisoners was a deliberate exploitation of the Islamic shame-based culture, heightening the sense of powerlessness of not only the direct victims of this violence, but also the broader Iraqi community.

While Saurette's (2007) and Fattah and Fierke's (2009) accounts tell us much about the tactical value of humiliation as an act of political violence, their analyses fail to explain why it is that *sexual* forms of humiliation are so often the mode employed.

The value of sexual violence must be seen through the lens of sexual politics. That is, the recognition that (the physical act of) sex and sexuality are deeply set within human social relations and comprehensible only in relation to 'the variety of attitudes and values to which culture subscribes' (Millet 1970: 23). Such a perspective invites us to critically interrogate the ways in which sexual violence is enacted within a system of sexual domination, which simultaneously inscribes meaning and power to violated/violating bodies and to the act itself. This meaning and power is not isolated to CRSV, but visible also in the typical link between cruelty and sexuality in our everyday 'peacetime' societies, as well (Millet 1970). That is because sexuality is a social construct borne out of patriarchal relations, and as such is 'defined by men, forced on women, and constitutive in the meaning of gender' (Mackinnon 1989: 316). Put another way, within the structural conditions of patriarchy, the seeming naturalness and inevitability of sex and sexuality must be understood as 'the product of gendered patterns of domination and submission intrinsic to patriarchal societies' (Jackson and Scott 1996: 16–17). As such, sexuality is made meaningful as a relation of dominance and submission, gendered through dichotomous symbolisms that associate dominance with the masculine and submission with the feminine. In this way, the gendered *nature* of sexual violence comes from its construction within a system of patriarchy, while the gendered *effects* are not limited to the biological sex of either the victim or perpetrator (Sjoberg 2016).

Given the intimate co-constitution of power and sexuality, we can begin to understand how particularly sexual forms of humiliation are made meaningful within sexual politics. Within social constructions of sexuality that understand the male body as 'phallic and impenetrable, as a war-body simultaneously armed and armoured, equipped for victory' (Waldby 1995: 268), the penetration or defilement of a masculine body carries significant import. Sexual violence perpetrated in the context of war represents a 'taboo violation' (Leatherman 2011). Taboos contravene the social order and engender disorder as they challenge established boundaries and prohibitions. According to Leatherman, taboo violations are central to patriarchy because hegemonic masculinity is constructed in a way that we value the surpassing of limits and 'boldly going where no man has gone before'. Power and patriarchal masculinity, in her words, manifest in taboo violations, since 'doing something that is prohibited and getting away with it demonstrates one's power much more fully than doing something acceptable' (Leatherman 2011: 141–142).

Sexual violence against men and boys in armed conflicts

While this framework is useful for understanding how bodies and value become (or are inherently) entwined in the politics of violence, an FPE analysis also pushes us further to ask the question: under what conditions might we see the value of CRSV against certain bodies (i.e. men and boys) exploited? How might the feminising/devaluing effects of this violence be tied to the material objectives of perpetrators in war?

To begin with, the effect of CRSV against men is similar to when an armed group perpetrates CRSV against women – the humiliation/feminisation is experienced by both the individual victim of this violence and their wider social group. When perpetrated against both men and women, sexual violence is humiliating – 'the victim is forced into passivity, acted upon, made helpless' (Lindner 2004: 40). The act constructs a political relationship between the perpetrator and victim, while simultaneously serving 'as a disciplinary site in the sense that others belonging to his community can take lessons from the bodily experiences of the victim' (Misra 2015: 30). The humiliation/feminisation extends to the collective body politic of the victim's community, and is (very often) effective in keeping them in a state of submission.

Despite the similar functioning of CRSV, regardless of the sex of the victim, there are some key distinctions in the way that sexual violence is perpetrated against men and boys versus that perpetrated against women and girls. Here, it is important to reiterate that while the *effects* of sexual violence may be similar, the fact that there are observable and distinctive patterns in the use of CRSV against men and boys, as opposed to against women and girls, speaks to a need for greater attentiveness to the work that gender does in this dynamic.

The first distinction is in the *location* of the perpetration of this violence. Most often, when men are victims of CRSV, it is perpetrated against them while in detention. Within this context, the most frequent forms of sexual violence used are means of sexual torture[2] and sexualised forms of humiliation.[3] Perpetrators ranging from Balkan state security forces during the wars of the former Yugoslavia to the US military, the Sri Lankan police, and the Syrian government have all reportedly used similar forms of sexual torture, rape, genital beatings, and sexualised humiliation as 'interrogation' tactics against detained men (Eisenstein 2004; Leiby 2009; Sivakumaran 2007; Sooka 2014; The Taguba Report n.d.).

The second distinction is in the intended *function* of the violence. Women may experience CRSV borne out of opportunism, bolstered by ideas of masculine virility (Enloe 2000; Eriksson Baaz and Stern 2009), and the male sex right (Mackenzie 2010; Moschetti 2005), as well as for strategic purposes. Male victims, on the other hand, are targeted for this violence not out of patriarchal constructions of the male sex right, but for their particular strategic value. Contrary to the argument that rape is about power and not sex, the FPE approach directs our attention to the intimate relationship between power and (the act of) sex, which necessarily manifests differently, under the condition of patriarchy, when enacted against men and boys and when it is against women and girls.

Thus, an FPE lens requires us to shift our attention from the direct effects of this violence (feminisation) to the material gains that may be achieved from its perpetration. On the structural level, the ability of the perpetrator to physically and sexually overpower his victims, whether male or female, both reinforces hierarchical gender relations and often results in material dividends, such as increased status, esteem, and even wealth (Meger 2016). That is, the perpetrators of CRSV against men and boys (as with women and girls) are not necessarily seeking power as an end in itself, but are often motivated by what that power can provide (e.g. strategic ends tied to the war objectives; expressions of cultural or inter-group dominance; (re)constitution of masculinity). Uncovering the motivations for CRSV against men and boys requires attention to how this violence is effective in demobilising opposition, terrorising civilian populations, and/or clearing valuable areas of strategic interest to the perpetrating group (Meger 2011), due to the differential and exploitable value assigned to gendered bodies.

Employing this FPE understanding of the function of sexual violence against men and boys allows us to trace the value of this violence in different conflicts and by different actors. In different conditions of armed conflict, the exploitation of CRSV against men and boys as taboo violations may serve quite different functions and take on different patterns and forms.

The final section explores the most common patterns of the perpetration of CRSV against men and boys and how an FPE lens can meaningfully account for different forms of CRSV by tying them to the material objectives of perpetrators.

Disaggregating CRSV: method of torture or instrument of war?

While international policy and scholarship has tended to focus on 'rape as a weapon of war', by far the most prevalent form of CRSV against men and boys occurs not in the field, by invading rebel groups, but behind the locked doors of state-run detention centres by state security forces. Most reports of sexual violence against men and boys subsume this violence under the name of 'torture'. While some may feel that this characterisation overlooks the sexual nature of this violence, it is important to distinguish the *function* of this violence perpetrated against men and boys in many conflicts from the types of sexual violence typified under the 'rape as a weapon of war' paradigm (Meger 2016).

What makes this form of sexual violence against men and boys particularly interesting for those who study CRSV is its prevalence in what some prominent scholars have dubbed 'non-event' cases, like the conflict (and post-conflict) in Sri Lanka (Wood 2009). Since the war officially ended in 2009, numerous reports have now begun to document the extent to which government forces have systematically used sexualised torture in its efforts to suppress the secessionist movement of the Liberation Tigers of Tamil Eelam (LTTE) (Amnesty International 2011; Asian Human Rights Commission 2010; Human Rights Watch 2013; Public Interest Advocacy Centre 2014; Sooka 2014; UN Committee Against Torture 2011). Most damning, evidence suggests that sexual torture is a strategic and deliberate tactic employed by the military and the police in the full knowledge and approval of senior officers, permitted by most security policy (Asian Human Rights Commission 2011).

Enloe (2000) characterises this form of CRSV as perpetrated by a 'nervous state' that is facing a significant challenge to its authority, control over territory and resources, or of the 'hearts and minds' of the general population. When used by agents of the state to enforce national security and quell opposition, sexual violence is typically employed to enforce submission, deter opposition, or force testimony (Farr 2009; Leiby 2009). A survey of reports from various countries found that more than a quarter of male detainees had experienced sexual abuse while in detention (Peel 2004) in the form of genital electrocutions, beatings, mutilations, and forced acts on guards and other detainees (Arieff 2010; Bastick, Grimm, and Kunz 2007). Inflicted against detainees, these forms of sexualised torture are used to extract information from prisoners or generally to instil fear both within the detainees themselves and among the wider community to which the victim belongs (Arieff 2010).

In inflicting sexualised forms of torture and abuse against men, perpetrators are able to express physical dominance and inflict deep humiliation on the victim in a way that speaks to the very heart of their individual and collective gendered identity. It is an expression of both the perpetrator's dominant masculinity and of the victim's inferiority. At the same time, the specifically sexual nature of this abuse illuminates the intent to feminise the victim, subjecting the victim to the type of physical treatment that is generally reserved for women. It thus works to 'install a disempowered masculinity as constitutive of the identities of the [group]'s men' (Hansen 2001: 60). What collects the victimised men together in such conflicts is their association with a political opposition group threatening to the state. Thus, the material objective that guides sexual violence as torture is the value derived from objectifying and feminising the masculine liberator (rebel group), towards the ends of counter-insurgency.

Yet, while men are most likely to experience CRSV as torture perpetrated by state security forces and proxy agents as a means of counter-insurgency, most international attention on sexual violence against men and boys in conflict is on how it can be a weapon of war. Reports from Sierra Leone (Human Rights Watch 2003), Sudan (Gingerich and Leaning 2004), Central African Republic (IRIN News 2005), Uganda, and the Democratic Republic of Congo (Dolan 2014; Refugee Law Project 2009) have all detailed cases of men experiencing sexual violence directly and causally linked to the conflicts in those countries.

The ongoing war in the eastern regions of the Democratic Republic of Congo has provided focus for the newly emerging attention to CRSV against men and boys. In their survey of households across the country, Johnson *et al.* (2010) found that nearly a quarter of men in the region had experienced sexual violence, most of which was conflict-related. Save the Children estimates that men and boys make up 10 per cent of survivors who seek treatment for sexual abuse in the DRC (Save the Children 2012).

While, in absolute numbers, this form of CRSV against men and boys is less common, like CRSV used as a means of torture, this violence is an effective instrument of war because of its exploitation of norms of masculinity within the country. A gender advisor for the Refugee Law Project explained,

> In Africa, no man is allowed to be vulnerable. You have to be masculine, strong. You should never break down or cry. A man must be a leader and provide for the whole family. When he fails to reach that standard, society perceives that there is something wrong.
>
> (Storr 2011)

Not only do the victims of this violence experience a loss of their masculine status for being made vulnerable, but in being forced into submission and pene-trated by invading soldiers, the male victims are also feminised. It is not simply, as Solangon and Patel (2012: 428) characterise, a stripping of the man's social status; rather, it's a conferring of a new status – being like a woman and thus Othered from and subordinate to men – that makes sexual violence against men an effective tactic of war.

Where it differs from sexual violence as torture is in *who* is targeted for this violence and how. First, the victims of CRSV as a weapon of war are almost exclusively civilians with no apparent ties to either side of the conflict, and this is due to the strategic value of civilian targeting in contemporary forms of war (Meger 2011). Second, it differs in its very public and brutal nature. That this form of violence is typically done in the open, with an audience, speaks to its communicative function: to absolutely demoralise both the immediate victim and the wider community associated with him, enforcing the community's submission or evoking sufficient fear within the wider population to displace the community and facilitate access to the land, to valuable resources, or to other materials that may be of strategic interest to the perpetrators. This function of CRSV was recognised in UN Security Council Resolution 1960, which explicitly recognised the way in which this violence has served to drive out settled populations or sufficiently enforce their submission to enable the armed group access to exploit natural resources.

Leatherman's analysis of CRSV as a potent 'taboo violation' that reinforces the power of the perpetrating actor is useful for understanding CRSV against men and boys as a weapon of war. As the exchange value of CRSV is derived from pushing ever further the boundaries of imaginable violence, the repeated use of the same form of violence comes with diminishing impact. Therefore, perpetrators must 'exercise even more cruelty, more extreme forms of defilement of the victim, more forceful penetration' or to turn to new categories of victims (Leatherman 2011: 143–144). Within this framework, male victims may be targeted in some contexts as the newer, bolder frontier of taboo violation, which multiplies the impact.

Yet, regardless of the function (torture or weapon of war), CRSV against men and boys is effective because it is explicitly sexual. CRSV against men and boys articulates directly one's masculine status in the gender hierarchy, and thus value. For the individual perpetrator, it is a demonstration of his dominance over the inferior masculine status of the victim and the group to which he belongs. For the victim, it denotes a valuation of being on a par with femininity, evidenced by submissiveness, passivity, and (often) penetrability. Fundamentally, the humiliation of sexual violence is tied to the loss of autonomous subject status and rendered sexual object, a designation typically reserved for women.

As 'sexual transactions often obey market principles' (Pinker 1998: 474) the political value of CRSV against men and boys may be generated from the degree of feminisation; in other words, as discussed above, greater value is generated from targeting *particularly masculine* (read: hegemonic forms of masculine) bodies for violation. So, too, is the value generated from the pushing of boundaries of taboo violations. Since, in many countries, male-to-male sex is a deeply held social taboo, the violation of it accesses a new source of power that can then be leveraged by the perpetrating group towards their ultimate conflict objectives.

Rather than the senseless violence that contemporary conflicts are often depicted to be, the perpetration of CRSV either as an instrument of torture or as a weapon of war forms 'an integral part of the daily systemic practices of capital accumulation and state building' (Turcotte 2011: 204; Meger 2015) in the global political economy. The seeming senselessness of sexual violence against men and boys is actually highly functional in that it enables the material ends of the armed groups, generally involving control of land, populations, and other (re)productive resources (Meger 2011; Leatherman 2011).

Conclusion

The FPE analysis put forward in this chapter to understand CRSV against men and boys has sought to understand this violence in terms of its politico-economic value. Contra to analyses that have de-gendered CRSV (Cohen *et al.* 2013; Eriksson Baaz and Stern 2013), this chapter has argued that, in order to address its causes and consequences, we must first look to how gendered violence is both political and productive in the context of armed conflict.

Violence is an instrument by which to contest or enforce power. As a form of political violence, CRSV's utility is determined by the objectives of its perpetrators. It is effective in this regard because of the multiple ways in which it constitutes the masculinity of the perpetrator and feminises the victim and his associated community, while also serving the politico-economic objectives of the perpetrating faction. Its value as an instrument of torture or weapon of war comes from its exploitation of deeply held norms regarding gender identities and gender roles. CRSV against men and boys produces dividends for the perpetrating actors not only in the reinforcement of their own gender identity, but also in terms of reinforcing socio-cultural hierarchies of gender and in terms of material pay-outs.

What makes particular bodies more *valuable* for the transmission of this message of dominance and power is in the function of humiliation that accompanies feminisation. This overtly *gendered* function of CRSV against men and boys was demonstrated in instances both as torture in state detention centres and in the field as a weapon of active combat. Against women and girls, CRSV also subordinates the wider population through the demonstration of their men's inability to fulfil their roles as masculine protectors. However, the transgression of heteronormative taboos to feminise directly the men of the targeted community communicates more emphatically both the superiority of the perpetrator's masculine identity (individually and collectively) and the failings of the victim's (individually and collectively).

Ultimately, this framework highlights the need for more critical analysis of the ways in which gender is a political category that shapes the identities and functions of actors in armed conflict. Instead of seeing CRSV as stemming from a singular cause, or determined by the same underlying normative constructions and motivations in all conflicts,[4] the FPE approach put forward here redirects our attention to structural conditions that shape relations between conflict actors and give meaning and *value* to multiple forms of violence, including sexual violence perpetrated against men and boys. It suggests that any hopes of eradicating this type of violence from future conflicts requires attention to the dividends that are produced from exploiting the abject value of CRSV for the perpetrating group(s).

Notes

1 I do not intend to revisit the considerable debate regarding the extent to which CRSV is strategic, or can be directly and causally linked to the wartime objectives of armed groups perpetrating this violence. For more on how and under what conditions CRSV can be linked to armed group objectives, see Meger (2015, 2016).
2 I am using 'torture' in the sense developed by the UN Convention against Torture:

> any act by which severe pain or suffering, whether physical or mental, is intentionally inflicted on a person for such purposes as obtaining from him, or a third person, information or a confession, punishing him for an act he or a third person has committed, or intimidating or coercing him or a third person, or for any reason based on discrimination of any kind, when such pain or suffering is inflicted by or at the instigation or with the consent or acquiescence of a public official or other person acting in an official capacity.

3 By the above definition, sexual forms of humiliation constitute a form of psychological torture.
4 For more on the development of scholarship and policy narratives of CRSV towards singular causal variables/motivations, see Meger (2016), Chapter 1.

References

Amnesty International. 2011. *Sri Lanka: Briefing to Committee Against Torture*. Report. London: Amnesty International.

Arieff, Alexis. 2010. *Sexual Violence in African Conflicts*. CRS Report for Congress, 30 November. Report No. R40956. Washington, DC: Congressional Research Service.

Asian Human Rights Commission. 2010. *The State of Human Rights in Sri Lanka in 2010*. Report No. AHRC-SPR-010–2010. Hong Kong: Asian Human Rights Commission.

Asian Human Rights Commission. 2011. *Case Studies of Torture Committed by the Police in Sri Lanka 1998–2011*. Report. Hong Kong: Asian Human Rights Commission.

Bastick, Megan, Karen Grimm, and Rahel Kunz. 2007. *Sexual Violence in Armed Conflict: Global Overview and Implications for the Security Sector*. Report. Geneva: Geneva Center for the Democratic Control of Armed Forces.

Carter, Kathleen R. 2010. 'Should International Relations Consider Rape a Weapon of War?'. *Politics & Gender* 6(3): 343–371.

Cohen, Dara K., Amelia H. Green, and Elisabeth J. Wood. 2013. *Wartime Sexual Violence: Misconceptions, Implications and Ways Forward*. United States Institute for Peace Special Report No. 323. Washington, DC.

De Beauvoir, Simone. 1949. *The Second Sex*. Paris: Editions Gallimard.

Del Zotto, Augusta, and Adam Jones. 2002. 'Male-on-Male Sexual Violence in Wartime: Human Rights' Last Taboo?'. Paper presented at the *Annual Convention of the International Studies Association*, New Orleans, LA, March 2002.

Dolan, Chris. 2014. 'Into the Mainstream: Addressing Sexual Violence Against Men and Boys in Conflict. Briefing paper prepared for workshop held at the Overseas Development Institute', London.

Eisenstein, Zillah. 2004. *Against Empire: Feminisms, Racism, and the West*. London: Zed Books.

Enloe, Cynthia. 2000. *Maneuvers: The International Politics of Militarizing Women's Lives*. Berkeley, CA: University of California Press.

Eriksson Baaz, Maria and Maria Stern. 2009. 'Why Do Soldiers Rape? Masculinity, Violence, and Sexuality in the Armed Forces in the Congo (DRC)'. *International Studies Quarterly* 53(2): 495–518.

Eriksson Baaz, Maria and Maria Stern. 2013. *Sexual Violence as a Weapon of War? Perceptions, Prescriptions, Problems in the Congo and Beyond*. London: Zed Books.

Farr, Kathryn. 2009. 'Extreme War Rape in Todays Civil War-Torn States: A Contextual and Comparative Analysis'. *Gender Issues* 26(1): 1–41.

Fattah, Khaled and K.M. Fierke. 2009. 'A Clash of Emotions: The Politics of Humiliation and Political Violence in the Middle East'. *European Journal of International Relations* 15(1): 67–93.

Franks, Mary Anne 2014. 'How to Feel Like a Woman, or Why Punishment is a Drag'. *UCLA Law Review* 61(3): 566–605.

Giacaman, Rita, N.M.E. Abu-Rmeileh, A. Husseini, H. Saab, and W. Boyce. 2007. 'Humiliation: The Invisible Trauma of War for Palestinian Youth'. *Public Health* 121(8): 563–571.

Gingerich, Tara and Jennifer Leaning. 2004. *The Use of Rape as a Weapon of War in Darfur, Sudan*. Paper prepared for the US Agency for International Development, Program on Humanitarian Crises and Human Rights, Harvard School of Public Health. Boston, MA.

Hansen, Lene. 2001. 'Gender, Nation, Rape: Bosnia and the Construction of Security'. *International Feminist Journal of Politics* 3(1): 55–75.

Hardt, Michael and Antonio Negri. 2004. *Multitude: War and Democracy in the Age of Empire*. New York: Penguin.

Heise, Lori L. 1998. 'Violence Against Women: An Integrated, Ecological Framework'. *Violence Against Women* 4(3): 262–290.

Human Rights Watch. 2003. *'We'll Kill You If You Cry': Sexual Violence in the Sierra Leone Conflict*. Report. New York.

Human Rights Watch. 2013. *'We Will Teach You a Lesson': Sexual Violence Against Tamils by Sri Lankan Security Forces*. Report. New York.

Human Security Report Project. 2012. *Human Security Report 2012: Sexual Violence, Education and War: Beyond the Mainstream Narrative*. Report. Simon Fraser University, Vancouver, BC.

IRIN News. 2005. 'Unending Misery of Rape Victims', 19 August. Accessed 5 October 2017. www.irinnews.org/feature/2005/08/19/unending-misery-rape-victims.

Jackson, Stevi and Sue Scott. 1996. 'Introduction'. In S. Jackson and S. Scott (eds), *Feminism and Sexuality: A Reader*. New York: Columbia University Press, 1–34.

Johnson, K., J. Scott, B. Rughita, M. Kisielewski, J. Asher, R. Ong, and L. Lawry. 2010. 'Association of Sexual Violence and Human Rights Violations with Physical and Mental Health in Territories of the Eastern Democratic Republic of Congo'. *JAMA: The Journal of the American Medical Association* 304(5): 553–562.

Leatherman, Janie L. 2011. *Sexual Violence and Armed Conflict*. Cambridge: Polity Press.

Leiby, Michele L. 2009. 'Wartime Sexual Violence in Guatemala and Peru'. *International Studies Quarterly* 53(2): 445–468.

Lindner, Evelin G. 2004. 'Gendercide and Humiliation in Honor and Human-Rights Societies'. In Adam Jones (ed.), *Gendercide and Genocide*. Nashville, TN: Vanderbilt University Press, 39–61.

Lindner, Evelin G. 2006. *Making Enemies: Humiliation and International Conflict*. Westport, CT: Praeger Security International.

Mackenzie, Megan. 2010. 'Securitizing Sex?'. *International Feminist Journal of Politics* 12(2), 202–221.

Mackinnon, Catherine A. 1989. 'Sexuality, Pornography, and Method: "Pleasure under Patriarchy"'. *Source: Ethics* 99(2): 314–346.

Meger, Sara. 2011. 'The Role of Globalization in Wartime Sexual Violence'. *African Conflict and Peacebuilding Review* 1(1): 100–132.

Meger, Sara. 2015. 'Toward a Feminist Political Economy of Wartime Sexual Violence: The Case of the Democratic Republic of Congo'. *International Feminist Journal of Politics* 17(3): 416–434.

Meger, Sara. 2016. *Rape Loot Pillage: The Political Economy of Sexual Violence in Armed Conflict*. New York: Oxford University Press.

Millett, Kate. 1970. *Sexual Politics*. New York: Doubleday.

Misra, Amalendu. 2015. *The Landscape of Silence*. London: Hurst & Co.

Moschetti, Carole O. 2005. *Conjugal Wrongs Don't Make Rights*. PhD Dissertation, School of Social and Political Sciences, University of Melbourne. Melbourne, Australia.

Peel, Michael. 2004. *Rape as a Method of Torture*. Report. Medical Foundation for the Care of Victims of Torture. London.

Peterson, V. Spike. 2010. 'Gendered Identities, Ideologies, and Practices in the Context of War and Militarism'. In L. Sjoberg and S. Via (eds), *Gender, War and Militarism: Feminist Perspectives*. Santa Barbara, CA: Praeger, 17–29.

Pinker, Steven. 1998. *How the Mind Works*. London: Penguin.

Public Interest Advocacy Centre. 2014. *Island of Impunity?: Investigation into International Crimes in the Final Stages of the Sri Lankan Civil War*. Report. Sydney, Australia.

Refugee Law Project. 2009. *Gender Against Men*. Report. Kampala: Refugee Law Project.

Russell, Wynne. 2008. 'Sexual Violence Against Men and Boys'. *Forced Migration Review* 27: 22–23.

Saurette, Paul. 2005. *The Kantian Imperative: Humiliation, Common Sense, Politics*. Toronto: University of Toronto Press.

Saurette, Paul. 2007. 'You Dissin Me?: Humiliation and Post 9/11 Global Politics'. Paper presented at the *Congrès de l'Association Française de Science Politique*. Toulouse, France.

Save the Children. 2012. *Hidden Survivors: Sexual Violence Against Children in Conflict*. Report. London: Save the Children.

Sivakumaran, Sandesh. 2007. 'Sexual Violence Against Men in Armed Conflict'. *European Journal of International Law* 18(2): 253–276.

Sjoberg, Laura. 2016. *Women as Wartime Rapists*. New York: New York University Press.

Solangon, Sarah and Preeti Patel. 2012. 'Sexual Violence Against Men in Countries Affected by Armed Conflict'. *Conflict, Security & Development* 12(3): 417–442.

Sooka, Yasmin. 2014. *An Unfinished War: Torture and Sexual Violence in Sri Lanka, 2009–2014*. Report. Sri Lanka: The Bar Human Rights Committee of England and Wales and the International Truth & Justice Project.

Storr, Will. 2011. 'The Rape of Men: The Darkest Secret of War'. *Guardian*, 17 July. Accessed 5 October 2017. www.theguardian.com/society/2011/jul/17/the-rape-of-men.

The Taguba Report. n.d. Article 15–6 Investigation of the 800th Military Police Brigade. Accessed 28 October 2014. www.npr.org/iraq/2004/prison_abuse_report.pdf.

Turcotte, Heather M. 2011. 'Contextualizing Petro-Sexual Politics'. *Alternatives: Global, Local, Political* 36(3): 200–220.

UN Committee Against Torture. 2011. *Concluding Observations of the Committee against Torture: Sri Lanka*. Report. New York: UN Committee Against Torture.

UN News. 2012. 'Eradicating Sexual Violence in Conflict Not 'A Mission Impossible' – UN Senior Official'. *UN News Centre*, 18 October. Accessed 5 October 2017. www.un.org/apps/news/story.asp?NewsID=43325&Cr=sexual%2Bviolence&Cr1#.UcEg-DOt6v3I.

Waldby, Catherine. 1995. 'Destruction: Boundary Erotics and Refigurations of the Heterosexual Male Body'. In E. Grosz and E. Probyn (eds), *Sexy Bodies: The Strange Carnalities of Feminism*. New York: Routledge, 266–277.

Wood, Elizabeth J. 2009. 'Armed Groups and Sexual Violence: When is Wartime Rape Rare?'. *Politics & Society* 37(1): 131–163.

Reflections

Reflections on sexual violence against men and boys in global politics[1]

Paul Higate and Nivi Manchanda

N: At the outset, it should be stated how much we welcome the attention to men who are subject to repeated and enduring sexual violence. This volume combines, in surprising and often contradictory ways, the familiar and the new. So, although the contributions deal with a problematique that has been relatively unexplored in the field of International Relations (IR) broadly conceived, they are also evocative and reminiscent of a familiar emotional and intellectual terrain – an asymmetrical, hierarchical, and deeply gendered world in which injustice is rife and oppression almost banal.

P: Absolutely. I concur. The intellectual terrain upon which critical scholars of gender operate (and for you Nivi, race) is growing rapidly. A constellation of wider social and cultural forces around gender fluidity and non-binary positionalities in both lived experience and academic discourse are making possible what feels like a radical opening up of how we think about sex, gender, and sexuality in current times. While the volume makes some vital interventions, it is fair to say that academics focused on sexual violence – and not just against men and boys – are generally behind the curve in regard to a (violent) empirical reality that has remained marginal for far too long.

N: Agreed, but let's start by thinking about what we bring to the texts as academics with different kinds of privilege. What about our own 'lenses'? You know, some of which are bestowed upon us or imposed externally (brown/ privileged woman in my case), and others (perhaps intuitively internalised and more private or personal) might be worth reflecting on.... What is the nature of our engagement with these contributions? How are we reading the violence? How far do responses to these two questions shape what it is acceptable/appropriate for us to say according to the political positionalities we occupy within the academy?

P: We could justify our reflection on lenses in the name of transparency and accountability as one way to draw attention to how we are embedded in different systems of power. I could say: 'I am a privileged white man and as such, must exercise humility in my interventions.' But actually, the first thing that strikes me concerns my/our status/role/subjectivity as an 'academic'. What would happen if we got 'non-academics' (a constituency that

I've heard one academic colleague refer to in rather patronising terms as 'civilians') to reflect on these chapters?

N: I'm guessing some outside of the academy (including a number of the authors in the volume), would probably say 'this is horrible. This is a problem! What is being done about it? How can we get involved and change stuff?' Meanwhile (us) academics get bogged down in the politics of the project in ways that divert both material and intellectual resources from – ultimately – the very real suffering of those subject to brutal and degrading violence. Indeed, my own scepticism of problem-solving approaches presents a real barrier to significant social transformation, even though radical change in both theory and praxis is precisely what we seek. I suppose our biggest contribution 'as academics', if you indulge me in this reification, in this respect is pedagogical – discussing violence (both epistemic and physical) in the classroom and outside are absolutely essential.

P: Yes. But there are both opportunities and constraints in thinking outside of the academy. Speculation I know, but opportunity because wider audiences outside of the so-called 'ivory tower' may be somewhat less interested or invested in the traditions, politics, and divisions of labour with which we are both encumbered and enlightened. It's an altogether less fraught process (maybe) for those outside the academy to implement and effect successful policy intervention. Having said that, masculinity is imbued with a universality that means questions of pride, shame, and masculinity's precarity mean that similarly – sexual violence against men – is also regarded more widely as a taboo topic and struck with policy marginality and thus stasis.

N: Though clearly important, let's not get diverted by policy change from which it is only a short step to institutional demands for the demonstrable 'impact' of our scholarship. What about change? We've already touched on the evolution of the sex/sexuality/gender/identity field … it strikes me that it is the way that change is conventionally framed and enacted that stands as a key hurdle to thinking beyond our current lexicons of sex and gender.

P: So what kind of (re)invigorated intellectual project are you advocating?

N: The concern here is that we have been largely unable to escape a sense of linear, incremental change that is – if I may be so provocative – driven largely by a (neo)liberal reformist agenda. First, sexual violence against women and girls is placed on the agenda. Next we identify men and boys as victims. This is rapidly followed by those who self identify as, or who are labelled queer and, lest we forget 'intersectionality' (a watered down understanding that forsakes systems of oppression for a focus on identity, often flattening structural prejudices and doing grave injustice to the original conception of intersectionality).... So, as categories burgeon and become increasingly complex and nuanced, we start adding brown and black women and perhaps, those identified as differently – abled. Guided by an impulse to taxonomise and in the name of inclusivity, we bring more people (we deem palatable) into our remit of social justice. Worthy and important, no doubt. But we (Western, privileged subjects) continue to bear, even embrace the mantle of 'saving', never really breaking from the lineages of inequality, 'rationality' and teleological progress that we have inherited. We might start not by devising a new lexicon to capture existing asymmetries of power, but rather by looking to other traditions, or alternate ontologies that do not have hierarchy inscribed in their very fabric. Without wishing to romanticise a pristine 'indigenous' existence, we might turn to other socio-political constellations and lifeways that do not conceive of gender in binaries, or have the same racialised logics girding all social interaction. There's some very interesting work being done by decolonial scholars in this vein and we have a growing archive (aural, visual, and written) that we can tap into in a manner that meaningfully evacuates hierarchy, asymmetry, and difference, at least as starting points and in the way that we currently conceive them, from our vocabulary when dealing with violence and not just as a way to pay lip service to 'diversity'.

P: The argument for transcending binaries is not new of course, and the current volume calls at certain junctures for exactly such a move. Since it begs rather more questions than it answers, a less ambitious – perhaps interim stage – might be to train our efforts on institutions rather than individual perpetrators and 'victims/survivors'. The (potential) prurience engendered by sexual violence against all actors has a tendency to pathologise both victim and perpetrator. This volume avoids this pathologisation deftly, and engages with sexual violence against men in a nuanced and eloquent way, all the while reminding us that the resounding reverberations of patriarchy structure the everyday not just of women, but also of men in insidious and deeply violent ways.

Note

1 The following is a result of a conversation between Paul and Nivi over a number of days at Queen Mary University and the University of Bath.

Homo interruptus

Paul Kirby

A few years ago, I travelled to Seoul, South Korea for a conference exploring wartime sexual violence and its many legacies. I had been asked to speak on UK government policy, and I emphasised the uncommon attention given by the then-Foreign Secretary William Hague to male survivors of rape and sexual violence. Since we had been convened partly to inform South Korean activists and civil servants of diverse national approaches to the Women, Peace, and Security agenda, my presentation was heavily descriptive, verging on the anodyne. My discussant took it otherwise, and challenged me forcefully on the status of male survivors. Wasn't it wrong to conflate their experiences with those of women, especially as it was obvious that sexual violence happened less often to men, and in any case wasn't nearly as serious, being comprised principally of lewd talk and adolescent hazing rituals? The idea that derogatory language used in basic training might belong in the same category as kidnapping, rape, coerced prostitution, and forced abortion was offensive, absurd, even dangerous. I countered that there were indeed grievous harms inflicted on men in conflict deserving of the term 'sexual violence', but that I had not been arguing any general comparative point. The exchange, though fleeting, precipitated an intense self-consciousness. I had been identified as a representative of the masculine condition, as if petitioning for relief on behalf of my kind. The role implied something oppositional: emphasising the victimhood of men and boys necessarily diminished the recognition of women and girls. Had I been expected to ventriloquise the perspective of a raped man? Was it anticipated (in some ways, *hoped*) that I would be a survivor myself?

The figure of the male victim disorients, obstructs, and interrupts.

Discussion of sexual violence against men is now welcomed in some quarters, not just for its contribution to a more representative map, but also because it helps dispel the notion of women's innate vulnerability. For others, the addendum of 'and men' portends a weakening of feminism by false equivalence. Wariness of the male victim-survivor is not without reason, as his existence can become the justification for diluting a decades-long stream of consciousness-raising and critical scholarship. And yet adjustments to feminist categories (e.g. Mesok on patriarchy, Ch. 3 in this volume) may also *renew* the case for a feminist analytic. Under these conditions, diverse explorations of gender violence are all too easily over-determined as partisan ammunition, even as they do not correspond neatly to positions 'for' or 'against' a settled and singular feminism (see Dolan 2014; on feminist narratives, see Hemmings 2011). The partisanship is not easily jettisoned, since claims about gender violence are suffused with politics at multiple depths. The tethering of injury to womanhood (Zalewski, Ch. 1 in this volume) has had its strategic uses as well as its feminist critics; the new-found recognition of men and boys will likewise generate disputes and discontents.

The political disorientation occasioned by the male survivor is paralleled by other ambiguities. As the opening chapters of this volume make clear, there is something evasive about men's wartime sexual trauma. While the penis and testicles are acknowledged as obvious and central referents for sexual violence against men, the character of the male wound – the inter-subjective and gendered connotation of a physical harm – both exceeds and undermines phallocentrism. The reduction of male experience to anxiety over the penis, or of masculine privilege to the symbolic authority of the phallus, is deeply inadequate. Maleness, no less than femaleness, is an amalgam of practices and performance, stereotype and demeanour, signal and noise. At one moment a commonsensical designation, at another the 'maleness' of an injury, its connection to a specifically *male* body, proves harder to specify. This is so even for the most basic conceptual link – between violence done to the reproductive organs or anus and the experience of emasculation.[1] The penis may plausibly be described as the most treasured body-object of masculine subjectivity, but it is also the least involved in practical masculine displays. The public performance of masculinity assumes a phallic presence, but inadequate masculinity is established primarily through judgements of utterance, posture, weaponry, costume, ethnicity, wealth, heritage, and fraternity. US military surgeons report that injured soldiers' first concern is the integrity of their genitals (Grady 2015). The concern is evidence of sexualisation (Hendershot, Ch. 2 in this volume). But the genitals may be understood as a consistent anchor (one anchor among others) for gendered personhood *in excess* of their sexual meaning: as a synecdoche for ideals of fatherhood (e.g. Kime 2014), a sense of manly citizenship, and able-bodied competence in such quotidian tasks as urination.

Bodily injury takes on meaning only in the context of a bodily imaginary: a series of ideas about what constitutes the limit of the self and its location within overlapping communities. On the evidence of these chapters, violence does not become sexual by virtue of genital or anal trauma alone. Rather, the sexual symbolism of an act of violence is secured by institutional, cultural, and psychological grids (wounded attachments for Zalewski; iterative sexualising for Hendershot; military masculinity for Mesok; 'languages of castration' for Myrttinen; and biomedical discourse for Cottet). The intelligibility of violence against men as inflicted for gendered motives, or enabled by a gendered vulnerability, is in turn produced by a coalition of medical experts, war biographers, gender studies academics, artists, propagandists, and in the everyday reparative work carried out by survivors and their supporters. One objective of academic labour is to make violent events recognisable and comparable by revisiting past atrocity in light of contemporary typologies. Definitions work to bind knowledge, demarcating kinds of violence even as violence relentlessly subverts stable meaning (famously Scarry 1985; cf. Cottet, Ch. 5 in this volume). Definitions do necessary conceptual work, but cannot salvage the inner life of gender violences past. Cases defined as torture in Peru (Leiby, Ch. 7 in this volume) may have involved feelings of emasculation and gendered humiliation on the part of male victims at the time, regardless of whether human rights groups coded them as 'sexual' or not, and without requiring that they now be coded as *really* sexual in nature. The indistinctness of the experience itself generates the desire to know.

Whether an injury to the penis or anus is sexual; whether the penis is indispensable to male sexuality; whether assaults on other body parts may be received as emasculating absent an attack on sexed organs; whether *any* bodily injury risks emasculation for the male soldier or conversely conveys hero status: such questions indicate the mobility of sexual meaning over the surface and interior of the body, and invite reflection on the associations between the vulnerable, the erotic, and the intimate in giving gender violence its force (see Butler 1993: 57–120). The shift in analytical focus from the generic male body towards intra-corporeal networks (the urinary tract, the endocrine system, brain matter) encourages a diversity of research strategies among the grids and sites where gender-sense emerges. One consequence is a drastic expansion in the set of injuries that may be considered gendered (for the purposes of this book, disproportionately affecting male and stereotypically masculine subjects). For example, traumatic brain injuries sustained in war can lead to 'sexual dysfunction' (Zeitzer and Brooks 2008: 350), and evidence points to a high prevalence of 'sexual problems' among veterans coping with post-traumatic stress disorder (reported by 63 per cent of respondents in one study – Badour, Gros, Szafranski, and Acierno 2015). Another consequence is fresh attentiveness to institutional fixes for the vulnerabilities of war-fighting, some of which would otherwise seem only distantly related to sexual violence (e.g. on armour, see MacLeish 2012).

The de-coupling of corporeal zones from a fixed binary designation (a choice between the male and female victim, or between men and boys) produces a broad field for critical inquiry. Yet the move away from the genital scene of sexual violence also risks a detachment that finds in empirical diversity an analytical weightlessness, as if libidinal significance may alight, randomly, on any conceivable part of the body. The danger may be navigated by means of relentless historicisation: the outlining of distinctive constellations of folk sexuality, bodily sense, and war/truth (see McSorley 2012; Barkawi and Brighton 2011), a recommendation more easily given than acted upon. The interruption occasioned by the male figure provokes a reconstitution of gender analysis bearing both peril and promise. There will be delight at what is imperiled, and anxiety over what is promised. In the fog lie new ways of knowing masculinity and war.

Note

1 There is insufficient space here to explore the differing meaning of violence against the penis as against forcible penetration of the anus. See Zalewski and Myrttinen, Ch. 1 and Ch. 4 in this volume, for prompts on the role played by heteronormativity (that is, the assumption of an underlying heterosexual formula for intercourse) in conceptualisations of sexual violence against men.

Bibliography

Badour, Christal L., Daniel F. Gros, Derek D. Szafranski, and Ron Acierno. 2015. 'Problems in Sexual Functioning Among Male OEF/OIF Veterans Seeking Treatment for Posttraumatic Stress'. *Comparative Psychiatry* 58: 74–81.

Barkawi, Tarak and Shane Brighton. 2011. 'Powers of War: Fighting, Knowledge, and Critique'. *International Political Sociology* 5(2): 126–143.

Butler, Judith. 1993. *Bodies That Matter: On the Discursive Limits of 'Sex'*. London: Routledge.

Dolan, Chris. 2014. 'Has Patriarchy been Stealing the Feminists' Clothes?: Conflict-Related Sexual Violence and UN Security Council Resolutions'. *IDS Bulletin* 45(1): 80–84.

Grady, Denise. 2015. 'Penis Transplants Being Planned to Help Wounded Troops'. *New York Times*. 6 December. Accessed 5 September 2017. www.nytimes.com/2015/12/07/health/penis-transplants-being-planned-to-heal-troops-hidden-wounds.html?mcubz=0.

Hemmings, Clare. 2011. *Why Stories Matter: The Political Grammar of Feminist Theory*. Durham, NC: Duke University Press.

Kime, Patricia. 2014. 'Wounded Troops Battle Obstacles to Sex and Intimacy'. *Military Times*. 29 December. Accessed 5 September 2017. www.militarytimes.com/news/your-military/2014/12/29/wounded-troops-battle-obstacles-to-sex-and-intimacy/.

McSorley, Kevin. 2012. 'Helmetcams, Militarized Sensation and "Somatic War"'. *Journal of War and Culture Studies* 5(1): 47–58.

MacLeish, Kenneth T. 2012. 'Armor and Anesthesia: Exposure, Feeling, and the Soldier's Body'. *Medical Anthropology Quarterly* 26(1): 49–68.

Scarry, Elaine. 1985. *The Body in Pain: The Making and Unmaking of the World*. Oxford: Oxford University Press.

Zeitzer, Mindy B. and J. Margo Brooks. 2008. 'In the Line of Fire: Traumatic Brain Injury Among Iraq War Veterans'. *Workplace Health and Safety* 56(8): 347–353.

Can our intellectual curiosity on gender cause harm?

Madeleine Rees

Tough! An unpleasant read for a Sunday, disturbing content, disturbing ideas, and above all: horrific. It is impossible to read what men will do to other men, (and to women too – but that was not, ostensibly, the topic of these papers) and not despair. In broad terms, I understand that this is the point of these essays … to understand causes, to better understand how to respond, and to place sexual violence against men in a broader context. If that was it, why do I feel so uncomfortable?

Part of that discomfort is that I am not sure we are right. Not to criticise the authors on their specific approaches and explanations, but I am growing in my concerns that through our intellectual curiosity, by looking at an issue from the perspective of our particular discipline, we may elevate issues, contextualise and explain in ways that have no resonance with what actually is happening to people in situations of extreme violence; if the terms we use can actually create harm where there might not have been.

To explain: I breathed a silent thank you to Heath and his demand, 'just make sure you explain it should never be a gendered thing' (Mesok, Ch. 3 in this volume), not because of what he actually said, but the intent behind it, or what I interpreted the intent to be. Don't make a comparison, take each violation for what it is. Why do we revert to the old default position of comparing men with women on this issue when self-evidently, each act of sexual violence is singular. No one experiences it in exactly the same way, interprets it the same way, and no one I have met who has endured such violence seeks to compare their own experience with any one else's as if to claim a hierarchy of horror. Yet external observers do, seeking to find within a comparator, a gendered understanding of cause, effect and hence the possible clue to ending it. It is not possible to find an equal harm for the castration of a male with a form of sexual violence to a woman and why should we? In the old days of sex discrimination, we had to compare the pregnant woman with a sick male in order to claim discrimination. It was ridiculous then and we should refuse it now. Inter alia this means making our understanding of Gender inclusive and yet specific, of looking at stigma and how we create it, at law and how the teleological approach has been both good and bad in reflecting our understandings of sexual violence, militarism, and of even greater importance: Looking at the crime itself and what we must do to understand, treat, respond – and just get it stopped!

The Nobel laureate, Leymah Gbowee is a practical, brilliant woman. At the 2014 Global Summit to End Sexual Violence, she told the assembled multitudes that they should not for one minute think they can stop sexual violence in armed conflict. The only way to stop sexual violence in conflict was to stop conflict. She is right. Unpacking it reads simply: ultimately we have militaries to fight wars, wars replace dialogue, dialogue ends early when you have a strong military that will assert your claims. Militarism is a way of thought, which needs and feeds off a masculinity prepared to do violence. It is not born but needs to be created and our societies do a pretty good job, but not as good as the 'controlled' violence taught in the military but re-enforced by the informal violence condoned so as to create a fighting male. Heath's torture was the product of that. Told to 'become a man' by taking it, or standing up to it. By taking it, he becomes stronger. The stigma he suffered was of a particular kind particularly potent in the military or prison environments.

If it should 'never be a gendered thing' then how do we explain gender so that it is relevant to the context without it overriding the actual experience of the abused? Social constructs, such as gender, are important as they do shape what we think and how we respond. Which is exactly why I think that our interventions must first and foremost ensure we do no harm. I am concerned that we are looking for sexual violence in armed conflict everywhere and describing it in ways that might not be reflective of the actual experience of the victim. Is it true that every time a man is beaten on his genitals it's sexual? Does it make a difference to him, the one who experiences it? If it is seen as torture, which it clearly is, why do we worry that it's sexual – which might then have a different impact on him, if his cultural milieu is not supportive? If he is penetrated then it's sexual violence, but most often, for men, it will be prosecuted as torture. Good, it should be. As a matter of law, we have no need for intimate descriptions of mechanical acts of 'invasion'.

This also shows how important it is to get our terminology right. Law follows a teleological approach, that is, it is shaped by social and scientific progress and thought. We need to ensure that we have law describe the lived experience of those who resort to its protection and redress; to mis-describe an act of torture as sexual violence because it involves abuse of particular body parts is to expose the victim to the next area of concern: stigma. Have we elevated sexual violence, creating stigma through our interventions? In Bosnia, I fear that we have, if not creating stigma then exacerbating it, as in a recent UN expert report that sought stigma in other complaints, misinterpreting ordinary acts – such as the refusal of a welfare benefit, ethnic, or language discrimination – as evidence of stigma when the cause is a discrimination totally unrelated to the existence of sexual violence. Note too that for the individual, and I have met many survivors, it is not always the sexual violence that is the issue (there are worse things that happen, horrific to say), but we do a disservice to their experience by our overzealous scrutiny. If we were to look into the possible stigma faced by men, then in actively seeking ways to address it, would we be creating it? I am not convinced that society in rem does stigmatise men who have suffered such violence, not least because it has, on the whole, been accurately categorised as torture.

If it is not a 'gendered thing' then what should our response be to the sexual violence experienced by men? Back to Heath. He wanted it to stop. He had a legitimate expectation that the Navy would protect him from his tormentors. They did not, and his incredulity that they would neglect him as they did was part of his torment – the rescue never came, the betrayal was complete. The men who did that to him should obviously have been prosecuted and punished, thus, sending the message to all that: if you commit crimes, no matter how you dress it up as initiation, hazing or whatever, it's a crime and is punishable. Strict enforcement, leadership. Job done! Why is it not dealt with that way? Can we change the military? I have good reason to doubt it.

Prosecution of perpetrators, adequate and appropriate health care, redress and reparation, guarantees of non-repetition. All are there in the principles underpinning transitional justice and are based on human rights. To understand human rights is to understand empathy; put yourself in the situation of the person who has suffered harm, and then think what you would need to recover. It's not hard. The hard part is that remedies are rarely freely given, and in the case of male sexual violence victims, not anticipated. That too must change and it must change in rem. Unless and until we really listen to the people who undergo the horrors of extreme violence, understand the fears, the needs, and translate those into appropriate rights driven responses, then I fear we will not get to the root of what Heath meant.

Gender, sex, and sexual violence against men

Laura J. Shepherd

I have an ambivalent relationship with writing about sexual violence. I understand the importance of witnessing, of being present for those who want – or need – to share their stories. I appreciate the desire to theorise carefully around the violations of bodies, to ensure we have conceptual tools adequate for the thinking work that we require of them and that our frameworks are not reproducing or perpetuating violence and exclusion. Intellectually, I recognise the value of these endeavours. But I find it hard to *feel* this value sometimes. I find it hard to feel anything beyond horrified and heartsick reading accounts of devastating trauma and abuse, though I also find it hard to reconcile this feeling with the knowledge that I have the privilege to turn the page, to turn away from these accounts, and to engage in other things, while the survivors whose stories are documented in these accounts have no such options. They have to sit with their experiences, to try to make some sense of them somehow, and so I in turn feel that perhaps I should sit with the discomfort as well, not out of some naïve sense of solidarity but because sometimes discomfort can be productive, even as it upsets and unsettles.

I cannot imagine that the authors of these chapters escaped such feelings of upset and unease. Their accounts and analyses are so thoughtful that they cannot but have been moved by the tales they recount, whether of combat trauma or ritualised abuse; this is evident in their efforts to derive meaning from the experience they document. Beyond, or perhaps in parallel to, the affective dimensions of these chapters, however, there is an analytical coherence that draws together this collection around what I identify as three key themes. These themes, and their exploration in these chapters, offer a productive utility surplus to witnessing, a form of engagement that feels – to me at least – significant.

The themes I identify are the institutional politics of sexual violence against men, the idea of wholeness, and the imbrication of violence in the maintenance of gender order. I will address each briefly in turn. In different ways, the chapters all speak to the institutionalisation of violation in certain contexts. As I read through this collection, I was reminded of feminist work on the violence of institutions: institutions as varied as the military, the church, and prisons. These institutions frequently rely on, and in some cases tacitly condone, sexualised violence both against men and perpetrated by men. Various studies, both academic and journalistic, have illuminated the extent to which sexualised violence in prisons, churches, and the military is endemic and often unchecked. The bodies of men and boys are, in these institutional contexts, broken down in service of the institution's need for order and hierarchy.

The brokenness of bodies subjected to sexual violence also brings to mind wholeness, which I identify as another theme. The analysis of sexual violence requires that due consideration be given to the question of bodily integrity, and the work that the assumption of, or desire for, integrity does in our cognitive architecture. There is a clear framework of normativity around discussions of gender/sex and sexual violence. These discussions hinge on the question of a body's *ought-ness*: a male body *ought to be* (sexually) desirable, (sexually) potent, (sexually) whole. And violence is violation: it ruptures not only the ought-ness ascribed to male bodies but also the figurative wholeness of the body. Hendershot's discussion of the disruption of the literal wholeness of the male body through urotrauma sustained in combat is an example *par excellence* of the centrality of integrity and wholeness in our thinking about bodies.

Stowing away in prevalent discourse on sexual violence against men then is perhaps a kind of ableism, an assumption that sexual violence happens to whole bodies to fracture or rent their wholeness and produce a fragmented body in place of the whole. But there are ways and ways of making un-whole: through adding something in (penetration) or taking something away (castration or rendering impotent). Violence can take the form of forced excess, or diminution, and we need to think through carefully what the different effects and affects might be of these violations.

So the final theme to which I turn is the question of gender order. One classic study of sexual violence against men articulates this ordering function most directly:

> Male rape victims often feel stigmatised as female or homosexual, whatever their sexual orientation. This was a major reason why men [in the study] did not report the offences to the police. When asked why he didn't tell the police, one man replied 'Only women are raped'.
>
> (Lees 1997: 95)

The fixity of the attachment between rape and the female body is a critical element, then of the way that bodies matter, as Butler (1993) would have it. Violence is a site at which gender is produced. The act of violence, its experience, a person's reaction to it, and the materiality of the body that survives are all related in, to, and through societal gender orders. Not only, then, is violence part of the (re)production of gender, but gender is inescapably a lens through which (our understanding of) violence is produced.

We 'read' violence – interpret its horror, make sense of it, insofar as sense can be made – through the prism of the ideas and ideals we hold about gender, which inform our cognitive architecture either consciously or otherwise. But perhaps it is a form of violence in itself to uphold, to adhere to, rigid constructions of gender norms (those ideas and ideals that I mentioned) that make 'sexual violence against men' an exceptional field of research, delineated against its binary other(s) to better serve our documentation and analysis of such violations. Perhaps we can capture with sufficient precision the dimensions that we desire to capture in our research on 'sexual violence against men' through the analysis of the violent ordering of gendered bodies, the violent reproduction of gender. But perhaps we cannot. Its framing and naming notwithstanding, each of these contributions prompts careful deliberation of the ways in which that which is so frequently taken for granted – the gendering of the body – is in fact violently enforced.

References

Butler, Judith. 1993. *Bodies that Matter: On the Discursive Limits of 'Sex'*. New York, London: Routledge.

Lees, Sue. 1997. *Ruling Passions: Sexual Violence, Reputation and the Law*. Buckingham: Open University Press.

Not for the faint of heart

Reflections on rape, gender, and conflict

Lara Stemple

Sexual violence against men and boys in armed conflict is not a topic for the faint of heart. For this and a myriad of other, more significant reasons laid out in the previous chapters, the subject has been woefully neglected. Clearly, that is now changing. From the vantage point of someone who has worked on sexual violence against men (and on gender issues generally) for many years, it's heartening, to say the least.

As Elizabeth Mesok points out, in the US military alone, sexual violence against men has received more attention in the last few years than in the institution's previous two-and-a-half centuries. Other chapters in this section find pieces of notable progress elsewhere in the world.

Yet a global hesitancy remains, and the authors determinedly bring a wide range of these hesitancies fully to light. We *know* that men have been violently sexually victimised during war, throughout time and across the planet. So, Marysia Zalewski rhetorically asks, why not simply include them alongside women, our collective victims of choice? Simply 'add men and stir' (Drumond 2017; Zalewski, Ch. 1 in this volume). Not so fast, it seems.

The sexual victimisation of men and boys (broadly defined in these chapters) is rife with complexity. Take the motives of its perpetrators. Henri Myrttinen looks at one particular form, violence towards men's genitals, and describes the varied messages and motives behind it: to destroy reproductive capacity, to impugn the masculinity of victims and groups, to intimidate and dominate populations, to take revenge, and so on.

Once victimised, men suffering from a range of sexualised harms are then poorly served by ill-equipped medical personnel who don't know what to look for or what to ask. Caroline Cottet pointedly contrasts this to reports from women in conflict zones who are relentlessly and invasively questioned about rape experiences, so as to amass data sufficient to justify additional funding.

Mesok explores how victimised men reconcile their experiences with 'military masculinity'. Perhaps the parameters of manliness can conveniently shift: warriors show strength by seeking help. And yet more than a third of victimised American servicemen describe their sexual assault as 'hazing', ensuring a distressingly tidy fit within military culture.

The chapters also touch on data-related issues, using numbers to tell part of the story. For instance, Chris Hendershot notes that nearly 1,400 American service men suffered wounds to the genitals in the wars in Iraq and Afghanistan (usually from IEDs), and at least several hundred locals also endured battle-induced urotrauma. And what to make of his 'unsettling realisation' that the US Department of Defense dispenses $25,000 per injured testicle and $50,000 per injured penis to injured American servicemen?

Setting aside official tallies of injuries by explosives (Hendershot explores sexual discourses around them) and turning to sexual violence by humans, we enter a world of numeric uncertainty. Zalewski describes an 'atmosphere of incredulity' regarding claims that victimisation rates among women and men are much less divergent than assumed. Indeed UN, NGO, and 'common sense' claims that women are vastly disproportionate victims persist, despite few researchers having included women and men together in empirical studies of conflict-related sexual violence (the few to have done so reveal a high prevalence among both women and men). Within the US military, more men than women report sexual victimisation, and there are many more serious assaults among men (Mesok, Ch. 3 in this volume).

Unfortunately, research methods generally remain limited. Cottet cites one study that, unbelievably, considered an act 'rape' only when perpetrated by the opposite sex, and she notes that, elsewhere, assumptions that male victimisation is comprised mainly of anal rape limit the scope of understanding. In reality, as these chapters detail, the forms of victimisation perpetrated in conflict seem limited only by cruel imaginings. Yet we know very little about non-penetrative sexual violence, as Myrttinen points out. What is the deeper significance of these harms for victims and perpetrators? How do they relate to gender and sexuality – and what of female perpetrators (increasingly but inadequately studied) and sexual minorities (still nearly wholly neglected in the field)? When is it rape? When is it torture? In short, the chapters ask, what ought to be the boundaries of this harm, so as to be both accurate and just?

We will, because we must, move toward approaches to sexual violence that are both gender inclusive *and* gender sensitive. By this I mean that a range of global actors will eventually come to acknowledge the necessity of including all victims and perpetrators of sexual violence, regardless of sex. And because of the gendered nature of sexual victimisation and the different ways men and women experience abuse, we must also remain gender sensitive, keeping a deep understanding of gender at the fore.

One of the most remarkable things about this collection of essays is the rich, layered thinking devoted to a topic typically treated as an afterthought. In fact, the section grapples with what Zalewski calls the 'complexities shrouded in simplicity'. She goes on to note that the 'hyper-celebrity fuelled attention' that sexual violence against women now receives is indebted to the herculean efforts of feminist scholars and activists who worked for decades to bring attention to it.

In this regard, I believe the collection of chapters in this section will do its part to advance work on sexual violence against men and boys. Here at UCLA

Law, the All Survivors Project aims to do likewise. These efforts are part of the tide's inevitable turning.

But will it turn quickly enough? These chapters help, not least because they add gravitas to an inquiry too often presented as equal parts titillating and gruesome. Moreover, because they advance the dialogue in ground-breaking ways and ask some of the hardest questions that arise in this work, the ensuing outcome promises to emerge as being well thought through.

Ultimately, however, it is the policymakers, UN officials, humanitarian groups, criminal justice professionals, and military leaders who will have to step up and take concrete and unflinching action to address sexual violence in conflict, including when its victims are men and boys.

Part II
Framing

7 Uncovering men's narratives of conflict-related sexual violence[1]

Michele Leiby

Despite recent advancements, the academic, policy, and practitioner communities have been slow to recognise conflict-related sexual violence (CRSV) against men and boys.[2] As a result, much of our understanding of the patterns, causes, and consequences of CRSV rests on the problematic assumption that women and girls are the sole or predominant targets for such violence. This article contributes to our understanding of CRSV by identifying *why* policymakers, practitioners, and scholars often miss or misrepresent sexual violence against men. Using Peru as an illustrative case, I discuss the challenges of collecting data on CRSV against men, and offer suggestions for overcoming them. I argue that commonly employed definitions of sexual violence are too narrow and may ultimately miss or misrepresent the sexualised nature of violence against men. While empirically situated in Peru, the lessons and implications of the study have general applicability to documenting and explaining conflict-related sexual violence.

In the section below, I provide a brief overview of the civil war in Peru and the subsequent work of the Peruvian Truth and Reconciliation Commission (PTRC) to document sexual, and other forms of wartime violence. Comparing the Commission's original figures to a new dataset based on a re-examination of 2,050 of the PTRC's testimonies provides a unique opportunity to examine the processes through which reports of human rights abuse are collected, information sorted, and statistics transmitted. I show that what we know about CRSV against men depends greatly on the choices we make in designing our investigations.

The Peruvian civil war

The civil war from 1980–2000 was one of the most violent periods in Peru since its independence. Informed by the politico-military ideology of Mao Zedong and led by Abimael Guzmán, the Communist Party of Peru-Shining Path (in Spanish, PCP-SL) launched a class-based insurgency, demanding the immediate overthrow of the regime, and an installation of a new revolutionary government led by Guzmán.

Unlike other insurgent groups in Latin America, the PCP-SL did not simply accept violence, it celebrated its use: 'Militants swore to die and kill for the revolution. They ... killed mayors, and massacred villagers to cross what Guzmán called the "river of blood" to destroy the "old state" and build a Maoist utopia in its place' (Starn, Kirk, and Degregori 2005: 320). The group's dogmatism dictated that anyone who was not an active militant was an enemy of the revolution. The legal political left and even the leftist-insurgent group, the Túpac Amaru Revolutionary Movement, (MRTA), were considered part of the old, reactionary order, and a threat to the *real* revolution. The PCP-SL perpetrated frequent and extreme acts of violence against the civilian population, members of the MRTA, and the state security forces.

The state, either unable or unwilling to distinguish between the civilian population and the PCP-SL, responded in kind. Illegal detention, torture, extrajudicial execution, and forced disappearance became a general practice of the state's counter-insurgency efforts (CVR 2003). Ultimately, the state captured Guzmán in 1992. Because the PCP-SL was organised vertically, with a high concentration of power at the top, Guzmán's capture dealt a significant blow to the armed group, and contributed directly to the war's end in 2000.

Creating an official narrative on conflict-related violence: the Peruvian Truth and Reconciliation Commission[3]

The PTRC was charged with clarifying the facts of the violences perpetrated during the war. To this end, the PTRC collected almost 17,000 testimonies from witnesses and survivors, and published a twelve-volume report detailing the patterns of violence perpetrated by all sides in the conflict.

At the urging of local feminist scholars and activists, the Commission appointed a gender unit to lead its investigation into CRSV. While initially defining sexual violence to include forced prostitution, forced marriage, sexual slavery, forced abortion, forced impregnation, rape, and sexual torture, the PTRC later narrowed its focus to cases of rape. All statistical figures cited by the Commission reflect only incidents of rape or gang rape, despite references to other forms of sexual violence in the final report.

The Commission registered 538 cases of rape, representing 1.53 per cent of all human rights violations recorded in their database. Ninety-eight per cent of victims of rape were women; only 2 per cent were men. The majority of victims were young (ten to twenty-nine years old) housewives and/or peasants, had a primary-level education, and spoke Quechua. Contrary to patterns of other forms of violence, the state was responsible for the overwhelming majority (83 per cent) of all rapes, and 100 per cent of those perpetrated against men.[4]

Re-evaluating the official narrative on CRSV in Peru

The analysis presented below is based on an independent re-coding of a random sample of 2,050 of the testimonies collected by the PTRC.[5] Each testimony ranges from twenty to fifty pages in length and provides a detailed recounting of the individual's experiences during the war.

Using these records, I created a new dataset on political violence in Peru. Information on the identity of the victim(s), perpetrator(s), and type(s) of violence was recorded. My dataset covers ten forms of non-sexualised political violence: arbitrary detention, forced disappearance, extrajudicial execution, combat-related deaths and injuries, forced recruitment into an armed organisation, kidnapping, and torture. The dataset also covers multiple forms of sexualised political violence: rape, gang rape, sexual torture, mutilation, sexual humiliation, threatened or attempted sexual violence, forced abortion, forced impregnation, and a general category for unspecified forms of CRSV. Additional details, such as the context in which the violence was perpetrated, and how the victim came to be targeted for violence, were recorded for each case. The resultant dataset covers more than 20,000 individual human rights violations, and about 14,600 unique victims of violence (Leiby 2011).

Re-examining the PTRC testimonies with a more complete conceptualisation of sexual violence reveals significant discrepancies about CRSV (see Table 7.1).

In addition to the testimony narrative, each case file includes several standardised in-take forms used by PTRC staff to describe the testimony and categorise the information contained therein. One such form provides information on the interview itself (see Figure 7.1).

Of particular value is Section 12: 'Information about the Violations'. Provided here is a series of boxes representing various human rights issues – death, disappearance, torture or cruel treatment, detention or kidnapping, sexual violence, violations of due process, destruction of private property, forced recruitment, discovery of mass grave, or other. After finishing the interview, the interviewer

Table 7.1 Comparing figures on CRSV

PTRC final report	Re-examination of PTRC testimonies
• 538 individual cases of rape (1.53% of all human rights violations) • 98% of victims were women; 2% were men[1] • 100% of cases of sexual violence were rape • 83% of sexual violence was perpetrated by state armed forces	• 903 incidents of sexual violence[2] • 71% of victims were women; 29% were men • 31% of incidents of sexual violence were rape; 13% gang rape; 11% sexual torture; 4% sexual mutilation; 33% sexual humiliation; 5% attempted or threatened acts of sexual violence; <1% forced abortion; 3% unspecified forms of sexual violence • 88% of sexual violence was perpetrated by state armed forces; 12% by non-state armed groups

Notes

1 While the PTRC's final report references 11 cases of sexual violence against men, there is only one such case in the Commission's statistical database, making the ratio of female to male victims of sexual violence closer to 99.9–0.01%. It is not clear where the error lies.

2 An incident is defined as an individual sexual assault perpetrated against an individual victim by an armed group(s). If an individual is subjected to more than one type of sexual violence at the same time, each would be recorded as a distinct sexual violation. If a victim is repeatedly sexually assaulted by the same perpetrator(s) within the context of a single event of violence (e.g. raped repeatedly during the course of one's incarceration), this is recorded as a single incident of sexual violence.

Testimonio N° 1

FICHA N° 1: DATOS DEL TESTIMONIO

1. Sede _Lima_   2. Fecha: 0 7 9 8 0 2 (Día Mes Año)   3. Hora inicio 11:31   4. Hora fin 2:00

5. Lugar de la entrevista:

Piura (Departamento)   _Sechura_ (Provincia)   _Bernal_ (Distrito)

Centro Poblado

6. Apellidos y Nombres de los entrevistadores

Apellido Paterno   Apellido Materno   Nombres

7. ¿Se autorizó que el testimonio sea grabado? ☒ Sí ☐ No   8. Número de cassettes grabados: 0 3

9. ¿En qué idiomas se realizó la entrevista?
☒ Castellano   ☐ Quechua   ☐ Aymara   ☐ Shipibo   ☐ Ashaninka   ☐ Mashiguenga
☐ Otro (especificar)

10. Durante la entrevista ¿se contó con un traductor? ☐ Sí ☒ No

11. Apellidos y Nombres del traductor:

Apellido Paterno   Apellido Materno   Nombres

12. Información sobre las violaciones:

Temas de la entrevista: Cantidad Total de víctimas:
☐ Muerte
☐ Desaparición   ☐ Cantidad Aproximada
☒ Tortura o malos tratos   ☐ Cantidad Aproximada
☒ Detención o secuestro
☐ Violencia sexual
☐ Procesos judiciales / Problemas judiciales
☐ Despojo o destrucción de bienes y propiedades
☐ Utilización forzada de personas
☐ Fosas
☐ Otros temas (especifique): _____

13. Relación de lugares y fechas en los que se cometieron las violaciones

Departamento		Provincia		Distrito		Día	Mes	Año
Piura		Piura		Piura		2	08	8
Piura		Piura		Tambogrande		17	08	92

14. Cantidad de Fichas Utilizadas:
Ficha 2: Datos del declarante 0 2   Ficha 3: Datos de la víctima 0 4   Ficha 4: Datos del Presunto Responsable Individual – –
Fichas premortem (EPAF) – –

15. Nivel de detalle sobre los hechos: ☒ Muy detallado ☐ Medianamente detallado ☐ Poco detallado

Figure 7.1 Author photograph, CVR n.d.

Source: Comisión para la Verdad y Reconciliación (CVR). No date. *Colección de Testimonios*. Lima, Peru: Centro de Información para la Memoria Colectiva y los Derechos Humanos.

marks each box corresponding to the types of violence reported in the testimony. These data allow us to compare the original testimony narrative presented to the PTRC, how the interviewer processed the information, and ultimately how the testimony was quantified and represented in the Commission's statistical database to identify at which stage(s) men's narratives of CRSV got lost or misrepresented.

Challenges to investigating CRSV against men

Any large-scale human rights data collection program confronts numerous practical and methodological obstacles (Ball 1996). In the case of the PTRC, for example, structural constraints, including an insufficient staff, budget, and time-frame, undoubtedly limited the Commission's work, and contributed to an official narrative of CRSV that was incomplete.[6]

The following sections address obstacles faced by the PTRC and other truth commissions when investigating CRSV, with a particular focus on how these obstacles affect what we know about sexual violence against men.

(Under)reporting by victims

It is well understood that female survivors[7] of sexual assault may be unable or unwilling to report the crime for a number of reasons. Many do not have access to the appropriate reporting agencies or care providers. If they do, survivors may fear harassment, humiliation or revictimisation by officials or staff.[8] Many worry about being abandoned by their partners, or ostracised by members of the community (Andersen 2008; Peterman, Cohen, and Hoover Green 2011).

Men may not report sexual abuse (or even acknowledge it to themselves) when such victimisation is viewed as a threat to their masculinity and heterosexuality. Norms of hegemonic masculinity exclude the very possibility of male weakness, victimisation, or sexual penetration. As a result, men and boys are less likely to disclose and openly discuss sexual violence – to do so would be to admit that one is no longer a 'real' man.

The norms and laws regulating gender roles and sexual behaviour not only affect *whether* a survivor reports sexual violence, but also *how* they talk about it (Lewis 2009). Victims may avoid direct language when recounting violent and traumatic events, particularly when the violence is of an intimate nature. Women in Peru, for example, often spoke about 'the difficult times' (*sassachacuy tiempu*), and the 'grief and sorrow' (*llaki*), or the 'craziness' that people suffered (*lukuyasca*). When reporting sexual violence, victims rarely used the Spanish word for rape (*violar*). Instead, they would describe abuse (*abusar*), disturbance or bother (*molestar, fastidiar*), being taken (*sacar*), or being offended (*ofender*) (Pedersen, Tremblay, Errázuriz, and Gamarra 2008).

Similarly, male survivors of sexual assault may not have access to the vocabulary to name and describe their violent experiences (Andersen 2008). The Defensoría del Pueblo in Peru notes that men often spoke only very briefly and circumspectly about their sexual victimisation:

> ... male torture victims recognize that they were beaten with fists or with objects before they had been victims of sexual violence. Including when they spoke of the beatings, they would generalize, saying that they were beaten all over their body, without detailing that they were also beaten on their genitals or on their buttocks. Only at the end of their declarations, and only in a brief, passing manner would they indicate that they had also been beaten on their sexual organs.
>
> (Dador Tozzini 2007: 14)

Men would not use phrases like 'he raped me', but instead would say: 'I was humiliated or disgraced' (*vejar*) (Dador Tozzini 2007).

Male survivors rarely labelled their experiences as *sexual* violence, instead referring to 'torture' and emphasising the physical nature of the attack. Violations like forced nudity are understood and framed as a form of torture, designed to make the subject physically uncomfortable, not as a form of *sexualised* violence, designed to humiliate, and denigrate the person's gender and/or sexual identity.

For example, a man from Abancay, Apurímac, accused of participating in the bombing of an army transport convoy, recounts his traumas in detention. Upon arrival at the military base, José was stripped and forced down on his knees. His hands were tied, and he was repeatedly beaten over seven days. In describing his experience, he pays specific attention to the physicality of the attack. He presents being forcibly stripped and left naked within the context of physical torture, as just one of the many methods the interrogators used to attack his body (CVR n.d.: testimony 5—).[9]

Fearing stigmatisation, a loss of social, intimate, and even economic relationships, fearing the 'taint of homosexuality' (Sivakumaran 2005), or even criminal prosecution, male survivors not only are less likely to report sexual violence, but also are less likely to describe it as *sexual* violence. Understanding these dynamics, and committing the time to build rapport and listen deeply is a crucial first step for human rights investigators to uncover men's narratives of CRSV.

(Under)reporting by investigators

Some of the same biases and misconceptions (of men as aggressors and women as victims) that affect victim underreporting of sexual violence also may affect investigators' willingness and ability to recognise such abuses when they *are* reported (Onyango and Hampanda 2011; Oosterhoff, Zwanikken, and Ketting 2004). Of the PTRC testimonies examined for this study, 336 included narratives of CRSV. Thirty-four per cent of testimonies included narratives of male sexual victimisation. Interviewers accurately recorded sexual violence (i.e. 'checked' the sexual violence box on the in-take form shown in Figure 7.1) in 30 per cent of all CRSV cases, but only in 10 per cent of cases against men.[10] Given the proportion of male to female victims of CRSV, and given interviewers' overall likelihood of recognising sexual violence when it was disclosed, interviewers were significantly less likely to do so when the victim was a man

Table 7.2 Probability that PTRC interviewers mark 'sexual violence' in testimony, by victim sex, sexual violation type, and interviewer sex

		Interviewer records SV (1 = yes, 0 = no)
SV Victim Sex		−0.438*
(1 = male, 0 = female)		(0.202)
Rape		0.691*
(1 = rape, 0 = other form of SV)		(0.287)
Interviewer Sex		−0.296
(1 = male, 0 = female)		(0.213)
Constant		−0.671**
		(0.248)
Model Stats	N	250
	χ^2 (3)	18.98***
	Log Likelihood	−150.097

Notes
Standard errors in parentheses;
* $p<0.05$;
** $p<0.01$;
*** $p<0.001$.

(Pearson $\chi^2(1)=38.2927$, $p<0.001$). This disparity holds regardless of the sex of the interviewer (see Table 7.2).

What counts as sexual violence?

Most work on CRSV focuses narrowly on rape and gang rape, overlooking the multiple ways in which men and women can be sexually victimised (Cohen 2013; CVR 2003; Wood 2009). The International Criminal Court recognises rape, sexual torture and mutilation, sexual slavery, enforced prostitution, enforced sterilisation,[11] and forced pregnancy in its definition of sexual violence as a war crime (ICC 2000). In this section, I provide a brief overview of different forms of sexual violence, and consider the ways in which how we define the problem may obscure male victimisation.

Rape and gang rape

Rape is defined as the invasion of:

> the body of a person by conduct resulting in penetration, however slight, of any part of the body of the victim or of the perpetrator with a sexual organ, or of the anal or genital opening of the victim with any object or any other part of the body.
>
> (ICC 2000)

According to my re-examination of the PTRC testimonies, rape and gang rape are the most common sexual violations perpetrated against women (62 per cent), but represent only 9 per cent of those perpetrated against men. The regression results in Table 7.2 show that PTRC interviewers were more likely to recognise sexual violence when the testimony concerned rape, compared to non-penetrative acts of sexual violence. In addition, there are often inconsistencies in how investigators and service providers treat rape of women and men. The PTRC dealt with male rape inconsistently. It was sometimes coded as physical (non-sexualised) torture, and in only one case coded accurately as rape. In most cases, however, male rape was missed altogether and not recorded in the database. To the extent that similar patterns are observed in other conflicts, our understanding of CRSV may be systematically under-representing male victimisation.

Sexual torture

Applying the UN Convention against Torture, sexual torture can be understood as any form of sexual violence that causes severe pain and suffering to the victim, whether physical or psychological. Sexual torture can be perpetrated during interrogations to intimidate or punish the victim, to obtain information, or to coerce a confession from the victim or a third party (UNGA 1984). However, as decided in the case of *Fernando and Raquel Mejía* v. *The Republic of Peru*, such acts need not be perpetrated in official detention centres in order to be considered torture (IACHR 1999). This decision was significant in recognising the environment in which irregular counter-insurgency conflicts are fought.

To create mutually exclusive categories of sexual violence, I use sexual torture here to refer to those abuses which satisfy the criteria for torture under the Convention against Torture, but exclude rape and gang rape, sexual humiliation, sexual mutilation, and threatened or attempted sexual violence (see the following sections, respectively named as sexual mutilation, sexual humiliation and threatened or attempted sexual violence), even though these offenses certainly can cause severe physical and/or mental trauma. Sexual torture may include offenses such as the application of electricity, beatings, or other injuries to the breasts, buttocks, and genitals.

Carlson found that during the war in the former Yugoslavia, blunt genital trauma, including testicular beatings, torsion, repeated strikes or restriction of blood flow to the genitals, was so common as to be considered 'an integral part of war-making itself' (2006: 16). Male genital trauma is not seen as a serious offense because, while extremely painful, it often does not result in permanent damage to the sex organs or loss of sexual function (Carlson 2006). Further, because male genital trauma occurs so frequently in some 'peacetime' activities (hazing, contact sports), it may not be recognised by investigators as a war crime.

Even if investigators recognise genital trauma as a human rights violation, they may equate it with other forms of physical assault, overlooking the *sexualised* nature of the violence (Agger 1989; Carlson 2006). Because the goals of sexual torture include not just physical and psychological pain, but also a concerted attack on the target's identity, sexuality, and an effort to impair future sexual function, it is crucial that investigators differentiate sexual and non-sexual forms of torture (Agger 1989: 307; Dador Tozzini 2007). One victim tells the PTRC how both he and his partner had been detained for years on suspicion of 'terrorism'. She was later released, and would visit him in prison. Both reported having problems with intimacy and sexual relations as a result of the police 'humiliation' they suffered (CVR n.d.: testimony 7—).

Sexual mutilation

Sexual mutilation, while similar, can be distinguished from sexual torture in that it involves the removal or permanent damage and scarring of sexual organs. In Peru, both the state armed forces and the PCP-SL committed sexual mutilation. These offenses followed different patterns of perpetration than other forms of CRSV. Sexual mutilation was often carried out in public, and resulted in visible signs of abuse on the victims' body (Leiby 2011).

Consider the following example. In February 1984, a group of thirty soldiers entered and searched the home of a suspected member of the PCP-SL. While interrogating the suspect's grandmother, the soldiers severely beat her and burned her vagina and anus. They later poured kerosene on her body and set her on fire. The soldiers also beat and interrogated the grandson, accusing him of terrorism. They stripped him and cut off his penis (CVR n.d.: testimony 2—). The PCP-SL also frequently punished men suspected of 'betraying the revolution' by forcibly stripping them in public and removing their testicles and/or penis (CVR n.d.: testimonies 1—, 2—, 2—, 2—, 2—, 2—).

That sexual mutilation follows qualitatively distinct patterns, coupled with the sheer brutality of the attack, warrants its treatment as a separate category of sexual violence. The PTRC's statistical database treats these cases inconsistently – coded as either sexual violence or non-sexual torture, or sometimes not coded at all.

Sexual humiliation

While not currently considered specifically in the ICC's definition of sexual violence as a war crime, I argue for the inclusion of sexual humiliation as a distinct category. Sexual humiliation can be defined as any offense of a sexual nature whose primary goal is to humiliate and degrade the victim, but which does not use direct physical violence, or does not result in physical injury. Arguably, all acts of sexual violence are designed to humiliate and debase the victim, and demonstrate his/her powerlessness relative to the aggressor. Examples of sexual humiliation include forced nudity and being subjected to sexual mockery.

US military personnel engaged in frequent acts of sexual humiliation against detainees at Abu Ghraib prison in Iraq. Detainees were often forcibly stripped and kept naked for prolonged periods. Some were forced to simulate sex acts alone or with other male detainees. Others were forced to wear women's underwear. Many were mocked in sexually explicit ways and photographed or video recorded (US Army 2004). While often perceived as a 'less severe' offense, the

Table 7.3 Probability that PTRC interviewers mark 'sexual violence' in testimony, by victim sex and sexual violation type

	Interviewer records SV
SV Victim Sex	−0.425*
(1 = male, 0 = female)	(0.215)
Sexual Humiliation	−0.700*
(1 = sexual humiliation, 0 = other form of SV)	(0.341)
Constant	−0.303
	(0.161)
Model Stats *N*	259
χ^2 (2)	15.62***
Log Likelihood	−157.507

Notes
Standard errors in parentheses;
* $p<0.05$;
** $p<0.01$;
*** $p<0.001$.

Army's own investigation documents the significant and long-term effects of sexual humiliation on one's mental and physical health (US Army 2004).

Similar acts of sexual humiliation were observed in Peru. Luis, a member of the PCP-SL, recounts how members of DINCOTE grabbed him off the street. He was detained for fifteen days, during which time he was tortured and interrogated about his subversive activities. Officers tied Luis' hands behind his back, and shoved his head in a bucket of urine, repeatedly questioning him about the location of rebel bases and weapons caches. He was forcibly stripped and hung with his arms extended overhead. A female officer then came in, and humiliated and degraded him in sexually explicit ways: 'She would make fun of me saying, "Look at this pathetic fool, look how tiny it is," while pulling on my penis' (CVR n.d.: testimony 7—).

Even though sexual humiliation was the most frequent form of CRSV perpetrated against men (see Table 7.4), interviewers were less likely to recognise it as such. Compared to other acts of CRSV, sexual humiliation was significantly less likely to be recorded in the PTRC database as sexual violence (see Table 7.3).

Threatened and attempted acts of sexual violence

Sexual threats include any threatened or attempted act of sexual violence. In some cases, threats of CRSV are made explicitly in an effort to coerce an individual to do something against their will, such as inform on the political activities of a neighbour, or confess to committing a crime. The following would be categorised as a sexual threat and sexual humiliation:

> On November 24, 1987, 60 soldiers arrived by helicopter and detained three people in [Moyobamba, San Martín]. They gagged, bound and detained the

victims at the local school. The soldiers hung and beat the three men on their backs with the butts of their guns. The soldiers then brought the men's wives and children into the school, stripped them, and threatened to burn them alive. The soldiers also threatened to 'abuse' the wives.... Later, [the men] were taken to the base in Tarapoto where they were accused of belonging to the PCP-SL ... [they] were freed on November 28, 1987.

(CVR 2003: case 1—)

The PTRC database reports that the three male victims were detained and tortured, but this is not a complete representation of the case. The soldiers intentionally used the sexual victimisation of their wives and children (by forcibly stripping them) *and* the threat of further sexual violence to coerce the men to comply with their orders, or to punish them for their suspected subversive affiliations. Recording realized, attempted, and threatened acts of sexual violence gives human rights investigators and service providers a more holistic understanding of wartime trauma.

Investigators should strive for the most complete documentation of CRSV possible. As is clear from the Peruvian case, it is likely that men and women are targeted for different types of sexual violence at different rates (see Table 7.4). Similarly, it is likely that different armed groups engaged in different forms of sexual violence, and perpetrate these offenses in different contexts. It is possible, for example, that the rape of women is perpetrated more often by soldiers when they are deployed in the field, whereas sexual torture may be more frequently perpetrated by the police against male political prisoners in detention centres. Failing to report on all types of sexual violence will severely limit what we know about the patterns and causes of CRSV.

Who counts as a victim?

The PTRC only recorded acts of violence against persons that could be identified by their full name. This is a common practice by human rights investigators in order to avoid duplicate cases (Ball 1996). This presents unique challenges to

Table 7.4 Most frequent types of CRSV against men and women

Most frequent sexual violations against women	*Most frequent sexual violations against men*
• Rape and gang rape (62%)	• Rape and gang rape (9%)
• Sexual torture (10%)	• Sexual torture (19%)
• Sexual mutilation (2%)	• Sexual mutilation (13%)
• Sexual humiliation (15%)	• Sexual humiliation (55%)
• Attempted and threatened acts of sexual violence (6%)	• Attempted and threatened acts of sexual violence (4%)
• Forced abortion (<1%)	• Unspecified acts of sexual violence (0%)
• Unspecified acts of sexual violence (5%)	

studies of sexual violence, a crime, as illustrated above, that survivors may be reticent to disclose publicly. Because of the stigma associated with being sexually violated, victims may report their attacks in the third person, as an event they witnessed or that happened to someone they know. Statements like the following are common: 'I heard that other girls had been raped, but not me' (CVR n.d.: testimony 7—).

Re-examining the original testimonies, I identified 249 cases of sexual violence against 222 unnamed or partially named victims. If events of violence including unnamed victims are qualitatively different from those where individuals can be identified by their first and last name, excluding anonymous accounts may underestimate a particular sub-group within the population of victims. Sexual violence that occurs in the context of massacres, battles between armed groups, or mass detentions may be more likely to include unidentifiable victims, and as a result, be disproportionately under-reported. For example, during a community sweep in the district of San Jose de Ticllas in Ayacucho, the military rounded up everyone in the village, and gathered them in the public square. Here, 'all the men' were stripped naked and beaten (CVR n.d.: testimony 2—). The witness does not know the exact number of victims, or their names. Excluding cases with multiple, unidentified victims, like this one, from our analyses biases our findings against sexual abuse associated with mass, indiscriminate acts of violence.[12]

Lastly, academics and policymakers almost always limit victims of CRSV to civilians (Cohen and Nordås 2014). This decision is puzzling given that international human rights and humanitarian law provides no context under which sexual violence against combatants is ever justified. Failing to recognise sexual violence against combatants is even more problematic when we recognise how conflict roles and dichotomies (civilian/combatant, victim/aggressor, innocent/guilty) are highly gendered. Historically, in Peru, men were more likely to occupy roles in public and political spaces; they were more active in trade unions, political parties, and peasant cooperatives (Jelin 2001).[13] Similarly, while women were incorporated into the PCP-SL and the MRTA in large numbers, men comprised a large majority of combatants. Ignoring sexual violence against combatants is not a gender-neutral choice.

If sexual violence is used as a tool of political repression, we might expect individuals who are members of organised opposition groups (armed or unarmed) to be at greater risk. For example, Mateo, who was accused of using his position in the agricultural co-op to buy ammonium nitrate for the PCP-SL, was detained by DINCOTE and repeatedly tortured, including with electricity on his genitals (CVR n.d.: testimony 7—). Ignoring cases of sexual violence against combatants is not supported by the law, is morally questionable, *and* may worsen our already gender-biased understanding of CRSV.

Conclusion

There are a number of methodological obstacles researchers confront when analysing sexual violence in conflict situations. Victim under-reporting is so pervasive that we must be especially careful to not 'lose' or misrepresent their stories in our investigations. The most common reasons human rights investigators miss sexual violence against men include: (1) working definitions of sexual violence that focus narrowly on penetrative rape; (2) limited understanding of how gendered social norms affect if and how men report sexual violence; (3) limited understanding of how these same norms also affect investigators' ability to recognise narratives of male sexual victimisation; and (4) working definitions of 'victim' that exclude individuals who cannot be identified, or choose to not disclose their full name, or that exclude combatants in armed conflict. More thoughtful consideration of these issues and how they affect our understanding of sexual violence against men must be a priority. The implications of a gender-biased understanding of conflict-related sexual violence may severely affect the efficacy of service programmes or prevention policies.

Notes

1 Special thanks to Gabriel Salazar Borja, Latrice Burks, Ronald Fernandez Contreras, Doris Leon Gabriel, Danica Genners, Sarah Huffman, and César Neruña for their research assistance. Thanks to Paula Drumond and Elisabeth Prügl for comments on earlier drafts of this paper. Funding was provided by the Feminist Research Institute, the Office of Graduate Studies, and the Latin American and Iberian Institute at the University of New Mexico; by the Council on Latin American and Iberian Studies at Yale University; and by an Andrew Mellon Foundation grant for interdisciplinary research through the College of Wooster.
2 Of course there are notable exceptions. For academic publications addressing CRSV against men and boys, see the works cited in this collection. Sivakumaran (2010) provides a review of UN statements on CRSV against men and boys since the passage of UNSC 1820 in 2008.
3 All figures cited in this section are from: CVR 2003, Tomo VI, Capítulo 1: 193–204.
4 State security agents include the Army, Navy, National Police, Civil Defense Organizations, and paramilitary groups. The DINCOTE and Sinchis counter-terrorist units within the National Police were singled out as particularly frequent perpetrators of sexual violence. Although formally prohibited by both groups, the Commission found that the PCP-SL and, to a lesser extent, the MRTA perpetrated sexual violence against civilians and other combatants.
5 As expected with a randomly drawn sample, the testimonies examined here do not differ systematically from the population of PTRC testimonies. It is important to recognise, however, that the collection of PTRC testimonies is a convenience sample, and as a result, may not be representative of all persons' experiences during the war.
6 Because of time constraints, 30 per cent of the testimonies received were never coded for non-lethal acts of violence, and thus not represented in the PTRC's final report.
7 I use the terms survivor and victim interchangeably to refer to individuals who have reported experiencing sexual violence, while recognising that these terms are fraught, and that not all victims survive the assault.
8 This is of particular concern when state security officials themselves are known perpetrators of sexual violence. Previous research has shown that state security forces are the most frequent perpetrators of CRSV (Cohen and Nordås 2014), and that among these institutions, the police – who are mandated to protect the civilian population, and uphold the rule of law – perpetrate sexual violence at rates disproportionately high, given their size (Leiby 2011).

9   All names have been changed, and any identifying information has been removed. Testimony numbers are redacted, but a complete list is on file with the author.
10 This figure includes testimonies of CRSV where at least one of the victims is male (but may also discuss CRSV against women). For testimonies where *only* male victims of CRSV are discussed, the probability of the interviewer correctly identifying the sexual assault plummets to 3 per cent.
11 Alberto Fujimori's government carried out coerced and forced sterilisations against more than 2,000 predominantly poor, indigenous women between 1996–2000 (DEMUS n.d.a, n.d.b).
12 Adding unnamed victims to datasets risks distorting the patterns of violence by over-counting cases that are duplicated within the dataset. De-duplication based on unique contextual details is possible, but time consuming, difficult, and error prone. At the very least, scholars should recognise the trade-offs associated with including/excluding unnamed victims of violence in their analyses.
13 Of course, it would be empirically false to suggest that women were absent from these spaces, and much work has been done looking at women's roles in social and political movements in Peru.

References

Agger, Inger. 1989. 'Sexual Torture of Political Prisoners: an Overview'. *Journal of Traumatic Stress* 2(3): 305–318.

Andersen, Torbjørn Herlof. 2008. 'Speaking about the Unspeakable: Sexually Abused Men Striving Toward Language'. *American Journal of Men's Health* 2(1): 25–36.

Ball, Patrick. 1996. *Who Did What to Whom?: Planning and Implementing a Large Scale Human Rights Project.* Washington, DC: AAAS.

Carlson, Eric Stener. 2006. 'The Hidden Prevalence of Male Sexual Assault during War: Observations on Blunt Trauma to the Male Genitals'. *British Journal of Criminology* 46: 16–25.

Cohen, Dara Kay. 2013. 'Explaining Rape during Civil War: Cross-National Evidence 1980–2009'. *American Political Science Review* 107(3): 461–477.

Cohen, Dara Kay and Ragnhild Nordås. 2014. 'Sexual Violence in Armed Conflict: Introducing the SVAC Dataset, 1989–2009'. *Journal of Peace Research* 51(3): 418–428.

CVR (Comisión para la Verdad y Reconciliación). n.d. *Collection of Testimonies*. Lima, Peru: Centro de Información para la Memoria Colectiva y los Derechos Humanos.

CVR (Comisión para la Verdad y Reconciliación). 2003. *Informe Final*. Accessed 10 September 2016. www.cverdad.org.pe/ingles/ifinal/index.php.

Dador Tozzini, María Jennie. 2007. *El Otro Lado de la Historia: Violencia Sexual contra Hombres, Perú 1980–2000.* Lima: Consejería en Proyectos.

DEMUS (Estudio para la Defensa de los Derechos de la Mujer). n.d.a. *Caso Esterilizaciones Forzadas'*. DEMUS: Casos Emblemáticos. Accessed 14 September 2016. www.demus.org.pe/casos-emblematicos/caso-esterilizaciones-forzadas/.

DEMUS (Estudio para la Defensa de los Derechos de la Mujer). n.d.b. '*Somos 2074 y Muchas Más'*. DEMUS: Campañas. Accessed 14 September 2016. www.demus.org.pe/campanas/somos-2074-y-muchas-mas/.

IACHR (Inter-American Commission on Human Rights). 1999. *Informe N 5/96 Case 10.970 Fernando y Raquel Mejía* v. *The Republic of Peru*. Washington, DC: IACHR.

ICC (International Criminal Court). 2000. Rome Statute of the International Criminal Court, Part 2: Jurisdiction, Admissibility and Applicable Law. Article 8(2) (e) (vi). Accessed 1 September 2016. http://legal.un.org/icc/statute/english/rome_statute(e).pdf.

Jelin, Elizabeth. 2001. 'El Género en las Memorias de la Represión Política'. *Mora: Revista del Instituto Interdisciplinario de Género* 7: 127–137.

Leiby, Michele. 2011. *State-Perpetrated Wartime Sexual Violence in Latin America*. PhD Dissertation. The University of New Mexico. ProQuest 896361190.

Lewis, Dustin. 2009. 'Unrecognized Victims: Sexual Violence Against Men in Conflict Settings under International Law'. *Wisconsin Journal of International Law* 27(1): 1–49.

Oosterhoff, Pauline, Prisca Zwanikken, and Evert Ketting. 2004. 'Sexual Torture of Men in Croatia and Other Conflict Situations: an Open Secret'. *Reproductive Health Matters* 12(23): 68–77.

Onyango, Monica Adhiambo and Karen Hampanda. 2011. 'Social Constructions of Masculinity and Male Survivors of Wartime Sexual Violence: An Analytical Review'. *International Journal of Sexual Health* 23: 237–247.

Pedersen, Duncan, Jacques Tremblay, Consuelo Errázuriz, and Jeffrey Gamarra. 2008. 'The Sequelae of Political Violence: Assessing Trauma, Suffering and Dislocation in the Peruvian Highlands'. *Social Science and Medicine* 67(2): 205–217.

Peterman, Amber, Dara Kay Cohen, and Amelia Hoover Green. 2011. 'Rape Reporting during War'. *Foreign Affairs*, 1 August. http://fsi-web1.stanford.edu/sites/default/files/Cohen_Rape_Reporting_During_War.pdf.

Sivakumaran, Sandesh. 2005. 'Male/Male Rape and the "Taint" of Homosexuality'. *Human Rights Quarterly* 27(4): 1274–1306.

Sivakumaran, Sandesh. 2010. 'Lost in Translation: UN Responses to Sexual Violence against Men and Boys in Situations of Armed Conflict'. *International Review of the Red Cross* 92(877): 259–277.

Starn, Orin, Robin Kirk, and Carlos Iván Degregori (eds). 2005. *The Peru Reader: History, Culture, Politics*. Durham, NC: Duke University Press.

UNGA (United Nations General Assembly). 1984. Convention against Torture and Other Cruel, Inhuman or Degrading Treatment or Punishment. UN A/RES/39/46. Accessed 11 September 2016. www.un.org/documents/ga/res/39/a39r046.htm.

US Army. 2004. 'The Taguba Report on Treatment of Abu Ghraib Prisoners in Iraq, Article 15–6 Investigation of the 800th Military Police Brigade'. Accessed 17 August 2016. https://fas.org/irp/agency/dod/taguba.pdf.

Wood, Elisabeth. 2009. 'Armed Groups and Sexual Violence: When is Wartime Rape Rare?'. *Politics & Society* 37(1): 131–162.

8 Sex, violence, and heteronormativity

Revisiting performances of sexual violence against men in former Yugoslavia

Paula Drumond

The former Yugoslavia saw unprecedented levels of sexual violence against men in the course of the conflicts that swept the federation throughout the 1990s. Existing reports give an indication of the pervasiveness of the phenomenon. A 2002 UNFPA publication affirms that 80 per cent of male inmates surveyed in Sarajevo camps suffered sexual assaults (Mudrovčić 2002: 6). In a survey of sixty male survivors from Bosnia and Croatia, Lončar, Henigsberg, and Hrabać found that about 68 per cent of the surveyed individuals were victims of physical torture on the genitals, most often severe beating to the testicles or penis (2010: 196). Grounded on data collected in three centres providing medical assistance to war victims, Oosterhoff, Zwanikken, and Ketting concluded that: 'sexual torture of men was a regular, unexceptional component of violence in wartime Croatia' (2004: 76).

Recently, scholars have traced how national and international law, the media and humanitarian policies have systematically ignored male victimisation in the Balkans (e.g. Carpenter 2006; Sivakumaran 2007; Zarkov 2007). Partially inspired by these findings, some authors have called for 'gender-inclusive' – or 'non-feminist' – lenses in policy and research on sexual violence (Dolan 2014; Carpenter 2002; Jones 2011). But scapegoating feminists and feminisms for the invisibility of men often leads to antagonistic narratives that shut down questioning of how particular sexual orders enable and perpetuate certain grammars of violence in the first place (see Zalewski, Ch. 1 in this volume).

As a social performance, sexual violence cannot be abstracted from the context, meanings, and logics of the interaction between victims, perpetrators, and audience (Schröder and Schmidt 2001; Fujii 2013). With this in mind, I propose to integrate a performance-oriented approach into analyses of sexual violence to help us move beyond the limited focus on sexed bodies, and towards the violent processes through which sexual violence comes into being. Inserting a performative approach into analyses of violence enables us to grasp how the 'sexual' is violently put on display (Fujii 2013), and therefore to identify the situated conditions of male vulnerability in war-making. In illuminating how violence unfolds in specific contexts, a performance-oriented analysis thus refines our understanding of logics that are specific to sexual violence against men.

Recently, Lee Ann Fujii has insightfully applied a performance-oriented framework to reveal the ways 'actors stage violence for graphic effects' (2013: 411). In her work, performances function as a useful heuristic tool for distilling 'the process of putting violence on display' without ignoring meaning-making processes and other social dynamics embedded in perpetrators' actions (Fujii 2013: 413). Building on Fujii, this chapter examines the way sexual violence is enacted while illuminating the ethno-sexualised logics evoked by these scripts. In analysing the contextual verbal and non-verbal dimensions of scripts of violence, the performative analysis herein conducted makes visible the 'grammar' that underpins particular scripts of violence and therefore contributes to a grounded understanding of how violence is produced and communicated in the scene. The premise of this chapter is that, as a social performance driven by heteronormativity, sexual violence against men gains its meaning through the aversion and abjection evoked by a penetrated/un-phallic/emasculated body. Therefore, doing away with feminist analyses and insights, as suggested by the 'gender-inclusive' enthusiasts, may lead to partial, and even misleading, knowledge about the gendered grammars underpinning these performances of violence.

Whereas previously scholars have alluded to the intimate connection between power and heterosexuality in their exploration of sexual violence against men (Zarkov 2001; Sivakumaran 2005; 2007; Misra 2015), existing debates on the topic have tended to excessively focus on *why* male-on-male sexual violence happens rather than on *how* particular heteronormative gender orders constitute and organise war-making. For example, Sivakumaran attributes the 'taint of homosexuality' provoked by male rape to widespread homophobia ingrained in social order (2005: 1275). In a similar direction, Misra goes as far as explaining male rape through the hidden homoerotic desire of specific perpetrators (2015: 111). Yet, thinking in terms of 'homophobia' places too much emphasis on the agency of individuals and gives the mistaken idea that certain types of violence can be eliminated if we change the behaviour of potential perpetrators (Chambers and Carver 2008: 145).

But rather than channelling the homophobic inclinations of certain individuals or military institutions, the sexual violation of male bodies is deeply imbricated in 'the normative power of heterosexuality' (Chambers and Carver 2008: 121) that percolates warfare practices. Although heteronormative scripts are widely diffused in war-making practices by a globalised military ethos (Eriksson Baaz and Stern 2009: 498), they are also performed in intimate articulation with local cartographies of enmity, which in former Yugoslavia was shaped by a genocidal ethno-national ideology.

Feminist literature has long argued that women's exposure to sexual violence is enmeshed in a complex and intersecting net of power relations. Crenshaw (1991), Buss (2009), and Peterson (2010), to name a few, have contributed in different ways to exposing the imbrications of race, ethnicity, class, and sexuality in making some women more vulnerable than others to different forms of violence and oppression. Yet, literature on sexual violence against men for the most part has not teased out the melding of contingent and multiple axes of differentiation that render particular male bodies vulnerable to sexual violation. Dubravka Zarkov's work is an exception that addresses the interplays between masculinity, sexuality, and ethnicity; her analysis focuses mainly on 'the exposures and invisibilities' of the sexually abused male bodies in the media and the discursive production of ethnic difference (2011, 2007). While unpacking performances of violence, I build on Zarkov's insights to crack open the way logics of ethno-nationality and sexuality intersect to produce difference and abjection in two distinctive forms of sexual violence against men: oral rape and genital violence.

Drawing on extensive archival research of cases handled by the International Criminal Tribunal for the former Yugoslavia (ICTY) since its creation, this chapter investigates performances of sexual violence against men as they were enacted in the conflicts in Bosnia (1992–1995) and Croatia (1991–1995). The first section presents the empirical landscape of conflict-related sexual violence against men based on a survey of the ICTY database. The following sections examine how this violence was performed by actors involved in the conflict, and locate the meaning of these scripts in a situated heterosexist, reproductivist, gender order.

Revisiting sexual violence against men through the ICTY database

The ICTY Court Records provide comprehensive descriptions of performances of violence collected as evidence for the prosecution of a range of human rights violations committed by all parties to the conflict in the Balkans. Documents available include judgements, hearing transcripts, and witness statements of cases tried by the ICTY since 1994. While surveying available evidence from the ICTY database, I found that a total of twenty cases include references to one or more forms of corporeal and psychological violence perpetrated against men that fit the tribunal's definition of 'sexual violence' – either because a man was forced to participate in anal or oral penetrative violence or because the performance involved the exposure or beating of the genitals.[1] This means that potential incidents of sexual violence against men appear in at least 32 per cent of the cases reviewed by the ICTY on Bosnia and Croatia. This figure is surprisingly high considering the hesitancy of male victims to report the crime, the stigmas surrounding the topic, and the invisibility of this debate in international criminal law.

With the help of qualitative data analysis software (NVivo), I surveyed the proceedings of the twenty ICTY cases containing evidence of sexual violence against men. Interestingly, and contrary to what was previously suggested in studies conducted by Lončar, Henigsberg, and Hrabać (2010), Oosterhoff, Zwanikken, and Ketting (2004) and Carlson (2006), the most prevalent form of sexual violence against men found in ICTY proceedings was not genital beating.

Instead, I found that oral rape was the most salient event in my codings. It would be premature to assert that fellatio was *the* most prevalent feature of sexual violence against men based only on this evidence. Yet, forcing men to engage in scripts of violence that graphically mimic acts associated with homosexual sex seems to be more common than previously assumed. Perhaps more importantly, these performances flag the circulation and mobilisation of sexual tropes in repertoires of violence deployed against men. In other words, if the sexual dimensions of genital beatings can be cloaked or even contested as 'just' torture, incidents of forced fellatio are particularly useful to illuminate how heteronormative tropes of sexuality organise war imaginaries and are played within the particular cartographies of enmity that animate the conflict, as further discussed in the following section.

In addition to oral rape, a wide range of patterns of sexual violence against men can be found in the proceedings of the tribunal. In particular, forced nudity, and genital violence – most notably, genital beating and genital mutilation – followed as the second and third most salient forms of sexual violence against men identified in court proceedings, respectively. My codings also revealed two important empirical findings. First, and similar to reported incidents of sexual violence against women, sexual violence against men was not isolated to specific armed groups or leadership levels: Serbs, Bosnians, and Croats were all involved as victims and perpetrators. For instance, Čelebići – a prison camp run by Bosnian and Croatian forces – is an emblematic example of how sexual violence against men was far from a monopoly of the Serbian army. In an infamous incident, Esad Landzo, a Čelebići camp guard, forced two Serb brothers to practise oral sex on each other and placed a burning fuse around their genitals in front of an audience of detainees.[2] Second, and in contrast to reported incidents of sexual violence against women,[3] only one pattern of sexual violence against men emerged during the coding: the sexual assault of men, individually or in group, in arrest-related circumstances.[4] These episodes occurred both during temporary arrest for investigation in police offices and, mostly, during incarceration in prison camps, detention centres, and other locations such as schools and cultural centres that were temporarily turned into detention facilities.

Taken together these findings reveal the pervasive, and yet particular dimensions of sexual violence against men in former Yugoslavia. Still, how these episodes unfolded and the ways sexual tropes circulated in scripts of violence targeting male bodies begs further attention.

Performing sexual violence against men in Bosnia and Croatia

The proceedings of the case against Dusko Tadić, a leader of the Serb Democratic Party, provides an outstanding illustration of how performances of sexual violence against men evolved in the conflicts that ravaged former Yugoslavia in the 1990s. The episode became one of the most emblematic cases of sexual violence against men and Tadić was eventually convicted for his participation in the incident,[5] which revolves around the forced fellatio Fikret Harambasić ('Hari') during his detention at the Omarska camp. The scene starts with Tadić's entourage beating a group of prisoners for a sustained period of time and then forcing them to do push-ups, jump into a canal, and drink oil,

> Then witness H heard: 'Hari, come here', and another man came into the canal. Though Witness H knew Fikret Harambasić, he did not recognise the naked man who was severely beaten, bloody, black. [...] *H was then ordered to lick Fikret's buttocks and G was ordered to suck Fikret's penis.* Then [witnesses] H, G and Fikret, were ordered out of the canal *and H had to first hold Fikret's hands, then hold Fikret's mouth shut as G was ordered to bite off Fikret's testicle.* [...] H did not know and did not see all of the people who were in that area. He could not see what was going on behind him or around him, but heard the Serbs yelling and acting as though they were at a sporting match being entertained by this horror.[6]

In this scene, sexual violence against men was performed as a spectacularised dramatisation of male-on-male fellatio that mobilised the sexual subjectivity of the victimised bodies and enabled a voyeuristic reception by the audience. The display of sexual/erotic scripts manifests in the words and deeds of Tadić and his cronies. While forcing male-marked bodies to engage in homoerotic behaviours, Tadić and the other guards were reportedly saying things such as 'are you enjoying [it] Hari, do you like it Hari, how do you feel Hari', while simultaneously insulting 'Hari's "*Turkish*" mother'.[7] On the same day, a witness recalls, Tadić also ordered two other prisoners, Emir and Jasmin, to fellate each other while laughing and saying 'look what the *Balija*s (Muslims) does [*sic*] to each other'.[8]

The verbal and non-verbal grammars deployed in the staging of oral rape described above suggest an implicit heteronormative gaze organising the script. For instance, Tadić and the other guards make reference to the potential sexual pleasure of Hari ('are you enjoying [it], Hari?') and use lines that put the spotlight on the transgressive nature of the scene when ironically remarking 'look what the *Balija*s (Muslims) does [sic] to each other'. Through these lines, Turks/Muslims/*Balija*[9] feature as sexually deviant and are measured against the untouched heterosexuality of the Serb ethnic self, casted by Tadić and his men, who purposefully kept their bodies at a distance during these enactments.

The lines delivered during the dramatisation of sexual violence illuminate how the positioning of victims in the heteronormative gender order melds with the ethno-national conflict architecture. As shown in the references to the victim's 'Turkish' mother and their '*Balija*' identity, the words, deeds and behaviours of perpetrators revolved around the demarcation of 'ethnosexual [bodily] frontiers' 'where ethnicity is sexualized, and sexuality is racialized, ethnicized, and nationalized' (Nagel 2003: 14).[10] The convergence between nationalism and heterosexism, as previously noted by Peterson, is part and parcel of the creation of 'hierarchical relations within and between imagined communities' and the ensuing subordination of those falling outside a rigid gender binary (Peterson 1999: 45).

Anchored in an ethno-national rhetoric, these scripts mobilised homoerotic stereotypes conjured around particular racialised male bodies. But more than transmitting gendered power and imposing hierarchisation, performances of sexual violence against men dramatise and produce that which does not conform to the prescribed sex/gender/desire order. By graphically displaying sexual relations associated with supposedly deviant sexual practices to spectators, who are forced to take part in the scene, these performances delimit the imaginaries around what a 'proper' sexual relation should look like, as also shown in the excerpts below:

> Some of the cruelest acts of torture (…) involved forced sexual acts. Slobodan Jacimovic – a Serb from Batkusa who called himself 'the Serbian inspector' – told two men, *'Let's see how Ustashas make children with each other,'* before forcing them to perform fellatio on each other.[11]

> As we were only separated by a part of the wall, (…) you could hear what was going on and the orders that had been given. (…) He said, 'Form two lines. Take the bottom part off. Turn towards each other.' And then he said quite clearly, *'You're going to perform oral sex* (…)' (…) And he would say, *'This one's a professional. This one's an amateur'.*[12]

In the first scene, male-on-male fellatio is used as a parody to represent how *'Ustashas'*,[13] that is, the ethno-sexual Other, engage in sexual relations and reproduce. In the second scene, the victims are mocked and 'evaluated' as professionals/amateurs in performances mimicking a homoerotic sexual engagement. Through the lens of heteronormativity, it is possible to grasp how the sexuality and sexual subjectivity of the ethnicised bodies are played within enactments that cast non-Serbs as deviants, grotesque, and bizarre, falling outside the norm of reproductive heterosexual encounters. Entangled in a sexualised ethno-national rhetoric, these scripts of violence incarnate the sexual politics of war, symbolised by the triumph of a Serbian-coded heteronormative sex/gender model that the ethno-sexual 'Other' does not embody and cannot become. In a context organised around heteronormative models of prowess, virility, and nationalism (Zarkov 2011; Bracewell 2000), the public display of forced fellatio involving the participation of non-Serbs thus cannot be merely reduced to a symbolic display of power from the ethnic self. Rather, in demarcating ethno-sexual Otherness, the display of fellatio was a productive form of violence that deprives *'Balijas'* and *'Ustashas'* of their hetero-normality. As driven by heteronormativity, it is precisely the fears and fantasies evoked by penetrated bodies displayed to an audience that provide these performances with its productive effects.

In these scenes, the display of violated male bodies to an audience transgresses established sexual norms while magnifying ethno-sexual 'abjection'

(Fujii 2013: 418; Diken and Laustsen 2005). These performances provoke bewilderment or consternation precisely because they produce difference by challenging the normative scripts of sexuality, unsettling bodily boundaries as envisaged and regulated in the sex/gender/desire system (Butler 2007). Consider, for instance, how witness 'R' strives to describe and make sense of an incident of forced fellatio involving two male bodies in the proceedings of the Čelebići case:

> *I do not know how to call it (...). It is not just a common incident.* (...) He ordered him to unbutton his pants and to put his genitals into his brother Vaso's mouth.[14]

As observed in the testimony above, the performance is portrayed by the spectator as unspeakable, 'not common', extraordinary – that is, in a way that sexual violence against women probably would not. Incidents of sexual violence against men, especially if penetrative, are unintelligible, repulsive, and startling as they involve two same-sexed bodies. In a somewhat similar direction, in a testimony of the case against Sikirica *et al.*, a victim recalls:

> One of the Banovics, I don't know which one, took off my sweatsuit, forced me to stand up. [...] And they got me – the trousers of my sweatsuit down, and then Tarzan had to kneel down. [...] And I apologise to all the listeners here, they got hold of my penis and put it in his mouth and beat him then [...]. Very degrading, very mean. [...] But it was very hard for me, *perhaps more than any other beatings, that humiliating, the degrading thing, very hard. I still have problems with that.*[15]

Interestingly, the performance of male rape is represented by the victim as the most abject and gruesome form of violence that one can possibly suffer. So grisly is this act that it stands out as worse than 'any other beatings' in his narratives and memories of sustained experiences of distress, torture, and humiliation. The sexual violation of male bodies thus gains its meaning and force from heteronormativity as it contravenes the prescribed impenetrability of the male body (Chambers and Carver 2008: 149). In overtly defying this prescription, these incidents thrive on the normative power of heterosexuality at the expense of the marginalisation and exclusion of that which does not conform to a binary sex/gender/desire order.

But beyond queering scripts of homosexualisation/feminisation, a performance-based analysis of this phenomenon also cracks open for analysis other productive dimensions of heteronormativity that operate in these violent displays. Observe, for instance, the excerpt below from a testimony provided during the trial of Ranko Cesić, a Bosnian Serb officer accused of forcing two Muslim brothers to orally rape each other:

> Ranko then said to my brother and I 'Take off your pants'. We did so. Ranko then ordered 'Start giving each other a "blow job" and don't stop

until we get back.' [...] The guard was laughing and said to soldiers, 'Come, see this.' We were begging them not to make us continue. This was so humiliating that I was ashamed to look at the guards. The guards stood and laughed at us.[16]

The performance revolves around two men from the same family being forced to engage in sexual intercourse through the explicit mobilisation of incestuous tropes. Similar performances can be found in the proceedings of other cases. In *Prosecutor* v. *Krajsnik*, for example, a witness reported that a group of Serb paramilitaries arrived at Dom Kulture, a cultural centre turned into a prison, headed by their Commander Dusan Repić, saying that they wanted to 'celebrate' the Bajram, a Bosnian Muslim holiday. They grouped two pairs of fathers and sons, who were taken to a stage and forced to fellate and then penetrate each other with a broom handle in front of other detainees, who were forced to watch the 'show'.[17]

In these episodes, heteronormativity illuminates not only the production of heterosexuality as the 'natural' ontology of sexual relations, but also of a wide range of pathologised sexual subjects and practices (Chambers and Carver 2008: 121). In her critique of the heterosexual matrix, Butler recognises how the incest taboo regulates society around exogamous opposite-sex marital and sexual arrangements (Butler 2002; see also Chambers and Carver 2008: 123–125). Therefore, the incest taboo 'works in the service of heteronormativity' by establishing only some forms of sexual arrangements as liveable and intelligible (Chambers and Carver 2008: 131). In this context, sex between fathers and their offspring is not only the symbolism of a despicable act or a demonstration of power of the Serbian self. Paired with violations of the incest taboo, these performances of sexual violence against men lack intelligibility by disturbing prescribed heteronormative kinship structures.

Therefore, in the production and direction of scripts involving male-marked bodies of the same family, perpetrators produce a 'kinship trouble' (Chambers and Carver 2008: 121) that disrupts the established domain of heterosexual practices and kinship norms of the 'Other', while simultaneously reaffirming the sexual norms attributed to the self. In this regard, what sexual violence against men signifies as a social performance transcends the bodily punishments and the 'emasculation' or 'homosexualisation' of the specific sexed bodies involved in the scene. Through the public display of transgressive sexual behaviours (as prescribed in the heterosexual matrix), these acts simultaneously unsettle and reiterate liveable sexual norms by violently forcing the targeted ethnic group to stand outside the intelligible sex/gender/desire matrix. In other words, through these performances of violence, constructions of gender, ethnicity, and sexuality intersect in the production of bodies that conjure a variety of pathologised sexual practices and behaviours, such as homosexuality, incest, and paedophilia (Puar 2007: xxiii; Nagel 2003). The intersection between ethno-national identity and sexuality in these violent displays creates not only ethnic difference, as Zarkov (2007) previously noted, but also operates in the (re)production and regulation of sexual and gender difference in reference to the heteronormative social organisation of sexuality (Butler 2011).

Beyond penetration: sex and heteronormativity in other performances of sexual violence

Heteronormativity also circulates in and organises other performances of sexual violence against men, as the script of genital mutilation of Harambasić further reveals:

> The man with the beard came back over and told [witness G] to take Hari's testicle out. G finally managed to get Hari's testicles in his hands. [...] The man with the beard was yelling 'harder, harder, harder'. G then was successful and bit one off [...] and the man with the beard then cursed Hari's mother and said to him '*make a Turk son now!*'[18]

A closer look reveals that the performative force of a castration script centres on anxieties that are different from those of oral or anal penetration. In forcing a male into the role of a penetrated body, the performance brings the sexual and reproductive subjectivity of the victim to the centre of the stage. Violent displays associated with male-on-male sexual penetration thrive on 'both aggressive and libidinal elements' that evoke 'the passive, receptive sexuality [of the victim], thereby provoking homosexual anxiety and identity feeling' (Agger 1989: 309). In contrast, while playing with the masculine morphology, scripts of genital violence and castration build on castration anxiety, that is, the fear of losing the phallus (Agger 1989: 309).

Embedded in phallic imaginaries, performances of genital violence in former Yugoslavia were mediated by a reproductivist gender logic contextually attached to the patrilineal formation of these different ethnic groups. As national reproduction directly depends on male sexed bodies, the integrity of male-marked sex organs is a constitutive component of modern nationhood in former Yugoslavia (Sofos 1996). A notable example of the entrenched connection between nationhood and manhood in this context emerges, for instance, in a statement by Dobrica Ćosic, one of the most prominent Serb nationalist intellectuals, who declared that 'a Serb is a man who is not a man unless he is also Serb' (Bracewell 2000: 577). While ironically reflecting on nationalism in the Balkans, Danilo Kiš, a Yugoslav writer observed, '*testicles are a national symbol, a trademark of the race*; other peoples have luck, tradition, erudition, history, reason – but we alone have balls' (Bracewell 2000: 570 – emphasis added).

This phallocentric and reproductivist syntax swirls around other transcripts and documents reporting genital violence and mutilation in Bosnia and Croatia. According to Carlson, references to the procreative capability of male victims, such as '*you will never again make Ustasha/Muslim children*', accompanied genital beatings in a vast number of reported incidents (Carlson 2006: 19 – emphasis added). Similarly, in the case against Blagoje Simić *et al.*, a witness recalls:

One night a group of Chetniks rushed into our detention room and started beating us. [...]. At one point, we were lined up and Milan Simić beat us in the genitals. *His men were laughing and said that we would not be able to make children any more (...)*.[19]

Following the cartographies of enmity of an ethno-national genocidal confrontation where the continuation of difference is situated in the male body and its capacity to procreate, 'ethno-sexual' articulations (Nagel 2003) around sexed matters moulded how these performances evolved. Thus, ethno-national grammar evoked in conjunction with physical attacks to the male genitalia are far from insignificant and play a central role in elevating these violent interactions into *sexual* violence (rather than 'just' physical torture).

During these displays of violence, the sexed body of the Muslim/Ustasha was the focus of the act, front and centre, precisely because it embodied the procreative power of the ethno-national group in heteronormative sexual encounters. In this particular scenario, the rhetoric of ethnic cleansing paired with heteronormative patrilineality shaped and produced the particular contours of sexual violence against men through enactments that bring the reproductive continuation of the other to the fore of the performance.[20]

Entailing the physical removal or permanent harming of the phallic marker of male bodies, these non-penetrative performances of sexual violence are also more than a symbol or a message of subordination (cf. Sivakumaran 2007; Goldstein 2001). They challenge existing morphological imaginaries as they involve the erasure of the bodily reference point of male-associated embodiment. As ' "persons" only become intelligible through becoming gendered' (Butler 2007: 22), the extirpation or damaging of the genitalia critically affects the binary parameters of gender intelligibility as the body no longer fits the male/masculine/ heterosexual construct. Particularly in cases of castration and penile amputation, the physical erasure of the biological sex disrupts boundaries of the victimised body, turning it into something else, a hybrid, that is neither feminine nor masculine (Wassersug, McKenna, and Lieberman 2012: 255–256). Even in cases where the reproductive organ does not completely vanish, such as in instances of partial genital mutilation, this performance of violence can profoundly affect masculine embodiment and subjectivity (see Hendershot, Ch. 2 in this volume).

Through a heteronormative gaze, penetrative and non-penetrative episodes of sexual violence deployed similar languages and references about the sexual and sexed integrity attributed to particular masculine bodies. Heteronormativity is deeply inscribed in war-making repertoires, underpinning how states and nations are imagined and how practices of violence and pain are dramatised and represented in conflict scenarios. Accordingly, sexual violence against men needs to be tackled as part of a militarised ethos of power and domination entrenched in 'sexualised orders of international relations' that shape and produce imaginaries and practices around citizens/foreigners, nations, and war-making (Weber 2016: 22). At the same time, as they intersect with different identity constructions, these performances of violence need to be analysed in the context in which they are produced. When seen in conjunction with other identity constructions, it is possible to identify how sexual violence may draw on different grammars that are specific to the violation of the male body. In Bosnia and Croatia, for example, the mobilisation of ethno-national figurations of the Muslim/Balijas/ Ustashas crafted the situated contours of sexualised scripts of violence against male-marked bodies.

Conclusion

In former Yugoslavia, heteronormative sexual politics was instantiated in scripts of bodily violence against male bodies ranging from male-on-male penetrative rape to the expunging of phallic and reproductive attributes through genital muti- lation. The analysis of these episodes of violence as performances illuminates both general and particular logics of the phenomenon. From a general per- spective, this chapter revealed *how* heteronormative tropes of sex and sexuality work as enabling conditions of episodes of sexual violence against men. The performative analysis of these scripts revealed that: 'sexuality is not the bar- ometer of exception, a situation out of control, or an unimaginable reality. Rather, it constitutes a systemic, intrinsic, and pivotal module of power rela- tions' (Puar 2007: 113). Therefore, sexual violence against men cannot be reduced to a 'bad apples' logic or explained by the existence of out-of-control individuals caught up in the frenzy of war. Driven by heteronormativity, these performances are intimately imbricated in militarised scripts of domination that shape and organise warfare practices. From a particular perspective that zooms in on the intricacies of performances of sexual violence against men in former Yugoslavia, this analysis also reveals that the manifestation of heteronormativity is a necessary but not a sufficient condition of sexual violence against men: the heteronormative ideology that fuelled episodes of sexual violence cannot be sep- arated from the identitarian rhetoric that animated the conflict. The mobilisation of ethno-national figurations was thus an integral and constitutive dimension of male sexual vulnerability, which is situated in an interlocking system of power relations. The intimate imbrication of ethno-national identity with sexuality also produces some important insights for policymaking: not all men are similarly vulnerable to sexual violence, and men are not necessarily targeted *because* they are men. Or as Ward has put it, sexual violence against men 'is not about men being targeted because of broad-based discrimination against them for being men; it is about men in particular social groups being targeted in order for their opponents to win wars' (Ward 2016: 293).

In order to grasp how multiple and intersecting axes of differentiation interact to make some men, including privileged men, vulnerable to sexual violence, ana- lytical and policy efforts need to unveil how sexual violence against men is per- formed and put on display. The insights gained this way must be considered in current debates around reshaping policy and programmes on sexual violence towards a 'gender-inclusive' approach. The temptation of automatically adding sexed bodies into purported inclusive frameworks of sexual violence might offer an apparently simple 'quick fix' to the formal acknowledgement of male victim-isation. Yet, the inclusion of men as victims cannot stand apart from a critical interrogation of how gender and sexuality circulate in these repertoires of violence through the continuing subordination of emasculated/homosexualised/feminised bodies. In failing to acknowledge how a heteronormative, male-privileging order operates in both war and 'peace', this approach risks reproducing the enduring gender hierarchies that enable sexual violence in the first place.

Notes

1 The twenty ICTY cases in which incidents of sexual violence against men were identified were the cases against Radoslav Brdjanin (IT-99-36); Ranko Cesić (IT-95-10); Zdravko Mucić *et al.* (IT-96-21); Anto Furundzija (IT-95-17/1); Enver Hadžihasanović and Amir Kubura (IT-01-47); Radovan Karadžić (IT-95-5-18); Momcilo Krajisnik (IT-00-39-T); Miroslav Kvocka *et al.* (IT-98-30/1); Milan Lukić and Sredoje Lukić (IT-98-32/1); Milan Martić (IT-95-11);. Mladen Naletilić and Vinko Martinović (IT-98-34); Jadranko Prlić *et al.* (IT-04-74); Sikirica *et al.* (IT-95-8); Blagoje Simić *et al.* (IT-95-9); Milan Simić (IT-95-9/2); Milomir Stakić (IT-97-24); Stanišić and Simatović (IT-03-69); Mićo Stanišić and Župljanin (IT-08-91); Dusko Tadić (IT-94-1); and Todorović (IT-95-9/1). Following the Akayesu Judgement at the International Criminal Tribunal for Rwanda, the ICTY considered sexual violence as 'broader than rape and includes such crimes as sexual slavery or molestation' as well as other acts that do 'not necessarily involve physical contact' (*Prosecutor* v. *Miroslav Kvocka et al.*, Case No. IT-98-30/1-T, Judgement, 2 November 2001, para. 180.
2 *Prosecutor* v. *Zdravko Mucić et al.*, Case No. IT-96-21-T, Trial hearing, 15 July 1997.
3 In its final report, the UN Commission of Experts found five main patterns of rape. The first pattern is rape perpetrated in conjunction with looting and intimidation of the target ethnic group 'before any widespread or generalized fighting breaks out in the region'. The second pattern 'involves individuals or small groups committing sexual assaults in conjunction with fighting in an area, often including the rape of women in public.' The third pattern involves sexual assaults of people held in detention, perpetrated individually or in groups. The fourth pattern of rape 'involves individuals or groups committing sexual assaults against women for the purpose of terrorizing and humiliating them often as part of the policy of "ethnic cleansing".' Finally, the fifth pattern 'involves detention of women in hotels or similar facilities for the sole purpose of sexually entertaining soldiers, rather than causing a reaction in the women' (UN Commission of Experts 1994, paras 11–16).
4 Among the identified places where sexual violence against men occurred were Omarska camp, Keraterm camp, Luka camp, Dom Kulture Celopek, Bosasnki Samac police station, Bosnanski Samac primary school, Čelebići camp, Orasac camp, Planjo's house, Kotor Varos police station, Batajnica, Hadzic's cultural centre, Banja Luka CSB police detachment, among others.
5 *Prosecutor* v. *Dusko Tadić*, Case No. IT-94-1-T, Opinion and Judgement, 7 May 1997.
6 *Prosecutor* v. *Dusko Tadić*, Case No. IT-94-1, Trial hearing, 25 November 1996, 8482 – emphasis added.
7 *Prosecutor* v. *Dusko Tadić*, Case No. IT-94-1, Witness statement, 24 and 25 January 1995, 5 – emphasis added.
8 *Prosecutor* v. *Dusko Tadić*, Case No. IT-94-1, Witness statement, 9–11 January 1995, 10 – emphasis added.

9 *Balija* is a derogatory term commonly used in the Balkans to refer to Bosnian Muslims. Inspired by a recollection of ethno-national memories, ultra-nationalist Serbs often referred to Bosnian Muslims as the 'Turks', that is, descendants of the Ottoman Empire, which was responsible for the downfall of the Serbian Empire in the fourteenth century (Boose 2002: 76).

10 The concept of 'ethno-sexual frontiers' offered by Nagel uses ethnicity as an encompassing term that refers to different forms of socially constructed identities used to differentiate individuals and groups. Therefore, in this conceptualisation, 'ethnicity subsumes both nationalism and race' (Nagel 2003: 6).

11 *Prosecutor* v. *Blagoje Simić et al.*, Case No. IT-95-9-T, Prosecution's final trial brief, 24 June 2003, para. 192 – emphasis added.

12 *Prosecutor* v. *Blagoje Simić et al.*, Case No. IT-95-9-T, Trial hearing, 16 October 2001, 2369 – emphasis added.

13 Croat separatist were associated with the 'Ustasha', a Croatian fascist movement responsible for the mass execution of Serbs following the Axis occupation of Yugoslavia in 1941 (Arfi 1998: 184).

14 *Prosecutor* v. *Zdravko Mucić et al.*, Case No. IT-96-21-T, Trial hearing, 15 October 1997, 7782 – emphasis added.

15 *Prosecutor* v. *Dusko Sikirica et al.*, Case No. IT-95-8, Trial hearing, 11 April 2001, 2346 – emphasis added.

16 *Prosecutor* v. *Ranko Cesić*, Case No. IT-95-10/1-S, Prosecution's sentencing brief, 12 November 2003.

17 *Prosecutor* v. *Momcilo Krajisnik*, Case No. IT-00-39-T, Trial hearing, 4 July 2005, 15726 – emphasis added; *Prosecutor* v. *Mico Stanisić and Stojan Zupljanin*, Case No. IT-08-91, Trial hearing, 27 March 2013, 27687.

18 *Prosecutor* v. *Dusko Tadić*, Case No. IT-94-1, Witness statement, 9–11 January 1995, 10 – emphasis added.

19 *Prosecutor* v. *Milan Simić et al.*, Case No.IT-95-9/2-S, Trial hearing, 22 July 2002, 16 – emphasis added.

20 Likewise, research observed how patrilineality and patriarchy facilitated the use of female-marked bodies as empty biological vessels for the reproduction of Serbian nationhood (Sofos 1996: 86; see also Allen 1996: 63). Accordingly, the practice of forced pregnancy of non-Serb women acts out as the corresponding counterpart of the genocidal logic to male castration.

References

Allen, Beverly. 1996. *Rape Warfare: The Hidden Genocide in Bosnia-Herzegovina and Croatia*. Minneapolis, MN: University of Minnesota Press.

Agger, Inger. 1989. 'Sexual Torture of Political Prisoners: An Overview'. *Journal of Traumatic Stress* 2(3): 305–318.

Arfi, Badredine. 1998. 'Ethnic Fear: The Social Construction of Insecurity'. *Security Studies* 8(1): 151–203.

Baaz, Maria Eriksson, and Maria Stern. 2009. 'Why Do Soldiers Rape?: Masculinity, Violence, and Sexuality in the Armed Forces in the Congo (DRC)'. *International Studies Quarterly* 53(2): 495–518.

Boose, Lynda E. 2002. 'Crossing the River Drina: Bosnian Rape Camps, Turkish Impalement, and Serb Cultural Memory'. *Signs: Journal of Women in Culture and Society* 28(1): 71–96.

Bracewell, Wendy. 2000. 'Rape in Kosovo: Masculinity and Serbian Nationalism'. *Nations and Nationalism* 6(4): 563–590.

Buss, Doris. 2009. 'Sexual Violence, Ethnicity, and Intersectionality in International Criminal Law'. In Emily Grabham, Davina Cooper, Jane Krishnadas, and Didi Herman (eds), *Intersectionality and Beyond: Law, Power and the Politics of Location*. London: Routledge, 105–123.

Butler, Judith. 2002. *Antigone's Claim: Kinship Between Life and Death*. New York: Columbia University Press.

Butler, Judith. 2007. *Gender Trouble: Feminism and the Subversion of Identity*, 1st edn. New York: Routledge.

Butler, Judith. 2011. *Bodies That Matter: On the Discursive Limits of Sex*, 1st edn. Abingdon: Routledge.

Carlson, Eric S. 2006. 'The Hidden Prevalence of Male Sexual Assault During War Observations on Blunt Trauma to the Male Genitals'. *British Journal of Criminology* 46(1): 16–25.

Carpenter, Charli. 2002. 'Gender Theory in World Politics: Contributions of a Nonfeminist Standpoint?' *International Studies Review* 4(3): 153–165.

Carpenter, Charli. 2006. *Innocent Women and Children: Gender, Norms and the Protection of Civilians*. New York: Ashgate.

Chambers, Samuel and Terrell Carver. 2008. *Judith Butler and Political Theory: Troubling Politics*. New York: Routledge.

Crenshaw, Kimberlé. 1991. 'Mapping the Margins: Intersectionality, Identity Politics, and Violence against Women of Color'. *Stanford Law Review* 43(06): 1241–1299.

Diken, Bülent and Carsten B. Laustsen. 2005. 'Becoming Abject: Rape as a Weapon of War'. *Body & Society* 11(1): 111–128.

Dolan, Chris. 2014. 'Has Patriarchy Been Stealing the Feminists' Clothes?: Conflict-Related Sexual Violence and UN Security Council Resolutions'. *IDS Bulletin* 45(1): 80–84.

Fujii, Lee Ann. 2013. 'The Puzzle of Extra-Lethal Violence'. *Perspectives on Politics* 11(2): 410–426.

Goldstein, Joshua S. 2001. *War and Gender: How Gender Shapes the War System and Vice Versa*. Cambridge: Cambridge University Press.

Jones, Adam. 2011. *Gender Inclusive: Essays on Violence, Men, and Feminist International Relations*. New York: Taylor & Francis.

Lončar, Mladen, Neven Henigsberg, and Pero Hrabać. 2010. 'Mental Health Consequences in Men Exposed to Sexual Abuse During the War in Croatia and Bosnia'. *Journal of Interpersonal Violence* 25(2): 191–203.

Misra, Amalendu. 2015. *The Landscape of Silence: Sexual Violence Against Men in War*, 1st edn. London: Hurst & Co.

Mudrovčić, Željka. 2002. 'Sexual and Gender-Based Violence in Post-Conflict Regions: The Bosnia and Herzegovina Case'. In *The Impact of Armed Conflict on Women and Girls: A UNFPA Strategy for Gender Mainstreaming 285 in Areas of Conflict and Reconstruction*. Bratislava: United Nations Population Fund (UNFPA), 60–76.

Nagel, Joane. 2003. *Race, Ethnicity, and Sexuality: Intimate Intersections, Forbidden Frontiers*. New York: Oxford University Press.

Oosterhoff, Pauline, Prisca Zwanikken, and Evert Ketting. 2004. 'Sexual Torture of Men in Croatia and Other Conflict Situations: An Open Secret'. *Reproductive Health Matters* 12(23): 68–77.

Peterson, Spike. 1999. 'Political Identities/Nationalism as Heterosexism'. *International Feminist Journal of Politics* 1(1): 34–65.

Peterson, Spike. 2010. 'Gendered Identities, Ideologies, and Practices in the Context of War and Militarism'. In Laura Sjoberg and Sandra Via (eds), *Gender, War, and Militarism: Feminist Perspectives*. Westport, CT: Praeger, 17–29.

Puar, Jasbir K. 2007. *Terrorist Assemblages: Homonationalism in Queer Times*. Durham, NC: Duke University Press Books.

Schröder, Ingo and Bettina E. Schmidt (eds). 2001. *Anthropology of Violence and Conflict*. New York: Routledge.

Sivakumaran, Sandesh. 2005. 'Male/Male Rape and the "Taint" of Homosexuality'. *Human Rights Quarterly* 27(4): 1274–1306.

Sivakumaran, Sandesh. 2007. 'Sexual Violence Against Men in Armed Conflict'. *European Journal of International Law* 18(2): 253–276.

Sofos, Spyros A. 1996. 'Inter-Ethnic Violence and Gendered Constructions of Ethnicity in Former Yugoslavia'. *Social Identities* 2(1): 73–92.

UN Commission of Experts. 1994. 'Final Report of the Commission of Experts for the Former Yugoslavia, Annex IX: Rape and Sexual Assault'. S/1994/674/Annex IX. United Nations.

Ward, Jeanne. 2016. 'It's Not about the Gender Binary, It's about the Gender Hierarchy: A Reply to "Letting Go of the Gender Binary"'. *International Review of the Red Cross* 98(901): 275–298.

Wassersug, Richard J., Emma McKenna, and Tucker Lieberman. 2012. 'Eunuch as a Gender Identity after Castration'. *Journal of Gender Studies* 21(3): 253–270.

Weber, Cynthia. 2016. *Queer International Relations*. New York: Oxford University Press.

Zarkov, Dubravka. 2001. 'The Body of the Other Man: Sexual Violence and the Construction of Masculinity, Sexuality and Ethnicity in Croatian Media'. In Caroline O.N. Moser and Fiona C. Clark (eds), *Victims, Perpetrators or Actors: Gender, Armed Conflict and Political Violence*. London: Zed Books, 69–82.

Zarkov, Dubravka. 2007. *The Body of War: Media, Ethnicity, and Gender in the Break-Up of Yugoslavia*. Durham, NC: Duke University Press Books.

Zarkov, Dubravka. 2011. 'Exposures and Invisibilities: Media, Masculinities and the Narratives of War in an Intersectional Perspective'. In Helma Lutz, Maria Teresa Herrera Vivar, and Linda Supik (eds), *Framing Intersectionality – Debates on a Multi-Faceted Concept in Gender Studies*. Aldershot: Ashgate, 105–120.

9 'Only a fool …' why men don't disclose conflict-related sexual violence in an age of global media

Chris Dolan

Introduction

What confronts the male victim who, in addition to the real people he encounters, discloses his experience of Conflict Related Sexual Violence Against Men (CRSVAM) to millions who view or listen on television, radio, or social media?[1] What comments does discussion of CRSVAM attract in virtual spaces – whether from 'netizens' (Murphy 2006) or 'trolls' (Manjikian 2010)? What narratives/ understandings of sexual violence against men underpin online reactions? Do online 'virtual world' interactions intensify 'real world' disclosure dilemmas confronting male survivors, or do they (also) subvert them? What might this intensification-subversion tension imply for the individual trying to decide whether to disclose or not?

This chapter considers these questions through a case study of two specific broadcasts (BBC Africa television[2] and BBC World Service Focus on Africa radio), which ran concurrently on 2 August 2017, and their online responses on Facebook over the following weeks. The clips contained material from a Congolese male survivor with whom I have worked for a number of years talking about his personal experience. I was also interviewed, in part as the author of a report that contained some statistics about disclosure of rape by South Sudanese men (Dolan 2017a) but also, more broadly, as a researcher and practitioner who has advocated widely both for greater recognition of CRSVAM, and for a fundamental rethink of what CRSVAM implies for the way in which 'gender' is done, particularly in humanitarian circles (Dolan 2014b, 2017b).

My reflections on this particular instance of disclosure and the reactions to it relate to one of my key advocacy concerns, the question of evidence – for without evidence CRSVAM can be (and is) readily dismissed as unimportant. Evidence in the absence of disclosure is not possible, hence my growing interest in exploring and identifying the multiple factors that inform the individual survivor's decision whether or not to disclose. In what follows, I am thus reflecting on a set of dynamics in on which I have had influence and continue to have a personal professional stake in, but that I believe are of more general relevance insofar as they exemplify the complex imbrications or overlaps of CRSVAM (and denial of it), nationalism, gender (and the way it is done), and sexuality.

My day-to-day work with hundreds of victims of CRSVAM indicates that the range and forms of such violence are very wide – but the spaces in which to disclose are very narrow.[3] While much of my practical experience relates to survivors from around the Great Lakes region of Africa, and some specific aspects of CRSVAM are undoubtedly context specific, the lack of disclosure by male survivors is a global one,[4] and remains a major practical obstacle to the development of urgently needed programming underpinned by appropriate laws, policies, and training. The data vacuum created by a lack of disclosure also muddies the theoretical and political waters when searching for inclusive understandings of gender and its multiple interconnections with other key dimensions of victims' identities, notably sexuality, ethnicity, and nationality.

Possible reasons for men's non-disclosure bear repeating here. Many victims, particularly in environments in which the issue is not discussed at all, are likely to believe that they are 'the only one' to whom such a thing has happened. In Africa's Great Lakes region, in cases where the sexual violence takes the form of anal rape, they will have been told by their perpetrators that 'we will make a woman of you' and indeed many victims, rather than say 'they raped me' will say 'they treated me as a woman' – in other (unspoken) words, 'those men penetrated me' (Neumann and Dolan 2009; Wierda and Otim 2011).

Within a logic that equates the act of penetration with masculinity and being penetrated with femininity, the fact of having been penetrated places the masculinity of male victims of rape in considerable jeopardy, not least in contexts with what Tadros describes as 'reified conceptions of masculinities in relation to gender-based violence' (Tadros 2016: 1). This can easily be reinforced by service providers who, for want of better training and information, when confronted with a male victim fall back on widespread male rape myths that it (rape) could not happen to a 'real man'.[5]

The challenge to a victim's masculinity is compounded in many countries, particularly those with penal codes established under British colonial rule,[6] by legal frameworks (Sivakumaran 2007 and 2005; Manivannan 2014; Mouthaan 2013). Although the Rome Statute recognises anal rape (whether of women or men, whether with a penis, another body part, or an object),[7] domestic legislations that define rape as the penetration of a vagina by a penis, do not.[8] Furthermore, penal codes in former British colonies view anal penetration by a man, regardless of the circumstances under which it occurs, as an 'act against the order of nature'; absence of consent by the penetrated man is no defence, rather it may impugn his masculinity (he 'permitted' another man to have carnal knowledge of him) – and, in some jurisdictions, place him at risk of life imprisonment.[9]

Important critiques of rape laws that privilege male defendants over female complainants[10] are intrinsic to the Rome Statute's emphasis on establishing the presence of coercion rather than an absence of consent. However, in jurisdictions like Uganda, proving absence of consent would never be enough; to get justice a male victim would first have to overturn a set of laws premised on gender beliefs positing men as being always in control and thus immune to sexual disempowerment. Rape laws thus work against men when they combine with laws criminalising all forms of same-sex intercourse to actively reinforce the vulnerabilities of men already victimised. By not recognising the rape of men, they imply that a man who is penetrated has not only been feminised, but must have consented to this act, and that therefore his sexual orientation is in question. Laws thus help create and reinforce widely held assumptions of a nexus between a normative gender identity or 'masculinity' and a normative (heterosexual) sexual identity.[11]

Zarkov's work, within a wider literature on gender, sexuality, and nationalism (e.g. Floya and Yuval-Davis 1989; McClintock 1993; Yuval-Davis 1997; Nagel 1998, 2003; Peterson 1999; Puar 2007) suggests further reasons for men not disclosing. While the discussion above indicates some ways in which masculinity and sexuality are mutually constituted, her exploration of 'The Body of the Other Man' (prompted by extensive silence about sexual violence against men despite its documentation in Bassiouni's 1994 report)[12] shows how in former Yugoslavia ethnicity was equally integral to constituting masculinity and sexuality. She also shows how sexual violence against men was systematically used to undermine all three to create 'the other man', who no longer belongs within particular geographic boundaries because his masculinity, sexuality, and ethnicity have all been thrown into question by his victimisation (Zarkov 2001).

Lack of medical training and specialisation constitutes another major obstacle to disclosure for male victims. While women survivors are referred to gynaecologists, there is no corresponding medical specialisation for responding appropriately to the specific medical needs of male survivors.[13] For male victims within humanitarian crises, the lack of services is compounded by the fact that since the 1990s 'gender' has for most humanitarians become synonymous with women and girls (Sivakumaran 2010; Dolan 2014b).[14] The resultant focus of services on women and girls is underpinned by theorisation of a 'continuum of violence' (against women and girls) between conflict and non-conflict settings.[15] In making the claim that there is *no* disconnect between peace and conflict for women, this theorisation obscures the possibility that when it comes to men who in peacetime conform to gender and sexuality norms, there *is* a major disconnect between peace and conflict experiences of vulnerability. In the absence of specialised projects and programmes, some men do seek and succeed in obtaining assistance, but same assistance can have the unfortunate effect of reinforcing the perception of having been feminised. A clear example of this latter dynamic would be when a male survivor seeks medical assistance and is sent to the gynaecology ward of a referral hospital (Men of Hope 2015).

These dilemmas reflect the fact that ignorance of the realities of CRSVAM is as widespread as its perpetration, as are (mis)understandings of gender and sexuality. They suggest that intimate and inter-personal reactions to disclosure are reiterated and reinforced by systemic and institutional silencing within bureaucratised systems of legal, medical, and humanitarian service provision. This combination of inter-personal and structural violations adds insult to injury. For many victims the likely costs are too high, the likely benefits too low to make disclosure a rational choice. As summarised by Stephen Kighoma, whose own disclosure on the BBC World Service is discussed below: '... most male survivors ask "when I open up, what happens? What is next?"'. If he discloses, will he be charged with a crime, mocked as a homosexual, abandoned by his wife, disrespected by his children, and excluded from decision-making by his community?

Notwithstanding these multiple obstacles, there is growing evidence that, under the right circumstances, male survivors are willing and able to disclose. Indeed, disclosure can be an important step in recovering from conflict-related sexual violence, involving activism to raise awareness of the phenomenon and the need to address it more appropriately (Edström, Dolan, Shahrokh, and David. 2016).[16] In what ways, then, does a growing global (social) media intersect with and affect these dynamics and dilemmas of disclosure?

Those focused on the progressive potential of the Internet have described cyberspace as a location for horizontally networked society (Castells in Murphy 2006: 1063), characterised by 'global citizen action' (Wong and Brown 2013), the formation of 'counter-publics' (Fraser 1990 in Salter 2013: 3), and a 're-democratised public sphere' (Fraser 1990 in Salter 2013: 3). Others see it as a site for reproducing nationalism and other forms of sectarianism (Manjikian 2010).[17] With regard to the disclosure of violence against women, Mantilla remarks that: 'The advent of online communities has enabled new forms of virulent sexism' and describes specifically misogynist patterns as 'Gendertrolling' (2013). Salter documents how, while online social media may provide an opportunity for women victims to challenge 'criminal justice system and "old media" [that] are underpinned by homosocial cultures and relations that can marginalise and disrupt the truth claims of girls and women', the success or otherwise is closely linked to the victim's social status (Salter 2013: 14). One analysis of 209 online responses to a discussion of CRSVAM triggered by the publication of 'The Rape of Men: The Darkest Secret of War' in 2011 (Pape 2012) focuses on showing 'how these discussions and exchange of views address gender norms and rules' (Murphy 2006), but, as the piece did not include the names of the victims, it cannot fully address what it means to disclose to a mass audience one's full identity as a survivor.

Background to the case study

After two civil wars in former Sudan (1955–1972, 1983–2005), the Republic of South Sudan finally attained independence on 9 July 2011. In December 2013, however, civil war broke out between President Salva Kiir's Dinka and Vice-President Riek Machar's Nuer factions of the new South Sudanese government. Following a peace agreement in August 2015, conflict erupted again in June 2016, prompting a mass influx of more than one million refugees into Uganda in the next twelve months.

From February to May 2017, prompted by various reports of extreme violence being perpetrated in South Sudan, the Refugee Law Project screened 937 South Sudanese refugees (46 per cent male, 54 per cent female) in the Adjumani,

Lamwo, Kiryandongo, and Kampala districts for experiences of violence – physical, psychological, sexual (Dolan 2017a). In early August, the BBC World Service broadcast a piece on television and radio, under the heading 'South Sudanese Rape: Government and Rebel Forces accused of Sex Offences'. These featured Stephen Kighoma, a Congolese refugee survivor of sexual violence in his country of origin, and myself as the author of the screening project report.

What was said in the BBC interviews

The television clip lasted six minutes and forty seconds, the radio clip lasted three minutes and nineteen seconds. The television newscaster announced that: 'a survey released today by the Ugandan Refugee Law Project reveals that *at least* one in twenty-five male refugees fleeing the latest conflict in South Sudan has suffered sexual violence'. I elaborated that: 'we were finding about 4 per cent of men *disclosing* that they have been victims of rape, and around 9 per cent *telling us* that they have suffered genital trauma' (emphasis added). Both the introduction and my first statement made it clear that the statistics reflected disclosure, not actual prevalence, and imply that the actual prevalence is likely to be higher than 4 per cent.[18]

In response to a question about the difficulties of getting medical help and legal recourse, I laid out the challenges highlighted in the introduction, namely, the lack of recognition of male survivors in law, the lack of medical service providers with appropriate training for working with male survivors, and the questioning of the victim's sexual orientation. Steven Kighoma, introduced by the news anchor as 'a Congolese refugee now living in Uganda who was also raped', disclosed that he had often thought that, after what happened to him, 'dying could be the best option'. He described the humiliation of disclosing to a medic:

> I explained to the doctor about my backache, but they looked at me, the way I was screaming when they told me to do exercises. The doctor told me 'no, this is not just a mere backache, you have something you are not talking about' (...). So I told him that I was used like a woman. (...) I told him that 'I'm bleeding, I have haemorrhoids'. (...) [B]ecause I said I was bleeding they took me to a doctor who was treating women.

During the radio interview, he spelled out the implications of disclosing rape for him, as an ethnic Nande:

> They [the Nande] will tell you, it's a taboo if a male says 'I was raped'. And secondly, as a man, you know in our traditions, I don't need to cry; why would I say that I'm suffering? ... they will tell you that 'you are a coward, you are weak, and you are stupid.'

Asked 'how can we better help male victims of rape?', Kighoma urges law reform so that male rape is recognised:

I want my fellow Africans, my fellow tribe mates, my fellow ethnic people to understand me. I'm not standing here for the gays ... they wish, they love ... they like it, it's theirs. [For] a person who is victimized like me: it was by force, I had a gun pointed at me; it was under the influence of someone's enforcement; ... [whether] in Congo, Uganda, South Africa, Kenya, Tanzania and South Sudan or anywhere, as long as a man says 'I was raped', the law should acknowledge, should listen, should attend, not judging.

Stephen's narrative touches on many of the reasons for non-disclosure outlined above. After disclosing to a physiotherapist that he had been 'used like a woman', he was promptly further feminised when he was referred to a medical doctor 'who was treating women'. Disclosure within his ethnic community could lead to being considered a 'coward', 'weak', and 'stupid', the opposite of idealised masculinity characterised by courage, strength, and intelligence. His primary concern is that his 'fellow Africans', 'fellow tribes-mates', and 'fellow ethnic people' understand him.

In addition to focusing on masculinity, ethnicity, and race, his remarks also explicitly address sexuality. When he says, 'I'm not standing here for the gays', he not only (re)asserts his own heterosexual identity (while acknowledging rather than denying the existence of homosexuality), but also emphasises that people must be able to distinguish between consensual and non-consensual sex – and that this requires a law that is 'not judging' before listening and attending to the victim. Indirectly, therefore, he further highlights the disincentive to disclosure created by existing legal frameworks.

The response

Once posted to BBC Africa's Facebook page, the clip was viewed a further 51,000 times over a three-week period. It was shared 253 times on individuals' timelines/accounts, receiving fifty-two primary comments and numerous secondary ones. Forty primary comments could be accessed while finalising this analysis: thirty-two from men, nine from women. Ten of the men's comments were negative, thirteen positive, eight unclear. Of the women's, none was negative, eight were supportive, one was unclear. The clip provoked the South Sudanese President's Press Secretary to argue that: 'Only a fool would believe men have been raped in South Sudan war.' Published on 8 August 2017 on the news site Hot in Juba,[19] this elicited another fifty-eight comments, of which fifty were published.[20] Forty-two were made by men (one commented twice), eight by women (one commented twice). While *all* the women's comments were supportive, over half (twenty-three) of the men's were negative, seventeen supportive, and two unclear.

The comments on BBC Africa's Facebook page included voices from many corners of the globe, including South Sudan itself, the USA, and Pakistan. The Hot in Juba Facebook page featured South Sudanese primarily, though some were clearly writing from the diaspora. Two comments appeared to come from

Kenya, one from Europe. Despite differences in geographic spread, responses in the two sites show considerable similarities. Most commentators fall into either the hostile 'trolls' or the supportive 'netizens' categories. The former attempt to discredit Stephen as a survivor, the report that gave rise to the BBC clips, and myself as the author of the report. The latter articulate understanding of and solidarity with male victims/survivors.

The BBC moderates comments on its Facebook postings[21] and it is therefore not possible to know how many more offensive comments were removed. Nonetheless, these figures give a sense of the overall distribution, particularly in terms of the predominance of male respondents and the fact that, unlike men who have very mixed reactions, women are almost exclusively writing in support of victims. They also indicate the wider range of nationalities engaging on the BBC Facebook page.

In the presentation that follows, all the quotations are copied direct from the BBC Africa Facebook page (FB) or from Hot in Juba (HIJ). I have made no changes to spelling or punctuation, though I have inserted clarifications in square brackets []. In the footnote to each quotation, I have ascribed a person's gender based on how they present themselves on Facebook.

Deny and discredit: sexual violence against men interpreted as a sign of homosexuality, an import from the West

A dominant theme on the hostile (denialist) side is the simultaneous recasting of male victimisation as an expression of homosexuality – and an Othering of these presumed homosexuals as non-South Sudanese: '… [N]o homosexuality in South Sudan, maybe he was gay from neighbouring country, trying to defame our culture and nation as whole, I'm South Sudanese, no such thing here.'[22] The urge to dissociate not just South Sudan, but indeed Africa as a whole from homosexuality is clear in the comment that: 'We are not gays (Robert Mugabe referred it to entire Africans in his unite nation address). It was demn liars brother.'[23] Equally, 'Did you say rape? Does it mean women now rape men? Because I know very well that there are no homosexuals in AFRICA. That cursed practices isn't and will never be part of our culture.'[24] This was put even more bluntly by another man; 'who da fuck got to do a shit like dat we are not fagy to stick a dick in a man. What a despicable report.'[25] Further instances of denialism included; 'No that thing [same sex rape] can never happen don't spoil our image by saying bullshit'[26] and 'Call it trash that all! Because we don't do such a thing at total.'[27]

These and similar comments demonstrate the close interconnections (in their authors' minds) between understandings of nationalism, sexuality, and gender, and the threat that the reality of sexual violence against men poses to their particular nationalist worldview. While the statement that male rape is a taboo is probably true, it forgets that taboos are a cultural response to an existing behaviour. It also fails to interrogate whether taboos that control actions in peace remain relevant in times of conflict, thus assuming a continuum of *non-violence* against men and boys (compared to the continuum of violence against women and girls discussed above).

The fusion of cultural nationalism with denialism about the possibility of penetration of men stands out in this Juba-originated comment:

> That man is a liar. We have no such male rape cases in South Sudan. The surveyor is biased because we don't have such a thing in our cultures. For a man to have a sex with another man is a taboo in South Sudan.[28]

Another combined cultural nationalism with an attempt to discredit the author of the report; 'Whoever thought of men being raped in South Sudan is straight up gay "South Sudanese men love pussy"'.[29] The connection in some people's minds between whiteness, gayness, and conspiracies to undermine South Sudan is again evident in the caution: 'be aware of white people seeking way to introduce gayness to our home. No men were raped.'[30] (Homo)sexuality is thus imagined as an entirely culturally constructed phenomenon: 'we don't have that culture in South Sudan',[31] along with an attempt to 'Other' the perpetrators:

> Ateny is right in this case.... Never in a million years would male male rape ever take place on South Sudan soil.... The army in question is well known for looting and grabbing civilian property, corruption and female rape which happens even with any other disciplined armies in the world but not male rape....[32]

Not only is homosexuality envisaged as a (Western) construct, it is regarded as one being purposefully deployed to attack South Sudan: 'Completely stupid report ... those whites devil have destroyed their culture and they are after African nation ...'[33] and '... I think this is another way for the western countries to defame and tarnish South Sudanese because male rape has never been one of our problems even if our ancestral history is traced ...'.[34] One person argued that: 'This is absolute nonsense, a foreigner conducting a survey n ends up interviewing another foreigner, thts absolute stupidity n I have lost respect for BBC, fake news.'[35] The message implicit in all these comments is captured by the man who wrote simply, 'BBC psychological ops'.[36] It is also echoed in the description of the clips as 'Febricated story and fake news at the same time',[37] remarks evoking an embattled nation whose defenses are porous and vulnerable to attack by state forces operating clandestinely through the BBC. Perhaps inevitably, attention turns to suspected traitors from within: 'Betrayal [betrayers?] are arming internationally communities with all the lies to dirty painted you guys. Tell them we don't have gay soldiers nor we culturally practiced it.'[38] Unsurprisingly, when challenged on the conflation of victimisation and homosexuality, one response was: 'Lesbian and gay form their west alliance, please my fellows black, keep your crazy freedom of love in the West. You African American are worst then troll.' He added that: 'You gay from west must stop this libel report please, we're not such evils people.'[39]

For the authors of such comments, the mutually constitutive interplay of gender, sexuality, and nationalism is neither academic abstraction nor self-perpetuating discourse; it is something actively shaped by external forces. Allegations of sexual violence are seen as part of a deliberate strategy (by an 'alliance') to 'libel' and 'defame our culture'.[40] The comments also elide gays with *Western*, and propose mutually exclusive 'African' and 'Western' sexualities. African Americans who acknowledge homosexuality and thus betray the belief that sexual orientation is not just a question of geographical location but also skin colour become the ultimate traitors. Not only have they shown a 'crazy' 'freedom of love', they are also 'worst then troll'.

The remark that 'We're not such evils people' passes moral judgement on same-sex intercourse as intrinsically evil and demonstrates how the author sees the allegations of same-sex sexual violence, reimagined as expressions of homosexuality, as coterminous with allegations against the whole South Sudanese *(male) people* that are fundamentally antithetical to the imagined *new* South Sudanese identity. In arguing that 'maybe he [Stephen Kighoma] was gay from neighbouring country', this particular commentator does not deny the existence of homosexuality; in contention for him is what – if the report were true – the existence of same-sex sex would imply for a collective *new* South Sudanese identity.

It should be mentioned that not all critics of the clip saw the issue as one of homosexuality. One person argued that: 'This people are just making their case stronger for resettlement nothing true, that is thr clue for those who haven't idea,'[41] and another that 'Looking for money 😢 that what they do is to make up lies.'[42] It is also worth highlighting the comment that exemplifies a common tendency to see CRSVAM as *torture* rather than sexual violence:

> Western Media are not report on accurate including BBC I have watching live Focus on Africa report on this case of rape but it is not rape but torture, since there is no standard code of punish criminals in South Sudan there are many ways of torture including male organs and I agree with Ateny Wek Ateny.[43]

Acknowledgement and solidarity

On the supportive side, several comments focused on delinking sexual victimisation, sexuality, and nationalism. They introduced an alternative interpretation of disclosure as a demonstration of courage rather than evidence of lying opportunism. For example, 'This brave young man is NOT talking about homosexuality. He is talking about a rape, an abuse of power, a hate crime.'[44] Others drew on the argument used for many years to counter misplaced attention (generally by the defence in court) on the sexuality of women rape victims, namely, 'rape is not about sex, it's about power'. As one commentator spelled out:

> It happens and we need to acknowledge that. This is not about consent [of the victim] or being turned on [on the part of the perpetrator] but dehumanizing

the victim, taking control, and theft of manhood. It is about power nothing less and nothing more. He [the victim] has more courage than most to be willing to show his face and tell his story.[45]

A number of comments from women challenge denialism. One said:

I don't know whether is true or false … [that men were raped in South Sudan] … but if it happened it was by force … in many war occasions the enemy soldiers would attack a family rape the women n girls n if a man resisted to protect his family, the ruthless soldiers would assault a man to teach him a lesson or belittle him. [46]

One reader of earlier comments noted:

I'm noticing a lot of men are denying that male rape even happens and are going strait to what their culture calls for or blaming the west rather than facing some cold hard facts.… Rather than continuing to live under a rock, let's come to terms with what's happening here and now and find a way to help these victims and prevent such atrocities.[47]

Another sought to frame the issue in terms of Africa and African men:

I am saddened by the level of some of our Africans especially most men thinking sexual violence is not happening to African men. Lots of atrocities happening and yet we are denying. Even stripping a man naked is sexual violence. Burning or torturing his genitals is considered as sexual violence etc.…[48]

Some pointed out that denial creates exceptionalist narratives without logical basis; 'hahahaha what is impossible in South Sudan. Many witnessed men being raped by unknown.'[49] Another stated:

'If wives can be lied on top of their husbands and raped, what if the wife is not available? Rape of men was one of the tools used during 22yrs liberation war especially in the most armless and vulnerable communities. 2ndly, if women can not disclose their rape status because it is a taboo, how can rapped man disclose his rape status?[50]

Some Hot in Juba comments targeted the President's Press Secretary Ateny Wek, with one of the women commentators stating that:

He [Ateny Wek] is a foil [fool?] … he does not know that in war rape is a weapon to weaken the opponents and especially prisoners of war are humiliated in that way. For … South Sudan … nothing is impossible when it comes to atrocities meted on its citizens.[51]

She later added that: 'in otherwards he [Ateny Wek] is re-echoing the fact that women are being raped unabated and it is ok for that to continue as long as it is not a male rape.[52] One of the few men to speak out against Ateny Wek did not mince his words: 'F@#k Ateny wek Ateny.... Vulnerable men could be rape victims ... stupid thought!.'[53]

Concluding reflections

While this piece focuses on how comments create incentives and disincentives to disclose, it is important to also note that the very nature of the reporting and online reactions, by making visible the issue of rape of men, also does considerable (probably unintended) work to perpetuate the invisibilisation of multiple other (non-rape) forms of CRSVAM. While denialist heteronormative visions of nationalism obsess about sexuality to the point that the violence itself is effectively erased, the supportive comments may, inadvertently, also undermine victims of *other* forms of CRSVAM. For example, the effort to clarify that the victims' sexual orientation is not the real issue and that a man's sexual victimisation cannot be explained away on those grounds, obscures the fact that the sexuality (regardless of orientation) of most male victims is profoundly impacted. While *Hidden Realities* covers a whole host of statistics from both women and men respondents, all of which should be of concern (Dolan 2017a), the global media focused in on the fact that 4 per cent of men had disclosed being *raped*. It thus reinforced rape as the iconic instance of conflict-related sexual violence against men, thus further consolidating the obstacles to survivors needing to disclose non-rape forms of CRSVAM.

With regard to the question of disclosure by male survivors of CRSV, and notwithstanding the limitations of analysing comments from which the most outspoken have already been removed by the media source in question,[54] the response to the clips discussed above provides food for thought when considering how globally accessible (social) media could influence the dynamics and dilemmas of disclosure. Disclosure of issues and experiences considered taboo in many 'real world' settings has never been easier nor had more reach than in this age of global media. At the same time, I would suggest, deciding to disclose has never been harder.

For the victim who discloses, the aggression of online denialists reproduces and amplifies the gender and sexuality norms encountered in the 'real world' reactions frequently by family, community, state duty bearers, and service providers; disbelief that men can be raped, questioning victims' sexual orientation, accusing victims of lying for financial gain or better resettlement prospects. The reproduction of norms is visible not just in terms of what is said, but who is saying it: far more men than women are engaged by the issue, and whereas approximately half the men seek to discredit the evidence, women tend to show solidarity with the victims.[55] The online aggression by men thus compounds the aggression of the original violations, which were also largely perpetrated by men.

For those (male) viewers/listeners who did not want to hear the content, or indeed who wanted to deny it, Kighoma's positionality as a non-francophone Congolese survivor and mine as a white British male reporting on disclosures of CRSVAM in South Sudan, provided a convenient opt-out to focus on shooting the messengers rather than dealing with the message. Where conceptions of the nation are threatened by victim narratives, denialists will respond by discrediting and blaming the victim.

What we represent in the eyes of the viewers, whether in terms of their notions of plausibility (how can a Congolese not sound Francophone and what is the BBC playing at by using him in a piece about South Sudanese survivors?) or position within (anti-)colonial hierarchies of privilege (why should we listen to a white man?), thus has considerable influence on how the information is received and interpreted, and thus on how it is (or is not) disseminated. Rather than adjusting received notions of nationalist masculinity, denialists paint survivors who disclose (and even those who are supportive towards those who disclose), as traitors to their country of origin. Paradoxically – when it comes to sexuality at least – ardent (denialist) nationalists seem to believe that 'Africa is a Country' and that the man who admits to victimisation thus betrays both his country of origin and the broader 'African' country. As the attacks, not just on Kighoma but also on pro-survivor African Americans and Africans based in the West reveal, denialists deem it necessary to deny survivors and their supporters both nationality AND race. They exploit the global space provided by the Internet to extend the control of and exclusion from the newly established – and visibly precarious – South Sudan. Had the survivor who disclosed on the BBC been South Sudanese rather than Congolese, the hostile reactions from Ateny Awek and others would have been (even more) intimidating; the fact that the presidential press secretary took note of and responded angrily in public to reports of disclosure by other South Sudanese male survivors, would trigger multiple issues of physical security and protection – and create a correspondingly strong disincentive to disclose.

Over and above 'real world' reactions, disclosure on global media such as the BBC, through its ability to reach people and spaces that are rarely, if ever, confronted by face-to-face disclosures, surfaces the intensely and overtly political dimensions of CRSVAM. Global (social) media thus 'up the ante' for survivors considering disclosure. In some contexts, this could escalate risk and further jeopardise survivors' protection and security, particularly for refugees living just across the border from where there violation happened. In the case of the South Sudanese men whose disclosure was discussed in *Hidden Realities*, to comment on the rape of men in South Sudan is to risk being interpreted as attacking the Government of South Sudan, which either through acts of omission or commission, bears responsibility for not protecting its own citizens.

Against the reactions to this highly political act of disclosure, there is very little protection, and the aggravated risks of further harassment and violation surely amplify existing disincentives to disclose. On the other hand, for the survivor for whom disclosure is an integral part of recovery (Edström *et al.* 2016), the existence of global media spaces, within which there are clearly numerous supportive voices, increases the prospects of a new sense of self as an activist confronting the forces that have tried to suppress him and, importantly, given the range of countries and contexts from which support emanates, can itself provide a sense of protection that is qualitatively different from the support provided in 'real life' responses to disclosure. In short, global media has the potential to simultaneously intensify the risks of global harassment *and*, through global expressions of solidarity, subvert them.[56]

Notes

1   The BBC claims a global audience of 348 million, see Mark Sweney, 'BBC's Global Audience Hits 348 Million', *Guardian*, 29 April 2016, www.theguardian.com/media/2016/apr/29/bbc-global-audience-hits-348-million. 'In Uganda, 1 in 5 adults (15 and older) consume BBC content each week … In Sierra Leone, the BBC World Service Group reaches 65 percent of the population.' from 'BBC Weekly Audience in Africa Rises to a Record 111 Million', BBC Media, 11 August 2016, www.bbc.co.uk/mediacentre/latestnews/2016/weekly-audience-in-africa. In 2015, the BBC had 100 million listeners in Africa, from 'BBC's Combined Global Audience Revealed at 308 Million', BBC Media Centre, 21 May 2015, www.bbc.co.uk/mediacentre/latest-news/2015/combined-global-audience.

2   See BBC Africa, on Facebook, www.facebook.com/bbcafrica/videos/101556812 74815229/. Accessed 25 September 2017.

3   For an elaboration of forms, see Dolan 2014c and Chapleau *et al.* 2008.

4   I have conducted numerous trainings on this topic in a wide range of locations in Africa, Europe, Latin America, Asia, and the Middle East, with participants from a correspondingly range of countries, and the participants consistently argue that they know that CRSVAM happens, but they don't know how to enable men to disclose.

5   For a discussion of male rape myths, see Dolan 2014a.

6   Uganda, Tanzania, India, all of which have very similar definitions established under British rule (Tadros 2016).

7   Rome Statute definition:

> The perpetrator invaded the body of a person by conduct resulting in penetration, however slight, *of any part of the body of the victim* or the perpetrator with a sexual organ or of the anal or genital opening of the victim with any object or any other part of the body. (emphasis added)

8   Article 123, Chapter XIV (Offences Against Morality) of the Ugandan Penal Code, for example, defines rape as:

> Any person who has unlawful carnal knowledge of a woman or girl, without her consent, or with her consent, if the consent is obtained by force or by means of threats or intimidation of any kind or by fear of bodily harm, or by means of false representations as to the nature of the act, or in the case of a married woman, by personating her husband, commits the felony termed rape.

9   Article 145c (Unnatural Offences) of the Ugandan Penal Code stipulates that: 'Any person who permits a male person to have carnal knowledge of him or her against the order of nature commits an offence and is liable to imprisonment for life.'

10   For example, Estrich 1987.

11   Sexual identity – the 'orientation' a person presents in public – may or may not be congruent with a person's internal sexual orientation. MSM (Men who have Sex with

Men), for example, are generally understood to present as heterosexual in public but have a same-sex attraction that they pursue in private.

It is worth noting that in Uganda, until recently, the Police Form (PF3) on which police were supposed to document injuries to complainants depicted a female body outline upon which the location of injuries could be marked by the police surgeon. This was amended in 2013. PF3A has both male and female body outlines.

12 See Bassiouni and McCormick 1996.

13 Medical students in Uganda, for example, have attested to the author that there is no place in their five-year curriculum where they are taught to respond to rectal and genital traumas frequently resulting from CRSVAM.

14 Decades of 'gender' work in the humanitarian sphere have made it as much a site of 'reified conceptions of masculinities in relation to gender-based violence' (Storr 2011) as some of the contexts humanitarians are supposed to be responding to.

15 See, for example, Aisling Swaine's discussion of CEDAW General Recommendation 35, blog, London School of Economics and Political Science, 12 September 2017, http://blogs.lse.ac.uk/wps/2017/09/12/cedaw-general-recommendation-35-draws-an-explicit-link-between-gender-discrimination-and-conflict-related-violence-against-women/.

16 See 5 'Journeys to Activism – Aime Moninga', Refugee Law Project, School of Law, Makerere University, Kampala, Uganda, https://refugeelawproject.org/component/allvideoshare/video/journeys-to-activism-aime-moninga?Itemid=151.

17 See Manjikian (2010: 384–387) for summary of 'utopian' and 'realist' theorisations of cyberspace, and a discussion of the Internet's power to mobilise an 'arena of ideological conflict' (Manjikian 2010: 396).

18 Despite these attempts to distinguish disclosure from prevalence, the statistic rapidly morphed into a claim about incidence: 'According to a research carried out by the Uganda Refugee Law Project released this month, 4% of men and 20% of women refugees in South Sudan have been raped' (Hot In Juba 2017).

19 See Masura, '"Only a Fool Would Believe Men have been Raped in South Sudan War," says Ateny Wek', Hot in Juba, 8 August 2017, http://hotinjuba.com/fool-believe-men-raped-south-sudan-war-says-ateny-wek/. Accessed 25 September 2017.

20 See www.facebook.com/hotinjuba/posts/1480525912014084. Accessed 25 September 2017.

21 As stated on the BBC website,

> At the BBC, we allow as much freedom as possible to have relevant debate on our website. However, we are also responsible for making sure that these discussions stay polite, safe and relevant and do not violate any laws or the BBC's Editorial Guidelines.
>
> (www.bbc.co.uk/social/moderation/faqs/moderation#faqitem-3-3)

22 FB-M (South Sudan).
23 HIJ-M (nationality not stated, living in Australia).
24 FB-M, 3 August 2017.
25 HIJ-M (Juba, South Sudan).
26 HIJ-M (Juba, South Sudan).
27 HIJ-M (Bor, South Sudan).
28 FB-M (South Sudan).
29 HIJ-Male (South Sudanese).
30 HIJ-Male (South Sudanese).
31 HIJ-M (Juba).
32 HIJ-M (South Sudanese in Uganda).
33 HIJ-M (Juba).
34 HIJ-M (South Sudanese in Uganda).
35 FB-M (South Sudanese in Uganda).

36 FB-M (Nigerian, New York).
37 FB-M (South Sudanese in US).
38 HIJ-M.
39 FB-M (South Sudan).
40 In the absence of studies of male perpetrators of CRSVAM, it is difficult to comment on their sexual orientation. Establishing the extent to which perpetrator orientation plays a role in such acts would be helpful in establishing the utility or otherwise of the view that: 'rape is not about sex, it's about power'.
41 FB-M (South Sudanese in UK). This was also stated in a HIJ comments that: 'Those are a bunch of idiots seeking for asylum to the western world' (HIJ-M, living in USA).
42 FB-M (South Sudanese).
43 HIJ-M (South Sudanese).
44 FB-F (Seattle).
45 FB-F (Bronx, New York).
46 HIJ-F.
47 FB-F (Florida).
48 FB-M (Uganda).
49 HIJ-M (Juba, South Sudan).
50 HIJ-M.
51 HIJ-F (Uganda).
52 HIJ-F (Uganda).
53 HIJ-M (Juba).
54 Even some of the moderated comments exemplify what has been described as the 'online disinhibition effect', namely, '... people say and do things in cyberspace that they wouldn't ordinarily say and do in the face-to-face world. They loosen up, feel less restrained, and express themselves more openly' (Suler 2004).
55 Whether women are more sympathetic to male survivors than men, or women in South Sudan have less access to the Internet than men, or women are not particularly interested in this story, is unclear. Certainly, those women who participated were well prepared and drew important parallels between the victimisation of women and men.
56 Following the enactment of the Anti-Pornography Act (2014), Uganda is procuring equipment with which to detect key words and phrases; it remains to be seen what impact such measures will have, whether on disclosure or denialism.

References

Bassiouni, Cherif. 1994. Final Report of the United Nations Commission of Experts Established Pursuant to Security Council Resolution 780, S/1994/674. New York: United Nations.

Bassiouni, M. Cherif and Marcia McCormick. 1996. Sexual Violence: An Invisible Weapon of War in the Former Yugoslavia. Occasional Paper #1, International Human Rights Law Institute, DePaul University.

Chapleau, Kristine M., Debra L. Oswald, and Brenda L. Russell. 2008. 'Male Rape Myths: The Role of Gender, Violence, and Sexism'. Journal of Interpersonal Violence 23(5): 600–615.

Dolan, Chris. 2014a. 'Into the Mainstream: Addressing Sexual Violence Against Men and Boys in Conflict'. Overseas Development Institute (May): 1–12.

Dolan, Chris. 2014b. 'Letting Go of the Gender Binary: Charting New Pathways for Humanitarian Interventions on Gender-Based Violence'. International Review of the Red Cross 96(894): 485–501.

Dolan, Chris. 2014c. *Report of Workshop on Sexual Violence Against Men*. New York: United Nations.

Dolan, Chris. 2017a. 'Hidden Realities: Screening for Experiences of Violence Amongst War-Affected South Sudanese Refugees in Northern Uganda', Refuge Law Project, Working Paper 25, Kampala. https://refugeelawproject.org/files/working_papers/RLP.WP25.pdf.

Dolan, Chris. 2017b. 'Inclusive Gender: Why Tackling Gender Hierarchies Cannot be at the Expense of Human Rights and the Humanitarian Imperative'. *International Review of the Red Cross*, 1–10.

Edström, Jerker, Chris Dolan, Thea Shahrokh, and Onen David. 2016. 'Therapeutic Activism: Men of Hope Refugee Association Uganda breaking the Silence Over Male Rape in Conflict-Related Sexual Violence'. *Brief Supporting Evidence Report* 182. Institute of Development Studies, 58.

Estrich, Susan. 1987. *Real Rape*. Cambridge, MA: Harvard University Press.

Floya, Anthia and Nira Yuval-Davis. 1989. *Woman-Nation-State*. London: Palgrave Macmillan.

Hot in Juba. 2017. '"Only a Fool Would Believe Men have been Raped in South Sudan War", says Ateny Wek'. Juba, South Sudan: Hot in Juba, 8 August. Accessed 9 November 2017. http://hotinjuba.com/fool-believe-men-raped-south-sudan-war-says-ateny-wek/.

McClintock, Anne. 1993. 'Family Feuds: Gender, Nationalism and the Family'. *Feminist Review* – Nationalisms and National Identities. 44: 61–80.

Manivannan, Anjali. 2014. 'Seeking Justice for Male Victims of Sexual Violence in Armed Conflict'. *Journal of International Law and Politics* 46: 635–679.

Manjikian, Mary M. E. 2010. 'From Global Village to Virtual Battlespace: The Colonizing of the Internet and the Extension of Realpolitik'. *International Studies Quarterly* 54(2): 381–401.

Mantilla, Karla. 2013. 'Gendertrolling: Misogyny Adapts to New Media'. *Source: Feminist Studies* 39(2): 563–570.

Men of Hope, 2015. *Men Can Be Raped Too*, Uganda: Refugee Law Project. Accessed 2 March 2018. https://refugeelawproject.org/component/allvideoshare/video/men-can-be-raped-too?Itemid=151.

Mouthaan, Solange. 2013. 'Sexual Violence against Men and International Law – Criminalising the Unmentionable'. *International Criminal Law Review* 13(3): 665–695.

Murphy, Emma C. 2006. 'Agency and Space: The Political Impact of Information Technologies in the Gulf Arab States'. *Third World Quarterly* 27(6): 1059–1083.

Nagel, Joane. 1998. 'Masculinity and Nationalism: Gender and Sexuality in the Making of Nations'. *Ethnic and Racial Studies* 21(2): 242–269.

Nagel, Joane. 2003. *Race, Ethnicity, and Sexuality: Intimate Intersections, Forbidden Frontiers*. New York: Oxford University Press.

Neumann, Daniel and Chris Dolan. 2009. *Gender Against Men*. 44-min advocacy documentary, June. Kampala, Uganda: The Refugee Law Project.

Otim, Patrick and Chris Dolan. 2011. *They Slept With Me, Uganda: Refugee Law Project*. Accessed 21 February 2018. www.refugeelawproject.org/component/allvideoshare/video/they-slept-with-me-community-reactions?Itemid=151.

le Pape, Marc. 2012. 'Follow-Up to "Wartime Rape: Men, Too"'. *Crash*. Paris: Fondation Médicins Sans Frontiers.

Peterson, V. Spike. 1999. 'Political Identities/Nationalism as Heterosexism'. *International Feminist Journal of Politics* 1(1): 34–65.

Puar, Jasbir K. 2007. *Terrorist Assemblages: Homonationalism in Queer Times*. Durham, NC: Duke University Press.

Salter, Michael. 2013. 'Justice and Revenge in Online Counter-Publics: Emerging Responses to Sexual Violence in the Age of Social Media'. *Crime, Media, Culture: An International Journal* 9(3): 225–242.

Sivakumaran, Sandesh. 2005. 'Male/Male Rape and the "Taint" of Homosexuality'. *Human Rights Quarterly* 27(2): 1274–1306.

Sivakumaran, Sandesh. 2007. 'Sexual Violence Against Men in Armed Conflict'. *European Journal of International Law* 18(2): 253–276.

Sivakumaran, Sandesh. 2010. 'Lost in Translation: UN Responses to Sexual Violence Against Men and Boys in Situations of Armed Conflict'. *International Review of the Red Cross* 92(877): 259–277.

Storr, Will. 2011. 'The Rape of Men: The Darkest Secret of War'. *Guardian*, 17 July. www.theguardian.com/society/2011/jul/17/the-rape-of-men.

Struckman-Johnson, Cindy and David Struckman-Johnson. 1992. 'Acceptance of Male Rape Myths Among College Men and Women'. *Sex Roles* 27(3–4): 85–100.

Suler, John. 2004. 'The Online Disinhibition Effect'. *CyberPsychology & Behavior* 7(3): 321–326.

Tadros, Mariz. 2016. 'Challenging Reified Masculinities: Men as Survivors of Politically Motivated Sexual Assault in Egypt'. *Journal of Middle East Women's Studies* 12(3): 323–342.

Wierda, Marieke and Michael Otim. 2011. 'Courts, Conflict and Complementarity in Uganda". In Carsten Stahn and Mohamed M. El Zeidy (eds), *The International Criminal Court and Complementarity: From Theory to Practice*. Cambridge: Cambridge University Press, 1155–1179.

Wong, Wendy H. and Peter A. Brown. 2013. 'E-Bandits in Global Activism: WikiLeaks, Anonymous, and the Politics of No One'. *Perspectives on Politics* 11(4): 1015–1033.

Yuval-Davis, Nira. 1997. *Gender and Nation*, London: Sage.

Zarkov, Dubravka. 2001. 'The Body of the Other Man: Sexual Violence and the Construction of Masculinity, Sexuality and Ethnicity in Croation Media'. In Caroline Moser and Fiona Clark (eds), *Victors, Perpetrators or Actors? Gender, Armed Conflict and Political Violence*. London: Zed Books, 69–81.

10 Masculine subjectivities in United Nations discourse on gender violence (1970–2015)

Absent actors, deviant perpetrators, allies, and victims

Gizeh Becerra

Sexual violence against men has increasingly become a subject of UN policy in the last decade, and efforts to address the issue have expanded, particularly in conflict and post-conflict situations. However, most conflict-related sexual violence initiatives still mainly target women and girls, bolstered in part by Security Council Resolution 1325 (2000) and its successors. Some have argued that the historic focus of UN discourse on women as victims of violence hinders the full recognition of sexual violence against men as a serious problem (Special Representative of the Secretary General on Sexual Violence in Conflict 2013: 10). Indeed, in United Nations discourse, conflict-related sexual violence (CRSV) has been primarily represented as a 'women's issue'; the question of men and violence, beyond their role as perpetrators, was rarely examined until recently. The increased attention that is now awarded to men and boys as victims of sexual violence and as 'allies' for the elimination of violence against women (VAW), has caused much debate about the way men and women are represented in discourses on VAW and CRSV. Changes in these discourses signal an important shift in the understanding of gender and violence more broadly, and it is important to examine how these issues are being conceptualised. I argue that problem representations that do not acknowledge the gendered roots of various forms of violence tend to obscure the systemic nature of gendered power imbalances. Failure to recognise that violence occurs as a result of imbalances in social power structures, leads to a focus on the role individuals play, either as perpetrators or victims, and narrows down the conversation to arguments over which groups deserve to be recognised as subjects of policy.

This chapter provides an overview of the representation of men and boys in UN discourse from the emergence of violence against women as an international public problem during the UN Decade for Women, to recent shifts in the conceptualisation of gender violence. It traces the evolving construction of masculine subjectivities in different gender violence discourses – from their invisibilisation in discourses on trafficking and domestic violence, to the representation of perpetrators as pathologically dysfunctional or socially isolated, to the emerging representations of men and boys as allies for the prevention of violence against women and as victims of sexual violence in conflict and post-conflict situations. The aim is to highlight frames, which have shaped the context into which the SVAM and CRSV debates emerged in the past decade. In the first and second sections, I argue that public health and criminal justice perspectives, which pervade in discourses on VAW, have tended to individualise the problem by focusing on the impact that multiple social and environmental factors have on victims and perpetrators and downplaying the influence of gendered power structures. In the third section, I show how a desire to highlight the social norms and systemic inequalities which result in and perpetuate male aggression, led to the emergence of the 'engaging men and boys as allies' frame in discourses on VAW. I argue that despite the factors which led to the frame's emergence, its use in awareness-raising campaigns reflects a much more limited problem representation. Finally, I discuss the factors which influenced the recognition that sexual violence can be directed at men or boys, and how this recent expansion has the potential to further research on violence and masculinity. I also note perspectives that tend to obscure the different dynamics that underlie male-to-male and male-to-female violence, and underplay the importance of power imbalances present in male-to-female violence. I hope to convey the fact that arguments which advance particular representations of gender violence over others should take into consideration the effects of their problem framings and subject constructions.

Absent perpetrators in discourses on violence against women

The issue of violence against women emerged in the mid-1980s to early 1990s, thanks to the advocacy of women's groups at the UN Women's World Conferences (1975–1985), the Vienna Conference for Human Rights (1993), and the International Conference on Population and Development (1994) (Fraser 1987; Bunch 1990; Bunch and Reilly 1994; Antrobus 2004; Pietila 2007; Joachim 2007). Documents issued from these international conferences focused mainly on the gravity of the problem and its impact on women's and children's lives. The reports of the Women's World Conferences often do not mention perpetrators of violence. When perpetrators are represented, their gender is not specified. Men and boys are mostly invisible in the discourse of the Decade for Women, hinted at through ambiguous language, their roles as perpetrators and/or victims of violence largely unexplored.

The 1975 Mexico report includes a resolution on *The Prevention of the Exploitation of Women and Girls*, which presents prostitution as 'one of the most grievous offences against the dignity of women' but attributes the prevalence of the problem to 'socio-economic conditions' (United Nations 1975). The gendered nature of the problem, its roots in the systemic inequality between men and women, and the link to male sexual entitlement to women's bodies is not mentioned. Moreover, the victims' gender is mentioned several times, but the perpetrators' is never specified.

The resolution on *Women Victims of Trafficking and Involuntary Prostitution* of the 1985 Nairobi Forward Looking Strategies contains a similar problem representation. It attributes the causes of the problem to the 'economic degrada-tion that alienates women's labour through processes of rapid urbanization and migration resulting in underemployment and unemployment' (United Nations 1985). However, a marked difference with respect to the past documents is the reference to 'women's dependence on men', appearing alongside economic factors as a cause of prostitution and trafficking. This reference signals a greater feminist influence, though the phrase is brief and isn't further explained. Focus-ing heavily on economic factors, the resolution recommends 'providing eco-nomic opportunities, training, employment and self-employment' for women in vulnerable communities (United Nations 1985). No measures are recommended to address 'women's dependence on men' as it is created by family law and other factors outside of economic ones.

Resolutions addressing partner violence also invisibilise the role of male per-petrators. The resolution on *Battered Women and Violence in the Family* of the 1980 Copenhagen Conference notes that:

> violence in the home and in the family (...) in particular physical, sexual and other forms of abuse of women, children and the elderly constitutes (...) a grave problem for the physical and mental health of the family as well as for society.

> (United Nations 1980)

The resolution refers to harm done to the family, which suggests a state per-spective that is preoccupied with maintaining family unity for the sake of social order. As scholar Pamela Pleck notes: 'the single most consistent barrier to reform against domestic violence has been the Family Ideal – that is, unrelated but nonetheless distinct ideas about family privacy, conjugal and parental rights and family stability' (Pleck 2004: 7). However, feminist ideas coexist with state perspectives, as paragraph 4 recognises that: 'long-held attitudes that diminish the value of women have resulted in virtual immunity from prosecution of persons who commit acts of violence against members of their families and against women in the care of institutions' (United Nations 1980). Despite this recognition, language again obscures who the perpetrators of violence are. More-over, it sets spousal violence and child abuse under the all-encompassing umbrella term of 'family violence', erasing the particularities of each issue and the very different needs that children and adults have, even when both are victims at the hands of the same perpetrator.

A shift in problem representation can be seen in the 1985 *Nairobi Forward Looking Strategies'* resolution titled *Abused Women*, which recommends provi-sions such as the 'suppression of degrading images and representation of women in society' as a means of preventing violence (United Nations 1985). This recog-nises that violence is tied to the objectification of women in society, and signals a shift away from a state perspective that presents economic and environmental factors as the primary causes of violence. However, even discourses that recog-nise broader patterns of discrimination against women do not explicitly address male privilege or its influence on how women are represented in the media. The resolution is brief and does not mention patriarchal structures shaping the representation of women for the male gaze.

In 1993, the *Declaration for the Elimination of All Forms of Violence Against Women* brought under one term various forms of violence against women and set out to provide an official definition for the problem, an explanation of its causes and consequences, and recommendations for its elimination. The Declaration is arguably the UN's most influential text on the subject, as the definition it provides is used by several UN agencies, programmes, and campaigns and has even entered mainstream discourses through its use by international and local NGOs and by some governments.

The language of the Declaration differs from UN Decade for Women resolutions; the text is clear on the gendered social roots of violence against women. The preamble states that:

> violence against women is a manifestation of historically unequal power relations between men and women, which have led to domination over and *discrimination against women by men* and to the prevention of the full advancement of women, and that violence against women is one of the crucial social mechanisms by which women are forced into a subordinate position compared with men.
>
> (United Nations 1993 – emphasis added)

This is the first instance of a UN document addressing the issue of gender violence explicitly, stating that women are discriminated against *by men*, that this relationship is one of power and domination over women, and that violence is not only a consequence of this domination but is also a mechanism which serves to perpetuate women's subordination. The language of the Declaration shows how a broader problem representation that considers the gendered nature of the problem leads to an examination of men's role in gender violence.

Moreover, as the Declaration's operative clauses recommend measures for the elimination of violence, the text serves to illustrate how the representation of men in the problem definition circumscribes the possibilities imagined for them in policy. While most recommendations focus on responding to the problem by protecting victims and providing them with adequate services, two measures address prevention. The first suggests developing legal, political, administrative, and cultural preventive approaches to violence (United Nations 1993, Art. 4f). The second recommends modifying 'the social and cultural patterns of conduct of men and women' and eliminating 'prejudices, customary practices and all other practices based on the idea of the inferiority or superiority of either of the sexes and on stereotyped roles for men and women' (United Nations 1993, Art. 4j.). Though these preventive measures are not as extensive as those included to respond to the problem, they nevertheless constitute the first recommendations that highlight the need to change masculine patterns of behaviour and stereotyped roles of men as well as women. Thus, the Declaration marks a change from the discursive patterns of previous UN resolutions and brings men into both definitional and policy discourses.

Counselling 'deviant' perpetrators

While the role of perpetrators was obscured in the majority of texts throughout the UN Decade for Women, in the few instances where they were discussed their behaviour tended to be represented as falling outside the norm. Discourses influenced by the public health and criminal justice fields focused on perpetrators' 'deviant' behaviour and methods that could act as deterrents for violators.

The 1980 Copenhagen resolution on *Battered Women and Violence in the Family* states that the causes of violence against women 'vary' but mentions the following 'contributing factors' without specifying whether they pertain to the perpetrator, the victim, or both: 'geographic and social isolation, financial difficulties, irregular employment, alcohol or drug abuse, and low self-esteem' (United Nations 1980). Similar to other resolutions of the decade, this document links economic factors such as poverty and lack of employment to violence. However, by highlighting factors like social isolation, substance abuse, and low self-esteem, it creates a portrait of the batterer as a troubled individual. It does not examine economic and environmental factors as macro-level forces that compound gender inequality, but considers them because of their psychological impact on the individual. The scholar Pamela Johnston refers to this perspective as the 'psychodynamic formulation', which portrays violence as an issue of sick individuals or sick relationships (Walker 1990: 78). The problem is 'seen as located and maintained within the individual' and as such calls for 'counselling or psychotherapy focused on intra-psychic and behavioural patterns' (Walker 1990: 78).

This type of frame is linked to the growing influence of the public health sector in creating policies to tackle various forms of violence, including against women and children. In several Western countries, refuges and rape crisis centres founded by women's groups and feminist activists were transformed into 'social agencies' during the late 1970s as many shelters needed funding from the state to expand or open in new areas. In the United States, the first services for batterers that were established in the 1970s were preceded by 'the counselling for male alcoholics provided by psychopathic hospitals' (Pleck 2004: 192). In France, the state-run Centre for Lodging and Social Reinsertion (CHRS in French), populated by social workers and psychologists, provided funding for the founding of shelters run by women's organisations (Delage 2015: 72). This link between state institutions and feminist organisations led to the increased influence of public health discourses which tended to explain domestic violence as the product of 'stress and frustration, compounded by alcoholism and drugs' (Pleck 2004: 195).

Later documents, such as the 1995 Beijing Platform for Action, do emphasise the roots of violence in gender inequalities – stating that it is a 'manifestation of the historically unequal power relations between men and women' (United

Nations 1995: 49). Yet the Platform for Action recommends addressing perpetrators' behaviour primarily through public health interventions. It suggests that states adopt legislation to provide remedies for the 'healing of victims and rehabilitation of perpetrators', recommends providing funding for 'counselling and rehabilitation programmes for the perpetrators of violence', and suggests promoting 'research to further efforts concerning such counselling and rehabilitation so as to prevent the recurrence of such violence' (United Nations 1995: 51).

It is also important to mention the influential work of the World Health Organization whose leading reports on partner violence (WHO 2002: 96, 2005: 8, 2010: 18) make use of the ecological framework created by developmental psychologist Jay Belsky (1980). In this framework, individual factors (e.g. women's previous victimisation, partner's employment status, whether the partner had witnessed violence as a child) and social factors (e.g. economic inequality between men and women, attitudes towards gender roles and violence against women) are all considered potential 'risk factors'. Though the aim of the framework is to 'conceptualize violence as a multifaceted phenomenon' (Heise 1998: 263–264), the framework does not differentiate between causal factors and factors which heighten the risk of violence. The framework is used by other influential institutions, like the European Union (EU) Commission, which in 2010 saw the need to modify it to emphasise the gendered nature of violence against women. In the modified EU version of the framework, certain factors are represented as having a higher level of influence than others; most high-influence factors are linked to gender power disparities and socialisation (Hagemann-White *et al.* 2010).

Towards the mid-2000s, public health perspectives were still influential, though these began to incorporate a gender element, and it is not clear whether these elements are grounded in feminist perspectives. The report of the Secretary General on the ten-year implementation of the Beijing Platform for Action notes that: 'prevention measures increasingly include rehabilitation of offenders: some countries provide psychological treatment and gender-sensitivity training' (CSW 2004: 45). The fact that gender-sensitivity training is mentioned is a tacit recognition that the root of violence lies within the construction of gendered identities. However, it is not clear what this training consists of, and the recommendation still targets individual behaviours rather than framing the problem as a problem with socialisation, masculinity, and power-structures that are biased in favour of men as a group.

Men and boys as allies for the prevention of violence

The 1995 Beijing Platform for Action marked a shift from the discursive obscuring of men or their representation as deviant to portraying them as potential allies in the prevention of violence against women. The Platform for Action is the first UN document to state that: 'men's groups mobilizing against gender violence are necessary allies for change' (United Nations 1995: 50). This shift in the representation of male subjects was influenced by the growing field of masculinity studies and the advent of gender mainstreaming within the UN system.

The work of scholars such as Carrigan, Connell, and Lee (1985) outlined the concept of hegemonic masculinity which linked problems of individual male behaviour to the larger social construction of masculine identities. Ways of 'being and behaving that are associated with dominance and power' became the focus of study, and work in this field revealed that: 'not all men benefit from and subscribe to dominant values' (Cornwall 1997: 11). 'Hegemonic masculinity' can be 'just as oppressive for those men who refuse, or fail to conform' (Cornwall 1997: 11). These concepts provided a social explanation for violence, which rooted the problem in the gendered socialisation of men and highlighted their privilege within social power structures. At the same time, it allowed for some men's participation in problem-solving by noting the value added of gender equality for men who didn't conform to hegemonic norms.

Moreover, the UN's efforts to mainstream gender equality into all policies caused a shift in the way women's rights were framed. On the one hand, 'attention to women-specific issues by women-specific machinery' remained a cornerstone of the organisation's work. On the other hand, UN officials pushed for a gender approach which reinforced 'an understanding that gender equality must be addressed as a strategic objective by society as a whole, rather than being a "women's concern"' (Office of the UN Secretary General 1998: 9). The launching of gender mainstreaming at the Beijing conference sought to achieve this objective; it also entailed the hope of 'co-opting new allies to gender equality' (Timothy 2008). Since then, several UN organisations have begun to incorporate initiatives to engage men in strategies to prevent violence against women.

UN Women, for instance, works closely with MenEngage 'a global alliance' that 'engages in information-sharing to capture the emerging techniques in engaging men and to assist one another in capacity-building' (MenEngage Alliance 2017). In 2014, UN Women participated in the 2nd MenEngage Global Symposium in New Delhi, India. The Delhi Declaration and Call to Action that resulted from the Symposium, stated that: 'it is essential to work with men and boys to transform social norms perpetuating GBV, to redress the effects of violence that boys experience and witness' (MenEngage Alliance 2014). The document identifies effective practices such as: 'group education methodologies that engage men and boys in challenging gender', 'school-based dating violence prevention programs', and 'bystander interventions which engage men to challenge other men's use of violence' (MenEngage Alliance *et al.* 2015: 32). In contrast to public health interventions, which attempt to modify perpetrators' pathological behaviour through counselling, these 'community-based' initiatives can target both perpetrators and non-violent men. They seek to eliminate violent behaviours by modifying traditional conceptions of masculinity held by men within a community. By focusing on the ways in which targeted interventions can reshape masculinities as opposed to individual behaviours, perpetrators are represented in discourse as violent but not deviant, since all men are somewhere along a spectrum of 'toxic masculinity' (Connell and Messerschmidt 2005).

Community-based initiatives have proved to be a popular way to engage men in the prevention of VAW, yet they are not the only approach employed by UN agencies. UN Women's awareness-raising campaign HeforShe describes itself as 'one of the key platforms to raise voice and take action in engaging men and boys' in promoting gender equality (UN Women 2014). One of the few initiatives that have emerged from the campaign, and is featured on the HeforShe website, is an event from 2015 in which a popular band from Dubai set up a stand at one of their concerts to take pledges from men in the crowd to support the HeforShe cause (HeforShe 2016). Since the goal of the campaign is to get men to pledge their commitment through action, it is puzzling that one of two actions featured on the website results in men taking more pledges.

Moreover, the band's song 'Fight for your Queen' illustrates a discursive trend that is all too common in awareness-raising campaigns that target men. The song reminds male listeners that 'this Earth is your mom/and that girl is your sister', and also that 'you are her man/you are her brother, her father, her friend/make her feel safe'. The chorus tells listeners to 'fight for what's right, fight for her life, fight for your queen' (Carl and the Reda Mafia 2015). In male-to-male discourses on gender violence, the appeal to respect women often does not derive from women's inherent right to life and security as human beings, but rather emerges out of an appreciation of the roles women play in men's lives. Thus the action and the message behind this event, though well intentioned, do not address the root causes of the problem.

The men-as-allies frame illustrates a complex understanding of the roots of gender violence and has the potential to 'reduce the hazard and harm associated with men's behaviour' by 'reforming violent men' (Cornwall 2014: 133). Yet the frame is not without drawbacks. It focuses on the noxious impact masculine behaviours have on women, but doesn't necessarily address the impact on male–male violence. Moreover, as Cornwall and Lindisfarne have observed, these approaches tend to be limited to the personal and have 'a tendency to forget the political and ignore the vested interest many men have in resisting change' (Cornwall and Lindisfarne 1994: 33). 'Much of the work in this field focuses more on men living in poverty and less on the men who occupy positions of power in the institutions that produce and sustain poverty and inequality' (Cornwall 2014: 134). Finally, there is significant concern about the 'diversion of an already small and ever-shrinking pot of funding' (Cornwall 2014: 134). The former Special Rapporteur on VAW, Rashida Manjoo, commented in a report to the Human Rights Council, that: 'although the shift to the men and boys agenda is fraught with difficulty, it appears to have attracted a great deal of funding, recognition and political support' (2014: 19). She notes the work of scholars who have remarked that: 'the increasing focus on men and men's organizations … is seen by some as a new fad, the latest silver bullet to achieving gender equality' and that: 'donor attention to men's organizations seems to signify a shift of support away from women's empowerment and women's leadership' (Manjoo 2014: 19). Thus, a further drawback to current frames representing men as allies for the elimination of gender violence, is the division created between men's and women's organisations over conceptual issues as well as competition for funding.

Men and boys as victims of sexual violence in conflict situations

In addition to men and boys being represented as allies, the turn of the century brought about another emerging frame. The conflicts in the former Yugoslavia, Rwanda, and Somalia drew attention to the high incidence of sexual violence perpetrated against women in conflict and post-conflict situations. UN bodies and agencies began to address CRSV against women in the mid- to late 1990s. In 1995, the United Nations High Commissioner for Refugees (UNHCR) drafted guidelines for the prevention and response to sexual violence against refugees. In 1997, the Division for the Advancement of Women held an Expert Group Meeting on 'Gender-Based Persecution' in armed conflict (DESA/DAW 1997). In 2000, the first of the Women, Peace and Security resolutions, Security Council Resolution 1325, highlighted the impact that conflict situations have on women and girls and stressed the importance of women's participation in the prevention and resolution of conflicts. The follow-up resolution 1820 highlighted that 'women and girls are particularly targeted by the use of sexual violence' (Security Council 2008). Though at first the focus of policies was exclusively on women as victims, reports from researchers and practitioners working with refugees, and testimonies heard at international criminal tribunals like that for the former Yugoslavia, reported a significant number of male victims of sexual violence (ICTY 2004, 2005). As these cases were disseminated in the early 2000s, a growing acknowledgement of men and boys as victims of CRSV emerged which then led to a shift in the way perpetrators of gender-based violence were portrayed.

First steps towards recognition

The 1995 UNHCR *Guidelines on Prevention and Response on Sexual Violence Against Refugees* state that they focus on sexual violence against female refugees and the pronouns are phrased accordingly 'since women and girls appear to be the ones most often subjected to sexual violence' (UNHCR 1995: 3). The UNHCR revised these guidelines in 2003 and this document still emphasised that 'while men and boys are often victims/survivors of sexual violence, statistics confirm that the majority of victims/survivors are women and girls' (UNHCR 2003: 6). However, both these documents provide brief examples of shifts beginning to occur which broadened discourse to include men and boys as victims of sexual violence. For instance, the 1995 text states that: 'reported cases of sexual violence against males are a fraction of the true number of cases' given the stigma attached to sexual assault and the difficulty of talking about that which has yet to be problematised (UNHCR 1995: 6–7). And according to the 2003 Guidelines, 'while gender-based violence has a devastating impact on the lives of women and girls who are the majority of victims/survivors, it also hinders the development of men and boys' (UNHCR 2003: 10). The document also recommends that humanitarian actors 'be sensitive to the fact that men and boys can also be victims/survivors of sexual and gender-based violence' and that they should 'create the space and conditions that allow men to discuss [the issue of sexual violence against men and boys]' (UNHCR 2003: 39). Although the amount of coverage dedicated to men and boys as victims of sexual violence is sparse, the UNHCR Guidelines nevertheless begin to create awareness of the phenomenon and link under-reporting to social taboos and conceptions of masculinity, thus highlighting a need for further research.

Expert group meetings acknowledge men and boys as victims

Awareness of the problem grew as UN officials convened expert meetings and workshops to assess the state of research on the problem, gaps and priority areas for action. A report from a 2008 expert meeting convened by the UN Office for the Coordination of Humanitarian Affairs (OCHA) notes that studying the problem can help to better understand 'the ways in which men and boys, as well as women and girls, are made vulnerable by rigid social norms of masculinity.' It emphasises that: 'a better understanding of the construction of models of masculinity' can improve our understanding of how these models 'reinforce, and are reinforced by, sexualized violence against men and boys' (OCHA 2008: 5). The problem representation emerges from an analysis of perpetrators' motivations, which researchers have painted predominantly as an expression of aggression, power, and dominance over the victim. The report emphasises that as in cases of sexual violence against women and girls, sexual violence against men and boys 'often involves purposeful action aimed at maintaining supremacy through intimidation, abuse and repression' (OCHA 2008: 4). Researchers noted that there is an intent to 'emasculate' the enemy, and that emasculation can take place through 'feminization', 'homosexualization', and/or the prevention of procreation (OCHA 2008: 5). Thus, the meeting report not only establishes that men are also victims of SGBV, but also clarifies that this type of violence is rooted in the same gender dynamics that result in sexual violence against women and girls.

The 2013 workshop of experts convened by the Special Representative of the Secretary General on Sexual Violence in Conflict further develops the notion of the gender-based nature of masculine aggression, stating that sexual violence is used 'as an instrument of humiliation and debilitation' (2013: 13). However, its report presents the focus on women and girls as a hindrance to combatting sexual violence: 'The discussion about gender has been blurred with and frequently subsumed into a necessary struggle for women's rights in the face of historical indifference to the widespread subordination of women.' It stresses the 'importance of the struggle' while acknowledging that the 'resultant discursive and policy focus on sexual and gender based violence as a women's rights issue has become [...] a serious obstacle to prevention of and response to conflict related sexual and gender-based violence against men and boys' (Special Representative of the Secretary General on Sexual Violence in Conflict 2013: 10). The document states that, in the few cases where sound research has been conducted, 'the disparity between levels of conflict-related sexual violence against women and levels against men is rarely as dramatic as one might expect' and raises questions 'about the usefulness of claims that women and girls are "disproportionately affected" by sexual violence' (Special Representative of the Secretary General on Sexual Violence in Conflict 2013: 10).

This oppositional representation fails to acknowledge the fact that sexual violence against women exists within a continuum of practices that result in their systemic discrimination as a group in all societies. While CRSV against men and boys seems to exhibit similar elements of shaming and control, the power imbalance between perpetrator and victim does not stem from systemic gender discrimination. In fact, in CSRV against men and boys, the source of this imbalance changes according to the context in which violence takes place – often it is tied to racial or ethnic divides (e.g. Rwanda, former Yugoslavia) and it can also be compounded by differences of power and status created within institutions such as the military or in detention facilities. The same perspective that highlights the gendered roots of masculine violence should be used to note the different dynamics that underlie male-to-male and male-to-female violence, as well as their different consequences.

Conclusion

This examination of gender violence discourses in the UN illustrates the impact of problem framing on the way subjects are represented. Problem framing can be used strategically by claims-making groups to push for the acknowledgement of an issue, though this can have unintended consequences on how subjects are represented and what types of policies are created. The analysis of the resolutions drafted during the UN Decade for Women shows how strategic framing by women's groups, coupled with state interests, obscured men's role as perpetrators of violence against women. Moreover, the need to legitimise activists' concerns through data and statistical evidence increased the types of actors involved in formulating policies on VAW. The involvement of public health professionals led to the popularisation of clinical language used to describe violent men, and to the widespread use of psychological behavioural models to analyse the factors that contribute to men becoming violent. These elements of public health framing unwittingly create a 'deviant' perpetrator representation, which downplays the influence of social norms as causes of gender violence.

Problem conceptualisation is dynamic, however, and shifts in frames can occur under propitious circumstances. The introduction of gender mainstreaming in the mid- to late 1990s opened the door to a more comprehensive representation of VAW. At the same time, the influence of scholars who deconstructed the concept of masculinity allowed this broader frame to include non-violent men as subjects of discourse and allies for change. However, as certain frames become pervasive they can also be transformed, and their application in practice is often devoid of the substantive context in which these frames emerged. The 'allies' frame, as it is used in many awareness-raising campaigns, often conveys messages that fail to incorporate a gender perspective.

Finally, the influence of external factors, such as the reports on the incidence of sexual violence against men and boys, which emerged out of criminal tribunals like the International Criminal Tribunal for the former Yugoslavia (ICTY) and International Criminal Tribunal for Rwanda (ICTR), also led to changes in the way sexual and gender-based violence is conceptualised. It led to a recognition of men and boys as victims of violence and the emergence of programmes which address their needs. However, some of these initiatives are also accompanied by a push for a more 'neutral' conceptualisation that obscures the way gender operates in contexts of CRSV.

As more representations coexist within discourses on gender violence, the validity or use of certain representations is being advanced by some against others. However, as this analysis of men's and boys' representation in discourses has illustrated, changes in a problem's conceptualisation often have unintended effects on the representation of subjects and policies. Thus, any argument that advances one representation over another should be formulated with a full consideration of the power effects generated through its problem definitions and subject constructions.

References

Antrobus, Peggy. 2004. *The Global Women's Movement: Origins, Issues and Strategies*. New York: Zed Books.

Belsky, Jay. 1980. 'Child Maltreatment: An Ecological Integration'. *American Psychologist* 35(4): 320–335.

Bunch, Charlotte. 1990. 'Women's Rights as Human Rights: Toward a Re-Vision of Human Rights'. *Human Rights Quarterly* 12(4): 486–498.

Bunch, Charlotte and Niamh Reilly. 1994. *Demanding Accountability: The Global Campaign and Vienna Tribunal for Women's Human Rights*. New York: United Nations Development Fund for Women.

Carl and the Reda Mafia. 2015. 'Carl & The Reda Mafia – Fight For Your Queen (HeForShe Campaign Song)'. YouTube video, 4:49. Posted 10 February 2015. www.youtube.com/watch?v=GmQpV9vrp3Y.

Carrigan, T., R. Connell, and J. Lee. 1985. 'Towards a New Sociology of Masculinity'. *Theory and Society* 14(5): 551–604.

Connell, R.W. and James W. Messerschmidt. 2005. 'Hegemonic Masculinity: Rethinking the Concept'. *Gender and Society* 19(6): 829–859.

Cornwall, Andrea. 1997. 'Men, Masculinity and "Gender in Development"'. *Gender & Development* 5(2): 8–13.

Cornwall Andrea. 2014. 'Taking Off International Development's Straightjacket of Gender'. *Brown Journal of World Affairs* 21(1): 127–139.

Cornwall, A. and N. Lindisfarne. 1994. 'Dislocating Masculinity: Gender, Power and Anthropology'. In A. Cornwall and N. Lindisfarne (eds), *Dislocating Masculinities: Comparative Ethnographies*. London: Routledge, 11–47.

CSW (Commission on the Status of Women). 2004. *Report of the Secretary General on the Review of the implementation of the Beijing Platform for Action and the outcome documents of the special session of the General Assembly entitled 'Women 2000: Gender Equality, Development and Peace for the Twenty-First Century'*. New York: United Nations. E/CN/6/2005/2.

Delage, Pauline. 2015. 'Des héritages sans testament: L'appropriation différentielle des idées féministes dans la lutte contre la violence conjugale en France et aux États-Unis'. *Politix* 109(1): 91–109.

DESA/DAW (Department of Economic and Social Affairs/Division for the Advancement of Women). 1997. *Expert Group Meeting on Gender-Based Persecution*. Toronto: United Nations Department of Economic and Social Affairs (DESA). Accessed 10 August 2017. www.un.org/documents/ecosoc/cn6/1998/armedcon/genderamen.htm.

Fraser, Arvonne. 1987. *The UN Decade for Women: Documents and Dialogue*. Boulder, CO: Westview Press.

Hagemann-White, Carol, Barbara Kavemann, Heinz Kindler, Thomas Meysen, Ralf Puchert, Mart Busche, Sandra Gabler, Bianca Grafe, Melanie Kungl, Gila Schindler, and Hartwig Schuck. 2010. *Review of Research on Factors at Play in Perpetration.* Prepared for the European Commission. Accessed 10 August 2017: http://ec.europa.eu/justice/funding/daphne3/multi-level_interactive_model/bin/review_of_research.pdf.

HeforShe. 2016. 'Rock Voices for Change'. Accessed 10 August 2017. www.heforshe.org/en/newsroom/safety/rock-voices-for-change.

Heise, Lori. 1998. 'Violence Against Women: An Integrated, Ecological Framework'. *Violence Against Women* 4(3): 262–290.

ICTY (International Criminal Tribunal for the former Yugoslavia). 2004. *Prosecutor* v. *Ranko Cesic (Sentencing Judgement).* The Hague: ICTY. IT-95-10/1-S.

ICTY (International Criminal Tribunal for the former Yugoslavia). 2005. *Prosecutor* v. *Slobodan Milosevic (Decision on Interlocutory Appeal on Kosta Bulatovic Contempt Proceedings)*. The Hague: ICTY. IT-02-54-A-R77.4.

Joachim, Jutta M. 2007. *Agenda-Setting, The UN, and NGOs: Gender Violence and Reproductive Rights.* Washington, DC: Georgetown University Press.

Manjoo, Rashida. 2014. *Report of the Special Rapporteur on Violence Against Women, its Causes and Consequences*. Geneva: UN Human Rights Council. A/HRC/26/38.

MenEngage Alliance. 2014. 'Men and Boys for Gender Justice: Delhi Declaration and Call to Action'. Accessed 11 March 2017. www.menengagedilli2014.net/delhi-declaration-and-call-to-action.html.

MenEngage Alliance. 2017. 'About Us'. Accessed 11 March 2017. http://menengage.org/about-us/.

MenEngage Alliance, UN Women, UNFPA. 2015. *Men, Masculinities, and Changing Power: A Discussion Paper on Engaging Men in Gender Equality From Beijing 1995 to 2015*. UNWomen. Accessed 4 March 2017. www.unwomen.org/~/media/headquarters/attachments/sections/news/in%20focus/engaging%20men/beijing-20-men-masculinities-and-changing-power-menengage-2014.pdf.

OCHA (Office for the Coordination of Humanitarian Affairs). 2008. *Meeting Report on the Use of Sexual Violence in Conflict: Identifying Research Priorities to Inform More Effective Interventions.* New York: OCHA.

Office of the UN Secretary General. 1998. *Integrating the Gender Perspective into the Work of United Nations Human Rights Treaty Bodies.* Tenth meeting of persons chairing human rights treaty bodies. New York: United Nations. HRI/MC/1998/6.

Pietila, Hilkka. 2007. *The Unfinished Story of Women and the United Nations*. New York: United Nations Non-Governmental Liaison Service.

Pleck, Elizabeth. 2004. *Domestic Tyranny: the Making of American Social Policy Against Family Violence from Colonial Times to the Present*. Chicago, IL: University of Illinois Press.

Security Council. 2000. *Security Council Resolution 1325 (2000) On Women and Peace and Security.* S/RES/1325.

Security Council. 2008. *Security Council Resolution 1820 (2008) On Acts of Sexual Violence Against Civilians in Armed Conflicts.* S/RES/1820.

Special Representative of the Secretary General on Sexual Violence in Conflict. 2013. *Executive Summary Report of the Workshop on Sexual Violence against Men and Boys in Conflict Situations.* New York: United Nations. https://ifls.osgoode.yorku.ca/wp-content/uploads/2014/01/Report-of-Workshop-on-Sexual-Violence-against-Men-and-Boys-Final.pdf.

Timothy, Kristen. 2008. 'Women's Engagement with Development and the United Nations: A Commentary'. *Forum for Development Studies* 35(2): 313–318.

UNHCR (United Nations High Commissioner for Refugees). 1995. *Sexual Violence Against Refugees: Guidelines on Prevention and Response.* Geneva: UNHCR.

UNHCR (United Nations High Commissioner for Refugees). 2003. *Sexual and Gender-Based Violence Against Refugees, Returnees and Internally Displaced Persons: Guidelines for Prevention and Response.* Geneva: UNCHR.

United Nations. 1975. *Report of the World Conference of the International Women's Year.* New York: United Nations. E/CONF/66.34.

United Nations. 1980. *Report of the World Conference of the United Nations Decade for Women: Equality Development and Peace.* A/CONF.94/35.

United Nations. 1985. *Report of the World Conference to Review and Appraise the Achievements of the United Nations Decade for Women: Equality, Development and Peace.* New York: United Nations. A/Conf.116/28/Rev.1.

United Nations. 1993. *Declaration on the Elimination of Violence Against Women.* New York: United Nations. A/RES/48/104.

United Nations. 1995. *Report of the Fourth World Conference on Women.* New York: United Nations. A/CONF.177/20/Rev.1.

UN Women. 2014. 'In Brief: UNWomen's Work with Men and Boys: 2nd MenEngage Global Symposium'. Accessed 4 March 2017. http://menengage.org/wp-content/uploads/2014/12/Global-Symposium-brief.pdf.

Walker, Gillian A. 1990. *Family Violence and the Women's Movement: The Conceptual Politics of Struggle.* Toronto: University of Toronto Press.

WHO (World Health Organization). 2002. *World Report on Violence and Health.* Geneva: World Health Organization.

WHO (World Health Organization). 2005. *WHO Multi-Country Study on Women's Health and Domestic Violence Against Women.* Geneva: World Health Organization.

WHO (World Health Organization). 2010. *Preventing Intimate Partner and Sexual Violence Against Women: Taking Action and Generating Evidence.* Geneva: World Health Organization.

11 Sexual violence or torture?

The framing of sexual violence against men in armed conflict in Amnesty International and Human Rights Watch reports

Thomas Charman

International non-governmental organisations (INGOs) and international legal tribunals have often described particular acts of violence against men as torture rather than sexual violence. Scholars argue that this is problematic since it perpetuates societal taboos surrounding male sexual victimisation and elides the gendered and sexual aspects of such crimes (Carlson 1997; Oosterveld 2014; Sivakumaran 2007). While the matter has been discussed in the language of international law and jurisprudence, there has been limited attention to the work of INGOs. However, I suggest that these organisations play a critical role in the discursive construction of sexual violence against both men and women in armed conflict through their advocacy programmes and necessitate further investigation.

The lack of an in-depth understanding of the framing and construction of sexual violence against men in armed conflict, and the theoretical and practical implications thereof, are particularly problematic in the context of the changing landscape of advocacy and policy discourses: male victims are increasingly surfacing in United Nations resolutions and programming (Sivakumaran 2010: 262) and international human rights instruments are increasingly employing gender-neutral terminology (Gorris 2015; Touquet and Gorris 2016), indicating they are increasingly cognisant of sexual violence against men. By bringing to bear insights from the practices of INGOs, I seek to contribute to a better understanding of the meaning and complexities of existing framing practices.

This chapter examines 131 conflict-specific reports produced between 2000 and 2016 by Amnesty International and Human Rights Watch, the two leading reporting organisations for human rights abuses in conflict settings. The analysis begins to map how INGO framing processes shape gendered understandings of sexual violence in conflict settings. The chapter is structured as follows. The first section delineates some of the scholarly perspectives on framing sexual violence against men in armed conflict as torture rather than sexual violence, as well as some of the conceptual and policy impacts this frame might have. The second section discusses the importance of INGOs as framers of the discourse around human rights abuses. It notes that both INGOs and international legal instruments play a significant role in constructing sexual violence in armed conflict, and mutually reinforce each other in this regard through the frequent use of international legal definitions of crimes in INGO-produced reports documenting human rights abuses. The third and final section consists of the analysis and discussion of the Amnesty International and Human Rights Watch reports.

Overall, the chapter demonstrates that both Amnesty International and Human Rights Watch, with a few exceptions, have constructed sexual violence against men in armed conflict as a form of torture in their advocacy literature: sexual violence against women, by way of comparison, is sometimes constructed as 'amounting to torture', but is more readily framed as 'sexual violence' than sexual violence against men. In this sense, existing literature on the subject of sexual violence against men in armed conflict is right to claim that the problem is frequently documented under the broader rubric of torture. However, I introduce further layers of complexity. First, I note that the context in which the violence is documented would appear to be significant. Sexual violence against men is most often recorded as occurring in the context of incarceration and detention and alongside other forms of violence that are seen to constitute torture. As such, the torture frame reflects the context in which the violence occurs. In addition, the topic of the reports appears to have some bearing on the framing of the violence, as reports that explicitly address sexual violence against women also tend to frame sexual violence against men specifically as sexual violence rather than torture. From this, while sexual violence against men is almost always framed as torture, it is noted that the concept can be somewhat fluid, in that it can be framed either as torture or sexual violence. Second, it is noted that when sexual violence against women is framed as torture, the sexual aspect of the violence is always acknowledged, in marked contrast to sexual violence against men. Furthermore, while sexual violence against men is related to torture in a consistent manner throughout the reports, sexual violence against women is only sometimes acknowledged as amounting to torture. In many cases, sexual violence against women is defined as a crime separate from torture. Finally, sexual violence against women is linked to and understood through a framework of gender subordination in the reports, whereas the relationship between sexual violence against men and gender is left unclear. While acknowledged in a few reports, gender is largely deemed to not play a role in conceptualisations of sexual violence against men, with the violence instead understood through the framework of torture. Furthermore, in the few cases where sexual violence against men is framed as sexual violence, the problem is often understood through the lens of violence against women. This, it is argued, may be problematic due to its potential to obscure the differing forms of sexual victimisation men and women suffer.

Sexual violence and torture frames in the literature

To date, there have been few scholarly discussions of the framing of sexual violence against men as torture. However, it is possible to draw upon themes in the existing literature to develop some initial insights on the conceptual and policy ramifications of such framing, highlighting the power these frames may hold over our conceptualisations and responses to the problem. In some cases, framing sexual violence against men as torture may be practically beneficial. First, it can draw attention to the fact that sexual violence in armed conflict frequently occurs in the context of detention alongside other forms of torture and violence (Carpenter 2006: 94). Furthermore, from a policy perspective, INGOs and funders have reportedly been reluctant to address the problem under a sexual violence frame, either for fear of the additional demands placed upon already limited and hard-won funds for addressing sexual violence against women (Féron 2015: 40; Storr 2011), or because of 'a lack of understanding of the issue and due to the difficulty of fitting the reality of sexual abuse [against men] into dominant gender perspectives' (Gorris 2015: 420). Conceptualising the problem as torture may provide a window for it to be adopted by INGOs without disrupting the already well-established and widely accepted campaigns surrounding sexual violence against women. Indeed, Catherine MacKinnon has argued in favour of conceptualising rape as torture in order to take advantage of the more stringent norms and legal instruments that relate to torture and to stimulate international action on recognising and combating the problem (2006: 17). This argument can also be applied to the case of male victims, given that there currently exist no strong international norms or legal frameworks explicitly prohibiting sexual violence against men.

But others have argued that international law on torture is inadequate, as existing instruments do not make any explicit reference to gender or sexual violence (Lewis 2009; Mouthaan 2012). In addition, beyond the scope of international law, the frequent conceptualisation of sexual violence as a form of torture by international organisations has been criticised because it risks obscuring the gendered aspects of certain forms of violence. For example, Sandesh Sivakumaran has argued that the repeated classification of sexual violence against men as torture risks reinforcing the idea that men cannot be the victims of sexual assault (2007: 256). This concern has now spread into the realm of international advocacy, with Amnesty International (2011) acknowledging that concepts of gender have, so far, played an inconsequential role in the analysis of the torture of women. Furthermore, sexual violence against men has specifically gendered consequences, such as confusion over sexuality, a sense of emasculation, social ostracism, and sexual dysfunction (Oosterhoff, Zwanikken, and Ketting 2004: 71), which may be obscured if considerations of gender are not incorporated into the framing of sexual violence.

The role of INGO framings and international law in issue construction

Human rights advocacy conducted by INGOs has a significant influence on our understandings of abuses. In the arena of transnational advocacy, INGOs are, according to some scholars, one of the principal driving forces behind the dissemination and reinforcement of international norms on human rights and standards of appropriate conduct (Risse and Sikkink 1999). These INGOs, and the transnational networks they form with similar organisations, engage in several strategies to achieve their policy and advocacy goals, inter alia, generating useable information on human rights abuses, seeking leverage with more powerful institutions and states, and holding states accountable for violations of international norms and legal obligations (Joachim 2003; Keck and Sikkink 1998; Simmons 2009). However, as these organisations lack the material power of states and inter-governmental organisations, INGOs and the strategies they employ instead rely on framing processes to garner support for problems they have identified and the solutions they propose (Joachim 2007: 19). Generally speaking, to frame something is to 'select aspects of a perceived reality and make them more salient in a communicating text, in such a way as to promote a particular problem definition, causal interpretation, moral evaluation, and/or treatment recommendation' (Entman 1993: 52). In the context of INGO framing processes as part of advocacy strategies, Rein and Schön argue that INGOs seek to provide 'a perspective from which an amorphous, ill-defined and problematic situation can be made sense of and acted upon' (1991, quoted in Joachim 2003: 250). INGOs are therefore actively engaged in the process of constructing the problems with which they concern themselves. They not only transmit meaning, but produce it as well (Joachim 2007; Snow and Benford 1988). 'Problems and solutions', as Joachim argues, 'do not simply exist out there' (2007: 19). INGOs define, categorise, and assign meaning to events and acts in order to render them both coherent and comprehensible to their audiences, and, in doing so, promulgate particular discursive constructions of problems on their agendas. While little research has been done into how INGOs frame and construct sexual violence against men, relevant examples can be found elsewhere. For example, Joachim (2003: 259) notes that the framing of women's rights as human rights in the early 1990s was a particularly powerful way of constructing the problem, one that resonated with various audiences, such as the media and the United Nations.

In the context of sexual violence in armed conflict, international law has played a significant role in the framing and construction of the phenomenon (Campbell 2007). There has been a trend in international jurisprudence and human rights advocacy towards incorporating sexual violence in armed conflict under the broader crime of torture. Case law from the International Tribunals for the Former Yugoslavia and Rwanda (ICTY and ICTR respectively) and the European Court of Human Rights has found that acts of sexual violence and rape can amount to torture (Mouthaan 2012; Sellers and Nwoye Ch. 12 in this volume). This development in international jurisprudence allowed for rape to be prosecuted under one of the most stringent protection regimes provided by international law (Fortin 2008: 146). However, sexual violence against both men and women is also specifically prohibited as a war crime and crime against humanity under international criminal law, such as the statutes of the ICTY and ICTR as well as the International Criminal Court (ICC). Furthermore, sexual violence against women, and to a lesser extent sexual violence against men (Lewis 2009), is also covered under international human rights law. The language used in these international legal instruments may hold significant sway over the framings of sexual violence promulgated by INGOs. Legal language, as Finley argues, 'through its definitions and the way it talks about events ... has the power to silence alternative meanings – to suppress other stories' (1989, quoted in Siva-kumaran 2007: 257).

It is important to note that the advocacy activities of INGOs and the texts and jurisprudence of international law do not operate separately from each other in the context of constructing and framing sexual violence in armed conflict. The norm-reinforcing activities and the focus on accountability politics of INGOs, whereby states and sub-state actors are held to account for breaches of their international legal and treaty obligations (Keck and Sikkink 1998), have resulted in advocacy programmes where there is a significant emphasis on international law. This, in turn, informs the frames promulgated in INGO reports. Human rights advocacy INGOs often base their definitions of human rights abuses on international legal definitions (e.g. Welsh 2000; Amnesty International 2014a), and documented abuses in advocacy reports are framed as breaches of relevant human rights standards. Furthermore, the legal frameworks outlined in reports act as a lens through which the violence and abuses are made comprehensible. By specifying which international legal instruments and treaties the abuses fall within the purview of, INGOs evoke associated conceptualisations and defini-tions and thus promote a particular reading of the documented violence. For example, Labonte (2013) argues that the strategic framing of mass atrocities using international humanitarian and human rights norms by INGOs has the potential to promote particular readings of said atrocities that may influence the decision to engage in humanitarian intervention on the part of policymakers. As such, it is likely that the use of international law and its associated language by INGOs plays a significant role in the framing and construction of sexual viol-ence against both men and women in armed conflict. The power that INGOs can exert over the discourse surrounding sexual violence warrants analysis of their framing practices.

Amnesty International and Human Rights watch: framings in advocacy reports

The empirical data presented in this chapter is derived from an analysis of 131 conflict-specific reports produced by Amnesty International and Human Rights Watch between 2000 and 2016. Amnesty International and Human Rights Watch are key cases because they play a highly influential role in setting the agenda of international advocacy networks concerning human rights and human security and researching and constructing the issues on those agendas (Bob 2002; Car-penter 2011). The collected documents primarily focus on abuses committed during conflicts in Africa, although conflicts in Europe, the Middle East, Asia, and South America are also covered. All the documents are freely accessible on the respective websites of both organisations, and were identified and collected through a keyword search for terms frequently used by INGOs when documenting cases of sexual violence against men, such as 'rape', 'genital', and 'testicle'. The topics of the selected documents either focused on sexual violence in armed conflict specifically, or on torture and human rights abuses as a part of armed conflict more generally. As discussed below, this is significant in the context of framing sexual violence against men in armed conflict. Once collected, the documents were coded, paying particular attention to how acts of violence against men were constructed, categorised, and described. Attention was also paid to the location of mentions of male victims and violence against men within the text, given that this plays a role in organising interpretations and structuring meaning (Shepherd 2008: 30). This included, for example, noting the titles, headings, and sub-headings under which mentions of sexual violence against men appeared.

The principal finding of the analysis of the documents is that, across a significant majority of the reports, acts of sexual violence against men are framed as forms of torture rather than sexual violence. That is, acts that could be construed as being sexual or having a sexual element, such as the application of blunt force trauma or electricity to the genitals or enforced nudity, are not described or framed in the documents as being sexual or gendered, but are instead positioned alongside other abuses such as stress positions or beatings and assimilated into the broader, non-sexual category of torture. To take but a few examples to illustrate this point, one respondent in Angola describes how soldiers 'beat me, squeezed my testicles and my tongue with a pincer, telling me to "say the truth"' (Human Rights Watch 2009b: 15). In Kenya, one individual recalled that: 'one [soldier] stood on both of my legs, and another held both of my hands, and a third caught me by the testicles. They tied a plastic cord around [my testicles] and pulled' (Human Rights Watch 2009a: 28). Amnesty International, in detailing torture committed by armed militias in the aftermath of the Libyan Civil War, described one victim as saying, '[the militia] started beating all over my body – including my genitals. They used an elastic black stick to beat me. They also kicked me' (2012b: 19). While these victims describe acts of torture that could be construed as sexual – in these examples the application of blunt force trauma to the genitals – neither Amnesty International nor Human Rights Watch describe them as such. Instead, as seen in the examples above, they assimilate them into the broader category of torture as a human rights abuse by positioning them alongside other forms of torture and not acknowledging the possible sexual and gendered dimensions of the violence.

While framing sexual violence against men solely as torture predominates throughout the documents, in a minority of cases, it was disaggregated from other forms of torture and categorised more specifically as 'sexual torture'. For example, Amnesty International, in referring to the varying forms of torture employed by the Syrian armed forces and security services during the ongoing civil war, notes that: 'rape and other torture and ill-treatment of a sexual nature have been reported more frequently than for many years' (2012a: 11). Human Rights Watch claims, in the context of the Sri Lankan Civil War, that:

there have long been reports that the Sri Lankan military and police forces rape and sexually abuse ethnic Tamils detained for alleged links to the secessionist Liberation Tigers of Tamil Eelam (LTTE), among other forms of torture and ill-treatment.

(Human Rights Watch 2013: 1)

Here, while still framing sexual violence against men as a form of torture, the modification of the noun 'torture' with the adverb 'sexual' opens up a discursive space in which the potentially sexual and gendered dimensions of some forms of violence can be articulated or acknowledged.

In an even smaller minority of reports, sexual violence against men was referred to explicitly as sexual violence with no or very limited references to the act of torture. For example, Human Rights Watch, in reporting on violence in Côte d'Ivoire, states that: 'men were forced to rape women and to witness rapes, but men and boys have also reportedly been raped and otherwise sexually assaulted by combatants' (2007: 35). In a report addressing sexual violence in Sierra Leone, it is noted that: 'according to FAWE Sierra Leone, boys and men were also raped by male rebels' (Human Rights Watch 2003: 42). Amnesty International reports exhibit similar frames, with one report detailing cases of rape in the Central African Republic noting that: 'in addition to the risks of injury, death or torture, men also suffered from sexual violence in some cases' (Amnesty International 2004: 5).

The importance of context

The context of the violence is apparently significant for the framing of sexual violence against men. In most reports, cases of sexual violence against men are documented as occurring almost exclusively in detainment facilities or in situations where the victim has been held captive by one of the belligerents. Furthermore, it is documented as being used alongside other torture that is not often viewed as having a sexual component, such as beatings, water torture, falaka,[1] and electrocutions. It is possible that the predominant frame applied to sexual violence against men, namely, torture, is a reflection of the context within which the violence is documented as occurring.

Furthermore, the topic of the documents appears to be significant in terms of contextualising and framing the violence. In almost all documents where sexual violence against men was framed as sexual violence, the report makes sexual violence in armed conflict the principal focus of its investigations. This is frequently reflected in the titles; to take but one example, in '"My Heart is Cut": Sexual Violence by Rebels and Pro-Government Forces in Côte d'Ivoire' (Human Rights Watch 2007), sexual violence against both men and women is framed explicitly as sexual violence. In contrast, documents where sexual violence against men was framed as torture focus either on torture specifically or human rights abuses more generally (see, e.g. Amnesty International 2012a, 2014b; Human Rights Watch 2012). While sexual violence against men is almost always framed as torture, there is an element of fluidity in the concept, in that it can be framed as either sexual violence or torture, depending on the context of both the violence and the subject of the reports.

Differences in the framing of sexual violence against women and men

This conceptual fluidity, however, is not entirely mirrored in the framings of sexual violence against women. In a manner similar to sexual violence against men, female victims are, in several cases, framed as victims of sexual torture. For example, Human Rights Watch describes how female detainees were subject to sexual abuse and rape in the context of their detainment and torture by Syrian government security forces (2012: 31–34). Notably however, the violence is not referred to as 'sexual torture', but rather 'sexual abuse' or 'sexual violence' that occurs in the context of torture. Furthermore, sexual violence against women has also been framed as 'amounting to torture' rather than as a subset of torture. This usually accompanies the outlining of the international and domestic legal frameworks applicable to the documented abuses. For example, when discussing sexual violence, Amnesty International frequently notes in its reports, alongside other international legal definitions of rape, that: 'rape committed by government officials or armed opposition during armed conflict – whether international or non-international – constitutes torture' (2000: 6). This differs somewhat from the torture frame applied to sexual violence against men, in that violence against women is almost always construed as sexual violence and is noted to meet the criteria for prosecution under international legal instruments prohibiting torture as well as sexual violence specifically, whereas violence against men that could be construed as sexual is largely not constructed as sexual violence, and is framed solely as torture.

Furthermore, while the framing of sexual violence against men as torture is consistent across a majority of documents, both Amnesty International and Human Rights Watch have related violence against women to torture in a less consistent fashion. In particular, they have also framed the problem as a crime and human rights abuse in itself, rather than attaching it to the broader problem of torture. In documenting acts of sexual violence and rape in Sudan and Chad, Amnesty International refers to these acts being 'recognised as war crimes and crimes against humanity' (2006: 1). Torture, or sexual violence amounting to torture, is not referenced in the report. Similarly, Human Rights Watch has framed sexual violence against women as being a separate human rights abuse from torture in several reports, such as describing acts of sexual violence and rape carried out in South Sudan as constituting war crimes without noting that rape can constitute torture (2015: 39). Again, this violence is neither framed nor defined in the context of torture.

Linking gender to sexual violence

The consistent framing of violence against women as being sexual in nature highlights a further difference in the framings of sexual violence against men and women. In cases of sexual violence against women, the violence is described, to take but one representative example, as '[reflecting] a dynamic of gender inequality and subordination. This power dynamic is deeply imbedded in societal attitudes' (Human Rights Watch 2007: 5). Sexual violence against women is viewed through a framework whereby the violence is the consequence of unequal power relations between men and women, and is therefore rendered as an explicitly gendered phenomenon.

Conversely, sexual violence against men and the motives behind it are largely understood through the non-gendered framework of torture. Current academic understandings view the sexual abuse of men in armed conflict through a gendered framework, conceptualising it as a symbolic attack on the masculine identity of the victim, rendering the victim as 'female' in the eyes of the perpetrators and society through the forcible association of the victim with traits considered 'un-masculine', such as victimhood and an inability to protect oneself (Sivakumaran 2007; Skjelsbæk 2001). However, in most reports, analyses of the motives of the perpetrators were left either unspecified or conceptualised in such a way as to subsume them into the broader motives seen to underpin torture – that of extracting information or punishing the victims. For example, in one case, the beating of a man's genitals, alongside other forms of violence, was described as being 'designed to make [the victims] confess and turn over guns' (Human Rights Watch 2009a: 3). In other cases, however, both Amnesty International and Human Rights Watch do provide information on the motives of the perpetrators that would appear to indicate a gendered or sexual dimension to the violence. For example, Human Rights Watch notes that, during the Chechen War, Russian soldiers would often assign female names to male victims of rape in detention facilities and use gendered language to insult them (2000), but these reports constitute a small minority of the total. Furthermore, the victims frequently articulated their own experiences in ways that constructed the violence as non-sexual. It has, however, also been argued that male victims may not recognise or experience the violence being perpetrated against them as being sexual or gendered in nature due to the taboos surrounding male sexual victimisation in society leading to an impression that 'men cannot be raped' (Sivakumaran 2005), as well as a lack of appropriate language to describe male sexual victimisation (Sivakumaran 2007). This is reflected in the testimonies provided by victims in the reports. Whereas women were far more likely to say they had been raped, male victims often did not refer to the violence as being sexual or gendered. Ultimately, however, the extent to which Amnesty International and Human Rights Watch communicate information concerning underlying dynamics, such as motives and social perceptions of sexuality, is somewhat limited.

In the few cases where sexual violence against men is framed as sexual violence and linked to gender, it is in the context of reports that deal specifically with sexual violence against women. This raises questions of whether it is possible that the only way in which sexual violence against men can be perceived as specifically sexual is when it is 'made sense of' through the lens of sexual violence against women. In the words of Grey and Shepherd, 'sexual violence against men is peripheral; akin to clothing for this body [of sexual violence against women], perhaps, or a surgical enhancement' (2012: 120). This would certainly seem to be the case in the analysed reports, where sexual violence against men is often treated as a subset of the broader problem of sexual violence against women. Furthermore, it has been noted that a significant obstacle to the documentation of male victims is that the sexual abuse of men is often assumed to mirror the act of sexual violence against women, namely, rape (Tienhoven 1993). As Oosterveld points out, while sexual violence against men and women are 'clearly interlinked' (2014: 118), there exist differences in the forms of violence men and women are exposed to, with men and boys potentially more vulnerable to abuses other than rape (2014: 117). By making sense of sexual violence against men through the lens of sexual violence against women, the reports may risk obscuring the differing harms which men and women can be exposed to during armed conflict.

Conclusions

The framing of sexual violence against men in armed conflict as a form of torture by Amnesty International and Human Rights Watch is perhaps a prudent means of addressing the problem; not only does it draw attention to the context in which the violence occurs, it also allows advocates to draw upon the strong international norms that surround torture. In contrast, while the sexual violence frame may proffer some fresh perspective on the problem, in practice, the relationship between sexual violence against men and gender is left uncertain in the reports, and the problem is almost always understood through the framework of torture. Sivakumaran argues there is 'a need to recognise the general – rape as torture, as well as the particular – rape as rape' (2007: 256–257). This argument could be applied to the cases of Amnesty International and Human Rights Watch in particular, and the wider question of whether to conceptualise sexual violence as sexual violence or as a form of torture in general. Both frames have their place within international discourse, and using both frames in parallel may be a more apt approach to conceptualising sexual violence against men in armed conflict, one that is better able to encapsulate the context in which the violence often occurs and take advantage of the strong legal frameworks that surround torture, while providing a discursive space in which the potentially sexualised and gendered nature of such violence, as well as the unique consequences and challenges faced by male survivors, can be articulated at the same time.

The purpose of this chapter has not been to offer a definitive overview of the framing practices of INGOs in the context of the documentation of sexual violence against men in armed conflict. Rather, it constitutes an initial foray into these framing practices with the goal of providing a foundation for further research and analysis. Several potential avenues of inquiry present themselves. First, our knowledge of INGO framing practices must be expanded. While Amnesty International and Human Rights Watch are particularly influential, they do not necessarily represent the entire range of potential framings of sexual violence against men. Second, the linking of gender to sexual violence against women but not men deserves further analysis, as this risks concealing the gender dimensions of this form of violence. Finally, the differences in framings of sexual violence against men and women, in particular the understanding of sexual violence against men through the lens of sexual violence against women, needs to be further problematised, given the potential this holds for obscuring the differences between these forms of violence.

Note

1 The beating of the soles of the feet with a rod or stick.

References

Amnesty International. 2000. *Sierra Leone: Rape and Other Forms of Sexual Violence against Girls and Women*. AFR 51/035/2000. London: Amnesty International. Accessed 5 April 2017. www.amnesty.org/download/Documents/132000/afr510352000en.pdf.

Amnesty International. 2004. *Central African Republic: Five Months of War Against Women*. AFR 19/001/2004. London: Amnesty International. Accessed 1 April 2017. www.amnesty.org/download/Documents/88000/afr190012004en.pdf.

Amnesty International. 2006. *'No One to Help Them': Rape Extends from Darfur into Eastern Chad*. AFR 54/087/2006. London: Amnesty International. Accessed 5 April 2017. www.amnesty.org/download/Documents/68000/afr540872006en.pdf.

Amnesty International. 2011. *Gender and Torture Conference Report*. IOR 50/001/2011. London: Amnesty International. Accessed 3 March 2017. www.amnesty.org/download/Documents/32000/ior500012011en.pdf.

Amnesty International. 2012a. *'I Wanted to Die': Syria's Torture Survivors Speak Out*. MDE 24/016/2012. Amnesty International. Accessed 1 April 2017. www.amnestyusa.org/sites/default/files/mde240162012en.pdf.

Amnesty International. 2012b. *Militias Threaten Hopes for New Libya*. MDE 19/002/2012. London: Amnesty International. Accessed 1 April 2017. www.amnesty.org/download/Documents/24000/mde190022012en.pdf.

Amnesty International. 2014a. *Torture in 2014: 30 Years of Broken Promises*. ACT 40/004/2014. London: Amnesty International. Accessed 3 April 2017. www.amnesty.org/download/Documents/4000/act400042014en.pdf.

Amnesty International. 2014b. *'Welcome to Hell Fire': Torture and Other Ill-Treatment in Nigeria*. AFR 44/011/2014. London: Amnesty International. Accessed 30 March 2017. www.amnesty.org.uk/sites/default/files/p4334_nigeria_report_complete_web.pdf.

Bob, Clifford. 2002. 'Globalisation and the Social Construction of Human Rights Campaigns'. In Alison Brysk (ed.), *Globalisation and Human Rights*. Berkeley, CA: University of California Press, 133–147.

Campbell, Kirsten. 2007. 'The Gender of Transitional Justice: Law, Sexual Violence and the International Criminal Tribunal for the Former Yugoslavia'. *The International Journal of Transitional Justice* 1: 411–432.

Carlson, Eric Stener. 1997. 'Sexual Assault on Men in War'. *The Lancet* 349: 129.

Carpenter, R. Charli. 2006. 'Recognizing Gender-Based Violence Against Civilian Men and Boys in Conflict Situations'. *Security Dialogue* 37(1): 83–103.

Carpenter, R. Charli. 2011. 'Vetting the Advocacy Agenda: Network Centrality and the Paradox of Weapons Norms'. *International Organization* 65(1): 69–102.

Entman, Robert. 1993. 'Framing: Towards Clarification of a Fractured Paradigm'. *Journal of Communication* 43(4): 51–58.

Féron, Élise. 2015. 'Suffering in Silence?: The Silencing of Sexual Violence Against Men in War Torn Countries'. In Ronald E. Anderson (ed.), *World Suffering and Quality of Life*. Dordrecht: Springer Netherlands, 31–44.

Fortin, Katharine. 2008. 'Rape as Torture: An Evaluation of the Committee Against Torture's Attitude to Sexual Violence'. *Utrecht Law Review* 4(3): 145–162.

Gorris, Ellen. 2015. 'Invisible Victims?: Where Are Male Victims of Conflict-Related Sexual Violence in International Law and Policy?' *European Journal of Women's Studies* 22(4): 412–427.

Grey, Rosemary, and Laura Shepherd. 2012. '"Stop Rape Now?": Masculinity, Responsibility, and Conflict-Related Sexual Violence'. *Men and Masculinities* 16(1): 115–135.

Human Rights Watch. 2000. '"Welcome to Hell": Arbitrary Detention, Torture, and Extortion in Chechnya'. New York: Human Rights Watch. Accessed 4 April 2017. www.hrw.org/reports/2000/russia_chechnya4/.

Human Rights Watch. 2003. '"We'll Kill You If You Cry": Sexual Violence in the Sierra Leone Conflict'. New York: Human Rights Watch. Accessed 5 April 2017. www.hrw.org/reports/2003/sierraleone/sierleon0103.pdf.

Human Rights Watch. 2007. '"My Heart Is Cut": Sexual Violence by Rebels and Pro-Government Forces in Côte d'Ivoire'. New York: Human Rights Watch. Accessed 5 April 2017. www.hrw.org/sites/default/files/reports/cdi0807webwcover.pdf.

Human Rights Watch. 2009a. '"Bring the Gun or You'll Die": Torture, Rape and Other Serious Human Rights Violations by Kenyan Security Forces in the Mandera Triangle'. New York: Human Rights Watch. Accessed 4 April 2017. www.hrw.org/sites/default/files/reports/kenya0609webwcover_0.pdf.

Human Rights Watch. 2009b. '"They Put Me in the Hole": Military Detention, Torture, and Lack of Due Process in Cabinda'. New York: Human Rights Watch. Accessed 30 March 2017. www.hrw.org/sites/default/files/reports/angola0609web.pdf.

Human Rights Watch. 2012. 'Torture Archipelago: Arbitrary Arrests, Torture and Enforced Disappearances in Syria's Underground Prisons since March 2011'. New York: Human Rights Watch. Accessed 3 April 2017. www.hrw.org/sites/default/files/reports/syria0712webwcover_0.pdf.

Human Rights Watch. 2013. *'We Will Teach You a Lesson': Sexual Violence against Tamils by Sri Lankan Security Forces*. New York: Human Rights Watch. Accessed 5 April 2017. www.hrw.org/sites/default/files/reports/srilanka0213webwcover_0.pdf.

Human Rights Watch. 2015. '"They Burned It All": Destruction of Villages, Killings, and Sexual Violence in Unity State, South Sudan'. New York: Human Rights Watch. Accessed 4 April 2017. www.hrw.org/sites/default/files/report_pdf/southsudan0715_web_0.pdf.

Joachim, Jutta M. 2003. 'Framing Issues and Seizing Opportunities: The UN, NGOs, and Women's Rights'. *International Studies Quarterly* 47(2): 247–274.

Joachim, Jutta M. 2007. *Agenda Setting, the UN, and NGOs: Gender Violence and Reproductive Rights*. Washington, DC: Georgetown University Press.

Keck, Margaret, and Kathryn Sikkink. 1998. *Activists Beyond Borders: Advocacy Networks in International Politics*. Ithaca, NY: Cornell University Press.

Labonte, Melissa. 2013. *Human Rights and Humanitarian Norms, Strategic Framing, and Intervention: Lessons for the Responsibility to Protect*. Abingdon: Routledge.

Lewis, Dustin A. 2009. 'Unrecognized Victims: Sexual Violence Against Men in Conflict Settings Under International Law'. *Wisconsin International Law Journal* 27(1): 1–49.

MacKinnon, Catharine. 2006. *Are Women Human?: And Other International Dialogues*. Cambridge, MA: Harvard University Press.

Mouthaan, Solange. 2012. 'International Law and Sexual Violence Against Men'. *Legal Studies Research Paper No. 2011–02*. Warwick: University of Warwick School of Law.

Oosterhoff, Pauline, Prisca Zwanikken, and Evert Ketting. 2004. 'Sexual Torture of Men in Croatia and Other Conflict Situations: An Open Secret'. *Reproductive Health Matters* 12(23): 68–77.

Oosterveld, Valerie. 2014. 'Sexual Violence Directed Against Men and Boys in Armed Conflict or Mass Atrocity: Addressing a Gendered Harm in International Criminal Tribunals'. *Journal of International Law and International Relations* 10: 107–128.

Risse, Thomas and Kathryn Sikkink. 1999. 'The Socialization of International Human Rights Norms into Domestic Practices: Introduction'. In Thomas Risse, Stephen Ropp, and Kathryn Sikkink (eds), *The Power of Human Rights: International Norms and Domestic Change*. Cambridge: Cambridge University Press, 1–38.

Shepherd, Laura J. 2008. *Gender, Violence, and Security: Discourse as Practice*. London: Zed Books.

Simmons, Beth A. 2009. *Mobilizing for Human Rights: International Law in Domestic Politics*. Cambridge: Cambridge University Press.

Sivakumaran, Sandesh. 2005. 'Male/Male Rape and the "Taint" of Homosexuality'. *Human Rights Quarterly* 27(4): 1274–1306.

Sivakumaran, Sandesh. 2007. 'Sexual Violence Against Men in Armed Conflict'. *European Journal of International Law* 18(2): 253–276.

Sivakumaran, Sandesh. 2010. 'Lost in Translation: UN Responses to Sexual Violence against Men and Boys in Situations of Armed Conflict'. *International Review of the Red Cross* 92(877): 259–277.

Skjelsbæk, Inger. 2001. 'Sexual Violence and War: Mapping Out a Complex Relationship'. *European Journal of International Relations* 7(2): 211–237.

Snow, David A. and Robert D. Benford. 1988. 'Ideology, Frame Resonance, and Participant Mobilization'. *International Social Movement Research* 1: 197–217.

Storr, Will. 2011. 'The Rape of Men: The Darkest Secret of War'. *Guardian*, 17 July. Accessed 14 December 2016. www.theguardian.com/society/2011/jul/17/the-rape-of-men.

Tienhoven, Harry van. 1993. 'Sexual Torture of Male Victims'. *Torture* 3(4): 133–135.

Touquet, Heleen and Ellen Gorris. 2016. 'Out of the Shadows?: The Inclusion of Men and Boys in Conceptualisations of Wartime Sexual Violence'. *Reproductive Health Matters* 24(47): 1–11.

Welsh, James. 2000. *Documenting Human Rights Violations: The Example of Torture*. ACT 75/04/2000. London: Amnesty International. Accessed 29 March 2017. www.amnesty.org/download/Documents/132000/act750042000en.pdf.

12 Conflict-related male sexual violence and the international criminal jurisprudence

Patricia Viseur Sellers and Leo C. Nwoye

Males and females are subjugated to sexualised violence during armed conflict. Nonetheless, conflict-related male sexual violence (CRMSV)[1] seldom is redressed at international courts. When intermittent adjudication of CRMSV does occur, it evinces neither a defined prosecutorial strategy nor a uniform judicial approach.

The current attention to CRMSV builds on the pursuit of surfacing rapes and other conflict-related female sexual violence (CRFSV), which has established an extensive body of international criminal jurisprudence that condemns female rapes as war crimes, crimes against humanity, and genocide (Brammetz and Jarvis 2016: 387–427).

This essentially female-focused jurisprudence emerged in the International Criminal Tribunal for the former Yugoslavia (ICTY) (Sellers 2009: 342), the International Criminal Tribunal for Rwanda (ICTR) (Bianchi 2013: 146–149), the Special Court for Sierra Leone (SCSL) (Oosterveld 2011), and the International Criminal Court (ICC) (Sellers 2016). The dearth of comparative CRMSV jurisprudence contrasts starkly with the critical attention allotted to CRFSV. As Simone Weil recognised, 'there is a wrong way of thinking that one has rights, and a wrong way of thinking that one has not any' (Weil 1956: 152).

Rectifying this insufficiency, first, entails acknowledgement of CRMSV as criminal conduct. Second, diligent investigation and competent prosecution must ensue, unwaveringly. And third, enlightened judicial deliberation must be conferred, consistently.

Thus far, modern CRMSV jurisprudence emerged primarily as ancillary to feminist perspectives on the enforcement of international criminal law (Aranburu 2016: 4–11). The feminist legal redress of rampant conflict-related sexual violence (CRSV) has encompassed CRMSV perpetrated in the Yugoslav wars and targeted the sexual abuse committed in the detention facilities established to facilitate ethnic cleansing policies.

At the Extraordinary Chambers in the Courts of Cambodia (ECCC), the Civil Parties Counsel's feminist legal filings raised the CRSV condoned by the Khmer Rouge regime, notably rapes against female prisoners and forced marriages that integrally comprised CRMSV (Oosterveld and Sellers 2016: 320, 326, 333–336).

Notwithstanding, recourse to feminist frameworks for CRFSV and discernment of key atrocities characteristics has not always sufficed. The SCSL yielded little CRMSV jurisprudence, even though the sexual abuse committed against girls within the context of recurrent recruitment of child soldiers was adjudicated. Similarly, a juridical void existed regarding the redress of CRMSV that occurred during the Rwandan genocide, even though prominent CRFSV jurisprudence abounds (Kaitesi 2014: 2 and 175).

The authors aver that CRSV simultaneously benefits from the current innovations in the redress of sexual violence under international criminal law yet suffers from an inconsistent legal focus. In response, this chapter proposes a survey of the legally significant, yet insufficient and unevenly developed CRMSV jurisprudence rendered by the modern international courts. The imbalance, seemingly, is produced by underwhelming prosecutorial attention to CRMSV and stultifying judicial pronouncements concerning CRMSV.

This survey highlights pertinent legal decisions about CRMSV whether as a war crime, a crime against humanity, or a component of genocide. Complex and strategic choices about which charges to bring, what facts to submit before the Trial Chamber, and how to interpret physical and psychological CRMSV evidence are of particular importance.

Challenges exist, such as establishing individual liability for CRMSV acts that usually do not physically involve the perpetrator or obfuscating CRMSV with other criminal conduct. Likewise, sentencing standards have yet to emerge. The authors' modest intent is to edge the initial conversation beyond the phenomena of CRMSV's occurrence, to a fuller legal deliberation. Ultimately, we urge judicial institutions to abate the incomplete redress of CRSV by confronting CRMSV crimes.

This chapter is divided into seven sections. The first section offers a brief historical overview of CRMSV adjudicated in the aftermath of World War II. The second, third, fourth, fifth, and sixth sections critically explore the irregular and varying CRMSV jurisprudence handed down by the ICTY, ICTR, SCSL, ECCC, and the ICC. The final section comments on and critiques the state of CRMSV jurisprudence and speculates about its evolution.

Historic precedent: CRMSV ubiquitous at Nuremburg and Tokyo military tribunals

Prior to the 1990s, redress of international crimes of sexual violence was disturbingly intermittent. However, contrary to urban legends, condemnations *did* transpire. In 1943, the United Nations War Crimes Commission catalogued the commission of such prohibitions during World War II.

Indeed, the military tribunals of Nuremberg (IMT) and Tokyo (IMTFE) investigated, prosecuted, and convicted individuals for sexual violence (Plesch, Sácouto, and Lasco 2014). IMT prosecutors tendered evidence of rapes against females committed in occupied France and at the Russian front. Yet, transcripts contained testimony of CRMSV, such as of blunt trauma to the genitals of male prisoners (Sellers 2000: 282–283). The governing law of the Nuremberg judgement, the London Charter, outlawed CRSV, including as prohibited acts under Article 3 of the 1929 Geneva Convention and Article 46 of the IV Hague Convention.[2]

The Nuremberg judges, having deliberated overwhelming evidence that established the commission of war crimes, expounded upon the war crimes of slave labour, the persecution of Jews, and the mistreatment of prisoners of war in the written judgement.[3] Notwithstanding, CRSV was condemned under the London Charter's provision for the war crime of 'ill treatment' and the provision for crimes against humanity provision of 'other inhumane acts' or of 'persecution' (Askin 2013: 32–33).

The IMT proceedings remarkably heard evidence of the Gestapo campaign that targeted homosexuals in the 1930s.[4] However, the Nuremberg judges did not explicitly opine upon persecution based on sexual orientation, leaving an enduring deficiency in international criminal law jurisprudence[5] (United States Holocaust Memorial Museum 2016; Giles 1992: 41–42, 55–57). Subsequent Nuremburg trials also redressed mass sterilisations of men and women as war crimes.[6]

The IMTFE judged CRSV crimes in the Asian theatre, including CRMSV acts such as: male rape; genital castration; electrical shocks, hot irons, burning candles or oil applied to sexual organs; men/boys forced to rape related females or the dead; and, collective sexual terrorisation. Based on the Tokyo Charter's proscription of war crimes, CRSV was indicted under torture, inhumane treatment, ill treatment, or 'failure to respect family honour and rights' (Askin 2013: 45; Chang 1997: 77, 88–89, 95).[7] The Tokyo judgement's more explicitly worded condemnation of CRSV presaged today's jurisprudential approaches to sexual violence, inclusive of CRMSV.

The International Criminal Tribunal for the former Yugoslavia

The ICTY rendered a burgeoning body of CRMSV jurisprudence (Campbell 2007: 422–427; Oosterveld 2014: 110). The UN Commission of Experts' Report, that foresaw the establishment of the ICTY, identified five patterns of conflict-related sexual violence (CRSV) that occurred in the armed conflict in the former Yugoslavia. The third pattern included CRMSV committed in detention (UN Security Council 1994, paras 232–253; Sharatt 2011: 10).

Upon the creation of the ICTY, the Experts' Report found receptive ground. Importantly, former commission investigators and lawyers joined the Office of the Prosecutor's (OTP) staff. Additionally, the OTP appointed a Legal Advisor for Gender – who utilised the aforementioned Annex 9 findings to devise investigation and prosecution strategies.

The OTP's strategic policies concerning CRSV, chiefly prompted by a feminist framework to CRFSV, were cognisant of CRMSV (Aranburu 2016: 6–7). For example, the OTP requested an amendment to Rule 96 (ii)(b) of the Rules of

Procedure and Evidence to remove 'she' as the presumed victim of sexual violence.[8]

The OTP's CRSV charging strategy advanced that acts of sexual violence could be indicted under the various provisions of the Statute, such as the war crimes of torture or cruel treatment, or such as the crimes against humanity provisions of torture, persecution, enslavement, or other inhumane acts, in addition to the express provision of rape as a crime against humanity. The OTP also forwarded a gender-neutral definition of rape, inclusive of male rape, in its pleadings.[9]

By 1995, the OTP's contacts with civil society included Dr Mladen Lončar's Medical Center for Human Rights in Croatia, which focused on CRMSV, and the International Rehabilitation Council for the Treatment of Victims of Torture, which treated CRMSV. The ICTY's Victim-Witness Unit similarly developed working relationships with organisations addressing CRMSV (relevant memos on file with the authors).

Tadić: *detention camps as incubators of CRMSV*

Pertinently, the OTP's initial prosecutions prioritised crimes committed against persons imprisoned in the vast network of detention facilities that were a prominent feature of the Yugoslav conflict. As a result, the simultaneous charging of CRFSV and CRMSV evidence emerged in several ICTY cases. By 1996, for example, the ICTY judiciary contemplated CRFSV and CRMSV evidence in the *Karadžić* Rule 61 Hearing Decision. The bench opined:

> [C]amps were nothing but 'specialised centers' for the rape of women. On a smaller scale, many men were also victims of rape and sexual assault by the Serbian Forces ... and the castration of men sometimes performed under duress by prisoners on one another was practiced.
>
> (*Prosecutor* v. *Karadžić & Mladić*, Decision on Review of Indictment pursuant to Rule 61, ICTY Case Nos. IT-95-5-R61 and No. IT-95-18-R61, 11 July 1996, p. 7)

Tadić, the ICTY's first case, typifies CRSV in detention facilities. The original indictment and two subsequent amended indictments alleged that: 'both female and male prisoners were beaten, tortured, raped, sexually assaulted, and humiliated'.[10] Moreover, *Tadić* exemplifies CRMSV conduct wherein guards forced male inmates to commit sexual acts upon each other and forced other inmates to watch.

Tadić, a low-level politician, belonged to a paramilitary force that captured Prijedor, Bosnia and detained its Muslim population in the Omarska camp.[11] Ultimately, only CRMSV evidence was presented at trial while the charges of CRFSV were withdrawn.

The persuasive CRMSV facts proved that *Tadić* and other Bosnian Serbs, ordered two Bosnian Muslim detainees, Witnesses 'H' and 'G', to jump into a pit with a third detainee, Harambasić, who was naked and bloodied from beatings. H was ordered to lick Harambasić's buttocks while G was told to fellate Harambasić. H was then ordered to shut Harambasić's mouth while G was told to lie between Harambasić's legs and to bite off his testicles. Only after G spat out Harambasić's testicle were they allowed to leave the pit. *Tadić* was found guilty of the customary war crime of cruel treatment and of the crime against humanity of 'other inhumane acts'.[12]

The Trial Chamber explicitly recognised the sexual mutilation of Harambasić as a form of CRMSV, however, it failed to pronounce upon the psychological sexual violence suffered by witnesses 'H' and 'G'.[13] *Tadić* received twenty years' imprisonment. On appeal, the convictions were affirmed. Additionally, the Appeals Chamber entered a conviction for the war crime of inhumane treatment in relation to the CRMSV conduct.[14] *Tadić*'s imprisonment was increased to twenty-five years' imprisonment.[15]

Čelibići: *CRMSV and command responsibility*

Delalić et al., the second ICTY case, commonly referred to as '*Čelibići*', continued the strategic pursuit of male and female CRSV perpetrated in detention centres. Notably, the case rendered *de novo* jurisprudence as a result of the prosecution charging strategy.

Delalić is the first case to characterise female rapes as the war crime of torture. It is also the first case to observe that if so alleged, forced male fellatio could constitute rape.[16] It is likewise the first modern case to hold a commander liable for CRSV, specifically for CRMSV because of the acts of his subordinates, as illustrated by *Zdravko Mucić*'s conviction for the crimes committed by *Esad Landžo*.[17]

Regarding CRFSV, *Hazim Delić*, a camp administrator, was convicted for the repeated rapes of Grozdana Ćećez and Milojka Antić. Ćećez was often raped – frequently in public – as punishment for concealing her husband's hideout. Milojka Antić was repeatedly raped, including when interrogated by *Delić*.[18] The Trial Chamber convicted *Delić* of torture for the rapes, because they were committed for such purposes as confession, intimidation, or based upon discrimination.[19] *Delić* was sentenced to fifteen years of imprisonment for the torture and eighteen years overall. *Mucić*, the camp deputy, likewise was convicted of torture for raping female detainees and sentenced to seven years' imprisonment.[20]

Regarding CRMSV, the indictment alleged that *Landžo* forced two brothers to perform fellatio in front of other detainees. *Landžo* also placed a slow-burning fuse cord against the bare genitals of two detainees.[21] Accordingly, *Mucić*, as a de facto superior, was charged with inhuman treatment and cruel treatment as war crimes because *Landžo*, his subordinate, forced two brothers to commit fellatio. The fellatio had not been charged as torture or rape.[22] The court also convicted *Mucić* of the war crimes of wilfully causing great suffering or causing serious injury to body or health, and cruel treatment for *Landžo*'s CRMSV act of placing a burning wire on the genitals of one detainee. He was acquitted of allegations that *Landžo* placed a burning wire on a second detainee's genitalia due to lack of proof.[23] *Mucić* was sentenced to seven years' imprisonment on these counts, and nine years overall. *Delalić* represents critical case law but yet remains woefully under-examined, especially in terms of CRMSV.

Furundžija: *CRMSV as psychological torture*

Furundžija, the ICTY's third case, often misunderstood for CRMSV, is renowned for its CRFSV jurisprudence. Nonetheless, *Furundžija* is illustrative of OTP strategy to jointly redress male and female sexual violence committed against detained persons.

Furundžija was charged with the war crimes of torture and outrages upon personal dignity for the perpetration of rapes (CRFSV). He was also convicted of torture for CRMSV.[24] *Anto Furundžija* commanded a Bosnian Croatian paramilitary unit, the Jokers, that committed CRSV against Witness A, a Muslim woman, and against Witness D, a Bosnian Croat soldier.

The Jokers arrested Witness A and transported her to their headquarters, where *Furundžija* and *Miroslav Bralo*, another Joker, undressed her, then interrogated her. Unsatisfied with Witness A's answers, *Furundžija* halted the interrogation and left, whereupon *Bralo* raped her multiple times in front of the other Jokers.[25]

Furundžija returned with Witness D, who was a Croat soldier that the Jokers arrested under the suspicion that he was assisting Muslims. *Furundžija* interrogated Witness D together with Witness A, who remained nude. Then, while *Furundžija* and the other Jokers watched, *Bralo* raped Witness A, vaginally, anally, and orally. *Furundžija* forced Witness D to watch the rapes in order to compel his confession. Even when he left the room or stood at the door, *Furundžija* knew the sexual abuse was being committed.[26]

Essentially, Witness A was repeatedly tortured *via* the rapes and Witness D was also subjected to torture, more specifically, psychological sexual torture because:

> [He] was then forced to watch Accused B's sexual attacks on Witness A [...]. The physical attacks upon Witness D, as well as the fact that he was forced to watch sexual attacks on a woman, in particular, a woman whom he knew as a friend, caused him severe physical and mental suffering.[27]

This is a frequent form of CRMSV, wherein detained males are constrained to witness or participate in the sexual abuse of others. Hence, *Tadić*, *Delalić*, and *Furundžija* demonstrate this psychological form of CRMSV that could be charged as torture.

Todorović: *CRMSV as rape*

The case against *Todorović* concerned the Bosnian-Serb takeover of the town Bosanki Šamac. Bosnian Croat and Muslim women and children were deported from Bosanki Šamac while the males were arrested. *Todorović*, the municipal Chief of Police, controlled prisoners held at the police station. On three occasions, *Todorović* forced detainees to fellate each other. On another occasion, he kicked a prisoner's genitals and then ordered him to bite another detainee's penis.[28]

Notably, for the CRMSV, the 1995 indictment charged *Todorović* and *Blagoje Simić*, his superior, with rape as a crime against humanity and the war crime of inhumane treatment.[29] This was only the second time that rape as a crime against humanity was charged at the ICTY. The first was in the *Tadić* indictment. However, *Todorović* is the first time rape was charged to characterise CRMSV. The Second Indictment, issued in 1998, added charges of persecution and torture for CRMSV and indicted *Todorović* both as a physical perpetrator and as a commander. *Blagoje Simić* was charged both as a superior and a perpetrator of CRMSV. Additionally, *Milan Simić*, a politician and a cousin of *Blagoje Simić* was charged with kicking prisoners in the genitals and threatening to cut off a prisoner's penis.[30]

In 2000, *Todorović* entered a guilty plea for persecution in exchange for the withdrawal of the other charges. The plea agreement encompassed the aforementioned CRMSV.[31] The recognition of CRMSV as persecution based on religious discrimination is noteworthy jurisprudence. The Trial Chamber ruled the CRMSV as an aggravating circumstance and sentenced *Todorović* to ten years' imprisonment.[32]

Several observations are pertinent. Although in 1998 *Furundžija* ruled that oral penetration of Witness A constituted rape as a war crime,[33] and the *Čelibići* judgement opined that fellatio was rape, it was the 1995 *Todorović* indictment that first confirmed a charge of rape as a crime against humanity for acts of fellatio, quickly followed by the same charge for similar conduct in the *Češić* case. This early charging of fellatio as rape accords with the OTP's gender-neutral definition of rape.

Sikirica et al.: *CRMSV as persecution*

Another ICTY case, *Sikirica et al.*, concerned crimes committed against Bosnian Muslims and Bosnian Croats detained at the Keraterm camp in the Prijedor municipality. The *Sikirica*-related cases stand for continued pursuit of CRSV in detention settings and the evolved charging OTP strategy, under genocide and persecution as a crime against humanity, especially for CRMSV. The ICTY had successfully pursued CRFSV under genocide.

The original indictment and subsequent amendments detailed abhorrent CRMSV. Detainees were killed, subjected to sexual assaults, torture, and inhuman treatment. The 1999 Amended Indictment consolidated, in one charging document, all of the crimes alleged to have been committed against detainees in the Keraterm, Omarska, and Trnoplje camps.

Duško Sikirica, Commander of Security at Keraterm, was charged with genocide, described as 'sexual assault and rape of Bosnian Muslims, Bosnian Croats and other non-Serbs in Prijedor, including those detained in the Keraterm.' He was also charged with persecution and inhumane acts as crimes against humanity and outrages upon personal dignity as a war crime.[34]

A Second Amended Indictment accused *Sikirica* of genocide and complicity to commit genocide. The commission of sexual assaults and forcing prisoners to witness sexual assaults entailed causing serious mental harm to members of the group, a genocide act.[35]

Sikirica and *Duško Knežević*, a camp interloper, committed CRMSV at Keraterm. They were indicted for persecution and inhumane acts as crimes against humanity and the war crime of outrages upon personal dignity. Two prisoners, Bahonjić and Jusufagić (alias 'Car') were severely beaten, and forced by *Knežević* and others to fellate other prisoners. Bahonjić and Jusufagić, then, had objects inserted into their anuses. They died from injuries sustained during such abuse.[36]

In September 2001, the genocide charge was dismissed[37] and *Sikirica*, together with *Damir Došen* and *Dragan Kolundžija*, both Keraterm shift commanders, pleaded guilty to the sexual assaults charged as persecution, a crime against humanity. *Sikirica* was sentenced to fifteen years' imprisonment. However, it remains inconclusive whether *Sikirica*'s conviction for CRMSV encompasses the crimes committed against Bahonjić and Jusufagić, since he exercised limited superior responsibility over *Knežević*.[38]

In July 2000, the prosecution combined the *Sikirica* and *Mejakić* indictments, thus consolidating the alleged crimes from the Omarska and Keraterm camps. The Consolidated Indictment seamlessly described CRMSV and CRFSV with other crimes. Paragraph 15 reads:

> The interrogations were frequently accompanied by beatings. Severe beatings, killings as well as other forms of physical and psychological abuse, including sexual assault, were commonplace at the Omarska and Keraterm camps....

Additionally, paragraph 29(a) states:

> [...] The persecutions included the:
> (a) Murder, beatings and sexual assault of Bosnian Muslims, Bosnian Croats and other non-Serbs detained in the Omarska and Keraterm camps [...]

The Consolidated Indictment also joined, in one charging document, the remaining defendants – *Dušan Fustar*, a Keraterm camp shift commander, *Knežević* and *Predrag Banović*, camp guards, from the *Sikirica et al.* case, with *Željko Mejakić*, the Omarska Camp Commander, and *Momčilo Gruban*, an Omarska camp shift commander. All accused were charged with persecution, murder, and other inhumane acts as crimes against humanity and murder and cruel treatment as war crimes.

However, the *Bahonjić* and *Jusufagić* incidents were veiled amid the generalised CRSV. Also, the Consolidated Indictment inexplicably dropped torture and rape as crimes against humanity against *Banović* and *Knežević* that were in the *Sikirica et al.* Second Amended Indictment.

Ultimately, in 2003, *Banović* pled guilty to persecution. The remaining charges were dropped. The plea agreement did not detail incidents of CRMSV.[39] *Banović* was sentenced to eight years' imprisonment. Crimes committed against Jusufagić, however, were addressed later, in the *Kvočka* case. The case against *Fustar, Knežević, Mejakić*, and *Gruban* were transferred to the Bosnia-Herzegovina's national criminal courts in 2006.

Stakić: *CRMSV and political liability*

Stakić, another ICTY case illustrated how local politicians and other members of a joint criminal enterprise were responsible for CRSV, including CRMSV.[40] *Milomir Stakić* was the President of the Prijedor Municipal Assembly where Omarska, Keraterm, and Trnoplolje camps were established. Unlike the *Sikirica* and *Mejakić* defendants, *Stakić* was physically removed from the sexual abuse and from the camps.

The case is indicative of the liability strategy to inculpate higher level political or military indictees accused of crimes of sexual violence. Indeed, *Stakić* is a rare case wherein the intended common purpose of the joint criminal enterprise encompassed CRSV as persecutory acts. The *Stakić* case, which is also similar to *Sikirica*, pursued a charging strategy that alleged, *inter alia*, genocide, complicity in genocide and persecution as crimes against humanity for detention related sexual violence.

The persecution entailed 'torture, physical violence, rape, constant humiliation and degradation.'[41] At the Keraterm camp, a group of male prisoners were made to remain naked from the waist down while another group half kneeled in front of them, as if engaged in sexual fellatio.[42] Other CRSV entailed the coercion of an elderly man to rape a girl. When he begged not to rape her, he was killed.[43] The Trial Chamber recognised this as sexual abuse, although it is unclear whether it considered the girl, the elderly man, or both as victims.

While *Stakić* was acquitted of genocide and complicity in genocide, he was convicted of persecution as a crime against humanity that encompassed the above-described CRMSV.[44]

Kvočka: *inconsistent evidence of CRMSV at detention camp*

The *Kvočka* case subsequently examined crimes committed at the notorious Omarska camp – the site of the genital mutilation that led to the first CRMSV conviction in *Tadić*. *Kvočka* originally was part of the 1995 *Mejakić* indictment. At Omarska, 'both female and male prisoners were beaten, tortured, raped, sexually assaulted, and humiliated.' Unlike *Stakić*, the accused were physically present at the camp. Allegations of CRMSV included acts of a prison guard who stripped a detainee and kicked his testicles, and of interlopers who maltreated male inmates.[45]

Notwithstanding, the plethora of criminal conduct, *Kvočka* exemplified inconsistencies in pleading and in adducing probative CRMSV evidence at trial. For example, *Zoran Zigić*, a taxi driver who mobilised as a reserve officer, frequented all three camps. He was charged with persecution and inhumane acts as crimes against humanity and with the war crime of outrages upon personal dignity for 'the sexual assault and rape of Bosnian Muslims, Bosnian Croats and other non-Serbs ... including prisoners in the Omarska, Keraterm and Trnopolje camps.' [46] He was also charged with the murders of Jusufagić and Bahonjić, but not the acts of CRMSV. Moreover, at trial, the CRMSV evidence regarding Jusufagić's and Bahonjić's sexual abuse was insubstantial. Hence, *Zigić* was convicted only of their murders.[47]

Kvočka, however, is renowned for liability of CRFSV based upon a theory of joint criminal enterprise. Therein, guilt for crimes, such as rape, was attributed to members of the joint criminal enterprise as a natural and foreseeable consequence of the criminal enterprise, the detention camp.[48]

Simić *and* Češić*: guilty pleas for CRMSV*

Milan Simić, a senior official in Bosanki Šamac, was originally indicted for CRMSV in the 1995 *Todorović* amended indictment. In 1998, *Simić* surrendered to the ICTY and pleaded guilty to torture as a crime against humanity for CRMSV alleged in the Fourth Amended Indictment. He admitted to kicking the arrested men in their genitals, to pulling down one prisoner's pants, and threatening to cut off his penis.[49] Detainees were made to stand with their arms outstretched and legs apart in order to receive forceful kicks to their genitals.

The *Simić* jurisprudence is insightful, not in the least because it is the result of a guilty plea for CRMSV of a direct perpetrator. Furthermore, the Trial Chamber held that sexual humiliation increased the mental suffering of victims, and that *Simić*'s position constituted aggravating factors. It dismissed his claim of intoxication as mitigating. *Simić* received five years' imprisonment.[50]

The *Češić* case persisted with the prosecution strategy to redress detention crimes, specifically those committed at the Luka camp in the Brčko municipality. *Češić* illustrates a familiar CRMSV pattern wherein an accused is not the physical perpetrator, yet commands male victims to sexually abuse each other in front of others inmates. Two Muslim brothers detainees were forced at gunpoint to fellate each other for forty-five minutes, while the guards mocked them. The 1995 *Češić* indictment adhered to a charging theory that was exhibited in 1995 *Todorović* indictment – that fellatio could constitute as rape, a crime against humanity.

In 2004, *Ranko Češić*, a member of the Bosnian Serb Territorial Defence and the Police Reserve Corps, pleaded guilty to the charge.[51] Significantly, the Trial Chamber recognised that *both* men were raped and deemed the public nature of the acts particularly serious.[52] *Češić* was sentenced to a single term of eighteen years' imprisonment.[53]

Brđanin: *indecisive CRMSV liability for a vice-president*

The *Brđanin* case continued seeking responsibility for detention-related CRSV by high-level politicians through a joint criminal liability theory. *Radoslav Brđanin* was the Vice-President of Republika Srpska and President of the Autonomous Region of Krajina Crisis Staff. Under his authority, Bosnian Muslim and Bosnian Croat prisoners faced CRSV throughout the Republika Srpska.

Brđanin was charged with genocide, however, CRMSV was not explicitly described in the count nor was rape as a crime against humanity expressly charged.[54] However, persecution, under crimes against humanity became the all-encompassing count that subsumed the CRSV and the CRMSV.

Facts included acts at the Kotor Varoš Police Station, where two males were forced to fellate each other in front of Bosnian Serb police officers and soldiers. At the Omarska camp, one of many CRMSV acts included a man being forced to 'cross the pista' naked while being whipped by a guard.[55]

Brđanin was convicted of aiding and abetting persecution as a member of a joint criminal enterprise. While the Trial Chamber proffered explicit acts of CRFSV, it only acknowledged CRMSV conduct in relation to its humiliating and degrading nature. *Brđanin* was sentenced to a single term of thirty-two years' imprisonment.[56]

Krajišnik *and* **Plavšić:** *mixed presidential liability for CRMSV*

Momčilo Krajišnik and *Biljana Plavšić*, as members of the Presidency of Republika Srpska, resided at the highest rungs of political power. Nonetheless they were indicted for the deportation and forcible transfer of Muslims out of the region as part of a criminal plan that eventually expanded to encompass other crimes, such as CRMSV.[57] As such, both were charged with genocide, complicity in genocide as well as deportation, extermination, murder, other inhumane acts, and persecution under crimes against humanity.

The factual allegations described male detainees at the Batković camp who were forced to perform degrading sexual acts on each other in the presence of other detainees. In Čelopek, at the Dom Kulture detention centre, two men were sexually mutilated. At Korto Vareš and Semizovac, male prisoners were forced to perform humiliating sexual acts in front of their captors.[58]

In 2002, *Plavšić* pleaded guilty to persecution, inclusive of the CRMSV, in return for the withdrawal of the genocide counts. The *Plavšić* judgement represents the first instance in international law that a head of state – on a shared presidency – pleaded guilty for CRSV, including CRMSV. The *Plavšić* guilty plea is also curious in that a female is guilty of CRSV of males and females. *Plavšić* was sentenced to eleven years' imprisonment.[59]

Krajišnik, to the contrary, was tried and convicted, *inter alia*, for CRMSV under persecution as a crime against humanity and acquitted of genocide and complicity in genocide.[60] He was sentenced to twenty-seven years' imprisonment. However, the Appeals Chamber reversed *Krajišnik*'s liability for CRSV, including CRMSV. It ruled that the Trial Chamber committed a legal error when it failed to specify the time period when the expanded crimes, including CRSV, entered into the criminal plan of the joint criminal enterprise. Accordingly, *Krajišnik* was re-sentenced to twenty years.[61] Thus, while one member of the Republic of Srpska presidency, *Plavšić*, was liable for CRSV, including CRMSV, another, *Krajišnik*, was exculpated.

Martić: *CRMSV as a foreseeable consequence of ethnic cleansing*

The *Martić* case is under-recognised for its CRMSV jurisprudence. *Martić* is notably a leadership case that pursued a varied crime-base, including detention-related abuse. Notably, *Martić* extends *Kvočka*'s liability analysis of sexual violence as a foreseeable consequence of an initial criminal plan to CRMSV.

Milan Martić was President of the Republic of Serbian Krajina, whose Ministry of Justice converted a hospital into a facility to detain Bosnian males. *Martić* was charged for persecution as a crime against humanity under joint criminal enterprise liability for the CRMSV. Prisoners were forced to mutually masturbate and fellate each other. Prison guards, also attempted to rape prisoners. The Serb Krajina leadership, including *Martić*, endorsed the mistreatment of detainees.[62]

CRSV was not intended within the original criminal plan to ethnically cleanse the region. However, the Trial Chamber held that such sexual abuse, including CRMSV, was the natural and foreseeable consequences of implementing the 'forcible removal of a majority of the Croat, Muslim and other non-Serb population … in order to make … a new Serb-dominated state.' The setting up of detention facilities was integral to the criminal enterprise.[63] *Martić*'s conviction for persecution and other crimes as well as his thirty-five-year prison sentence were affirmed on appeal.[64]

Stanišić and Župljanin: *CRMSV affirmed as persecution*

The *Stanišić and Župljanin* case surfaced CRMSV directed against the Bosnian Muslim men prisoners – perpetrated by Serb paramilitaries and reserve policemen. The jurisprudence confirms the utility of CRSV joint criminal enterprise theory. In *Stanišić and Župljanin*, the common purpose was to remove non-Serbs from the territory to establish the Republic of Srpska. As in the *Martić* case, the detention related CRSV, including CRMSV, was not part of the original plan, and yet was a natural and foreseeable consequence of ethnic cleansing. Hence, liability was attributable to the accused.[65]

Stanišić and Župljanin jurisprudence is also reminiscent of *Furundžija*. Here, the Trial Chamber ruled that the psychological suffering caused when forced to watch a close female relative being raped amounted to torture, cruel treatment, and other inhumane acts.[66] *Stanišić and Župljanin* is among the rare cases to acknowledge the secondary psychological harm caused by witnessing CRSV.

Mićo Stanišić was the Minister of the Interior of Republika Srpska. Stojan Župljanin was Stanišić's direct subordinate. Both of the accused facilitated the establishment and operation of detention facilities[67] and were participants in the joint criminal enterprise.[68]

CRMSV crimes previously prosecuted in *Krajišnik* and *Brđanin* were alleged against *Stanišić and Župljanin*, such as: forced nudity; anal rape using a broom handle; forcing a man to watch a close female relative being raped; attachment of electrical wires to genitals or nipples; forced fellatio among inmates; stomping on genitals; forced sexual acts between related inmates; severing a penis; and forcing detainees to ingest a penis under threat of death.[69]

The Trial Chamber convicted *Stanišić and Župljanin* of persecution as a crime against humanity and torture as a war crime based upon CRFSV and CRMSV evidence. Each accused received twenty-two years' imprisonment.[70] On appeal, the convictions for persecution, including CRMSV were upheld,[71] confirming modern international criminal law's characterisation of CRMSV as persecution, a crime against humanity.

Karadžić: *CRMSV for the highest level accused*

Radovan Karadžić, a Bosnian Serb former politician, was a founding member of the Serbian Democratic Party – a nationalist party originally established to, *inter alia*, unify the Bosnian Serbs in the former Yugoslavia and lead them in remaining part of Yugoslavia in the event of secession by Bosnia-Herzegovina and Croatia from the federation. He was the President of the Presidency of Serbian Republic of Bosnia and Herzegovina (renamed Republika Srpska on 12 August 1992) and later the sole President of the Republic of Srpska during the Bosnian War.[72]

Karadžić was charged with genocide, crimes against humanity, and war crimes. The genocide charge that alleged serious bodily or mental harm and the crimes against humanity charge of persecution examined CRMSV conduct.[73]

Although a certain amount of CRMSV evidence emanated from previous ICTY cases, *Karadžić's* CRMSV evidence revealed a much more complete, if not complex, rendering of CRSV.[74] Some of the evidence elicited was that Batković camp detainees were 'forced to have sexual intercourse with each other, often in front of other detainees.'[75]

The detainees from the Rasadnik camp (in the town of Rogatica) testified that guards forced 'male prisoners to perform unnatural sexual acts' and that 'female detainees were forced (…) to strip and perform sexual acts with (male) elderly detainees.'[76] Omarska camp detainees testified that the guards 'attempted to force a male detainee to rape another female detainee.'[77] At the Hadžići facility, Ljiljia, a female perpetrator 'removed one man's pants and told another man to "suck the first man's sexual organ".' She then, forced 'the second man to lick her buttocks, threatening to slit the men's throats if they did not comply.'[78]

At the Bunker in Vogošća, paramilitary men, 'forced the two Bosnian Muslim men to have oral sex and sexual intercourse.'[79] The Trial Chamber also held that: 'some Bosnian Muslim male detainees, including a 13-year-old boy, were also raped by Serb Forces who used police truncheons and similar objects' in the town of Rogatica.[80] The thirteen-year-old boy in question (as well as women and girls as young as seven) were taken out of the classrooms from the Veljko Vlahović Secondary School and raped by the police and soldiers who guarded the camp almost every night for a period of two and a half months. One male detainee was taken to a basement 'at least 30 times and raped on almost every occasion.'[81]

Concerning genocide, the Trial Chamber concluded that CRMSV and CRFSV 'were of such a serious nature as to contribute or tend to contribute to the destruction of the Bosnian Muslims and Bosnian Croats.'[82] However, it ultimately found *Karadžić* guilty of genocide only in relation to the Srebrenica events and not the detention-related sexual violence.

Karadžić nonetheless was guilty for all of the CRMSV and CRFSV acts perpetrated. He was convicted of persecution as a crime against humanity because the CRMSV (and other sexual violence crimes) was a natural and foreseeable consequence of the ethnic cleansing and detention.[83] *Karadžić* was sentenced to forty years' imprisonment.[84] An appeal is currently pending, at the time of writing, under the jurisdiction of the Mechanism for International Criminal Tribunals.

The *Karadžić* case, a historic case concluded against a very high-level perpetrator at the ICTY, provided a more integrated approach to CRSV evidence by demonstrating the unrelenting and pervasive existence of CRMSV. While all sexual violence was alleged jointly, persecution as a crime against humanity was the basis of the charge even though it is not a sexually explicit crime.

The International Criminal Tribunal for Rwanda: missed opportunities to address CRMSV

CRSV against males and females happened during the Rwandan genocide. Notwithstanding, the prosecutorial and judicial focuses were, archetypally, on female sexual violence and essentially overlooked CRMSV. Until 2000, the ICTR and the ICTY functioned with one Prosecutor and shared the same Legal Advisor for Gender. The recognition of CRFSV as acts of genocide was paramount to the inaugural ICTR case of *Akayesu*.

Subsequently, the ICTR Prosecutor appointed advisors for gender-related crimes but not for sustained periods, prompting merited critiques from feminists who raised concerns about impunity for CRFSV. By mid-2005, the ICTR established a Sexual Assaults Team to investigate CRFSV, yet, the largely male composed team was not well trained and lacked the requisite skills. This team was eventually dissolved and its members reassigned into the other investigation teams. As such, CRMSV ultimately transpired as a background narrative without legal consideration (Sivakumaran 2010: 273–274).

The *Bagosora* case implicitly nods to the intertwined occurrence of male and female CRSV in Roméo Dallaire's poignant testimony:

> Female victims were left lying on their back[s] with their legs spread and stained with semen. Dallaire saw objects crushed or implanted in vaginas, breasts cut off, stomachs opened and the mutilated genitals of men.
>
> (*Bagosora et al. Trial Judgement*: para. 1908)

The OTP focused purely on CRFSV. No line of questioning surfaced CRMSV.[85] Indeed, CRMSV was rampant during the Rwandan genocide but was absent from the dominant discourse of sexual violence in Rwanda:

> Some were forced to have sexual intercourse with their children, parents, and enemies. They were mutilated, castrated, hanged by their sexual organs and forced into sexual relations with dead animals. Some middle aged men were in different places laid down nude and forced to have sex with dead animals like dogs ... while the family members of the victims were forced to watch....
> (Kaitesi and Haveman 2011: 387 and 406)

Only CRMSV acts committed against Assiel Kabanda, an influential Tutsi trader, were prosecuted. In *Muhimana*, the town councillor for Gishyita secteur, who actively participated in the killing of Kabanda, was merely charged with murder as a crime against humanity.[86]

In the *Niyitegeka* case, charges of genocide and crimes against humanity, although framed broadly, only included CRFSV and did not address sexual assaults against males.[87] Niyitegeka was the Minister of Information, who 'was jubilant and rejoicing' while Kabanda was killed and his genitalia were mutilated.[88] *Niyitegeka*'s encouragement of the killing, decapitation, and castration of Kabanda constituted 'aiding and abetting' in genocide.

Additionally, the mutilation of Kabanda and Niyitegeka's orders to paramilitaries that they insert sharpened wooden sticks into the genitalia of a dead Tutsi female were legally characterised as other inhumane acts, under crimes against humanity. The conviction and the sentence of life imprisonment were affirmed on appeal.[89]

The ICTR hence represents missed opportunities to redress impunity for CRMSV and develop a fuller body of sexual assault jurisprudence commensurate with the veritable scope of the genocide.

Special court for Sierra Leone: CRMSV insufficiently and inconsistently assessed

Inadequate attention was given to CRMSV at the SCSL, despite the fact that its case law illustrated that in general, sexual violence was employed against males and females, separately or concurrently, as a means of terrorising the civilian population. *Prosecutor* v. *Sesay et al.* recognised such gendered 'patterns and effects.' In the town of Bomboafuidu, the Revolutionary United Front (RUF) undressed male and female civilian captives and ordered them to have sex with each other. RUF rebels mutilated the genitals of civilian males and females.[90]

The Trial Chamber also regarded CRMSV as psychological harm suffered when RUF fighters forced a husband and his children to watch the rape and subsequent death of his wife and their mother.[91] Moreover, they deemed CRSV and gender-based violence against males or females admissible, if 'clear, timely and consistent' prior notice was given to the defence counsel.[92]

It is noteworthy that the leadership cases of the Armed Forces Revolutionary Council (AFRC), the RUF, and Charles Taylor explicitly charged rapes, sexual slavery, or sexual violence crimes committed against females.[93] However, the CRMSV that surfaced during the trials[94] was inconsistently treated by the Trial Chambers. In *Taylor*, and ostensibly in *Brima et al.*, the Trial Chamber left CRMSV ill defined, as they were restricted by the indictment.[95]

All the same, in spite of the insufficiency and inconsistency of the SCSL's treatment of CRMSV, there was some advancement in CRMSV jurisprudence, albeit limited.

The International Criminal Court: mixed results for CRMSV

The prosecution of CRMSV cases at the ICC has produced varied outcomes. In *The Prosecutor* v. *Jean-Pierre Bemba Gombo*, the ICC charged rape as a crime against humanity for men, women, and children. Significantly, it is the ICC's first conviction for sexual violence and a rare case that characterises CRMSV as rape, like *Simić* and *Češić*. *Bemba* is also important, together with *Čelibići*, for holding a superior, liable for CRSV.

The case concerned a campaign of atrocities committed by rebel forces in the Central African Republic. Armed fighters successively raped a male victim, while family members watched. Subsequently, he witnessed his wife and his three daughters' rape and heard his granddaughter's cries when raped by fighters.[96] Another man suffered anal and oral rape by two armed fighters in his home – after he had protested about the prior vaginal and anal rape of his wife.[97]

Bemba, as a superior, was convicted of rape (*inter alia*) because of his failure to prevent or punish the rapes (and other criminal conduct) that the fighters under his effective control, perpetrated. An appeal is pending.

In *Prosecutor* v. *Kenyatta et al.*, the CRSV committed during the Kenyan post-election violence from late 2007 to early 2008 included forced circumcision of Luo males. The prosecution alleged that forced circumcision constituted 'other forms of sexual violence' as a crime against humanity. The prosecution submitted that forced circumcision and penile amputation occurred in a broad context with other forms of sexual violence:

> [E]ight Luo men had their genitals chopped off and ... boys, some ... as young as 11 and 5 years old had their genitalia cut with blunt objects such as broken glass.[98]

The prosecution contended that the attacks on Luo men targeted their virility and were 'designed to destroy their masculinity':

> In committing rape and mutilation of genital organs, individuals are assaulted and wounded in ways that are socially gendered, in their identities as women and men as such, and in the social roles that they occupy, identify

with, and anticipate filling as gendered members of their communities. (...) Men who were castrated were deprived of their manhood and debased in front of their families.[99]

Nevertheless, the Pre-Trial Chamber's sexual analysis focused on female rapes, not penile mutilation, forced nudity or the specific gendered cultural practice of circumcision within the ethno-political milieu of the crimes.[100] The Pre-Trial Chamber held that: 'not every act of violence which targets parts of the body associated with sexuality should be considered an act of sexual violence.' It opined that: 'the acts were motivated by ethnic prejudice and intended to demonstrate cultural superiority of one tribe over the other.'[101]

Ultimately, the Pre-Trial Chamber rejected the characterisation of forced circumcision as other sexual violence, stating that forcible circumcision more properly equated 'other inhumane acts' under crimes against humanity.[102] The Pre-Trial Chamber, hence, likened such genital mutilation to a physical bodily injury, holding it 'not sexual enough' to be sexual violence. It did not proffer guidance about when such genital mutilations amounted to sexual violence. Arguably, the Pre-Trial Chamber's interpretation was responsive to the Prosecutor's insufficient elucidation about the link between sexual norms, gender, and sexual organs (Oosterveld 2014: 124).

The ICC case of the *Prosecutor* v. *Bosco Ntganda* alleges CRSV, wherein male prisoners were ordered to rape female prisoners and three male victims were raped anally. These acts were charged as rape as crimes against humanity and as a war crime.[103] The case, as of this writing, is in the Defence phase and it appears that the prosecution did not present any CRMSV evidence.

Notwithstanding the ICC's prosecutorial challenges and mixed results, given its potential caseload, the ICC should be a substantial actor in the maturing evolution of CRMSV analysis and jurisprudence – especially given the Office of the Prosecutor's its recent adoption of a mandatory gender inclusive analysis that implements the 2014 Policy Paper on Sexual and Gender-Based Crimes.

Extraordinary chambers in the Courts of Cambodia: new ground for CRMSV

While CRMSV jurisprudence of the ECCC is limited, evidence of thousands of forced conjugal relations between men and women, ordered by the Khmer Rouge regime, is being tendered.[104] Such 'forced marriages' entailed:

[M]en and women [often between the ages of 15–30] ... complete strangers, forced to commit to each other at mass wedding [of between 5–100 or more couples] officiated by actors of the Khmer Rouge state.... [A]ssigned husbands and wives publically promised to have a child within one year. Married couples stayed with each other a few days ... often with Khmer Rouge spies, or *chhlob*, making sure they consummated the marriage with sexual relations.
(De Langis, Strasser, Kim, and Taing 2014: 28; Ye 2011: 469–470)

Marriages required the regime's approval. Punishment for refusing to marry ranged from receiving a warning, to imprisonment or to execution. Such CRSV contextualises the regime's true objectives in directing males and females to sexually violate each other. Pregnancy and childbirth were the expected outcomes. The regime, then, removed the children from their biological progenitors to be raised by the state. In essence, the Khmer Rouge regime executed a state policy of sexual violence in order to breed children. It thus ensured a mass of indoctrinated citizens for the new Khmer society (Oosterveld and Sellers 2016: 322).

Commentary: an imperative need for strategic forethought

It is patently obvious that judicial recognition of CRMSV begs judicial clarity, uniformity, and consistency. CRMSV has confronted many biases and taboos since the modern re-emergence of the adjudication of sexual violence under international humanitarian and international criminal law. While it has 'given' rights regarding sexual integrity, there is insufficient attention on how to make those rights redress CRMSV and acknowledge the victims.

A principally feminist approach to CRFSV led to piecemeal international jurisprudence for CRMSV. However, that jurisprudence is problematic: it is woefully uneven at the ICC and the ICTY; absent at the ICTR; rife with unsatisfactory assessments at the SCSL; or stunted and tardy (while covering new CRMSV terrain) at the ECCC. The *Kenyatta* jurisprudence that characterised genital mutilation as non-sexual physical violence defies common sense. Mature judicial attention about CRMSV must be secured (Gorris 2015: 413).

Legal characterisation of CRMSV is significant. Trial Chambers can enter cumulative or multiple convictions based upon different statutory provisions that have 'materially distinct elements.'[105] Cumulative charging is laudable when it captures the implicit sexual nature of crimes like persecution, inhumane treatment, or torture. Nonetheless, concerns remain. Feminists and increasingly male advocates on CRSV often prefer that sexual violence conduct be indicted under explicitly sexual assault provisions, such as rape or sexual slavery. The authors suggest that both approaches to CRFSV and CRMSV are strategically viable and legally complementary.

Furthermore, OTPs in international courts can critically advance gender CRSV jurisprudence. At a minimum, designating investigative and legal advisors for gender in the OTP appears indispensable. Investigative strategies usually concentrate on factual patterns endemic to an armed conflict, such as detention systems, exterminations, forced recruitment, or enslavement. Irrespective of the distinctive factual patterns, competently uncovering CRMSV acts should inform, if not determine investigation strategies.

Likewise, prosecution litigation strategies must not intentionally nor inadvertently result in impunity for CRMSV. Strategies that address CRFSV might omit or inadequately address CRMSV. Framing forced marriages as crimes only inflicted upon females, while appropriately capturing CRSV in Sierra Leone, ignores how forced marriages entailed CRMSV under the Khmer Rouge regime. Moreover, prosecutorial discretion to select CRMSV charges must comprehensively capture the criminal conduct. *Delalić* omitted to charge torture for genital mutilation, while *Tadić*, although groundbreaking, did not charge the psychological nature of the sexual torture suffered by H and G who were forced to mutilate Harambasić.

A gender-inclusive analysis of CRSV (like the aforementioned ICC OTP's new mandatory approach) necessitates deciphering physical and psychological sexual violence that targets males and females, sequentially, simultaneously, consequentially, or alternatively. A holistic examination of CRSV intricately contextualises and reveals the scope of war crimes, crimes against humanity, or genocide. For example, the military occupation of a village during armed conflict might purposely entail forced recruitment and deliberate sexual abuse of boys and girls as a means to exercise control over families through sexual terrorisation. Therein, individual and collective suffering of physical or psychological sexual violence reveals an endemic factual pattern. Any resulting jurisprudence should comprehensively rule upon the complexities of CRMSV and CRFSV that reinforces this military occupation.

Opportunities abound to progress beyond intermittent acknowledgement of CRMSV under international criminal law: yet legal inertia could prevail. Refined prosecution strategies must precede the deliberation and delivery of lucid CRMSV jurisprudence that is integral, not incidental, to CRSV. International courts are mandated to examine the sexual violence within their jurisdiction, without discrimination. The aversion to execute such mandates occludes the destructive extent of wartime sexual violence and profoundly offends the international community. The competent adjudication of CRMSV crimes committed in Central African Republic, the Democratic Republic of Congo, Syria and Libya teeters upon this legal chasm.

Coda

On 30 May 2016, Hissein Habré, the President of Chad between 1982 and 1990, was convicted by the Extraordinary African Chambers in the Senegalese Courts (EAC), *inter alia* of crimes against humanity of intentional homicide, sexual slavery, rape, torture, and inhumane treatment perpetrated by his regime and sentenced to life imprisonment.[106] The torture conviction encompassed CRMSV meted out on several prisoners who were from certain ethnic groups or who were perceived as political enemies.[107]

Intriguingly, Habré is the first former head of state to be condemned for international crimes exclusively under the universal jurisdiction of another African state. The EAC breaks new ground and offers insights into the possibility of a regional approach to international criminal justice in Africa.

More recently, on 22 November 2017, the ICTY Trial Chamber convicted General *Ratko Mladić*, the highest ranked Bosnian Serb military commander, of, *inter alia*, persecution as a crime against humanity, based in part, on the CRMSV inflicted in detention camps that defined the Yugoslav armed conflict.[108] *Mladić* was sentenced to life in prison.[109]

Notes

1 Scholars draw on the World Health Organization (2002) to define sexual violence against men:

> Sexual violence against men includes actions directed at the victim's sexual or reproductive health or identity, for example: rape, whether oral or anal, involving objects, the perpetrator or two victims; enforced sterilization; enforced nudity; enforced masturbation and other forms of sexual humiliation; castration; genital violence (for example beatings of genitals or the administration of electric shocks to the genital area); and enforced incest or enforced rape of female or male others.
>
> (Solangon and Patel 2012: 418)

2 IMT (International Military Tribunal, Nuremberg). 1945. *Trial of Major War Criminals before the International Military Tribunal.* Vol. I, 14 November 1945–1 October 1946. Accessed 10 October 2016. www.loc.gov/rr/frd/Military_Law/pdf/ NT_Vol-I.pdf. 53; 253.
3 Ibid., 226–228.
4 Ibid., transcript 25 April 1946, 200.
5 *United States* v. *Karl Brandt, Siegfried Handloser, Paul Rostock, Oskar Schroeder, Karl Genzken, Karl Gebhardt, Rudolf Brandt, Kurt Blome, Joachim Mrugowsky, Helmut Poppendick, Wolfram Sievers, Gerhard Rose, Siegfried Ruff, Hans Wolfgang Romberg, Viktor Brack, Hermann Becker-Freyseng, Georg August Weltz, Konrad Schaefer, Waldemar Hoven, Wilhelm Beiglboeck, Adolf Pokorny, Herta Oberheuser and Fritz Fischer.* 1946. IMT (International Military Tribunal, Nuremberg). Case No. 1, 'The Doctors Trial' or 'Medical Case'. 511; 993.
6 Ibid., 14; 694–738.
7 IMTFE (International Military Tribunal for the Far East, Tokyo). 'Judgement of 4 November 1948'. In John Pritchard and Sonia M. Zaide (eds), *The Tokyo War Crimes Trial*, Vol. 22. Accessed 10 October 2016. www.alpha-canada.org/wp-content/ uploads/2012/08/IMTFE-Judgement-4Nov1948.pdf {49,664}; {49,666}–{49,667}; {49,674}.
8 ICTY (United Nations International Criminal Tribunal for the former Yugoslavia). Rules of Procedure and Evidence – as amended, IT/32/Rev.3/Corr.4. 3 May 1995.
9 *Prosecutor* v. *Anto Furundžija*, Case No. IT-95-17/1-T, Judgement, 10 December 1998, para. 174.
10 *Prosecutor* v. *Duško Tadić*, Case No. IT-94-1-I, Initial Indictment, 13 February 1995, para. 2.6.
11 *Prosecutor* v. *Duško Tadić*, Case No. IT-94-1-T, Opinion and Judgement, 7 May 1997, paras 137, 151.
12 Ibid., paras 726, 730.
13 *Prosecutor* v. *Duško Tadić*, Case No. IT-94-1-T, Sentencing Judgement, 14 July 1997, para. 22.
14 *Prosecutor* v. *Duško Tadić*, Case No. IT-94-1-Tbis-R117, Second Sentencing Judgement, 11 November 1999, paras 30–31.
15 Ibid., para. 32; *Prosecutor* v. *Duško Tadić*, Case No. IT-94-1-A, Appeal Judgement, 15 July 1999, paras 170–171.
16 *Prosecutor* v. *Zejnil Delalić, Zdravko Mucić, Hazim Delalić and Esad Landžo*, Case No. IT-96-21-T, Judgement, 16 November 1998, para. 1066.
17 Ibid., paras 767, 770, 774–775.
18 Ibid., paras 926, 946.
19 Ibid., paras 943, 965.
20 Ibid., Disposition, 442.

21 *Prosecutor* v. *Zejnil Delalić, Zdravko Mucić, Hazim Delalić and Esad Landžo*, Case No. IT-96–21, Indictment, 19 March 1996, para. 31; *Prosecutor* v. *Zejnil Delalić, Zdravko Mucić, Hazim Delalić and Esad Landžo*, Case No. IT-96–21-T, Judgement, 16 November 1998, paras 1038, 1041, 1062–1065.

22 Ibid., paras 1066, 1072.

23 Ibid., paras 1038–1040, 1045.

24 *Prosecutor* v. *Anto Furundžija*, Case No. IT-95–17/1-T, Judgement, 10 December 1998, paras 86–87, 127–128.

25 Ibid., paras 82–83, 124–125.

26 Ibid., paras 86–87, 127–128.

27 Ibid., para. 267(ii).

28 *Prosecutor* v. *Stevan Todorović*, Case No. IT-95–9/1-S, Sentencing Judgement, 31 July 2001, paras 9, 14, 34, 38–40, 45–46.

29 *Prosecutor* v. *Stevan Todorović*, Case No. IT-95–9-I, Indictment, 29 June 1995, Counts 36–38, 51–53.

30 *Prosecutor* v. *Stevan Todorović*, Case No. IT-95–9-I, Second Amended Indictment, 19 November 1998, Counts 1, 16–24, 28–32.

31 *Prosecutor* v. *Stevan Todorović*, Case No. IT-95–9/1-S, Sentencing Judgement, 31 July 2001, paras 4, 7, 12, 17, 64–64, 80.

32 Ibid., paras 64, 66, 115.

33 *Prosecutor* v. *Anto Furundžija*, Case No. IT-95–17/1-T, Judgement, 10 December 1998, paras 182–185.

34 *Prosecutor* v. *Duško Sikirica*, Case No. IT-95–8-PT, Amended Indictment, 24 August 1999, Counts 1, 3–5, paras 19, 24–25, 30 (c).

35 *Prosecutor* v. *Duško Sikirica, Damir Došen, Dusan Fustar, Dragan Kolundžija, Nenad Banović, Predrag Banović and Duško Knežević*, Case No. IT-95-8-PT, Second Amended Indictment, 3 January 2001, paras 30 and 31.

36 Ibid., Count 3–5, paras 9, 24–26, 30, 32–38, 46.

37 *Prosecutor* v. *Duško Sikirica, Damir Došen and Dragan Kolundžija*, Case No. IT-95-8-T, Judgement on Defence Motions to Acquit, 3 September 2001, paras 96–97.

38 *Prosecutor* v. *Duško Sikirica, Damir Došen and Dragan Kolundžija*, Case No. IT-95-8-S, Sentencing Judgement, 13 November 2001, paras 18–22.

39 *Prosecutor* v. *Predrag Banović*, Case No. IT-95-9/1-S, Sentencing Judgement, 31 July 2001, paras 9, 12-19; *Prosecutor* v. *Predrag Banović*, Case No. IT-95-9/1-S, Sentencing Hearing Transcript, 3 September 2003.

40 *Prosecutor* v. *Milomir Stakić*, Case No. IT-97-24-A, Appeal Judgement, 22 March 2006, Disposition, 141, paras 72, 73, 104.

41 *Prosecutor* v. *Milomir Stakić*, Case No. IT-97-24-PT, Fourth Amended Indictment, 10 April 2002, paras 48–49, 54.

42 *Prosecutor* v. *Milomir Stakić*, Case No. IT-97-24-T, Judgement, 31 July 2003, paras 7, 241.

43 Ibid., paras 234, 236.

44 Ibid., paras 228, 556, 560–561, 821, 826.

45 *Prosecutor* v. *Željko Mejakić, Miroslav Kvočka, Dragoljub Prcać, Mlađo Radić, Milojica Kos, Momčilo Gruban, Zdravko Govedarica, Gruban, Predrag Kostić, Nedjeljko Paspalj, Milan Pavlić, Milutin Popović, Draženko Predojević, Željko Savić, Mirko Babić, Nikica Janjić, Dušan Knežević, Dragomir Šaponja and Zoran Žigić*, Case No. IT-95-4-I, Indictment, 13 February 1995, paras 2.6, 29.1.

46 *Prosecutor* v. *Miroslav Kvočka, Milojica Kos, Mlađo Radić, Zoran Žigić, Dragoljub Prcać*, Case No. IT-98-30/1, Amended Indictment, 21 August 2000, paras 23, 25(c), 37(a); *Prosecutor* v. *Miroslav Kvočka, Milojica Kos, Mlađo Radić, Zoran Žigić, Dragoljub Prcać*, Case No. IT-98-30/1-T, Judgement, 2 November 2001, para. 4.

47 Ibid., para. 691.

48 Ibid., para. 327.

49 *Prosecutor* v. *Milan Simić*, Case No. IT-95-9/2-S, Sentencing Judgement, 17 October 2002, para. 4.

50 *Prosecutor* v. *Milan Simić*, Case No. IT-95-9/2-S, Sentencing Judgement, 17 October 2002, paras 63, 113, 115, 122.

51 *Prosecutor* v. *Ranko Češić*, Case No. IT-95-10/1-S, Sentencing Judgement, 11 March 2004, paras 7, 13–14.

52 Ibid., paras 13–14, 35, 52.

53 Ibid., para. 111.

54 *Prosecutor* v. *Radoslav Brđanin*, Case No. IT-99-36-T, Sixth Amended Indictment, 9 December 2003, paras 37(2), 42, 47, 55.

55 Ibid., paras 13, 42; *Prosecutor* v. *Radoslav Brđanin*, Case No. IT-99-36-T, Judgement, 1 September 2004, paras 516, 824, 845; *Prosecutor* v. *Milomir Stakić*, Case No. IT-97-24-T, Judgement, 31 July 2003, para. 236.

56 *Prosecutor* v. *Radoslav Brđanin*, Case No. IT-99-36-T, Judgement, 1 September 2004, paras 1002–1018, 1050, 1055–1061, 1152–1153.

57 *Prosecutor* v. *Momcilo Krajišnik and Biljana Plavšić*, Case No. IT-00-39 & 40-PT, Amended Consolidated Indictment, 7 March 2002.

58 *Prosecutor* v. *Momcilo Krajišnik*, Case No. IT-00-39-T, Judgement, 27 September 2006, paras 4, 304, 372, 461, 600.

59 *Prosecutor* v. *Biljana Plavšić*, Case No. IT-00-39 & 40/1-S, Sentencing Judgement, 27 February 2003, paras 5, 134.

60 *Prosecutor* v. *Momcilo Krajišnik*, Case No. IT-00-39-T, Judgement, 27 September 2006, paras 745, 800, 803–806, 1126, 1145, 1181.

61 *Prosecutor* v. *Momcilo Krajišnik*, Case No. IT-00-39-A, Appeal Judgement, 17 March 2009, para. 178, Disposition 279.

62 *Prosecutor* v. *Milan Martić*, Case No. IT-95-11-T, Judgement, 12 June 2007, paras 2, 174–181, 277, 288 (n. 899), 412–416, 454–455.

63 Ibid., para. 442.

64 Ibid., paras 454–455, 480; *Prosecutor* v. *Milan Martić*, Case No. IT-95-11-T, Appeal Judgement, 8 October 2008, paras 189–190.

65 *Prosecutor* v. *Mićo Stanišić and Stojan Župljanin*, Case No. IT-95-8-PT, Second Amended Consolidated Indictment, 10 September 2009, paras 24–28, 32–36; *Prosecutor* v. *Mićo Stanišić and Stojan Župljanin*, Case No. IT-08-91-T, Judgement, 27 March 2013 (Vols 1–3), paras 8–9, 523–528, 776–779.

66 Ibid., paras 1214, 1235, 1246.

67 *Prosecutor* v. *Mićo Stanišić and Stojan Župljanin*, Case No. IT-95-8-PT, Second Amended Consolidated Indictment, 10 September 2009, paras 2–3, 18, 56; *Prosecutor* v. *Mićo Stanišić and Stojan Župljanin*, Case No. IT-08-91-T, Judgement, 27 March 2013 (Vols 1–3), paras 2–3.

68 *Prosecutor* v. *Mićo Stanišić and Stojan Župljanin*, Case No. IT-95-8-PT, Second Amended Consolidated Indictment, 10 September 2009, paras 24–28, 32–36; *Prosecutor* v. *Mićo Stanišić and Stojan Župljanin*, Case No. IT-08-91-T, Judgement, 27 March 2013 (Vols 1–3), paras 8–9.

69 Ibid., paras 401, 404, 475, 959, 1048, 1211, 1221, 1235, 1560, 1599, 1663, 1685, 1687–1690.

70 Ibid., Vol. 1, paras 1214, 1235, 1246; Vol. 2, paras 955–956.

71 *Prosecutor* v. *Mićo Stanišić and Stojan Župljanin*, Case No. IT-08-91-A, Appeal Judgement, 30 June 2016, Disposition, 496.

72 *Prosecutor* v. *Radovan Karadžić*, Case No. IT-95-5/18-T, Judgement, 24 March 2016, paras 58, 2635–2654.

73 Ibid., paras 3–6, 537, 597, 994.

74 Ibid., para. 1021.

75 Ibid., para. 653.

76 Ibid., paras 1016–1017.

77 Ibid., Trial Judgement para. 1771.
78 Ibid., para. 2104.
79 Ibid., para. 2406.
80 Ibid., para. 2501.
81 Ibid., paras 990–991.
82 Ibid., para. 2582.
83 Ibid., paras 2518, 3521.
84 Ibid., Disposition, 2537.
85 *Prosecutor* v. *Theonéste Bagosora, Gratien Kabiligi, Aloys Ntabakuze, Anatole Nsengiyumva*, Court transcript of 20 January 2004, 32, ln 3–17.
86 *Prosecutor* v. *Mikaeli Muhimana*, Case No. ICTR-95-1B-T, Judgement and Sentence, 28 April 2005, paras 444, 450, 570, 583.
87 *The Prosecutor* v. *Eliézer Niyitegeka*, Case No. ICTR-96-14-I, Amended Indictment, 26 June 2000, 60–67, paras 5.38, 6.59–6.61, 6.69.
88 *The Prosecutor* v. *Eliézer Niyitegeka*, Case No. ICTR-96-14-T, Judgement and Sentence, 16 May 2003, para. 303.
89 Ibid., paras 312, 417, 462–467; *The Prosecutor* v. *Eliézer Niyitegeka*, Case No. ICTR-96-14-A, Appeal Judgement, 9 July 2004, para. 270.
90 *Prosecutor* v. *Issa Hassan Sesay, Morris Kallon and Augustine Gabo*, Case No. SCSL-04-15-T, Judgement, 2 March 2009, paras 1207–1208.
91 Ibid., paras 1125, 1347–1351.
92 *Prosecutor* v. *Issa Hassan Sesay, Morris Kallon and Augustine Gabo*, Case No. SCSL-04-15-T, Judgement, 2 March 2009, paras 1303–1304.
93 *Prosecutor* v. *Alex Tamba Brima, Brima Bazzy Kamara and Santigie Borbor Kanu*, Case No. SCSL-04-16-PT, Further Amended Consolidated Indictment, 18 February 2005, paras 51–57; *Prosecutor* v. *Issa Hassan Sesay, Morris Kallon and Augustine Gabo*, Case No. SCSL-04-15-PT, Corrected Amended Consolidated Indictment, 2 August 2006, paras 54–60; *Prosecutor* v. *Issa Hassan Sesay, Morris Kallon and Augustine Gabo*, Case No. SCSL-04-15-T, Judgement, 2 March 2009, n. 2519; *Prosecutor* v. *Charles Taylor*, Case No. SCSL-03-01-T, Prosecution's Second Amended Indictment, 29 May 2007, paras 14–17.
94 *Prosecutor* v. *Alex Tamba Brima, Brima Bazzy Kamara and Santigie Borbor Kanu*, Case No. SCSL-04-16-T, Judgement, 20 June 2007, paras 991, 1023.
95 *Prosecutor* v. *Charles Taylor*, Case No. SCSL-03-01-T, Judgement, 18 May 2012, paras 124–134.
96 *The Prosecutor* v. *Jean-Pierre Bemba Gombo*, Case No. ICC-01/05-01/08, Judgement pursuant to Article 74 of the Statute, 21 March 2016, paras 487–495.
97 Ibid., paras 498–501.
98 *Prosecutor* v. *Francis Kirimi Muthaura, Uhuru Muigai Kenyatta and Mohammed Hussein Ali*, Case No. ICC-01/09-02/11, Transcript of 22 September 2011, 89.
99 Ibid., 84, 88.
100 Ibid., 88–91; *Prosecutor* v. *Francis Kirimi Muthaura, Uhuru Muigai Kenyatta and Mohammed Hussein Ali*, Case No. ICC-01/09-02/11, Decision on the Confirmation of Charges Pursuant to Article 61(7)(a) and (b) of the Rome Statute, 23 January 2012, paras 258–266.
101 Ibid., paras 226–266, 270.
102 *Prosecutor* v. *Francis Kirimi Muthaura, Uhuru Muigai Kenyatta and Mohammed Hussein Ali*, Case No. ICC-01/09-02/11, Decision on the Prosecutor's Application for Summonses to Appear for Francis Kirimi Muthaura, Uhuru Muigai Kenyatta and Mohammed Hussein Ali, 8 March 2011, para. 27.
103 Situation in the Democratic Republic of the Congo in the case of the *Prosecutor* v. *Bosco Ntaganda*, Case No. ICC-01/04-02/06, Decision Pursuant to Article 61(7)(a) and (b) of the Rome Statute on the Charges of the Prosecutor Against Bosco Ntaganda, 9 June 2014, paras 50, 52.

104 Extraordinary Chambers in the Courts of Cambodia, *Co-Lawyers for the Civil Parties*, Fourth Investigative Request Concerning Forced Marriages and Sexually Related Crimes,' Case No. 002/19-09-2007-ECCC/OCIJ, 4 December 2009, para. 38.
105 *Prosecutor* v. *Zejnil Delalić, Zdravko Mucić, Hazim Delalić and Esad Landžo*, Case No. IT-96-21-A, Appeal Judgement, 20 February 2001, paras 412–413.
106 *Ministère Public* v. *Hissein Habré*, Chambre Africaine Extraordinaire D'assises, Judgement, 30 May 2016, XI. Dispositif, p. 536.
107 Ibid., paras 610–624, 1565–1570, 1806, 2278.
108 *Prosecutor* v. *Ratko Mladić*, Case No. IT-09-92-T, Judgement, 22 November 2017, paras 551, 565, 1128, 1493, 1506, 3291, 3297, 3312, 5214.
109 Ibid., para. 5215.

References

Aranburu, X.A. 2016. 'The Old, the New and The Newer: Shifting Paradigms in the Understanding of War-Time Sexual Crimes'. Paper presented in June 2016 at the seminar *Traps and Gaps: the Politics of Generating Knowledge.* SVAC (International Research Group Sexual Violence in Armed Conflict).

Askin, Kelly D. 2013. 'Treatment of Sexual Violence in Armed Conflicts: A Historical Perspective and the Way Forward'. In A.-M. de Brouwer, C. Ku, R. G. Römkens, and L. J van den Herik (eds), *Sexual Violence as an International Crime: Interdisciplinary Approaches.* Transitional Justice Series 12. Cambridge: Intersentia.

Bianchi, Linda. 'The Prosecution of Rape and Sexual Violence: Lessons from Prosecutions at the ICTR'. In A-M. de Brouwer, C. Ku, R. G. Römkens, and L. J van den Herik (eds), *Sexual Violence as an International Crime: Interdisciplinary Approaches.* Transitional Justice Series 12. Cambridge: Intersentia.

Brammertz, Serge, and Michelle Jarvis (eds). 2016. *Prosecuting Conflict-Related Sexual Violence.* Oxford: Oxford University Press.

Campbell, Kirsten. 2007. 'The Gender of Transitional Justice: Law, Sexual Violence and the International Criminal Tribunal for the Former Yugoslavia'. *The International Journal of Transitional Justice* 1(3): 411–432.

Chang, Iris. 1997. *The Rape of Nanking: The Forgotten Holocaust of World War II.* New York: Basic Books.

de Langis, Theresa, Judith Strasser, Thida Kim, and Sopheap Taing. 2014. *Like Ghost Changes Body – A Study on the Impact of Forced Marriage under the Khmer Rouge Regime.* Phnom Penh: Transcultural Psychosocial Organization of Cambodia.

Giles, Geoffrey J. 1992 '"The Most Unkindest Cut of All": Castration, Homosexuality and Nazi Justice'. *Journal of Contemporary History* 27(1): 41–61.

Gorris, Ellen Anna Philo. 2015. 'Invisible Victims? Where are Male Victims of CRSV in International Law and Policy?' *European Journal of Women's Studies* 22(4): 412–427.

International Criminal Court – Office of the Prosecutor. 2014. 'Policy Paper on Sexual and Gender Based Crimes', June 2014. Accessed 30 July 2017. www.icc-cpi.int/iccdocs/otp/OTP-Policy-Paper-on-Sexual-and-Gender-Based-Crimes-June-2014.pdf.

Kaitesi, Usta. 2014. *Genocidal Gender and Sexual Violence: The Legacy of the ICTR, Rwanda's Ordinary Courts and Gacaca Courts.* Cambridge: Intersentia.

Kaitesi, Usta and Roelof Haveman. 2011. 'Prosecution of Genocidal Rape and Sexual Torture before the Gacaca Tribunals in Rwanda'. In R. Letschert, R. Haveman, A.-M. de Brouwer, and A. Pemberton (eds), *Victimological Approaches to International Crimes: Africa.* Cambridge: Intersentia.

Oosterveld, Valerie. 2011. 'The Gender Jurisprudence of the Special Court for Sierra Leone: Progress in the Revolutionary United Front Judgments'. *Cornell International Law Journal* 44(1): 49–74.

Oosterveld, Valerie. 2014. 'Sexual Violence Directed Against Men and Boys in Armed Conflict and Mass Atrocity: Addressing a Gendered Harm in International Criminal Tribunals'. *Journal of International Law and International Relations* 10: 107–128.

Oosterveld, Valerie and Sellers, Patricia. 2016. 'Issues of Sexual and Gender-Based Violence at the ECCC'. In S. M. Meisenberg and I. Stegmiller (eds), *The Extraordinary Chambers in the Courts of Cambodia – Assessing Their Contribution to International Criminal Law*. International Criminal Justice Series, Volume 6. T.M.C. Asser Press.

Plesch, Dan, Susana Sácouto, and Chante Lasco. 2014. 'The Relevance of the United Nations War Crimes Commission to the Prosecution of Sexual and Gender-Based Crimes Today'. *Criminal Law Forum* 25(1–2): 349–381.

Sellers, Patricia. 2000. 'The Context of Sexual Violence: Sexual Violence as Violations of International Humanitarian Law'. In G.K. McDonald and O.Q. Swaak-Goldman (eds), *Substantive and Procedural Aspects of International Criminal Law – The Experience of International and National Courts*. Boston, MA: Kluwer Law International.

Sellers, Patricia. 2009. 'Gender Strategy is Not Luxury for International Courts Symposium: Prosecuting Sexual and Gender-Based Crimes before International/ized Criminal Courts'. *American University Journal of Gender, Social Policy & the Law* 17(2): 327–335.

Sellers, Patricia. 2016. 'Sexual Violence and Commanders' Responsibilities during Conflict'. Just Security. Accessed 30 May 2017. www.justsecurity.org/tag/jean-pierre-bemba/.

Sharratt, Sara. 2011. *Gender, Shame and Sexual Violence: The Voices of Witnesses and Court Members at War Crimes Tribunals*. London: Routledge.

Sivakumaran, Sandesh. 2010. 'Lost in Translation: UN Responses to Sexual Violence against Men and Boys in Situations of Armed Conflict'. *International Review of the Red Cross* 92(877): 259–277.

Solangon, Sarah and Preeti Patel. 2012. 'Sexual Violence Against Men in Countries Affected by Armed Conflict'. *Conflict, Security & Development* 12(4): 417–442.

United Nations Security Council. 1994. *Final Report of the Commission of Experts Established Pursuant to Security Council Resolution 780*. Accessed 10 October 2016. www.icty.org/x/file/About/OTP/un_commission_of_experts_report1994_en.pdf.

United States Holocaust Memorial Museum. *Persecution of Homosexuals*. Accessed 22 September 2016. www.ushmm.org/learn/students/learning-materials-and-resources/homosexuals-victims-of-the-nazi-era/persecution-of-homosexuals.

Weil, Simone. 1956. *The Notebooks of Simone Weil, Volume 1*, Translated from the French by Arthur Wills. London: Routledge.

WHO (World Health Organization). 2002. *World Report on Violence and Health*, edited by E. G. Krug, L. L. Dahlberg, J. A. Mercy, A. B. Zwi, and R. Lozano. Geneva: World Health Organization.

Ye, Beini. 2011. 'Forced Marriages as Mirrors of Cambodian Conflict'. *Peace Review: A Journal of Social Justice* 23(4): 469–475.

Reflections

Familiar stories, the policing of knowledge, and other challenges ahead

Maria Eriksson Baaz

How may we fit conflict related sexual violence against men (SVAM) into existing explanatory frameworks about conflict related sexual violence (CRSV), which until recently focused almost exclusively on women and girls? Can we fit it in? Should we fit it in? In particular, what are the potential stakes involved in (not) doing so?

The ways in which efforts to make sense of SVAM are haunted by dominant understandings of CRSV against women is lucidly reflected in this book. Sexual violence against women clearly emerges as the inescapable constitutive framework in relation to which we are trying to make sense of SVAM – a constitutive framework which, paradoxically then, is also partly responsible for the long silence that has surrounded SVAM. To recap, the familiar story: in the dominant policy and scholarly understanding of CRSV as a gendered weapon of war rooted in men's domination over women, male victims have for long been rendered 'uncomfortable subjects' (Eriksson Baaz and Stern 2013; Dolan 2014). This, in turn, further complicates the queries above: is it possible to understand SVAM through the same lens that contributed to it being silenced and neglected for such a long time?

While not posing the question in this manner, the contributions in this edited volume offer different responses to this puzzle. Some reject a conclusive response and highlight the specificity of SVAM and the various contexts in which it is enacted. Yet, others – and reflecting one central trend in the CRSV and SVAM literature – propose that we answer the question through a unanimous 'yes'. In short, we appear to partly be moving from not being able to fit SVAM into our explanatory frameworks to squeezing the 'uncomfortable subjects' into the frame (i.e. showing how SVAM is a gendered weapon of war rooted in patriarchy).

While not refuting the relevance of the 'yes' – the ease and certainty with which it is formulated is, arguably, a cause for concern. Or rather, it is the 'yes, if' – the lingering idea that we can only address SVAM insofar as we make it fit into what we already know (or rather want to know) about CRSV against women – which is unsettling. Moreover, resonating with other efforts to 'establish the truth', the 'yes, if' position worryingly tries to establish the truth by instilling fear and by policing potential contenders through the prospect of shame and exclusion. Here it appears to work by instilling a fear of being named and shamed as a non-feminist, who 'trivialise the influence of hierarchical gender relations as a cause of wartime rape' (Meger, Ch. 6 in this volume) or argues that 'men's victimisation or women's perpetration of sexual violence in war is sufficient evidence of an equality between the sexes' (Meger, Ch. 6 in this volume); in short, a traitor, who must be expunged from the community of feminist and gender scholars, unless he/she repents.

This politics of marking terrain highlights the need for more critical self-reflection on feminist ethics. Such reflections need also to include a critical interrogation into the global political economy within the, by now, quite lucrative but highly unequal field of CRSV which, in a familiar manner, benefits certain actors (i.e. Northern-based academics, policymakers, practitioners, and celebrities) over others (Masika Bihamba 2017; Eriksson Baaz and Stern 2013). Yet, in addition to the power/knowledge and epistemic violence embedded in the efforts of marking terrain and policing knowledge, a crucial problem with the 'yes, if' position lies in the ways in which it has confined how we can think about CRSV and clearly risks doing the same in relation to SVAM.

The entrance of alleged non-feminist (or not-feminist enough) suspects into the CRSV field has added crucial knowledge that previously was largely missing in the field (partly reflecting the same logic: i.e. that certain 'Other' perspectives are irrelevant or even dangerously misleading). In particular, we have seen a partial bridging of the research gap between, on the one hand, research addressing violence against civilians in war more generally, including the sociology of military organisations (which often has omitted gender, at times simply mentioning sexual violence in passing), and, on the other hand, research on CRSV (which has attended only to violence defined as gendered a priori in a specific way and focused mainly on the gendered logics of sexual violence). Inputs from the former field into CRSV have, for instance, convincingly demonstrated that the occurrence of CRSV varies and that in order to understand logics and variation, we also need to probe into, for example, military ideologies and military organisation – aspects which are also clearly gendered in a myriad of ways (Wood 2006, 2009; Hoover Green 2016; Cohen 2013; Eriksson Baaz and Stern 2013). Such insights do not rely on refuting *that* CRSV is always already gendered.

This trend in which CRSV is explored from various angles will hopefully continue and shape our more recent efforts to make sense of, and redress, SVAM. Some contributions in this book highlight precisely this need for multiple explanatory frameworks and the importance to 'unveil how sexual violence against men is performed and put on display', 'in order to grasp how multiple and intersecting axes of differentiation interact to make some men, including privileged men, vulnerable to sexual violence' (Drumond, Ch. 8 in this volume).

Yet, as several contributions highlight, the field of SVAM is marked by a number of methodological challenges, emanating from our preconceptions as scholars – and relatedly, the difficulties to access survivor narratives. Moreover, another major challenge ahead mentioned in the book is to recognise and include sexual violence against combatants. Given that (scarce) research indicates that the levels of SVAM against military men is often higher than that committed against civilians, attending to SVAM committed within and against men in other military organisations appears paramount.

Yet, also the absence of certain perspectives and forms of data in the book bear witness to the challenges that lie ahead in our efforts to make sense of SVAM. One of these is to address the absence (in comparison to CRSV against women) of data based on perpetrator accounts – an absence also reflected in this edited collection. While the inclusion of perpetrators' voices by no means can be read as offering a magic key to further knowledge, it can nevertheless shed important light on the discursive practices and contextual circumstances surrounding SVAM.

Moreover, one of the most urgent tasks ahead appears to be to further unpack the concept of SVAM itself. This challenge remains, of course, in relation to CRSV against women. As for CRSV against women, SVAM is marked by a remarkable variation in the repertoire of acts that are regrouped under the label. Yet, the attention so far has mainly been directed to torture committed in detention (now increasingly acknowledged as sexualised and gendered) and anal rape. The latter fits exceptionally well into existing frameworks through the notion of feminisation (by penetration), which is reflected also in the ways in which many survivor make sense of these acts. Yet, SVAM takes many other forms, such as mutilations, castration, forced sterilisation and sexual slavery, acts committed in various contexts (public or secluded, in combat and non-combat situations, as a single act or repeatedly, etc.) that might not fit as easily into the dominant frames.

The astounding variation in the forms and contexts in which SVAM is committed require a further unpacking of the category of SVAM itself. Yet, above all, it calls for more open-ended queries – like many of those that are reflected in this book – that do not reject, but remain open to both unexpected testimonies and colleagues.

References

Cohen, Dara K. 2013. 'Explaining Rape During Civil War: Cross-National Evidence (1980–2009)'. *American Political Science Review* 107(3): 461–477.

Dolan, Chris. 2014. 'Has Patriarchy been Stealing the Feminists' Clothes?: Conflict-Related Sexual Violence and UN Security Council Resolutions'. *IDS Bulletin* 45(1): 80–84.

Eriksson Baaz, Maria and Maria Stern. 2013. *Sexual Violence as a Weapon of War?: Perceptions, Prescriptions, Problems in the Congo and Beyond.* London: Zed Books.

Hoover Green, Amelia. 2016. 'The Commander's Dilemma: Creating and Controlling Armed Group Violence'. *Journal of Peace Research* 53(5): 619–632.

Masika Bihamba, Justine. 2017. 'The "Rape Capital of the World"? We Women in Congo Don't See It That Way'. *Guardian*, 9 October, www.theguardian.com/

global-development/2017/oct/09/the-rape-capital-of-the-world-we-women-in-democratic-republic-congo-dont-see-it-that-way.

Wood, Elisabeth J. 2006. 'Variation in Sexual Violence During War'. *Politics & Society* 34(3): 307–342.

Wood, Elisabeth J. 2009. 'Armed Groups and Sexual Violence: When is Wartime Rape Rare?' *Politics & Society* 37(1): 131–161.

Reflections on the slippery politics of framing

Harriet Gray

The chapters in this section offer compelling interventions which advance our understandings of how sexual violence against men has been framed across different discursive spaces. Such frames shape, we learn from the chapters, whether harmful acts perpetrated against men can be recognised as 'sexual' by post-war justice mechanisms (Leiby), and how such violence is understood to be related to conflict and to subjectivity (Drumond), among other things. As such, in various ways, the chapters help us to understand how framings of sexual violence *matter* – how they have significant, material implications in shaping policy responses to sexual violence, and in delineating which subjects can be recognised as victims and as perpetrators of sexual violence and, as a result, who can access support and who is liable to prosecution.

Reading the chapters, I was reminded that the framings through which we make sense of violence, perhaps inevitably, involve compromises and silences. In particular, the chapters demonstrate one of the perhaps unavoidable compromises entailed in framing sexual violence: namely, how to balance the necessity of highlighting a form of violence which has so often been obscured with the recognition that it is embedded in and enabled by so many other power structures and forms of harm. That is, while drawing attention specifically to sexual violence against men is politically and analytically crucial, the act of doing so also runs the risk of isolating 'sexual' from 'non-sexual' violence. Such an abstraction is unlikely to be empirically grounded; indeed, several of the chapters, in noting that sexual violence against men takes place mainly in detention, themselves indicate that it is experienced as embedded in multiple violences. In abstracting sexual violence from its context, we risk, among other things, losing sight of the fact that 'non-sexual' forms of violence are *also* gendered and gendering, and have gendered effects. That is, in analysing sexual violence against men in isolation from other forms of violence, we may lose sight of the *multiple* ways in which masculinised soldier bodies are targeted, violated, maimed, and killed in war *specifically as masculine bodies*, as well as the inherent leakiness, unruliness, and vulnerability of masculine bodies themselves (Basham 2013: 87) and, in so doing, we risk reproducing the very narratives of idealised masculine impenetrability which, as several of the chapters compellingly argue, sexual violence against men exploits to devastating effect.

In addition, the chapters also demonstrate how framings of sexual violence against men slip and slide about: how, for example, representations of men within UN framings have emerged and changed over time (Becerra), and how even those frames which we might think of as definitively pinned down within international law are always subject to interpretation (Sellers and Nwoye). Perhaps the main site at which sexual violence against men slips over and through other violences – a site which appears in almost all the chapters but which emerges most strongly in the chapter by Charman (as well as that by Meger in the previous section) – is at the borders and overlaps between 'sexual violence' and 'torture'. Torture itself is a slippery category, open to (re)interpretation (Birdsall 2016), and its overlaps with sexual violence are well recognised in the wider literature, where the question of where, or indeed *if*, lines should be drawn between the two has been subject to politically charged debate (e.g. Edwards 2011; MacKinnon 2006: 17–27; McGlynn 2008; Sivakumaran 2007). In regards to framing, this overlap also raises pertinent questions about the conditions through which a particular act of violence comes to be understood as 'sexual'. Is it because the act is experienced as 'sexual' by the victim? Or by the perpetrator? Or because it is targeted at, or deploys as a weapon, 'sexualised' parts of the body? These possible conditions do not always align with one another, and the lines we draw between sexual violence and torture – and the *meanings* attached to violent acts – are likely to shift considerably depending on which we emphasise. Moreover, of course, the internal content of each of these conditions also shifts: body parts are not stable in their status as 'sexual' or 'non-sexual' but can 'become eroticized' during violence (Cahill 2001: 139–140); 'sexual' and 'non-sexual' violence/torture may be similarly experienced by victim-survivors as a devastation (however temporary) of their subjectivity (du Toit 2009: 86–100; Sussman 2005); and the question of whether perpetrators experience sexual *pleasure* in rape is intensely politically loaded and often obscured in scholarship (Eriksson Baaz and Stern forthcoming). The point here is that violences do not objectively fall into one or another neat definitional box, and the task at hand is not therefore to find the objectively 'correct' label for each harmful act; rather, our framing and our categorisation of violence is *political*, and it has important political implications. The ways in which terms such as 'torture' and 'sexual violence' are filled with meaning in any given example, then, is a politically charged process, the stakes of which require focused interrogation. The chapters in this section provide valuable material through which to reflect on these questions, enabling us to make sense of SVAM through a reflexive, critical, and *gendered* lens.

References

Basham, Victoria M. 2013. *War, Identity and the Liberal State: Everyday Experiences of the Geopolitical in the Armed Forces.* London: Routledge.

Birdsall, Andrea. 2016. 'But We Don't Call It "Torture"!: Norm Contestation During the US "War on Terror"' *International Politics* 53(2): 176–197.

Cahill, Ann J. 2001. *Rethinking Rape*. Ithaca, NY: Cornell University Press.

Edwards, Alice. 2011. *Violence Against Women under International Human Rights Law*. Cambridge: Cambridge University Press.

Eriksson Baaz, Maria and Maria Stern. Forthcoming. 'Curious Erasures: The "Sexual" in "Wartime" Sexual Violence'. *International Feminist Journal of Politics*.

McGlynn, Clare. 2008. 'Rape as "Torture"?: Catherine MacKinnon and Questions of Feminist Strategy'. *Feminist Legal Studies* 16(1): 71–85.

MacKinnon, Catharine. 2006. *Are Women Human?: And Other International Dialogues*. Cambridge, MA: Harvard University Press.

Sivakumaran, Sandesh. 2007. 'Sexual Violence Against Men in Armed Conflict'. *European Journal of International Law* 18(2): 253–276.

Sussman, David. 2005. 'What's Wrong with Torture?' *Philosophy & Public Affairs* 33(1): 1–33.

du Toit, Louise. 2009. *A Philosophical Investigation of Rape: The Making and Unmaking of the Feminine Self*. New York: Routledge.

Male victims

A blind spot in law

Charu Lata Hogg

This collection of chapters brought home some stark truths for me, for example, that conflict-related sexual violence against men and boys is so often conflated with torture given that national laws routinely contain provisions which de facto promote impunity and prevent all victims of this violence from accessing justice (Leiby, Ch. 7 in this volume). As such existing national legal frameworks often pose a significant impediment in allowing justice for male survivors of sexual violence making it difficult, if not dangerous, for survivors to come forward.[1] The lack of criminalisation of male rape and corresponding criminalisation of same-sex sexual conduct impact heavily on male survivors, exposing them to prosecution for their victimisation. In most countries where the All Survivors Project works, lawyers are not trained to challenge legal frameworks that make it impossible for male victims to seek redress through the courts. In fact, lawyers would not even ask the men they are representing whether they were sexually abused. As a result, the cycle of under-reporting, under-documenting and under-acknowledging sexual violence against men and boys has been perpetuated (OSRSG 2013). In situations of conflict and conflict-related displacement 'national protection mechanisms are frequently disrupted or inadequate to address acute protection risks' (UNHCR 2015: 8) such as sexual violence, thus exacerbating impunity further.

The argument that humiliation lies at the core of the use of sexual violence against men and boys has a good deal of credibility given it can work to feminise and degrade men. But this use of humiliation to render the victim an unautonomous, sexual object is unlawful in international standards. Additional Protocol I to the Geneva Conventions provides that 'outrages upon personal dignity, in particular humiliating and degrading treatment, enforced prostitution and any form of indecent assault', are 'prohibited at any time and in any place whatsoever, whether committed by civilian or by military agents' (ICRC 1977a, Article 75.2.b). In non-international armed conflicts, common Article 3 to the four Geneva Conventions outlaws 'violence to life and person, in particular (...) mutilation, cruel treatment and torture' as well as 'outrages upon personal dignity, in particular humiliating and degrading treatment' (ICRC 1949). Additional Protocol II (AP II) prohibits 'outrages upon personal dignity, in particular humiliating and degrading treatment, rape, enforced prostitution and any form of indecent assault' for 'all persons who do not take a direct part or who have ceased to take part in hostilities' (ICRC 1977b, Article 4.2.e). Notably, this is the first international humanitarian law provision which explicitly prohibits rape without distinction between women and men.

The interaction and intersection of power relations in creating vulnerabilities for sexual violence against men cannot be ignored, but international responses, including judicial approaches, have been patchy at best in acknowledging and addressing these vulnerabilities. It remains a fact, and an opportunity lost, that psychological sexual violence, which was intrinsic to offences against men and boys, were not fully recognised by the International Criminal Tribunal on the former Yugoslavia (ICTY). Most notable is the case of Duško Tadić, who was found guilty of involvement in forcing a male camp detainee to perform oral sex on another detainee and then bite off his testicles (see Drumond, Ch. 8 in this volume; Sellers and Nwoye, Ch. 12 in this volume).[2] These acts were defined as cruel treatment (a violation of the laws and customs of war) and inhumane acts (a crime against humanity) but their sexual nature was not acknowledged in either the indictment or judgement. Only in two indictments (*Prosecutor* v. *Češić*, 1995; *Prosecutor* v. *Blagoje Simic et al.*, 1995)[3] was conflict-related sexual violence against men specifically characterised as such (see Sellers and Nwoye, Ch. 12 in this volume).

One of the issues, as pointed in the Sellers and Nwoye's chapter (Ch. 12 in this volume) on international criminal jurisprudence on sexual violence against men and boys, lies in the framing of the definition of rape in the ICTY statute, which although gender-neutral, seems to require the perpetrator to be physically involved in an act of penetration whether by the penis or another object. As such, this element of the definition risks excluding from the crime of rape one of the most common forms of sexual violence against men perpetrated during the Yugoslav wars, that of forced oral sex or sexual intercourse between male detainees.

Yes, impunity will thrive for abhorrent sexual crimes being committed against men and boys in situations of armed conflict, in the Central African Republic, the Democratic Republic of Congo, Syria, and Libya, but also in Afghanistan, South Sudan, and Colombia. Until we are able to acknowledge fully that widespread institutional gaps exist in responding to sexual violence against men and boys, and that gender norms have resulted in silencing these specific forms of abuse, and that our laws and their implementation discriminate on the basis of gender, we will have little hope for change.

Notes

1 Sixty-seven countries criminalise male victims of rape or sexual assault, see Dolan (2014: 6).
2 *Prosecutor* v. *Dusko Tadić*, Case No. IT-94-1-A, Appeal Judgement, 15 July 1999.
3 *Prosecutor* v. *Češić*, Case No. IT-95-10/1, Indictment, 21 July 1995; *Prosecutor* v. *Simić et al.*, Case No. IT-95-9, Initial Indictment, 21 July 1995.

References

Dolan, Chris. 2014. 'Into the Mainstream: Addressing Sexual Violence against Men and Boys in Conflict'. Briefing paper prepared for the workshop held at the *Overseas Development Institute*. London, 14 May 2014. Accessed 11 November 2017. www.refugeelawproject.org/files/briefing_papers/Into_The_Mainstream-Addressing_Sexual_Violence_against_Men_and_Boys_in_Conflict.pdf.

ICRC (International Committee of the Red Cross). 1949. *Geneva Convention Relative to the Protection of Civilian Persons in Time of War (Fourth Geneva Convention)*, 12 August 1949, 75 UNTS 287. Accessed 6 November 2017. www.refworld.org/docid/3ae6b36d2.html.

ICRC (International Committee of the Red Cross). 1977a. *Additional Protocol I – Protocol Additional to the Geneva Conventions of 12 August 1949, and relating to the Protection of Victims of International Armed Conflicts*. 8 June 1977. Accessed 6 November 2017. https://ihl-databases.icrc.org/applic/ihl/ihl.nsf/INTRO/470.

ICRC (International Committee of the Red Cross). 1977b. *Additional Protocol II – Protocol Additional to the Geneva Conventions of 12 August 1949, and relating to the Protection of Victims of Non-International Armed Conflicts*. 8 June 1977. Accessed 6 November 2017. https://ihl-databases.icrc.org/applic/ihl/ihl.nsf/INTRO/475?OpenDocument.

OSRSG (Office of the Special Representative of the Secretary General). 2013. Sexual Violence in Conflict. Report of *Workshop on Sexual Violence Against Men and Boys in Conflict Situations*. New York, 25–26 July 2013.

UNHCR (United Nations High Commission for Refugees). 2015. 'Protection and Accountability to Affected Populations in the Humanitarian Programme Cycle', Guidance Note. *Global Protection Cluster and IASC*. Accessed 6 November 2017. www.globalprotectioncluster.org/_assets/files/tools_and_guidance/protection_of_civilians/edg-aap_protection_guidance_note_2016.pdf.

Sexual violence against men and boys in the Congo

Ilot Muthaka

In the Democratic Republic of Congo (DRC), in conflict-affected areas and non-conflict settings alike, sexual and gender-based violence against men and boys is ignored not because people are not willing to learn about it, but because they have little information about the issue in general. This situation gets worse during violent conflicts when men are tortured and sexually abused, but the community does not recognise them as victims. Male victims also do not identify themselves as victims of sexual violence but as victims of torture, crimes, and mistreatment.

In my country, we have gender-neutral laws against sexual violence. Recent assessment reports show that there is a growing number of men and boys reported as victims of sexual violence, and this is promising because according to our cultures and traditions men are not supposed to say they are hurt or abused as it detracts from their male identity.

One question that should be addressed is to what extent men and boys who are victims of sexual violence have also perpetrated violence on women and children. In our work at Comen, we have observed that men and boys who have been victims of any type of violence are potential violence perpetrators. When a man rapes and abuses another man, he tells the victim that he is a woman – that is why he cannot defend himself. The male victim feels powerless and this leads to frustration and trauma. Once he recovers from this painful situation, we have found that he sometimes tries to prove his masculinity in committing violence mostly against women and girls.

I think the reason why the UN and INGOs are hesitant on this issue of sexual violence against men is that they fear competition in terms of funds for gender equity. Many women lobbyists have expressed their concerns regarding reducing funds to address gender equality issues in order to accommodate men's issues. For me, sexual violence is a neutral issue; when addressing it, no consideration should be put on sex but rather it should be put on trying to address the specific needs of each group.

The current effort to make sexual violence against men a global issue sets up a competition between male and female victims that will reduce international attention to women survivors. This is pernicious; men are beginning to claim that they are victims of the same violence as women. In many villages I have worked, men were arguing that they are more vulnerable than women regarding gender-based violence in order to excuse themselves from joining the fight against sexual and gender-based violence against women.

The authorities and justice systems also lack understanding of sexual violence against men and boys, especially in conflict settings. In the DRC, for instance, even if our laws, policies, and plans use gender-neutral language, they do not specify the needs of male and female survivors. In practice, the law was made in an emergency situation and the focus was put on female victims. Thus, the police and judges face interpretation challenges when it comes to male survivors.

Given this situation I would suggest that:

- Laws punishing sexual and gender-based violence are revised using clear language, taking into account women's and men's specific needs and vulnerability;
- Men and boys benefit from community outreach programmes to be able to report and raise awareness;
- Donors reach a common understanding of the problem and support programmes and projects addressing female and male survivors with holistic support as well as prevention activities.

SGBV against men and boys as a site of theoretical and political contestation

Jill Steans

This collection of thought-provoking, engaging, diverse, and wide-ranging chapters spark reflections on a myriad of puzzles of how gender, sex, and violence are related to the production and reproduction of international order. Here, I focus on just a few questions that arise for me as particularly salient in current discussions and as potentially fruitful avenues for further investigation. First, what challenges are posed to feminist theorising on sexual violence in conflict by the growing visibility of men and boys as victims and survivors? Binary constructions of male perpetrators and female victims that underpin both mainstream approaches to war and so too strands of feminist literature on conflict are evidently belied by more complex realities. The need to tell more complicated, nuanced, and often troubling stories about women and men, masculinities and femininities, sexual violence and torture, humiliation and shame, and accountability and justice cannot be denied. Yet, as contributors to this collection insist, it is a mistake to posit, as did the UN Senior Official Zainab Bangura (UN News Centre 2012) and the authors of the Human Security Report (Human Security Research Group 2012), a kind of gender equivalence in the enactment of sexual violence and in the suffering inflicted on the targets of violence that renders gender obsolete in understanding and responding to this pervasive harm.

Herein, individual authors mount compelling defences of gender analyses that shift attention from the perverse criminal actions and alleged pathologies of 'a few bad apples' to the higher echelons of hierarchal and still profoundly male-dominated political and military chains of command, to the strategic role that sexual violence often (though not always) plays in conflicts and to the importance of social and institutional norms in not only regulating, but also in reproducing the larger architecture and organisation of international politics. However, beyond this consensus on the need to link embodied experiences and local enactments, or performances, of sexual violence to the violent reproduction of the 'national' and 'international', there is theoretical divergence and indeed contestation. Is identity politics the driver of sexual violence against both women and girls and men and boys? Is it part and parcel of boundary marking processes and integral to the creation of hierarchical relations within and between imagined communities? Or is sexual violence central to the construction and reproduction of hierarchical relations marked by differential distributions of resources, status and wealth, and stark disparities in the value attached to differently sexed, gendered, classed, and ethnically marked bodies? This division reflects a wider schism in contemporary feminist theory between approaches that foreground the discursive and practices of signification and those that emphasise the material and structural determinants of gendered and sexual violence. Is it possible to bring together and combine insights from these approaches? If not, what are the implications for how academic discourse and debates inform future practice?

I was struck by the tendency, observed by several contributors, for violence with a sexual component to be classed as sexual violence when visited on women and girls and yet more often recorded as torture when inflicted on men and boys. Why is this? Does the answer again lie in prevalent norms and common-sense understandings which, even in the face of burgeoning evidence to the contrary, continue to support gender binaries and representations of war that circumscribe the repertoire of identities and roles women perform (as civilians, passive bystanders, collateral damage, victims) and constructions of men and masculinity as inherently aggressive, controlling, and violent and which serve to script men as the principal and natural actors, agents, and threats in war, albeit in these instances prior to their detention?

The International Criminal Court (ICC) does not stand outside or above the violence that is seemingly endemic to international order, but rather implements, further develops, and polices the rules and norms that proscribe some forms of violence while legitimising others. As such, ultimately, the ICC is complicit in normalising violence as an entrenched and seemingly intractable feature of the contemporary social, political, and economic relations that collectively constitute world order. Feminist scholars have long understood that international humanitarian law, the primary source of these rules and norms, is predicated on antithetical categories of combatant (actors/agents) and civilian (bystanders/victims) that are profoundly gendered both in conception and in how they are operationalised (e.g. Kinsella 2015). The convergence of international humanitarian law and international human rights law from the 1990s onwards promised to open up space for advocacy on behalf of individual victims and thus – potentially at least – create space for more complex stories about sexual violence; specifically in this case, the embodied experience of men and boys to be spoken and heard. In actuality, as victims of sexual violence, men and boys continue to be largely silenced. Individually and taken together, these chapters offer distinctive and valuable insights into why non-governmental organisations and advocates tend to frame egregious harms of sexual violence and torture in ways that reinforce gendered understandings of war. It is important to probe further, I think, how power relations in specific institutional contexts shape advocacy in the name of the victims of violence. We might then better understand why advocates strategise and frame issues in ways that accord with dominant understandings and that resonate with public perceptions and 'common sense'. Appeals to the latter are seemingly crucial to the legitimacy of the Court and indeed to the work of the broader epistemic community that has formed around this prominent and currently crisis-ridden organisation.

And so to my final question: what do we actually learn from narratives and testimonies on experiences of rape and sexual violence in war? Performances of sexual violence are indeed modes of communication framed in a particular way and put on display for an audience and so it is important to ask, who is the audience? I think this question is pertinent not only with respect to exalted national(ist) communities and abject 'Others', but also in all cases where narratives and testimonies are articulated in public spaces. Scholars working in and across the social sciences have struggled to carve out spaces in the study of war for people hitherto marginalised to be made visible and for their voices to be heard, or, in Cynthia Enloe's terms, to make the private, public and international (1992). Where once women and girls were the sole focus of concern, the experiences of men and boys are now taken seriously in feminist scholarship. This is undoubtedly a change for the better. Yet it seems the problems attendant on translation and appropriation when stories are told in public forums are not dissimilar whatever the sex or gender of the subject. It is well known that the ostensibly 'authentic' testimonies of women and girls articulated in public domains become a source of bitter contestation when, as is invariable if not inevitable, they become entangled in national and international politics. How men and boys are able to articulate their experiences and, more to the point perhaps, how they are represented and spoken for in public forums are critical questions. In this regard, the contributors to this collection mark out the terrain of further investigation into not only the continuing invisibility and under-representation of men and boys, but also how norms of hegemonic masculinity, the gendered norms of conflict and war, and also the politics of representing perpetrators and victims to specific audiences, enable and constrain the possibilities for making visible and public male sexual victimisation in war.

References

Enloe, Cynthia. 1992. *Bananas, Beaches and Bases: Making Feminist Sense of International Politics.* Berkeley, CA: University of California Press.

Human Security Research Group. 2012. *Human Security Report 2012 – Sexual Violence, Education and War: Beyond the Mainstream Narrative.* Vancouver: Simon Fraser University.

Kinsella, Helen. 2015. *The Images before the Weapon: A Critical History of the Distinction between Combatant and Civilian.* Ithaca, NY: Cornell University Press, 2015.

UN News Centre. 2012. 'Eradicating Sexual Violence in Conflict Not "a Mission Impossible" – UN Senior Official'. United Nations, 18 October. Accessed 9 November 2017. www.un.org/apps/news/story.asp?NewsID=43325#.WgWEtbbOqu4.

'People You May Know'[1]

Kevin Kantor

When my rapist showed up under the People You May Know tab on Facebook, it felt like the closest to the crime scene I've ever been.

That is if I don't count the clockwork murder that I make of my own memory every time that I drive down Colfax avenue.
Still, I sit in my living room, I sift for clues.
Click; I see myself caught in his teeth.
He's dancing with his shirt off in a city that I've never been to.
Click; he is eating sushi over a few beers with friends and I am under his fingernails.
Click; I know that alley.
Click; I killed the memory of that t-shirt.
Click; this is an old photograph. It's a baby picture. There's also an older man, presumably his father, they are both round and right and still smiling.
Click; he is shirtless again and I catch my reflection in the weight room mirror. '#beastmode selfie'
I call him the wolf when I write about him. The wolf, so as to make him as storybook as possible.
The wolf when I write about him which is to say, when my memory escapes the murder, or when the internet suggests it.
Facebook informs me that we have three mutual friends.
Which is to say, that he is People You May Know.
Which is to say that I am People You May Know,
and there are people that know, and people that don't know.
And people that don't know, I want to know, I'm afraid to let know.
And probably people that know him, know of me, that know.
The word 'know', 'know' 'know'
Know is a flock of sleeping sheep sitting in my mouth and now,
now I know the wolf's middle name and what he listens to on Spotify.
And the all too familiar company that he keeps,

and he can no longer be a wolf. Or the nameless grave that I dig for myself
on bad days.

We have three mutual friends on Facebook, and now it feels like they are
holding the shovel.

64 people liked the shirtless gym pic.

and four people have told me they'd rather I had said nothing.

Two police officers told me, that I must give his act a name or it didn't
happen.

That obviously I could have fought back.

Which is to say, no one comes running for young boys who cry rape.

When I told my brother, he also asked me why I didn't fight back.

Adam, I am. Right now. I promise.

Everyday I write a poem titled 'Tomorrow'

it is a handwritten list of the people I know that love me

and I make sure to put my own name at the top.

Note

1 Author's recitation of the poem is available on YouTube, at: www.youtube.com/
watch?v=LoyfunmYIpU.

Index

ableism 130
abortion, forced 122, 138–9
Abu Ghraib 29, 60, 80, 105–6, 145
Afghanistan 9, 35, 43–5, 48, 133
aggression, as distinctly male trait 94
Ahmed, S. 32
Alison, M. 58
All Survivors Project 134
Always Loyal (Stokes) 48–9
American servicemen, genital harm suffered by 43–53 (*see also* battle-induced urotrauma)
Amnesty International reports, framing of sexual violence against men in armed conflict 198–208
anal rape: focus of the SVAMB debate on 71; impact on masculinity 168 (*see also* feminisation); recognition of by the Rome Statute 168; *see also* male rape; rape

Baartman, Sara 36
Bassiouni, C. 169
Battered Women and Violence in the Family (UN) 186, 188
battle-induced urotrauma: and American servicemen 43–53; casualty numbers 45; definition 43; examples of 46; and health insurance coverage 46; and infertility 52; loss or injury of the penis 45–6; and militarised sexuality 46–50; official tallies 133; as one of war's cruellest injuries 49; *see also* castration; male genital mutilation in conflict; penile amputation and castration
Beijing Platform for Action 8, 188–9
Belkin, A. 61, 65
Belsky, J. 189
Bemba, Jean-Pierre 4, 29, 226, 233

blunt genital trauma 72, 83, 144, 203
bodily integrity 130
'The Body of the Other Man' (Zarkov) 169
Bosnian War: acts of male genital mutilation 76, 78; *see also* former Yugoslavia; International Criminal Tribunal for the former Yugoslavia (ICTY)
Bourke, J. 31
Braidotti, R. 32
Brecić, P. 96
Brown-Miller, S. 62
Buss, D. 153
Butler, J. 44, 130, 159

Carlson, E. 71, 83, 85, 144, 160
Carrigan, T. 190
castration: female equivalent 126; historical perspective 72; *see also* battle induced urotrauma; male genital mutilation in conflict; penile amputation and castration
Central African Republic 110
Cesić, Ranko 158
Chad 205
Chechen War 206
circumcisions, forced 72–3, 75, 79, 226–7
Cixous, H. 29
conflict-related sexual violence (CRSV): disclosure of experiences *see* disclosure of CRSV experiences; feminist political economy *see* feminist political economy of CRSV; investigative challenges 141–3; men's narratives 137–49; representation as women's issue in UN discourse 184 (*see also* United Nations discourse on gender violence)
Connell, R. 7, 190

context, significance of for the framing of sexual violence against men 204–5
Coomaraswamy, Radhika 92
Cornwall, A. 191
Côte d'Ivoire 204
Cottet, C. 132
courage, disclosure of CRSV experiences as a demonstration of 175–7
Cramer, C. 74
Crenshaw, K. 153
Cuvier, Georges 36

Dahomey 79
Daly, M. 27
Declaration for the Elimination of All Forms of Violence Against Women (UN) 8, 187
Democratic Republic of the Congo (DRC): castrations and penectomies committed by militias in 74; Eriksson Baaz and Stern's study on perpetrators' narratives 7; male survivors of sexual abuse 110; sexual and gender-based violence against men and boys 249–50
destruction of reproductive capacity, as motive behind SVAMB 78, 132
detention centres 109
deviant behaviour, sexual violence as evidence of 6
Disasters of War (Goya) 26, 27
disclosure of CRSV experiences: in an age of global media 167–79; BBC interviews 171–2; as a demonstration of courage 175–7; Facebook responses 172–3; and the interpretation of sexual victimisation as sign of homosexuality 12, 65, 142, 153, 159, 170, 173–5; lack of medical services and 169; possible reasons for non-disclosure 168–9
Dolan, C. 32
Drumond, P. 4, 77
Dworkin, A. 27

Egypt 79
El Salvador 124; prison inmates subjected to blunt trauma to the genitals 83
electrocutions 204
electrodes, attached to penis and testicles 80
Elkins, C. 79
emasculation, violence done to the reproductive organs or anus and the experience of 123
Enloe, C. 93, 109, 253

Eriksson Baaz, M. 7
The Evolution of Sex 90
Extraordinary Chambers in the Courts of Cambodia (ECCC), CRMSV jurisprudence 227–8

Facebook: responses to disclosure of CRSV experiences 172–3; when your rapist shows up under the People You May Know tab 254–5
falaka 204
Fattah, K. 104, 106
Fausto-Sterling, A. 90
fellatio: forced 155, 157–8; as rape 217
feminisation of male victims/survivors: accompanying humiliation 112; the concept 29, 105; as demobiliser of the enemy 106; experienced by the social group 107–8; and loss/change of status 105–6, 110–11; as political value of CRSV 111
feminism, and the concealment of women's violence 30–1
feminist political economy of CRSV: against men and boys 107–9; economic politics of sexual violence 104; function of the FPE approach 103–7; method of torture *vs* instrument of war 109–12
Fierke, K.M. 104, 106
former Yugoslavia 192; ethnicity and masculinity 169; levels of sexual violence against men during the 1990s conflicts 152; performances of sexual violence against men in 95, 152–63; use of blunt genital trauma 144; *see also* International Criminal Tribunal for the former Yugoslavia (ICTY)
framing of sexual violence against men: the politics of 243–4; significance of context 204–5; *see also* INGO framings of sexual violence against men

gang rape, definition 143
Geddes, P. 90
gender: intellectual curiosity on 126–8; linking to sexual violence 206–7; as a neutral tool 31, 33; and sexual violence against men 129–31
gender hierarchy 3, 104, 106, 111
gender inclusivity 32
gender mainstreaming 189–90, 194
gender-based violence: General Recommendation 19 definition 8; UN discourse on 184–95

gender-sensitivity training 189
genital integrity, as injured soldiers' first concern 123
genital mutilation, suffered by American servicemen 43–53 (*see also* battle-induced urotrauma)
genocide, and the destruction of reproductive capacity 78
Global Study on the implementation of Resolution 1325 8
Global Summit to End Sexual Violence 5, 8, 26
Goetz, A.M. 31
Goldstein, J.S. 6, 79
Graham, R. 28
Grey, R. 207
'Guidelines for Investigating Conflict-Related Sexual and Gender-Based Violence Against Men and Boys' (IICI) 98
'Guidelines for Medico-Legal Care for Victims of Sexual Violence' (WHO) 98
Guzmán, Abimael 137
gynaecology 34

Hague, William 122
Harambašić, Fikret 156
Hardt, M. 104
hazing 7, 63–6, 128, 132, 144
HeforShe 191
hegemonic masculinity 7, 106–7, 111, 141, 190, 253
help, showing strength by seeking 132
Hendershot, C. 133
Henderson, C. 75
Henigsberg, N. 96
heterosexual masculine sexual impulses, as driver of rape of female civilians 92
Hidden Realities: Screening for Experiences of Violence amongst War-Affected South Sudanese Refugees in northern Uganda (Dolan) 177–8
homoerotic behaviours, forcing male-marked bodies to engage in 155–6
homosexuality: same-sex sexual conduct as expression of 175; sexual violence against men interpreted as a sign of 12, 65, 142, 153, 159, 170, 173–5
Hottentot Venus 36
Hrabać, P. 96
Human Rights Watch reports, framing of sexual violence against men in armed conflict 198–208

humiliation: as central device of political violence 104; experiences of at Abu Ghraib 105; routinely used at Abu Ghraib 106; value to an FPE analysis 105

impregnation, forced 138–9
improvised explosive devices (IEDs) 45, 72–4, 83–4, 133
Inca Empire 79
INGO framings of sexual violence against men: in advocacy reports 202–7; Amnesty International and Human Rights Watch reports 198–208; literature review 199–200; role of in issue construction 200–2
institutions, violence of 129–30
International Criminal Court (ICC): case of Jomo Kenyatta 79; case of the DRC 74; case of the FLDR 81; case of Uhuru Muigai Kenyatta 73; conviction of Jean-Pierre Bemba 4; CRMSV jurisprudence 226–7; definition of sexual violence as a war crime 143, 201; female-focused jurisprudence 211; role in the normalisation of violence 252
international criminal jurisprudence: CRMSV and 211–29; female-focused 211
International Criminal Tribunal for Rwanda (ICTR) 78; CRMSV jurisprudence 224–5
International Criminal Tribunal for the former Yugoslavia (ICTY) 78; Brđanin case 221; Čelibići case 215–16; CRMSV jurisprudence 213–24; examples of sexual violence against men in Bosnia and Croatia 155–60; Furundžija case 216; Karadžić case 223–4; Krajišnik and Plavšić cases 221–2; Kvočka case 219–20; Martić case 222; revisiting sexual violence against men 154; sex and heteronormativity in other performances of sexual violence 160–2; Sikirica case 217–19; Simić and Češić cases 220; Stakić case 219; Stanišić and Župljanin case 222–3; Tadić case 214–15; Todorović case 216–17
International Protocol on the Documentation and Investigation of Sexual Violence in Conflict 3
intersectionality 37, 120
Iraq 9, 43–5, 48, 80, 133, 145

Jacimovic, Slobodan 157
Johnson, K. 110
Johnson, M. 79
Johnston, P. 188

Kenya 203; forced circumcisions of ethnic
    Luo men 79–80; male genital mutilation
    in conflict 76; Mau-Mau uprising 79
Kenyatta, Uhuru Muigai 73
Kighoma, Stephen 169, 175
Kiš, Danilo 160
Kramer, L. 38

the law, treatment of SVAMB 168–9,
    246–7
Leatherman, J.L. 107, 111
Lebanese Civil War, male genital
    mutilation 79
Lee, J. 190
Leiby, M. 83, 85
LGTBQI+ people 35, 243
Libyan Civil War 203
Lindisfarne, N. 191
Linker, B. 48
Linos, N. 96
Lončar, M. 95–6

MacKinnon, C. 62
male genital mutilation in conflict: blunt
    trauma to the genitals 83, 144, 203; case
    of the Vietnamese woman combatant
    cutting off a US Marine's penis and
    testicles 75–6; cultural meanings 82;
    destruction of reproductive capacity 78;
    examples 78–80, 82–3; as a form of
    revenge 81–2; indirect messages 82;
    interpreting the meaning of 73–6; lack
    of research on perpetrator motivations
    75; languages of genital violence 77–84;
    Lebanese Civil War 79; messages and
    audiences 76–7; not related to SVAMB
    83–4; ritualistic eating of genitals 75,
    82; symbolic questioning of masculinity
    79–80; *see also* battle-induced
    urotrauma; castration; penile amputation
    and castration
male rape, denial of 61–3, 206
male victims/survivors of rape and sexual
    violence: awareness of in medical
    practices 95–7; comparison with women
    122; figures for rape in the former
    Yugoslavia 96; reluctance to report 93;
    UNHCR guidelines 92–3
male violation, proliferation of evidence 8

Manjoo, Rashida 191
Mantilla, K. 170
Marcus, S. 63
Marine Corps photo scandal 60
'Marine Sniper' (Henderson) 75
marriages, forced 138, 211, 227–8, 234–5
Martin, E. 27
masculinity: as conduit for damage 29–30;
    hegemonic 7, 106–7, 111, 141, 190,
    253; heterosexual masculine sexual
    impulses as driver of rape of female
    civilians 92; impact of anal rape on 168
    (*see also* feminisation); male genital
    mutilation in conflict and the symbolic
    questioning of 79–80; masculine
    subjectivities in UN discourse on
    gender violence 184–95; as a social
    construct 7
Mau-Mau uprising, Kenya 79
medical responses to sexual violence
    89–98; biological justification of gender
    roles in war 91–2; hormonal system
    91–2; medical and social understandings
    of sex 92–7; medicine and biological
    sex 90–2; natural urge argument 92;
    practices 95–7; UNHCR guidelines
    92–4
medical specialisms for women 33–4
men, as natural perpetrators of sexual
    violence 92–3
Men Can Be Raped Too (Kithima/King)
    89, 97
MenEngage Alliance 190
Mesok, E. 132
#metoo 6
militarisation and gender, through a
    feminist lens 104
militarised sexuality, battle-induced
    urotrauma and 46–50
military sexual violence, importance of
    non-gendered discourse 58
Minh-ha, T. T 36
Misra, A. 79, 106, 153
Mugabe, Robert 173
' "My Heart is Cut": Sexual Violence by
    Rebels and Pro-Government Forces in
    Côte d'Ivoire' (Human Rights Watch)
    204
Myrttinen, H. 133

national security, impact of sexual assaults
    in the armed forces on 59
natural urge argument, for rape of female
    civilians 92

Negri, A. 104
Nuremburg military tribunal, CRMSV
    ubiquitous at 212–13

obstetrics 34
Oosterveld, V. 207

Patel, P. 110
patriarchy 8, 38, 107–8, 239, 241
peacetime sexual violence, growing
    attention to 6
penetration, as military test of endurance
    65
penile amputation and castration 72–3, 75,
    78–9, 81, 83, 161, 226; *see also* battle-
    induced urotrauma; castration; male
    genital mutilation
Persian Empire 79
Peru 124
Peruvian Truth and Reconciliation
    Commission (PTRC): the civil war
    137–8; and the creation of an official
    narrative of CRSV 137–49; identifying
    victims 147–8; rape cases registered
    138; re-evaluating the official narrative
    on CRSV 138–41; treatment of male
    rape 144; treatment of sexual
    humiliation 145–6; treatment of sexual
    mutilation 145; treatment of sexual
    torture 144–5; treatment of threats of
    sexual violence 146–7; under-reporting
    by investigators 142–3; under-reporting
    by victims 83, 141–2
Peterson, V.S. 105, 153, 156
phallocentrism 123
Phillips, Heath 57–8, 61, 63–4
Pleck, P. 186
political economy of CRSV *see* feminist
    political economy of CRSV
prostitution, forced 138
Prügl, E. 4

race: public castration of black men by
    white colonial forces 79; and sexual
    violence 35–8
RAND Military Workplace Study
    (RMWS) 59–60, 64–5
rape: attachment between the female body
    and 130; cases registered by the PTRC
    138; definition 143; denial of male rape
    61–3, 206; feminist theorisations 62–3;
    ICC charges sexual violence against
    men under the rubric of 4; weapon of
    war paradigm 109

rape laws, gendered perspectives 168–9,
    246–7
'The Rape of Men: The Darkest Secret of
    War' (Storr) 170
Reemtsma, J.-P. 74
refugees, UNHCR guidelines on sexual
    violence against 92–4
'The Rehabilitation of War Victims'
    (WHO) 98
reporting figures for sexual assaults, men
    vs women 60 (*see also* under-reporting)
reproductive capacity, destruction of as
    motive behind SVAMB 132
Rwanda 92, 192; *see also* International
    Criminal Tribunal for Rwanda (ICTR)

Salter, M. 170
same-sex sexual conduct: criminalisation
    169, 246; as expression of
    homosexuality 175
Saurette, P. 106
Security Council Resolutions 1325 26,
    184, 1960 111, 2106 1–2, 26, 2122 26;
    dealing with sexual violence in armed
    conflicts 14n9
Sendero Luminoso, castration and penile
    amputation of a civilian man 83
Serbian detention camps, Croat and
    Bosnian male victims of sexual violence
    95
sex, relationship between violence and 25
sex organs, the biological 'truth' of 33–4
sexual abuses against men, legal treatment
    of 2
sexual assaults, percentage of male
    inmates in Sarajevo camps suffering
    152
sexual dysfunction, caused by traumatic
    brain injury 124
sexual humiliation: definition 145–6;
    examples of 145
sexual mutilation, definition 145
sexual politics 31, 33, 48, 106–7, 157,
    162
sexual slavery 138, 143, 226, 228–9, 241
sexual torture: definition 144–5; use of in
    Sri Lanka 109
sexual violation, practices of 6
sexual violence: classic gendered framing
    2–3; frequency and impact comparison
    between men and women 28–30;
    General Recommendation 19 definition
    8; ICC definition 143; PTRC definitions
    138; scope of first appearance on the

international agenda 8; source of gendered nature 107; as a weapon of war 6

sexual violence against men and boys (SVAMB): defining 96; focus of literature 71

'Sexual Violence against Men and Boys in Conflict' (workshop) 3

'Sexual Violence Against Refugees: Guidelines on Prevention and Response' (UNHCR) 92

sexual violence against women: artistic and literary representations 26; comparison of reporting figures with SVAMB 60; distinctions between SVAMB and 108; framing differences between SVAMB and 205; making sense of sexual violence against men through the lens of 206–7; reason for the focused attention on 28

sexual violence in armed conflicts: Security Council Resolutions 14n9; women and girls as primary victims of 29

sexual violence in the US military 57–66; characterisation as hazing ritual 63–6; DOD plan to address 60; epidemic 59; Heath Phillips' experiences 57–8, 61, 63–4; and the men cannot be raped myth 61–3; role of American military masculinity 59–61

Shepherd, L.J. 2, 203, 207

al-Shweiri, Dhia 29, 105

Sierra Leone 110, 204; *see also* Special Court for Sierra Leone (SCSL)

Simić, Bjagoje 160

Simić, Milan 161

Sivakumaran, S. 6, 28, 84, 207

Sjoberg, L. 76, 79

social construction 33, 37, 107, 190

social media, and the disclosure of CRSV experiences 167–79

Solangon, S. 110

Somalia 92, 192

South Sudan 72; disclosure of CRSV experiences 167–79; male genital mutilation 78; war crimes 205

Special Court for Sierra Leone (SCSL), CRMSV jurisprudence 225–6

Špirić, Ž. 96

Sri Lanka, government use of sexualised torture 109

Sri Lankan Civil War 203

Staidum, Frederik Charles, Jr 37

Stern, M. 4, 7

Stop Rape Now 5

Sudan 110, 205

Sustainable Development Goals 26

Syria 205, 229, 247

taboo violations: centrality of to patriarchy 107; CRSV as 111; value generated by 111

Tadić, Dusko 155–6, 214–15

Tadros, M. 168

Thomson, J.A. 90

threats of sexual violence, definition 146–7

Tokyo military tribunal, CRMSV ubiquitous at 212–13

Tomlinson, B. 26–7

torture: examples of 203–4; framing of sexual violence against men as 73, 199–200, 203–5; sexual violence as part of 73

transgender service members 61

'Tribulations' (Harouna) 20–1

Tuana, N. 34

Túpac Amaru Revolutionary Movement 138

Uganda, legislation on rape 168

under-reporting: general pattern 83; by investigators 142–3; legal frameworks and 246; paucity of data due to 2; in Peruvian and Salvadoran truth and reconciliation commissions 83; UNHCR guidelines 93, 193; by victims 141–2; *see also* disclosure of CRSV experiences

UNHCR (United Nations High Commissioner for Refugees), guidelines on sexual violence against refugees 92–4

United Nations: instruments on sexual violence 26; *see also* Security Council Resolutions

United Nations discourse on gender violence: absent perpetrators 185–8; counselling 'deviant' perpetrators 188–9; men and boys as allies for prevention of violence 189–92; men and boys as victims of sexual violence 192–4

urotrauma, battle-induced *see* battle-induced urotrauma

US military: as equal-opportunity employer 61; *see also* sexual violence in the US military

van Tienhoven, H. 96
victims, identifying 147–8
Vietnam 92
violence, relationship between sex and 25

war crimes 74, 143–5, 201, 205, 211–13, 215, 217–18, 223, 227, 229
Ward, J. 65, 162
water torture 204
Weil, S. 211
White, S.C. 31
WHO (World Health Organization) 98
witch-hunts, of the sixteenth–nineteenth centuries 34
women: comparison of male victims/ survivors of rape and sexual violence with 122; feminism and the concealment of women's violence 30–1; medical specialisms for 33–4; as natural victims of sexual violence 92–3; as perpetrators of male genital mutilation 75–6; UN work on violence against 185–8; *see also* sexual violence against women
Women, Peace, and Security (WPS) 5
Women Victims of Trafficking and Involuntary Prostitution 185
Wool, Z. 47–8, 51
'Working with Men and Boy Survivors of Sexual and Gender-Based Violence in Forced Displacement' (UNHCR) 97

Yugoslavia *see* former Yugoslavia; International Criminal Tribunal for the former Yugoslavia (ICTY)

Zalewski, M. 4, 132–3
Zarkov, D. 6, 152, 159, 169
Zeeland, S. 65